JUDGES

THE OLD TESTAMENT LIBRARY

Editorial Advisory Board

Susan Niditch

Judges

A Commentary

Westminster John Knox Press
LOUISVILLE • LONDON

Book design by Jennifer K. Cox

First edition
Published by Westminster John Knox Press
Louisville, Kentucky

This book is printed on acid-free paper that meets the American National Standards Institute Z39.48 standard. ∞

PRINTED IN THE UNITED STATES OF AMERICA

08 09 10 11 12 13 14 15 16 17 — 10 9 8 7 6 5 4 3 2 1

Library of Congress Cataloging-in-Publication Data

Niditch, Susan.
    Judges : a commentary / Susan Niditch.—1st ed.
        p. cm.—(The Old Testament library)
    Includes bibliographical references and index.
    ISBN 978-0-664-22096-9 (alk. paper)
    1. Bible. O. T. Judges—Commentaries.   I. Title.
BS1305.53.N53   2008
222'.32077—dc22   2007031689

CONTENTS

PREFACE

As a student of biblical literature who is deeply influenced by studies of oral-traditional literatures and folklore, I have always sought to explore the writings of the ancient Israelites in terms of "text," "texture," and "context." These categories or rubrics, as developed by Alan Dundes (1980: 20–32), frame (1) the study of the content and structure of any piece of traditional literature as preserved; (2) a description of the material's tone and style; and (3) an effort to set the material in its historical and social setting and to understand it in the larger and evolving tradition to which it belongs. Related to such approaches are concerns with audience, performance, and worldview. How did a work convey meaning to people within particular cultural settings? What are the ways in which the written texts of the Bible were rooted in and functioned in oral worlds?

The field of biblical studies has many of the same goals, methodologies, and interests as the field of folklore and the study of oral literatures. To be a good biblicist is, in fact, to be a good folklorist. Since the publication of my book *Oral World and Written Word* in 1996, interest in oral and traditional literatures has grown among biblicists, and a number of scholars have explored the implications of oral literary theory for understanding the content, themes, genres, and genesis of the Hebrew Bible (see Person 1998, 2002; Carr 2005; Schniedewind 2004; Greenstein 2002: 460–65).

The present commentary on the book of Judges offers an exciting opportunity to study closely one rich collection of biblical tales from the perspective of the field of early and oral literatures. The conviction that Judges reflects a traditional-style culture has important implications for the way one goes about doing a commentary, touching upon text-critical approaches, translation, format, and the exegesis itself. I hope that readers find the volume enjoyable, thought-provoking, and capable of sustaining and enriching their interest in one of the liveliest books of the Bible.

ACKNOWLEDGMENTS

I want to express deep appreciation to friends who have offered valuable comments, criticisms, and suggestions that have influenced my thinking about Judges and the final shape of the commentary: Dan Ben-Amos, Howell D. Chickering, John J. Collins, Rebecca E. Doran, John Miles Foley, Edward L. Greenstein, Jo Ann Hackett, Yehudit Heller, Peter Machinist, Joseph Falaky Nagy, Paul V. Rockwell, Lawrence E. Stager, Richard J. Staley, Phyllis Trible, Robert R. Wilson, and members of the Colloquium for Biblical Research. Portions of the introduction draw upon material presented more fully in "The Challenge of Israelite Epic," an essay that I contributed to *A Companion to Ancient Epic* (2005). Some of the ideas developed in this volume began to take shape when I prepared a brief commentary on Judges for *The Oxford Bible Commentary* (New York: Oxford University Press, 2001). John Barton, my editor for that project, provided thoughtful comments that have influenced in helpful ways my subsequent work. I would also like to thank my students at Amherst College who have explored Judges with me. Their questions and comments always move me to fresh insights. My former student Suzie Park was an enormous help with various logistical aspects of the project and served ably as research assistant. I thank my editors at Westminster John Knox: Jon L. Berquist, who convinced me to undertake the commentary; Carey C. Newman, who was encouraging during a period of delay; and William P. Brown, who beautifully guided the manuscript to completion. My husband, Robert Doran, was, as always, my greatest support. He and I spent many hours looking at the Greek and Latin manuscript traditions, and his sensitivity to the nuances of the Greek and Latin and his erudition were invaluable and enriching. I also thank my beautiful and talented daughters, Rebecca and Elizabeth, for their support, suggestions, and for always keeping me in touch with reality.

Over the last decade, as I worked on Judges, my family and I had to deal with some challenges due to bouts of illness and injury. As I complete this work, I am grateful for wellness and hope that the publication of the commentary is a propitious omen for my family and my friends.

ABBREVIATIONS

A	Codex Alexandrinus
AB	Anchor Bible
ABD	*Anchor Bible Dictionary*. Edited by David Noel Freedman. 6 vols. New York: Doubleday, 1992.
AnOr	Analecta orientalia
ANET	*Ancient Near Eastern Texts Relating to the Old Testament*. Edited by J. B. Pritchard. 3rd ed. Princeton: Princeton University Press, 1969.
BA	*Biblical Archaeologist*
BAR	*Biblical Archaeology Review*
BASOR	*Bulletin of the American Schools of Oriental Research*
BDB	F. Brown, S. R. Driver, and C. A. Briggs, *A Hebrew and English Lexicon of the Old Testament*. Repr. Oxford: Clarendon, 1968.
Bib	*Biblica*
BibInt	*Biblical Interpretation*
BN	*Biblische Notizen*
BR	*Bible Review*
BWANT	Beiträge zur Wissenschaft vom Alten und Neuen Testament
BZAW	Beihefte zur Zeitschrift für die alttestamentliche Wissenschaft
CBQ	*Catholic Biblical Quarterly*
DCH	*The Dictionary of Classical Hebrew*. Edited by David J. A. Clines. Sheffield: Sheffield Academic Press, 1993– .
FFC	Folklore Fellows Communications
GBS, OT	Guides to Biblical Scholarship, Old Testament
HBD	*Harper's Bible Dictionary*. Edited by Paul J. Achtemeier. San Francisco: Harper & Row, 1985.
HSM	Harvard Semitic Monographs
HTR	*Harvard Theological Review*
HUCA	*Hebrew Union College Annual*
ICC	International Critical Commentary
JAF	*Journal of American Folklore*

JAOS	*Journal of the American Oriental Society*
Jastrow	Marcus Jastrow, *Dictionary of the Targumim, the Talmud Babli and Yerushalmi, and the Midrashic Literature.* New York: Pardes, 1950.
JBL	*Journal of Biblical Literature*
JJS	*Journal of Jewish Studies*
JNES	*Journal of Near Eastern Studies*
JNSL	*Journal of Northwest Semitic Languages*
JPS	Jewish Publication Society
JSNTSup	Journal for the Study of the New Testament, Supplement Series
JSOT	*Journal for the Study of the Old Testament*
JSOTSup	Journal for the Study of the Old Testament, Supplement Series
Kittel	Rudolf Kittel, ed., *Biblia Hebraica.* Stuttgart: Württembergische Bibelanstalt, 1966.
KTU	*Die keilalphabetischen Texte aus Ugarit.* Edited by M. Dietrich, O. Loretz, and J. Sanmartín. Neukirchen-Vluyn: Neukirchener Verlag, 1976.
LXX	Septuagint
MT	Masoretic Text
NRSV	New Revised Standard Version of the Bible
OBT	Overtures to Biblical Theology
OG	Old Greek version
OL	Old Latin version
RevQ	*Revue de Qumran*
RHR	*Revue de l'histoire des religions*
SBLDS	Society of Biblical Literature Dissertation Series
SBLSCS	Society of Biblical Literature Septuagint and Cognate Studies
UT	*Ugaritic Textbook.* C. H. Gordon. AnOr 38. Rome: Pontifical Biblical Institute, 1965.
Vat	Codex Vaticanus
VT	*Vetus Testamentum*
VTSup	Vetus Testamentum, Supplements
ZAW	*Zeitschrift für die alttestamentliche Wissenschaft*

BIBLIOGRAPHY

I. Commentaries (cited by author's name and pages)

Boling, Robert. *Judges: Introduction, Translation, and Commentary.* AB. Garden City, NY: Doubleday, 1975.

Burney, C. F. *The Book of Judges.* London: Rivingstons, 1918.

Gray, John. *Joshua, Judges and Ruth.* New Century Bible. London: Nelson, 1967.

Kaufmann, Yehezkel. *Sefer Shoftim (The Book of Judges).* (Hebrew). Jerusalem: Kiryat-Sefer, 1962.

Lindars, Barnabas. *Judges 1–5: A New Translation and Commentary.* Ed. A. D. H. Mayes. Edinburgh: T&T Clark, 1995.

Moore, George Foot. *A Critical and Exegetical Commentary on Judges.* ICC. Edinburgh: T&T Clark, 1895.

Soggin, J. Alberto. *Judges: A Commentary.* Trans. John Bowden. OTL. Philadelphia: Westminster, 1981.

II. Monographs and Edited Volumes

Ackerman, Susan. 1992. *Under Every Green Tree: Popular Religion in Sixth-Century Judah.* HSM 46. Atlanta: Scholars Press.

———. 1998. *Warrior, Dancer, Seductress, Queen: Women in Judges and Biblical Israel.* New York: Doubleday.

Albright, W. F. 1968. *Yahweh and the Gods of Canaan.* London: Athlone.

Alter, Robert. 1981. *The Art of Biblical Narrative.* New York: Basic.

———. 1985. *The Art of Biblical Poetry.* New York: Basic.

———. 2004. *The Five Books of Moses: A Translation with Commentary.* New York: W. W. Norton.

Amit, Yaira. 1999. *The Book of Judges: The Art of Editing.* Trans. Jonathan Chipman. Biblical Interpretation 38. Leiden: Brill.

Beissinger, Margaret, Jane Tylus, and Susanne Wofford, eds. 1999. *Epic Traditions in the Contemporary World: The Poetics of Community.* Berkeley: University of California Press.

Bodine, Walter Ray. 1980a. *The Greek Text of Judges: Recensional Developments*. HSM 23. Chico, CA: Scholars Press.

Brettler, Marc. 1995. *The Creation of History in Ancient Israel*. London: Routledge.

———. 2002. *The Book of Judges*. London: Routledge.

Bright, John. 1981. *A History of Israel*. 3rd ed. Philadelphia: Westminster.

Bynum, David. 1978. *The Daemon in the Wood*. Cambridge: Harvard University Press.

Campbell, Antony F., and Mark A. O'Brien. 2000. *Unfolding the Deuteronomistic History: Origins, Upgrades, Present Text*. Minneapolis: Fortress.

Campbell, Joseph. 1949. *The Hero with a Thousand Faces*. Bollingen Series 17. Princeton: Princeton University Press.

Carr, David M. 2005. *Writing on the Tablet of the Heart: Origins of Scripture and Literature*. Oxford: Oxford University Press.

Coote, Robert B., and Keith W. Whitelam. 1987. *The Emergence of Early Israel in Historical Perspective*. Social World of Biblical Antiquity 5. Sheffield: Almond.

Crenshaw, James L. 1978. *Samson: A Secret Betrayed, a Vow Ignored*. Atlanta: John Knox.

Cross, Frank Moore. 1973. *Canaanite Myth and Hebrew Epic*. Cambridge: Harvard University Press.

———. 1998. *From Epic to Canon: History and Literature in Ancient Israel*. Baltimore: Johns Hopkins University Press.

Cross, Frank Moore, and David Noel Freedman. 1975. *Studies in Ancient Yahwistic Poetry*. SBLDS 21. Missoula, MT: Scholars Press.

Cross, Frank Moore, and Shemaryahu Talmon, eds. 1975. *Qumran and the History of the Biblical Text*. Cambridge: Harvard University Press.

Culley, Robert C. 1976. *Studies in the Structure of Hebrew Narrative*. Semeia Supplement 3. Missoula, MT: Scholars Press.

Dahood, Mitchell J. 1968. *Psalms II. 51–100*. AB. Garden City, NY: Doubleday.

Daube, David. 1965. *Collaboration with Tyranny in Rabbinic Law*. Riddell Memorial Lectures, 1965. London: Oxford University Press.

Day, John. 1989. *Molech: A God of Human Sacrifice in the Old Testament*. University of Cambridge Oriental Publications 41. Cambridge: Cambridge University Press.

Dearman, Andrew, ed. 1989. *Studies in the Mesha Inscription and Moab*. Society of Biblical Literature Archaeology and Biblical Studies 2. Atlanta: Scholars Press.

Dever, William G. 1986. *Gezer IV: The 1969–71 Seasons in Field VI, the "Acropolis."* Jerusalem: Annual of the Nelson Gluck School of Biblical Archaeology.

Dever, William G., H. Darrell Lance, and G. Ernest Wright. 1970. *Gezer I: Preliminary Report of the 1964–66 Seasons*. Jerusalem: Hebrew Union College Biblical and Archaeological School.

Dundes, Alan. 1980. *Interpreting Folklore*. Bloomington: Indiana University Press.

Eilberg-Schwartz, Howard. 1990. *The Savage in Judaism: An Anthropology of Israelite Religion and Ancient Judaiśm*. Bloomington: Indiana University Press.

Eliade, Mircea. 1954. *The Myth of the Eternal Return: or Cosmos and History*. Bollingen Series 46. Princeton: Princeton University Press.

Engnell, Ivan. 1969, *A Rigid Scrutiny: Critical Essays on the Old Testament*. Trans. and ed. John T. Willis with Helmer Ringgren. Nashville: Vanderbilt University Press.

Finnegan, Ruth. 1988. *Orality and Literacy*. Oxford: Basil Blackwell.

Foley, John Miles. 1991. *Immanent Art: From Structure to Meaning in Traditional Oral Epic*. Bloomington: Indiana University Press.

———. 1993. *Traditional Oral Epic: The Odyssey, Beowulf, the Serbo Croatian Return Song*. Berkeley: University of California Press.

———. 1995. *The Singer of Tales in Performance*. Bloomington: Indiana University Press.

Fontaine, Carole R. 1982. *Traditional Sayings in the Old Testament: A Contextual Study*. Bible and Literature 5. Sheffield: Almond.

Fox, Everett. 1995. *The Five Books of Moses: Genesis, Exodus, Leviticus, Numbers, Deuteronomy: A New Translation with Introductions, Commentary, and Notes*. New York: Schocken.

Gaster, Theodore H. 1977. *Thespis: Ritual, Myth, and Drama in the Ancient Near East*. New York: Norton.

———. 1981. *Myth, Legend, and Custom in the Old Testament: A Comparative Study with Chapters from Sir James G. Frazer's Folklore in the Old Testament*. 2 vols. 1969. Repr. Gloucester, MA: Peter Smith.

Geller, Steven A. 1979. *Parallelism in Early Biblical Poetry*. HSM 20. Missoula, MT: Scholars Press.

Gottwald, Norman. 1979. *The Tribes of Yahweh: A Sociology for the Religion of Liberated Israel 1250–1050 BC*. Maryknoll, NY: Orbis.

Gunkel, Hermann. 1895. *Schöpfung und Chaos in Urzeit und Endzeit*. Göttingen: Vandenhoeck & Ruprecht.

———. 1913. *Reden und Aufsätze*, Göttingen: Vandenhoeck & Ruprecht.

———. 1966. *The Legends of Genesis*. New York: Schocken Books.

Gzella, Holger. 2003. *Cosmic Battle and Political Conflict: Studies in Verbal Syntax and Contextual Interpretation of Daniel 8*. Biblica et Orientalia 47. Rome: Pontifical Biblical Institute.

Hadley, Judith M. 2000. *The Cult of Asherah in Ancient Israel and Judah.* Cambridge: Cambridge University Press.

Halpern, Baruch. 1988a. *The First Historians: The Hebrew Bible and History.* San Francisco: Harper & Row.

Hanson, Paul D. 1975. *The Dawn of Apocalyptic: The Historical and Sociological Roots of Jewish Apocalyptic.* Philadelphia: Fortress.

Heinemann, Isaac. 1954. *Darkhei ha-Aggadah.* Jerusalem: Magnes.

Hobsbawm, Eric. 1969. *Bandits.* New York: Delacorte.

Honko, Lauri. 1998. *Textualising the Siri Epic.* FFC 264. Helsinki: Suomalainen Tiedakatemia.

Hurvitz, Avi. 1982. *A Linguistic Study of the Relationship between the Priestly Source and Ezekiel: A New Approach to an Old Problem.* Cahiers de la Revue biblique 20. Paris: Gabalda.

Japhet, Sara. 1989. *The Ideology of the Book of Chronicles and Its Place in Biblical Thought.* Beiträge zur Erforschung des Alten Testaments und des antiken Judentums 9. Frankfurt am Main: Peter Lang.

Kang, Sa-Moon. 1989. *Divine War in the Old Testament and in the Ancient Near East.* BZAW 177. Berlin: de Gruyter.

Katzenstein, H. J. 1973. *The History of Tyre, from the Beginning of the Second Millennium B.C.E. until the Fall of the Neo-Babylonian Empire in 538 B.C.E.* Jerusalem: Schocken Institute for Jewish Research of the Jewish Theological Seminary of America.

Kempinski, Aharon. 1989. *Megiddo: A City-State and Royal Centre in North Israel.* Materielen zur Allgemeine und Vergleichenden Archäologie 40. Munich: Beck.

King, Philip J., and Lawrence E. Stager. 2001. *Life in Biblical Israel.* Library of Ancient Israel. Louisville: Westminster John Knox.

Klein, Lillian R. 1988. *The Triumph of Irony in the Book of Judges.* JSOTSup 68. Sheffield: Almond.

Knoppers, Gary N., and J. Gordon McConville, eds. 2000. *Reconsidering Israel and Judah: Recent Studies on the Deuteronomistic History.* Sources for Biblical and Theological Study 8. Winona Lake, IN: Eisenbrauns.

Kugel, James L. 1981. *The Idea of Biblical Poetry: Parallelism and Its History.* New Haven: Yale University Press.

——. 1997. *The Bible as It Was.* Cambridge: Harvard University Press.

——. 2003. *The God of Old: Inside the Lost World of the Bible.* New York: Free Press.

Lambdin, Thomas O. 1971. *Introduction to Biblical Hebrew.* New York: Charles Scribner's Sons.

Levenson, Jon. 1993. *The Death and Resurrection of the Beloved Son: The Transformation of Child Sacrifice in Judaism and Christianity.* New Haven: Yale University Press.

Lévi-Strauss, Claude. 1973. *From Honey to Ashes*. Trans. John and Doreen Weightman. New York: Octagon.

Lord, A. B. 1988. *The Singer of Tales*. 1960. Repr. Cambridge: Harvard University Press.

McCarter, P. Kyle. 1986. *Textual Criticism: Recovering the Text of the Hebrew Bible*. GBS, OT. Philadelphia: Fortress.

Mayes, A. D. H. 1974. *Israel in the Period of the Judges*. Studies in Biblical Theology 2/29. Naperville, IL: Allenson.

Mazar, Amihai. 1992. *Archaeology of the Land of the Bible: 10,000–586 B.C.E.* New York: Doubleday.

Mazar, Benjamin, ed. 1971. *Judges*. Vol. 3 of *The World History of the Jewish People: First Series: Ancient Times*. New Brunswick, NJ: Rutgers University Press.

Mendenhall, George E. 1973. *The Tenth Generation: The Origins of the Biblical Tradition*. Baltimore: Johns Hopkins University Press.

Miller, Patrick D. 2000. *The Religion of Ancient Israel*. Louisville: Westminster John Knox.

Mowinckel, Sigmund. 1967. *The Psalms in Israel's Worship*. Trans. D. R. Ap-Thomas. 2 vols. 1962. Repr. New York: Abingdon.

Nagy, Gregory. 1996. *Homeric Questions*. Austin: University of Texas Press.

———. 2003. *Homeric Responses*. Austin: University of Texas Press.

Nelson, Richard D. 1997. *Joshua: A Commentary*. OTL. Louisville: Westminster John Knox.

Niditch, Susan. 1980. *The Symbolic Vision in Biblical Tradition*. HSM 30. Chico, CA: Scholars Press.

———. 1987. *Underdogs and Tricksters: A Prelude to Biblical Folklore*. San Francisco: Harper & Row.

———. 1993a. *Folklore and the Hebrew Bible*. Minneapolis: Fortress.

———. 1993b. *War in the Hebrew Bible: A Study in the Ethics of Violence*. New York: Oxford University Press.

———. 1996. *Oral World and Written Word: Ancient Israelite Literature*. Louisville: Westminster John Knox.

———. 1997. *Ancient Israelite Religion*. New York: Oxford University Press.

Niditch, Susan, ed. 1990. *Text and Tradition: The Hebrew Bible and Folklore*. Semeia Studies. Atlanta: Scholars Press.

Noth, Martin. 1930. *Das System der zwölf Stamme Israels*. BWANT 4/1. Stuttgart: W. Kohlhammer.

———. 1957. *Uberlieferungsgeschichtliche Studien*. 2nd ed. Tübingen: Max Niemeyer.

———. 1966. *The Old Testament World*. Trans. Victor I. Gruhn. Philadelphia: Fortress.

Obeyesekere, Gananath. 1981. *Medusa's Hair: An Essay on Personal Symbols and Religious Experience*. Chicago: University of Chicago Press.

O'Callaghan, Roger T. 1948. *Aram Naharaim: A Contribution to the History of Upper Mesopotamia in the Second Millennium B.C.* AnOr 26. Rome: Pontifical Biblical Institute.

O'Connell, Robert H. 1996. *The Rhetoric of the Book of Judges.* VTSup 63. Leiden: Brill.

O'Connor, M. 1980. *Hebrew Verse Structure.* Winona Lake, IN: Eisenbrauns.

O'Keeffe, Katherine O'Brien. 1990. *Visible Song: Transitional Literacy in Old English Verse.* Cambridge: Cambridge University Press.

Parry, Milman. 1971. *The Making of Homeric Verse.The Collected Papers of Milman Parry.* Ed. Adam Parry. Oxford: Clarendon.

Pepicello, W. J., and Thomas A. Green. 1984. *The Language of Riddles.* Columbus: Ohio State University Press.

Person, Raymond F., Jr. 2002. *The Deuteronomic School: History, Social Setting, and Literature.* Society of Biblical Literature Studies in Biblical Literature 2. Atlanta: Society of Biblical Literature.

Polzin, Robert. 1976. *Late Biblical Hebrew: Toward an Historical Typology of Biblical Hebrew Prose.* HSM 12. Missoula, MT: Scholars Press.

Radcliffe-Brown, A. R. 1965. *Structure and Function in Primitive Society.* New York: Macmillan.

Richter, Wolfgang. 1963. *Traditionsgeschichtliche Untersuchungen zum Richterbuch.* Bonner biblische Beiträge 18. Bonn: Peter Hanstein.

Robert, Ulysse. 1900. *Heptateuchi partis posterioris versio latina antiquissima e codice Lugdunensi: Version latine du Deutéronome de Josué et des Juges antérieure à Saint Jerôme, publié d'après le manuscript de Lyon.* Lyon: Rey.

Robertson, David A. 1972. *Linguistic Dating in Early Hebrew Poetry.* SBLDS 3. Missoula, MT: Society of Biblical Literature.

Römer, Thomas, ed. 2000. *The Future of the Deuteronomistic History.* Bibliotheca ephemeridum theologicarum lovaniensium 147. Louvain: Peeters.

Rowlett, Lori L. 1996. *Joshua and the Rhetoric of Violence: A New Historicist Approach.* JSOTSup 226. Sheffield: Sheffield Academic Press.

Schearing, Linda S., and Steven L. McKenzie, eds. 1999. *Those Elusive Deuteronomists: The Phenomenon of Pan-Deuteronomism.* JSOTSup 268. Sheffield: Sheffield Academic Press.

Schniedewind, William M. 2004. *How the Bible Became a Book: A Textualization of Ancient Israel.* Cambridge: Cambridge University Press.

Smith, Morton. 1971. *Palestinian Parties and Politics That Shaped the Old Testament.* New York: Columbia University Press.

Thompson, Stith. 1955–1958. *Motif-Index of Folk-Literature.* Rev. ed. 6 vols. Bloomington: Indiana University Press.

Thompson, Stith, ed. 1973. *The Types of the Folktale.* FFC 184. Helsinki: Suomalainen tiedeakatemia. (An extended edition of Antii Aarne's *Verzeichnis der Märchentypen.*)

Tov, Emanuel. 2001. *Textual Criticism of the Hebrew Bible*. 2nd ed. Minneapolis: Fortress.

Trible, Phyllis. 1978. *God and the Rhetoric of Sexuality*. OBT. Philadelphia: Fortress.

————. 1984. *Texts of Terror: Literary-Feminist Readings of Biblical Narratives*. OBT. Philadelphia: Fortress.

————. 1994. *Rhetorical Criticism: Context, Method, and the Book of Jonah*. GBS, OT. Minneapolis: Fortress.

Turner, Victor. 1969. *The Ritual Process*. Ithaca, NY: Cornell University Press.

Ulrich, Eugene. 1999. *The Dead Sea Scrolls and the Origins of the Bible*. Grand Rapids: Eerdmans.

Van Seters, John. 1983. *In Search of History: Historiography in the Ancient World and the Origins of Biblical History*. New Haven: Yale University Press.

————. 1992. *Prologue to History: The Yahwist as Historian in Genesis*. Louisville: Westminster John Knox.

Vermeule, Emily. 1979. *Aspects of Death in Early Greek Art and Poetry*. Sather Classical Lectures 46. Berkeley: University of California Press.

Walls, Neal. 1992. *The Goddess Anat in Ugaritic Myth*. SBLDS 135. Atlanta: Scholars Press.

Webb, Barry G. 1987. *The Book of Judges: An Integrated Reading*. JSOTSup 45. Sheffield: JSOT Press.

Westermann, Claus. 1984. *Genesis 1–11. A Commentary*. Trans. John J. Scullion, S.J. Minneapolis: Augsburg.

————. 1985. *Genesis 12–36. A Commentary*. Trans. John J. Scullion, S.J. Minneapolis: Augsburg.

Wright, G. Ernest. 1965. *Shechem: The Biography of a Biblical City*. London: Duckworth.

Younger, K. Lawson, Jr. 1990. *Ancient Conquest Accounts: A Study in Ancient Near Eastern and Biblical History Writing*. JSOTSup 98. Sheffield: JSOT Press.

Zobel, H.-J. 1965. *Stammesspruch und Geschichte: Die Angaben der Stammessprüche von Gen 49, Dtn 33 und Jdc 5 über die politischen und kultischen Zustände im damaligen "Israel."* BZAW 95. Berlin: Töpelmann.

III. Articles and Chapters

Ackerman, Susan. 1993. "The Queen Mother and the Cult in Ancient Israel." *JBL* 112:385–401.

Aharoni, Yohanan. 1970. "New Aspects of the Israelite Occupation of the North." Pages 254–67 in *Near Eastern Archaeology in the Twentieth Century: Essays in Honor of Nelson Glueck*. Ed. James A. Sanders. Garden City, NY: Doubleday.

————. 1972. "The Stratification of Israelite Megiddo." *JNES* 31:302–11.

Albright, W. F. 1922. "Earliest Forms of Hebrew Verse." *Journal of the Palestine Oriental Society* 2:69–85.

————. 1936. "The Song of Deborah in the Light of Archaeology." *BASOR* 62:26–31.

————. 1950–1951. "A Catalogue of Early Hebrew Lyric Poems (Psalm LXVIII)." *HUCA* 33:1–38.

Alt, Albrecht. 1966. "The Settlement of the Israelites in Palestine." Pages 133–69 in *Essays on Old Testament History and Religion*. Trans. R. A. Wilson. Oxford: Blackwell (originally published in German, 1953).

Alter, Robert. 1983. "From Line to Story in Biblical Verse." *Poetics Today* 4:615–37.

————. 1990. "Samson Without Folklore." Pages 47–56 in *Text and Tradition*. Ed. Susan Niditch. Atlanta: Scholars Press.

Amit, Yaira. 1984/85. "'There was a man . . . . and his name was . . .': Editorial Variations and Their Tendenz" (Hebrew). *Beth Mikra* 30:388–99.

————. 2000. "Bochim, Bethel and the Hidden Polemic (Judg 2, 1–5)." Pages 121–31 in *Studies in Historical Geography and Biblical Historiography, Presented to Zecharia Kallai*. Ed. Gershon Galil and Moshe Weinfeld. VTSup 81. Leiden: Brill.

Auld, A. G. 1975. "Judges and History: A Reconsideration." *VT* 25:261–85.

Bal, Mieke. 1984. "The Rhetoric of Subjectivity." *Poetics Today* 5:337–76.

Baly, Denis. 1985. "Succoth." *HBD* 996–97.

Barré, Michael L. 1991. "The Meaning of *PRŠDN* in Judges 3:22." *VT* 41:1–11.

Ben-Amos, Dan. 1976. "Analytical Categories and Ethnic Genres." Pages 214–42 in *Folklore Genres*. Ed. Dan Ben-Amos. Austin: University of Texas Press.

Blenkinsopp, Joseph. 1961. "Ballad Style and Psalm Style in the Book of Judges." *Bib* 42:61–76.

Bloch-Smith, Elizabeth. 2003."Israelite Ethnicity in Iron I: Archaeology Preserves What Is Remembered and What Is Forgotten in Israel's History." *JBL* 122:401–25.

Bodine, Walter Ray. 1980b. "*Kaige* and Other Recensional Developments in the Greek Text of Judges." *Bulletin of the International Organization for Septuagint and Cognate Studies* 13:45–57.

Brandfon, Fredric. 1992. "Beth Shemesh." *ABD* 1:696–698.

Brettler, Marc. 1989. "The Book of Judges: Literature as Politics." *JBL* 108:395–418.

————. 1991. "Never the Twain Shall Meet? The Ehud Story as History and Literature." *HUCA* 62:285–304.

Burns, Thomas A. 1976. "Riddling: Occasion to Act." *JAF* 89:139–65.

Bynum, David E. 1990. "Samson as a Biblical *phēr oresxōos*." Pages 57–73 in *Text and Tradition*. Ed. Susan Niditch. Atlanta: Scholars Press.

Camp, Claudia V., and Carole R. Fontaine. 1990. "The Words of the Wise and Their Riddles." Pages 127–51 in *Text and Tradition*. Ed. Susan Niditch. Atlanta: Scholars Press.

Coogan, Michael D. 1978. "A Structural and Literary Analysis of the Song of Deborah." *CBQ* 40:146–66.

Craigie, P. C. 1968. "A Note on Judges V 2." *VT* 18:397–99.

———. 1972a. "A Reconsideration of Shamgar Ben Anath (Judg 3:31 and 5:6)." *JBL* 91:239–40.

———. 1972b. "Some Further Notes on the Song of Deborah." *VT* 22:349–53.

———. 1977. "Three Ugaritic Notes on the Song of Deborah." *JSOT* 2:33–49.

Cross, Frank Moore. 1968. "The Structure of the Deuteronomistic History." *Perspectives in Jewish Learning* 3:9–24.

Danielus, Eva. 1963. "Shamgar ben ʿAnath." *JNES* 22:191–93.

Day, Peggy L. 1989. "From the Child Is Born the Woman: The Story of Jephthah's Daughter." Pages 58–74 in *Gender and Difference in Ancient Israel*. Ed. Peggy L. Day. Minneapolis: Fortress.

Dearman, J. Andrew. 1985. "Amelek." *HBD* 25.

Dehan, Na'im. 2000. "Concerning מחצצים and בפרע פרעות in the Song of Deborah" (Hebrew). *Beth Mikra* 45:171–76.

Dorson, Richard M. 1978. "Introduction." Pages 1–6 in *Heroic Saga and Epic: An Introduction to the World's Great Folk Epics*. Ed. Felix J. Oinas. Bloomington: Indiana University Press.

Dothan, Moshe. 1992. "Acco." *ABD* 1:50–53.

Drews, Robert. 1989. "The 'Chariots of Iron' of Joshua and Judges." *JSOT* 45:15–23.

Dundes, Alan. 1981. "On the Structure of the Proverb." Pages 43–64 in *The Wisdom of Many: Essays on the Proverb*. Ed. Wolfgang Mieder. New York: Garland (originally published in *Proverbium* 25 [1975] 961–73).

Dundes, Alan, with Robert A. Georges. 1975. "Toward a Structural Definition of the Riddle." Pages 95–102 in *Analytic Essays in Folklore*. Studies in Folklore 2. The Hague: Mouton (originally published in *JAF* 76 [1963] 111–18).

Exum, J. Cheryl. 1981. "Aspects of Symmetry and Balance in the Samson Saga." *JSOT* 19:3–29.

———. 1983. "The Theological Dimension of the Samson Saga." *VT* 33:30–45.

———. 1992. "Delilah." *ABD* 2:133–34.

Fensham, F. Charles. 1961. "Shamgar Ben ʿAnath." *JNES* 20:197–98.

Fernández Marcos, Natalio. 2003. "The Hebrew and Greek Texts of Judges." Pages 1–16 in *The Earliest Text of the Hebrew Bible: The Relationship between the Masoretic Text and the Hebrew Base of the Septuagint Reconsidered*. Ed. Adrian Schenker. SBLSCS 52. Atlanta: Society of Biblical Literature.

Finkelstein, Israel. 1985. "Response." Pages 80–83 in *Biblical Archaeology Today*. Ed. A. Biran. Jerusalem: Israel Exploration Society.

———. 1988. Pages 25–234 in *The Archaeology of the Israelite Settlement*. Jerusalem: Israel Exploration Society.

Fuchs, Esther. 1985. "The Literary Characterization of Mothers and Sexual Politics in the Hebrew Bible." Pages 117–36 in *Feminist Perspectives on Biblical Scholarship*. Ed. Adela Yarbro Collins. Chico, CA: Scholars Press.

Gal, Zvi. 1982. "The Settlement of Issachar: Some New Observations." *Tel Aviv* 9:79–86.

Geertz, Clifford. 1973. "Religion as a Cultural System." Pages 87–125 in *The Interpretation of Cultures*. New York: Basic.

Gerleman, Gillis. 1951. "The Song of Deborah in the Light of Stylistics." *VT* 1:168–80.

Glock, Albert E. 1992. "Taanach." *ABD* 6:287–90.

Grayson, A. Kirk. 1980. "Histories and Historians." *Orientalia* 49:150–94.

Greenstein, Edward L. 2002. "Some Developments in the Study of Language and Some Implications for Interpreting Ancient Texts and Cultures." Pages 441–79 in *Semitic Linguistics: The State of the Art at the Turn of the Twenty-First Century*. Ed. Shlomo Izre'el. Israel Oriental Studies 20. Winona Lake, IN: Eisenbrauns.

Grimm, D. 1981. "Der Name der Gottesboten in Richter 13." *Bib* 62:92–98.

Gunn, David M. 1974a. "The 'Battle Report': Oral or Scribal Convention?" *JBL* 93:513–18.

———. 1974b. "Narrative Patterns and Oral Tradition in Judges and Samuel." *VT* 24:286–317.

———. 1987. "Joshua and Judges." Pages 102–21 in *The Literary Guide to the Bible*. Ed. Robert Alter and Frank Kermode. Cambridge: Harvard University Press.

———. 1990. "Threading the Labyrinth: A Response to Albert B. Lord." Pages 19–24 in *Text and Tradition*. Ed. Susan Niditch. Atlanta: Scholars Press.

Gurewicz, S. B. 1959. "The Bearing of Judges on i-ii 5 on the Authorship of the Book of Judges." *Australian Biblical Review* 7:37–40.

Hackett, Jo Ann. 1985. "In the Days of Jael: Reclaiming the History of Women in Ancient Israel." Pages 15–38 in *Immaculate and Powerful: The Female in Sacred Image and Social Reality*. Ed. Clarissa W. Atkinson, Constance H. Buchanan, and Margaret R. Miles. Boston: Beacon.

———. 1996. "Canaan and Canaanites." Pages 408–14 in vol. 1 of *The Oxford Encyclopedia of Archaeology in the Near East*. Ed. Eric Meyers. 5 vols. New York: Oxford University Press.

———. 1998. "'There Was No King in Israel': The Era of the Judges." Pages 177–218 in *The Oxford History of the Biblical World*. Ed. Michael D. Coogan. New York: Oxford University Press.

Halpern, Baruch. 1983. "The Resourceful Israelite Historian: The Song of Deborah and Israelite Historiography." *HTR* 76:379–401.

———. 1988b. "The Assassination of Eglon: The First Locked-Room Murder Mystery." *BR* 4, no. 6:32–41.

Hamilton, Jeffries M. 1992. "Kiriath-arba." *ABD* 4:84.

Hendel, Ronald. 2001. "The Exodus in Biblical Memory." *JBL* 120:601–22.

Herr, Denise Dick, and Mary Petrina Boyd. 2002. "A Watermelon Named Abimelech." *BAR* 28, no. 1:34–37, 62.

Herion, Gary A., and Dale W. Manor. 1992. "Debir." *ABD* 2:112.

Hess, Richard S. 1999. "Judges 1–5 and Its Translation." Pages 142–60 in *Translating the Bible: Problems and Prospects*. Ed. Stanley E. Porter and Richard S. Hess. JSNTSup 173. Sheffield: Sheffield Academic Press.

———. 2003. "Israelite Identity and Personal Names from the Book of Judges." *Hebrew Studies* 44:25–39.

———. 2004. "The Name Game." *BAR* 30, no. 6:38–41.

Hillers, Delbert. 1965. "A Note on Judges 5, 8a." *CBQ* 27:124–26.

Humbert, Paul. 1919. "Les métamorphoses de Samson." *RHR* 80:154–70.

Hurvitz, Avi. 2000. "Can Biblical Texts Be Dated Linguistically? Chronological Perspectives in the Historical Study of Biblical Hebrew." Pages 143–60 in *Congress Volume: Oslo 1998*. Ed. A. Lemaire and M. Sæbø. VTSup 80. Leiden: Brill.

Hymes, Dell. 1989. "Ways of Speaking." Pages 433–51, 473–74 in *Explorations in the Ethnography of Speaking*. Ed. Richard Bauman and Joel Sherzer. 2nd ed. Cambridge: Cambridge University Press.

———. 1994. "Ethnopoetics, Oral-Formulaic Theory, and Editing Texts." *Oral Tradition* 9:330–70.

Ishida, Tomoo. 1979. "The Structure and Historical Implications of the Lists of Pre-Israelite Nations." *Bib* 60:461–90.

Jackson, Kent. 1989. "The Language of the Mesha Inscription." Pages 96–130 in *Studies in the Mesha Inscription and Moab*. Ed. Andrew Dearman. Atlanta: Scholars Press.

Janzen, J. Gerald. 1989. "The Root *pr*ᶜ in Judges V 2 and Deuteronomy XXXII 42." *VT* 39:393–406.

Japhet, Sara. 1968. "The Supposed Common Authorship of Chronicles and Ezra-Nehemia Investigated Anew." *VT* 18:330–371.

Lasine, Stuart. 1984. "Guest and Host in Judges 19: Lot's Hospitality in an Inverted World." *JSOT* 29:37–59.

Leach, Edmund R. 1967. "Magical Hair." Pages 77–108 in *Myth and Cosmos: Readings in Mythology and Symbolism*. Ed. John Middleton. Garden City, NY: Natural History Press (repr. from *Journal of the Royal Anthropological Institute* 88 [1958]: 147–64).

Lindars, Barnabas. 1983. "Deborah's Song: Women in the Old Testament." *John Rylands University of Manchester Bulletin* 65:158–75.

Little, David. 1995. "Introduction," Pages 3–9 in David R. Smock, *Perspectives on Pacifism: Christian, Jewish, and Muslim Views on Nonviolence in International Conflict.* Washington, DC: U.S. Institute of Peace Press.

McCarter, P. Kyle. 1987. "Aspects of the Religion of the Israelite Monarchy: Biblical and Epigraphic Data." Pages 137–55 in *Ancient Israelite Religion: Essays in Honor of Frank Moore Cross.* Ed. P. D. Miller, Paul D. Hanson, and S. Dean McBride. Philadelphia: Fortress.

McCarthy, William Bernard. 2002. "Lang Lang May the Ladies Stand: A Ballad Motif in the Book of Judges." *Acta Ethnographica Hungarica* 47:7–18.

MacDonald, John. 1976. "The Status and Role of the *Na'ar* in Israelite Society." *JNES* 35:147–70.

McGovern, E. 1992. "Beth-Shan." *ABD* 1:693–96.

Machinist, Peter. 1991. "The Question of Distinctiveness in Ancient Israel: An Essay." Pages 196–212 in *Ah, Assyria . . . ! Studies in Assyrian History and Ancient Near Eastern Historiography Presented to Hayim Talmon.* Ed. Mordechai Cogan and Israel Eph'al. Scripta hierosolymitana 33. Jerusalem: Magnes.

———. 1994. "Outsiders or Insiders: The Biblical View of Emergent Israel and Its Contexts." Pages 35–60 in *The Other in Jewish Thought and History.* Ed. Laurence J. Silberstein and Robert L. Cohn. New York: NYU Press.

———. 2000. "Biblical Traditions: The Philistines and Israelite History." Pages 53–83 in *The Sea Peoples and Their World: A Reassessment.* Ed. Eliezer D. Oren. Philadelphia: University Museum, University of Pennsylvania.

———. 2005. "Hosea and the Ambiguity of Kingship in Ancient Israel." Pages 153–81 in *Constituting the Community: Studies on the Polity of Ancient Israel in Honor of S. Dean McBride Jr.* Ed. John T. Strong and Steven S. Tuell. Winona Lake, IN: Eisenbrauns.

Malamat, A. 1954. "Cushan Rishathaim and the Decline of the Near East around 1200 B.C." *JNES* 13:231–42.

Margalith, Othniel. 1985. "Samson's Foxes." *VT* 35:224–29.

———. 1986a. "Samson's Riddle and Samson's Magic Locks." *VT* 36:225–34.

———. 1986b. "More Samson Legends." *VT* 36:397–405.

———. 1987. "The Legends of Samson/Heracles." *VT* 37:63–70.

Mattingly, Gerald. 1992a. "Aroer." *ABD* 1:399–400.

———. 1992b. "Chemosh." *ABD* 1:895–97.

Mazar, Benjamin. 1965. "The Sanctuary of Arad and the Family of Hobab the Kenite." *JNES* 24:297–303.

Merwe, C. H. J. van der. 1999. "The Elusive Biblical Hebrew Term *WYHY*: A Perspective in Terms of Its Syntax, Semantics, and Pragmatics in 1 Samuel." *Hebrew Studies* 40:83–114.

Michalowski, Piotr. 1983. "History as Charter: Some Observations on the Sumerian King List." *JAOS* 103:237–48.

Miller, Patrick D. 1970. "Animal Names as Designations in Ugaritic and Hebrew." *Ugarit-Forschungen* 2:177–86.

Mobley, Gregory. 1997. "The Wild Man in the Bible and the Ancient Near East." *JBL* 116:217–33.

Mosca, Paul. 1975. "Child Sacrifice in Canaanite and Israelite Religion: A Study of *mulk* and *mlk*." Unpublished Ph.D. dissertation. Harvard University.

Nel, Philip. 1985. "The Riddle of Samson (Judg 14:14–18)." *Bib* 66:534–45.

Niditch, Susan. 1982. "The 'Sodomite' Theme in Judges 19–20: Family, Community, and Social Disintegration." *CBQ* 44:365–78.

———. 1989. "Eroticism and Death in the Tale of Jael." Pages 43–57 in *Gender and Difference in Ancient Israel*. Ed. Peggy L. Day. Minneapolis: Fortress.

———. 1990. "Samson as Culture Hero, Trickster, and Bandit: The Empowerment of the Weak." *CBQ* 52:608–24.

———. 2001. "Judges." Pages 176–91 in *The Oxford Bible Commentary*. Eds. John Barton and John Muddiman. New York: Oxford University Press.

———. 2005. "The Challenge of Israelite Epic." Pages 277–87 in *A Companion to Ancient Epic*. Ed. John Miles Foley. Oxford: Blackwell.

Noy, Dov. 1968. "Riddles in the Wedding Meal" (Hebrew). *Maḥanayim* 83:64–71.

O'Connor, M. 1986. "The Women in the Book of Judges." *Hebrew Annual Review* 10:277–93.

Olyan, Saul. 1998. "What Do Shaving Rites Accomplish and What Do They Signal in Biblical Ritual Contexts?" *JBL* 117:611–22.

Person, Raymond F., Jr. 1998. "The Ancient Israelite Scribe as Performer." *JBL* 117:601–9.

Polak, Frank H. 1998. "The Oral and the Written: Syntax, Stylistics and the Development of Biblical Prose Narrative." *Journal of the Ancient Near Eastern Society* 26:59–105.

Porter, Stanley. 1992. "Amorites." *ABD* 1:199–203.

Prausnitz, M. W. 1992. "Achzib." *ABD* 1:57–58.

Rabin, Chaim. 1955. "Judges 5:2 and the 'Ideology' of Deborah's War." *JJS* 6:125–34.

———. 1974. "The Origin of the Hebrew Word *Pilegeš*." *JJS* 25:353–64.

Reed, Stephen A. 1992. "Perizzite." *ABD* 5:231.

Rendsburg, Gary A. 2002. "Some False Leads in the Identification of Late Biblical Hebrew Texts: The Cases of Genesis 24 and 1 Samuel 2:27–36." *JBL* 121:23–46.

Richter, Wolfgang. 1965. "Zu den 'Richtern Israel.'" *ZAW* 77:41–71.

Roberts, J. J. M. 1985. "Horites." In *HBD* 404–5.

Rofé, Alexander. 1982. "The End of the Book of Joshua according to the Septuagint." *Henoch* 4:17–36.

Rubin, Gayle. 1975. "The Traffic in Women: Notes on the 'Political Economy' of Sex." Pages 157–210 in *Toward an Anthropology of Women*. Ed. Rayna R. Reiter. New York: Monthly Review Press.

Rudman, Dominic. 2000. "The Second Bull in Judges 6:25–28." *JNSL* 26:97–103.

Schloen, J. David. 1993. "Caravans, Kenites, and Casus Belli: Enmity and Alliance in Song of Deborah." *CBQ* 55:18–38.

Selms, A. van. 1964. "Judge Shamgar." *VT* 14:294–309.

Shulman, David D. 1986. "Battle as Metaphor in Tamil Folk and Classical Traditions." Pages 105–30 in *Another Harmony*. Ed. Stuart M. Blackburn and A. K. Ramanujan. Berkeley: University of California Press.

Speiser, E. A. 1967. "The Shibboleth Incident (Judges 12:6)." Pages 143–50 in *Oriental and Biblical Studies: Collected Writings of E. A. Speiser*. Ed. J. J. Finkelstein and Moshe Greenberg. Philadelphia: University of Pennsylvania Press (originally published in 1942).

Stager, Lawrence E. 1988. "Archaeology, Ecology and Social History: Background Themes to the Song of Deborah." Pages 221–34 in *Congress Volume: Jerusalem 1986*. Ed. J. A. Emerton. VTSup 40. Leiden: Brill.

———. 1989. "The Song of Deborah: Why Some Tribes Answered the Call and Others Did Not." *BAR* 15, no. 1:50–64.

———. 1998. "Forging an Identity: The Emergence of Ancient Israel." Pages 123–75 in *The Oxford History of the Biblical World*. Ed. Michael D. Coogan. New York: Oxford University Press.

———. 2003a. "The Shechem Temple: Where Abimelech Massacred a Thousand." *BAR* 29, no. 4:26–35, 66–69.

———. 2003b. "Key Passages." *Eretz-Israel*. 27:240–45. *Hayim and Miriam Tadmor Volume*. Ed. Israel Eph'al, Amnon Ben-Tor, and Peter Machinist. Jerusalem: Israel Exploration Society.

———. 2006. "The House of The Silver Calf of Ashkelon." Pages 403–10 in *Timelines. Studies in Honour of Manfred Bietak*. Vol. 2. Ed. Ernst Czerny, Irmgard Hein, Hermann Hunger, Dagman Melman, and Angela Schwab. Leuven: Uitgeverij Peeters.

Sweeney, Marvin A. 1997. "Davidic Polemic in the Book of Judges." *VT* 47:517–29.

Talmon, Shemaryahu. 1961. "Synonymous Readings in the Textual Traditions of the Old Testament." Pages 335–83 in *Studies in the Bible*. Ed. Chaim Rabin. Scripta hierosolymitana 8. Jerusalem: Magnes.

———. 1964. "Aspects of the Textual Transmission of the Bible in the Light of Qumran." *Textus* 4:95–132.

————. 1970. "The Old Testament Text." Pages 159–231 in *From the Beginning to Jerome*. Ed. P. R. Ackroyd and C. F. Evans. Vol. 1 of *The Cambridge History of the Bible*. Cambridge: Cambridge University Press.

Täubler, Eugen. 1947. "Cushan-Rishathaim." *HUCA* 20:136–42.

Trebolle Barrera, Julio. 1989. "Textual Variants in 4QJudg[a] and the Textual and Editorial History of the Book of Judges (1)." *RevQ* 14:229–45.

————. 1991. "Édition préliminaire de 4QJuges[b]: Contribution des manuscripts qumrâniques des Juges à l'étude textuelle et littéraire du livre." *RevQ* 15:79–100.

————. 1993a. "The Authoritative Functions of Scriptural Works at Qumran." Pages 95–110 in *The Community of the Renewed Covenant: The Notre Dame Symposium on the Dead Sea Scrolls*. Ed. Eugene Ulrich and James Vanderkam. Notre Dame, IN: University of Notre Dame Press.

————. 1993b. "Textual Affiliation of the Old Latin Marginal Readings in the Books of Judges and Kings." Pages 315–24 in *Biblische Theologie und gesellschäftlicher Wandel für Norbert Lohfink S.J.* Ed. Georg Braulik, Walter A. Gross, and Sean McEvenue. Freiburg: Herder.

Ulrich, Eugene. 1993. "The Bible in the Making: The Scriptures at Qumran." Pages 77–93 in *The Community of the Renewed Covenant: The Notre Dame Symposium on the Dead Sea Scrolls*. Ed. Eugene Ulrich and James Vanderkam. Notre Dame, IN: University of Notre Dame Press.

VanderBilt, Deborah. 1998. "Translation and Orality in the Old English Orosius." *Oral Tradition* 13:377–97.

Van der Toorn, Karel. 1986. "Judges XVI 21 in the Light of Akkadian Sources." *VT* 36:248–53.

Van Seters, John. 1972. "The Conquest of Sihon's Kingdom: A Literary Examination." *JBL* 91:182–97.

Weitzman, Steven P. 1999. "Reopening the Case of the Suspiciously Suspended Nun in Judges 18:30." *CBQ* 61:448–60.

————. 2002. "The Samson Story as Border Fiction." *BibInt* 10:158–74.

Wenning, Robert, and Erich Zenger. 1982. "Die siebenlockige Held Simson: Literarische und ikonigraphische Beobachtungen zu Ri 13–16." *BN* 17:43–55.

Wright, G. Ernest. 1946. "The Literary and Historical Problem of Joshua 10 and Judges 1." *JNES* 5:105–14.

————. 1962. "The Lawsuit of God." Pages 26–67 in *Israel's Prophetic Heritage: Essays in Honor of James Muilenburg*. Ed. Bernard W. Anderson and Walter Harrelson. New York: Harper & Row.

Yadin, Y. 1970. "Megiddo of the Kings of Israel." *BA* 33:66–96.

Yee, Gale A. 1995. "Ideological Criticism: Judges 17–21 and the Dismembered Body." Pages 146–70 in *Judges and Method*. Ed. Gale A. Yee. Minneapolis: Fortress.

Younger, K. Lawson, Jr. 1994. "Judges 1 in Its Near Eastern Context." Pages 207–27 in *Faith, Tradition, and History: Old Testament Historiography in Its Near Eastern Context*. Ed. A. R. Millard, James Hoffmeier, and David W. Baker. Winona Lake, IN: Eisenbrauns.

Zertal, Adam. 1992. "Bezek." *ABD* 1:717–18.

Zimmerman, Frank. 1952. "Reconstruction in Judges 7:25–8:25." *JBL* 71:111–114.

INTRODUCTION

1. Story, Characters, and Themes: Epic Implications

Judges is one of the most exciting portions of the grand traditional history of the people Israel that runs from Genesis through 2 Kings, especially to those who share a deep appreciation for epic-style literature. By the time the narrative reaches Judges, Israel has been engendered by the ancestral heroes and heroines. The group has been promised the land of Israel as its inheritance, enslaved in Egypt, and rescued by God. They have received laws, spent forty years wandering in the wilderness, and, as told in one strand of the book of Joshua, conquered the promised land.

Judges describes the attempt by various Israelite groups to achieve liberation from oppressors and to gain political and geographic control of the land. On a basic level, the book is a series of stories about conflict, containing themes that are typical of the foundation tales of many cultures. In the biblical chronology, the judges' experiments in statehood are followed by the establishment of a monarchy. Judges thus describes a formative and transitional period in the biblical version of Israelite political history.

The Judges

The "judges," protagonists of the tales that give the book its name, are swashbuckling, charismatic military leaders. What does it mean to call such leaders "judges," a term that in English evokes images of those who resolve disputes, assess damages, and mete out punishments by rendering legal decisions? As Jo Ann Hackett has noted in a careful overview, the root *špṭ*, "to judge," usually has a "decision-making context" in the Hebrew Bible (1998: 187–88). Extrabiblical uses of cognate terms refer to various "judicial" and "administrative" functions (188–89). Hackett points out that the judge was "not only responsible for the administration of justice but could also perform duties that include some sort of governing" (189). To appreciate fully the role of the judge in Judges, one needs to return to the root meaning of decision making in its narrative and religious contexts. How do biblical writers outside of Judges understand the term, and how is it contextualized in the book of Judges? Material in 1 and 2 Samuel is especially helpful, although additional allusions are relevant.

Ruth 1:1; 2 Kgs 23:22; and Isa 1:26 all imply that the "judges" demarcate a particular era and a particular form of polity—of political "decision making"— that existed before the monarchy. This theme is echoed in versions of the recurring refrain that frames the final five chapters of Judges: "In those days there was no king in Israel. . . ."

Judges 2, a theologically oriented excursus, understands the judge to be a leader who models proper covenantal behavior, inspiring Israel to maintain loyalty to Yhwh (2:17, 19). The judge is also a military "deliverer" in ch. 2 (v. 1) and frequently elsewhere in the book (e.g., 3:9, 15; 6:14; 8:22; 10:1, 2, 3; 13:5). Valuable detail begins to emerge, however, in the descriptions of the judges Othniel and Deborah. The phrase indicating that Othniel "judges Israel" is preceded by the formulaic allusion to his God-sent charisma (3:10). The descent of the divine spirit is also said to be experienced by Jephthah (11:29) and by Samson (14:19; 15:14). Charisma, the status as judge, and military success are all interrelated. The fuller description of the activities of Deborah contributes further to this portrait of the judge. She is said to be "judging Israel," and Israelites come to her for "judgment" (4:4–5). She is also called a "prophet," a mediator between God and humans (4:4), a person who offers oracles, predicting that Sisera will fall by the hands of a woman. She offers oracles under the "palm of Deborah," a sacred grove, an oracular site (see commentary at 4:4–10; 9:1–7). One returns, then, to the root meaning "decision maker." The judge can offer decisions, whether to go to war or how to conduct the battle (e.g., Deborah, Ehud, Gideon), and his or her advice is followed because it is believed to be God-sent knowledge. This oracular capacity also allows him or her to adjudicate more mundane matters, to "judge" in a more workaday fashion. The judge is endowed with the divine spirit. Thus Gideon receives his call to leadership under the oak at Ophrah, another sacred space where a divine messenger appears (6:11). War itself is also an indicator of where the divine will lies. God arbitrates in war and through war (11:27).

Samuel's various roles as judge are also instructive as we seek to understand the range of meanings of the term. Like the other judges, Samuel, who "judges" the people of Israel at Mizpah (1 Sam 7:6), mediates between God and the people. The people continue to sin, as in the view that frames the careers of other judges. Under Samuel, the people gather, pour out water, fast, and confess in a ritual, rich in the symbolism of cleansing. To oversee this ritual is also to act as judge, an intermediary who prays to the Lord on Israel's behalf (7:8). First Samuel 7:17 adds that Samuel built an altar. Judging is framed in religious terms. To translate Samuel's activities as a circuit judge, "administering justice," as does NRSV (1 Sam 7:17), is perhaps too bureaucratic. Samuel, like Samson, is a *Nazir,* a charismatic, divinely ordained figure. The judge is enabled to lead and make decisions not because of legal wisdom but because of a divinatory capacity, a spirit critical to the conduct of war. Even Gideon, who may seem less "spirited" in this sense than some of the other judges, hears a *klēdōn*, an overheard prophecy placed in the mouth of a passerby (Judg 7:13–14), and receives signs (6:36–40). He creates a sacred space and oversees ritual (8:24–27).

Epic Heroes

The judges are frequently regarded as epic heroes. Folklorist Richard Dorson provides a brief but masterful overview of traits that recur in various traditions. He notes that many of the works that might be regarded as epic are "stirring traditional narrative(s) of perilous adventure, daring, and manhood" (1978: 4). He observes that heroes manifest human qualities such as bravery or physical might, that they often have divine helpers, and that they may use "guile" as well as strength to vanquish enemies. Underlying story patterns involve conquests, travels, and valor, but the relationship of epic to history varies, for "the hero of history attracts splendid legends and the hero of fiction assumes a realistic and historical dimension, so that they tend to converge over the course of the epic and saga process" (4).

Dorson's observations apply well to tales of the judges and the early kings. Whether one uses the term *epic* or not, the Israelites produced a literature entirely comparable to those of the many cultural traditions explored by Dorson. Such narratives had their appeal within ancient Israel as elsewhere and were employed in culturally specific ways as a deeply expressive means of asserting and declaring national and ethnic identity. Also relevant to a discussion of judges as "epic heroes" is the character of international folklore that Eric Hobsbawm (1969) dubs the "social bandit."

Social Bandits

A warrior chief endowed with charisma and empowered by God, the judge has a special social and political function in Judges as defender of the weak against the strong. The judge fights for those who are marginalized and against the interests of the establishment. The "deliverers" of Judges compare well with Eric Hobsbawm's "social bandits" or "primitive rebels." Robin Hood is perhaps the most famous primitive rebel in Western folklore. As a social historian, Hobsbawm relates tales of social bandits to particular types of sociopolitical contexts. Hobsbawm locates social banditry "in all types of human society which lie between the evolutionary phase of tribal and kinship organization, and modern capitalist society" (1969: 14). While the rise of capitalism is not an issue in biblical material, the tales of the judges and early kings do mark a significant transition between a socio-structural group identity based upon kinship and one based upon allegiance to a state, such as the monarchies of the ancient Near East. Admired by their communities, social bandits are "champions, fighters for justice, perhaps even leaders of liberation" (13).

Young men of rural origins, bandits arise during periods of transition and flux. They are often marginal figures in their own societies, sometimes victims of injustice, and are characteristically rebels. They kill in just vengeance or self-defense and, in Israelite versions, are tricksters who often succeed through deception. The judges and early kings, Saul and David, suit this list of criteria beautifully, although Moses as well might qualify as a social bandit in the narratives of Exodus. Gideon, Saul, and David all have agrarian or pastoral roots. Jephthah is an illegitimate son of a prostitute, denied rights by his brothers; and Deborah is a female leader, an unusual role in this literature about men. Ehud is a left-handed man in a symbolic world in which the "normal," preferred side is the right; and David, a youngest son, is an enemy of the Saulide establishment. All of these heroes qualify in ancient Israel for the designation "marginal." Samson is an explosive hero, a type of bandit Hobsbawm calls "the avenger" because his warring boils over into uncontrolled manifestations of violence. He takes shelter in caves, kills with his bare hands, and is Israel's weapon against the powerful and oppressive Philistines. The judges, plus Saul and David, confront Israel's political and cultural enemies in war and save their people. Thus the judge, the epic hero, and the social bandit converge as one seeks to characterize the stories of Judges and their protagonists. The prominence of war in these tales is another critical element in understanding Judges as a national foundation narrative.

War and the Judges

Warring in tales of the early Israelite heroes, including the biblical judges and the early kings, is characterized by a specific bardic ideology, by certain roles played by women, and by the juxtaposition of themes of eroticism and death. War is sport to these "men of valor," as Gideon, David, and his men are called (Judg 6:12; 1 Sam 14:52; 16:18; 2 Sam 17:10; 23:20; 24:9). Combat is a contest in which heroes use special, sometimes unusual, weapons and skill (see Beniah, 2 Sam 23:20–21; 1 Chron 11:23; Elhanan, 2 Sam 21:19; David and Goliath, 1 Sam 17; Ehud, Judg 3:12–30; Shamgar, Judg 3:31; Samson, Judg 14:6; 15:15). Abner, the general of Saul, proposes to Joab, David's general, that the lads on each side "rise up and make sport before us" (2 Sam 2:12–16). They do so, but the contest between warriors ends in all of their deaths. Opponents frequently engage in taunting behavior before or during battle (e.g., Goliath and David) and nevertheless respect the skill of their enemies. A certain code applies whereby men of comparable experience and skill are expected to confront one another in battle. Goliath thus resents the young man David in the cameo scene in 1 Sam 17:41–49, and Abner hesitates to kill Joab's younger brother, Asahel, who insists upon pursuing him in battle (2 Sam 2:21–22). Respect for the enemy is also evident in the conversation between Gideon and the captured Midianite kings (Judg 8:20). They comment on the noble demeanor of Israelites they have killed in battle and ask that Gideon be the one to kill them, because his son, a less experienced warrior, is not up to the task.

Much of the fighting in Judges through 2 Samuel is between Israelites and non-Israelite enemies, but battle frequently erupts among Israelites themselves over the distribution of booty, leadership rights, or perceived insults. The civil war between the forces of Saul and David is one of the lengthiest of these accounts, but also in this category are Gideon's vengeance in Judges 8, Abimelech's rebellion in Judges 9, Jephthah's confrontation with the men of Ephraim in Judges 12, and the civil war in Judges 20–21.

Central in the relationships between warriors are women. They frequently serve as prizes of war and as valuable items of exchange. Michal is David's reward, promised by King Saul, her father, in return for a hundred Philistine foreskins (1 Sam 18:25). Achsah is the prize meted out by Caleb to the hero Othniel (Judg 1:12–15). The women create relationships between the men. In the case of Saul and David, however, as in the cases of Samson's marriage to the Philistine Timnite woman and his affair with Delilah, the relationship leads to or reflects enmity rather than accord. The sacrifice of Jephthah's daughter as a war vow in Judg 11:29–40 also reflects this theme of exchange between males, but in this case the recipient of the valuable woman prize is God. The girl is offered as a sacrifice to the Lord in return for Jephthah's success in battle. Jael, slayer of the enemy general Sisera, is mistakenly perceived by Sisera as a helper because of his king's relationship to her husband (4:17). The characters are portrayed as assuming the existence of certain kinds of bonds between men of power, bonds often mediated by women. Instead of serving as a mediator of this positive relationship, however, Jael serves the cause of the Israelites, a subversive manifestation of the folk motif of "the iron fist in the velvet glove."

The treatment of women sometimes sets the occasion for war, as in the case of the rape and murder of the Levite's concubine in Judges 19. This crime leads to civil war when the men of Benjamin side with their kinsmen in Gibeah, where the heinous incident occurred, rather than back pan-Israelite vengeance. In 1 Samuel 30 David attacks and defeats the Amalekites who had stolen his women in a raid. Women are also involved in the process of reconciliation even while their voices and experiences offer a critique of men's wars. It is the stealing of the women of Shiloh at the end of the war and the forced marriage of daughters from the town of Jabesh-gilead that close the hostilities in Judges 21. The words of Sisera's mother and her ladies in waiting in Judges 5 serve as an implicit critique of the phenomenon of war, which creates heroes but eliminates sons and enslaves daughters.

Finally, the Israelite war tradition equates death on the battlefield with sex. As shown by Emily Vermeule for Homeric material, the defeated warrior is metaphorically the woman who has been raped (1979: 101). The language and imagery of the tale of Jael and Sisera purposefully commingle military death and sexual conquest. Terms such as "kneel" and "lie," and the phrase "between her legs," found in Judg 5:27, create the double entendre in a traditional Israelite medium (Niditch 1989). Tales of the heroes Ehud (Judg 3:12–30) and Samson (Judg 16) are similarly informed (see Niditch 1993b: 113–19; 1990: 616–17).

2. Judges and History

American and European biblical scholars in the twentieth century expressed an understandable interest in matching the narratives of Joshua and Judges with actual historical origins of the Israelites in the land. The Bible itself seems to offer two versions. One, represented in Joshua (e.g., the summaries in Josh 10:40–42; 11:23; 18:1; 24:8–13), suggests that Israelites swept into the land in an unbeatable military wave in which all enemies fell before Joshua and the Israelites, portrayed as a unified, successful commando force, aided by the divine warrior and assorted miracles. The other version, well represented in the middle chapters of Joshua (e.g., 13:1–7; 15:63; 16:10; 17:12) and throughout Judges, offers a more halting and disjunctive portrayal of the Israelites' early presence in the land, describing successes and failures in establishing themselves. Judges includes both alternating periods of subjugation and of subjugating and a more tribal accounting, as Israelite groups are seen in various geographic locations, north to south, living side by side with non-Israelite groups who have not been rooted out. What is one to make of such contrasting pictures?

Various models for Israelite origins have been offered, several of which are directly relevant to the study of Judges. The "infiltration model" articulated in the work of German scholars including Albrecht Alt (1966) and Martin Noth (1966) matched the nontriumphalist thread in Judges, also found in portions of Joshua, with a particular evolutionary view of civilization involving the gradual settlement of nomads to become agrarian villagers. Alt pointed to archaeological evidence suggesting that the central highlands of Israel were sparsely populated in the Late Bronze Age and available to these would-be settlers, and theorized that as the settlers increased in number, they found themselves in competition with other local groups and claimants to the land, fighting them for control. In this model, the battles described in Judges are viewed as a reflection of the Israelites' defensive wars, for the infiltration had been gradual and nonaggressive, and Israelites defended themselves by unifying in a league or amphictyony, consisting of various segments or tribes of Israel.

This model has come under criticism. While it appears to match Judges better than the triumphalist thread in Joshua, even Judges contains no description of peaceful infiltration, only scenes of what Alt would have to call subsequent tensions; and, of course, many of these tensions are among Israelites themselves, an important and revealing aspect of the book.

From American scholars of the mid-twentieth century such as W. F. Albright and his students John Bright and G. Ernest Wright emerged the "conquest model." ②
These scholars employed archaeological data to suggest confidently that Israelites did take over the land through sweeping military actions, as suggested by portions of the book of Joshua (e.g., the accounts in Josh 1–9; 10:40–42; 11:23; 18; 24:8–13). For Wright (1946: 114), the linear conquest and halting takeover are not mutually exclusive; rather, portions of Joshua describe the Israelites' initial rapid successes, while Judges describes later attempts to hold or consolidate power. Links between specific stories in Joshua and archaeological evidence of destruction and burning in biblically named locations of the appropriate era have proven elusive, although one thread in modern scholarship, evidenced, for example, in the work of several archaeologists cited in the commentary on chapter 1, still tries to match biblical accounts with the warring actions of certain ancient Israelite groups at specific locations (see also the orientation offered in B. Mazar, 1971).

In contrast to "infiltration" and "conquest" models, the "peasant revolution" ③ model, first suggested by George Mendenhall (1973) and later developed more fully by Norman Gottwald (1979), suits one collection of biblical stories quite well, namely, the tales of Israelite "social bandits." The many accounts in Judges describe politically marginal, poorly armed guerrilla forces of Israelites combating well-equipped, king-led oppressors by means of the warfare of trickery or banditry. The "liberation" or "peasant revolt" model holds that the Israelites engaged in a war of liberation to free themselves from various feudal overlords who reigned at least nominally as vassals of the superpower Egypt. In this way Gottwald and Mendenhall link tales of Judges to certain aspects of Late Bronze Age/Early Iron Age sociopolitics as reconstructed by historians.

The "pioneer settlement" model, evidenced, for example, in the work of ④ Robert Coote and Keith Whitelam, regards Israelites as native to the land and does not rely at all on the biblical story to reconstruct Israelite origins (1987: 16, 19–20, 176–77). Building instead on archaeological data and pertinent ethnographic models from other cultures, Coote and Whitelam hypothesize that Israelites were composed of elements that left the more settled urban lowland to deforest and tame the highlands. The movements of these pioneers were motivated by economic issues, especially the collapse of trade in the difficult times of the Late Bronze Age. Coote and Whitelam, however, resist matching their model to suggestions in Judges 5, for example, about banditry on the highways and economic deprivation that would seem to suit such a portrayal.

Lawrence Stager and others offer a more nuanced version of the "pioneer settlement" model, namely, a "ruralization hypothesis." Stager explores a conflu- ⑤ ence of economic, archaeological, and biblical data to explain the emergence of early Israel and "the proliferation of agricultural villages in frontier areas" within the framework of the "economic decline of the Late Bronze city-state" (1998: 141–42). Stager carefully suggests links between the process of rural-ization and situations described in Judges. He finds a degree of historical verisimilitude, for example, in the reference to economic contractions in Judg 5:6–7, in the competition with the Philistines that dominates the tales of Samson (the Philistines settled on the Mediterranean coast in the 12th century B.C.E.), and in the description of the Danites as employed in seafaring (Judg 5:17; Stager 1988, 1989).

Other approaches to ancient Israel treat the question of Israelite history differently. Some regard the earliest period of Israelite history as impossible to reconstruct, suggesting that the Bible reflects a much later vision from the period of the monarchy or postmonarchy. An example of this approach to Judges is found in Marc Brettler's excellent study that postulates an exilic or postexilic, pro-Davidic ideology behind the work (2002). Others downplay historical questions or ignore them altogether, finding the meaning of a text in the reader's response or treating biblical works as literary wholes to be appreciated. Sensitive holistic analyses of Judges are offered by Barry G. Webb (1987) and by David Gunn (1987).

In this commentary I offer a theoretical approach that is interested in history and takes seriously the idea that Judges includes material that would have been meaningful in some form to Israelite audiences before there were kings in Israel (pre–tenth century B.C.E.), during the northern and southern monarchies (tenth–sixth centuries B.C.E.), and after the collapse of the southern kingdom (586 B.C.E.). Judges is multilayered and multivoiced, and in the commentary I am concerned with the ways in which material preserved in Judges both reflects various periods and resonated in those settings. The approach is thus historical in this sense, but matching narrative details with specific historical events or testing for historical verisimilitude is not at the foreground of the approach. In the commentary I try to listen closely to the stories themselves in the form they have been preserved, to the meanings and messages conveyed by style, content, and structure, asking what sort of Israelites they might have shaped and reflected. In this work I seek to understand the relationship between the stories and the variegated threads in Israelite culture.

3. Redaction History: Voices

Judges is a series of narratives, rich in characterization, dramatic tensions, protagonists, and enemies. As one explores these narratives, questions concerning implicit worldviews are critical. Is a particular political ethic at work, a view of war, a prevailing attitude to gender roles? Where do the tales stand in contrast with or in comparison to material in the larger biblical tradition? The answers to some of these questions begin to reveal certain trajectories in Israelite thought and to suggest hypotheses about the people who produced and received this tradition of narratives.

Judges does not feature the triumphalist tradition so apparent in Joshua. The triumphalist voice may be attributed to monarchic-period writers extolling the victories of the people and their leader, as is common in the war accounts of many ancient Near Eastern victory steles. Such an orientation may have been preserved also by writers composing long after the heyday of the centralized monarchies, northern and southern. Such writers were royalists who longed for renewal. They believed that God was on their side, a view promulgated and validated by stories of ancient victories, justifying rights to the land now in the control of oppressors. Judges, however, does not perpetuate this triumphalist view. Instead, within Judges, three major voices are discernible: the epic-bardic voice, the voice of the theologian, and the voice of the humanist. The voices are characterized by considerable overlaying and intertwining as would be expected in a traditional corpus of literature that has been made and remade many times orally and in writing.

The Epic-Bardic Voice

The epic-bardic voice may be as old as the stories themselves and as old as Israel's origins in the latter part of the second millennium B.C.E. The world as pictured is richly comparable to the depiction of ancient classical epic worlds with long-haired warriors, the use of a prophetic *klēdōn* (whereby the future is divined from another person's overheard words), a character akin to Hercules, a story comparable to that of Iphigeneia, a tale reminiscent of the rape of the Sabine women, and epic-style encounters of heroes in battle and in death. This list is not to suggest direct borrowing from Aegean cultures but rather to acknowledge that more than one epic tradition enlivened the ancient Mediterranean world, and that cross-fertilization between various traditions is to be expected.

In this trajectory of Judges, heroes supported by the divine helper (Yhwh) battle enemies, sometimes on their own as in the case of the rogue Samson, sometimes with the help of a band of warriors comparable to that of Robin Hood. Narrative interests include the distribution of booty, the workings of temporary charismatic leadership and a decentralized polity, and aspects of religious life that sometimes differ, for example, from portrayals in the book of Deuteronomy.

Judges 5, the "Song of Deborah," belongs to this trajectory and for reasons of texture, text, and context may date to the twelfth century B.C.E., a very early date. It speaks in a particular stylized register that may have been available to composers in early Israel. Most of the book of Judges, however, reflects the influence of later receivers, preservers, and transmitters of the early tales. One of the most important is the voice of the theologian.

The Voice of the Theologian

A second layer or voice in Judges is usually recognized among biblicists as that of "Deuteronomic" or "Deuteronomistic" writers. The former term usually refers to the fifth book of the Bible and its qualities of language and theme, while the latter term more broadly refers to Deuteronomic-style biblical contributors who are typically represented in the corpus that runs from Deuteronomy through 2 Kings and who are often regarded as responsible for the compilation of that corpus.

An interesting and important history of scholarship has been devoted to exploring the identity and compositional activities of these writers whose style and worldview share much with the book of Deuteronomy. Theories about a Deuteronomistic History are relevant to views of the redaction history of Judges. Martin Noth (1957) thought that much of the material in Judges was incorporated into a grand history of Israel running from Deuteronomy through 2 Kings and created by an exilic author of the mid-sixth century B.C.E. This author wrote introductory material in Judges 2 and composed or framed Judg 3:7–13:1. In Noth's view, this core was then expanded and revised by later contributors. Continuing in the spirit of Noth's work, Wolfgang Richter (1963) provided perhaps the most detailed theory of the various Deuteronomistic layers as they pertain to Judges. In later groundbreaking work, Frank Moore Cross (1968; 1973: 274–89) suggested that the Deuteronomistic History was the creation of a composer who gathered and shaped a history of the people Israel as a propagandistic and nationalistic contribution to the reform of Josiah, the seventh-century B.C.E. Judean king. This work was later revised and updated by an exilic-period author. Thus in Judges one might look for evidence of these two Deuteronomistic layers. In his Anchor Bible commentary, Robert Boling accepted and applied Cross's theory to Judges. Barry G. Webb (1987) cogently reviewed these and other theories concerning the Deuteronomistic History and their implications for Judges. Scholars, however, have been reassessing the influence of Deuteronomistically oriented writers on the formation of smaller and larger portions of the Hebrew Bible (see articles in Knoppers and McConville 2000; Römer 2000; and Schearing and McKenzie 1999). In the present work I will treat the Deuteronomic-style material in Judges holistically under the heading of the "voice of the theologian," identifying material in Judges that has been recognized as "Deuteronomic" or "Deuteronomistic" in style, content, and message. In contrast to the work by Antony Campbell and Mark O'Brien (2000), I will not attempt to distinguish between various contributors within this layer or to deal with the knotty larger issue of Deuteronomism, a subject of much current debate.

Strongly covenantal in orientation, the voice of the theologian regards Israel's history as dependent upon the relationship with Yhwh. Faithfulness brings success, military, economic, and political, whereas unfaithfulness and covenant breaking bring defeat and oppression. Successes and failures in war—and the book of Judges is primarily a collection of war stories—are viewed strictly in terms of Israel's covenant faithfulness, in contrast to other explanations of failure such as inferior weapons or inexperience. The intellectual ancestors of the Deuteronomic-style writers of the Hebrew Bible are probably to be found in conservative Levitical northern circles such as those that supported the prophetic careers of Elijah and Elisha. Such groups, many of whose members headed southward after the conquest by the Assyrians (721 B.C.E.), may have influenced the reform of the seventh-century B.C.E. king Josiah, who is said to have reinvigorated the covenant with God, eschewing all idolatry and prohibiting other practices that would have been rejected as non-Yahwistic (2 Kgs 22–23).

The language of Judges 2 and other recurring literary structures that set the history of the judges and individual tales about them in a theological framework (3:7–15; 4:1–3; 6:1–10; 10:6–16; 13:1) are, as noted above, reminiscent of the style and content of the book of Deuteronomy, the classic statement of Deuteronomic thought. These strong covenantal frameworks, however, also serve to preserve fascinating descriptions of precisely the sort of popular religious practices that Deuteronomists are supposed to have rejected. They briefly condemn Gideon's ephod, even though other non-Deuteronomic features of religious practice are presented without commentary or negative evaluation. The sacrifice of Jephthah's daughter, for example, is narrated without condemnation. The voice of the theologian in Judges is less dominant and intrusive than is often asserted (Amit 1999: 363–67), and its appreciation for the old stories is irrepressible. Like Deuteronomy 17, the book of Judges is also critical and suspicious of kings (cf. Amit 1999: 114–18). Writers of a Deuteronomistic orientation appear to have been particularly influential during the late southern monarchy and the early exilic period. One might imagine their stamp to have been set on traditions of the judges during the seventh to sixth centuries B.C.E., but earlier or later dates are possible.

The Voice of the Humanist

A third voice, most prominently represented in Judges 1 and 17–21, can be detected in the work of those who preserve the ancient stories. Telling tales of "olden times," this voice is noncritical about the ancient protagonists. It lets the tales speak for themselves. Perhaps contributors to this third voice or layer regarded their compositions as works of fiction written in a traditional mode, designed to put a spin on early history. Or perhaps the authors regarded themselves as preservers of ancient history. In either case, they preserved and shaped tales that purport to tell about ancient times. Many of these stories may have circulated among Israelites in various forms for centuries before the formation of the book of Judges. I do not mean to suggest that the stories in any form were necessarily true representations of the earliest Israelite culture or religion, but rather that they had validity as one way in which Israel viewed itself even in early times.

Whereas the dominant responsibility for framing the hero stories of chs. 3–16 belongs to the contributor I call "the theologian," this third trajectory is well represented in chs. 1 and 17–21. Material in these chapters is formally different from the stories of the individual judges in chs. 3–16, which are introduced by a recurring, covenantally oriented frame. Judges 3–16, moreover, explore Israel's early history by tracing the careers of heroic and charismatic individuals. As go their adventures and victories, so goes the nation. Judges 1 and 17–21, however, provide foundation tales that tend not to feature heroic individuals. The voice that dominates is aware of tensions in Israelite worldview and lets the tradition as framed reveal them. We are allowed to see two options in polity: one centralized and one decentralized, one state-led, the other kin-based and tribal. The view of Israel's conquest of the land is ambivalent and contrasts with the portrayal found in portions of Joshua that project uncomplicated self-assurance. The voice of this trajectory is particularly attuned to the vagaries of power, the transience of political and military control, themes that emerge strongly in the introductory first chapter and the foundation tales of the last five. Messages about the ways in which power comes and goes are, of course, thematically important in many epic traditions and make for powerful stories about heroic human beings. The third voice of Judges embraces and intensifies such messages. I call this measured and thoughtful contributor the "humanist" voice, whose worldview is congruent with those of some Persian or early Hellenistic period biblical writers.

Despite the limited and edited nature of the preserved corpus, biblical works from the late sixth–fourth centuries B.C.E. reveal a wide array of genres and points of view. Proto-apocalyptic works such as Zechariah 14, Joel, and Isaiah 24–27 coexist with writings such as Ezra and Nehemiah, which reflect a sober "collaboration with tyranny," to use a phrase of David Daube (1965). Tales of simple things and people with a positive view of foreigners, such as Ruth, coexist with Esther, a tale of people in high places who survive by using their wisdom to manipulate unwise and evil courtly foreigners. God stands in the distance in the book of Ruth but is nowhere mentioned in Esther. Pious wisdom works such as Proverbs coexist with radical works such as Job and Ecclesiastes that question God's justice. Much has been written about the sources of these works and the differences in worldview that they reflect. The social realities are, no doubt, much more complex than Paul Hanson (1975) or Morton Smith's (1971) two-party maps allow. The former suggests "visionary" and "pragmatist" parties, while the latter offers a contrast between "Yahweh-aloners" and "assimilationists." Smith does, however, offer observations germane to suggesting a final Persian-Hellenistic layer in Judges. He writes of "belletristic material" stemming from members of a "lay circle enjoying wealth, leisure, and considerable culture" who are "in touch with the intellectual and artistic developments of the hellenistic world" (121–22). Such authors are responsible in his view for the finest stories of the late biblical or early postbiblical period, such as Ruth, Jonah, Esther, and Judith.

Smith sees this group of literati as initially being part of the assimilationist party, a cosmopolitan religiously "liberal" group that gradually comes to accept views of their opponents in the "Yahweh-alone party," those religiously conservative groups represented in Ezra–Nehemiah. Again, the "parties" of this difficult-to-reconstruct period were probably far more complex and varied than such dichotomies allow. Nevertheless, Judges 1 and 17–21 do reflect a worldview that is not messianic or apocalyptic, nor strongly pro-monarchic. The writers who are responsible for Judges 1 and 17–21, and ultimately for the preservation of the rest of Judges—tales of the heroes framed by the theologian—are able to imagine a time without kings. Like the voice of Deuteronomy 17 and the theologian's voice that frames the central tales of the judges, the humanist voice suggests that the monarchy is inevitable if not always glorious. This voice is responsible for the significant refrain in the last five chapters of Judges, "In those days there were no kings in Israel," and thereby appears to be recalling a long-ago past. In portions dominated by the voice of the humanist, human beings are largely on their own, although God is always in the background, the ultimate controller of events. This voice is nationalistic and interested in showing that Israelites can reconcile even after the worst civil war. It describes a world without temple or priesthood in which individuals exercise leadership when needed, and it appreciates the epic world, perhaps influenced by comparable Greek traditions. I suggest that a postexilic writer or writers has appreciatively preserved and shaped the inherited traditions of Judges, with a light hand. This voice is heard best at the beginning and end of Judges, and, like the rest of the book, preserves older material. Tales of chs. 1 and 17–21, however, were not previously collected and shaped by the "theologian."

The three hypothesized voices carry redactional significance for Judges. Ancient stories have been reworked, and those who have done the reworking are more obviously represented in some passages than in others. By the same token, Judges is a whole. Both the theologian and the humanist have embraced the epic-style tales they have inherited as ancient Israelite tradition, while all three voices would agree on essential features of Yahwism, emphasizing, for example, God's role in Israel's fate. As elsewhere in the ancient world, political and military successes depend upon the favor of the Deity.

4. Texture: Recurring Language, Orality, Verbal Art, and Registers

Repetition and Epic Language

A full appreciation of tales of the judges, their characters, themes, and settings, is possible only with an understanding of the way in which they are expressed. An analysis of texture in Judges and of the presuppositions behind matters of style points back to the oral-traditional and to the notion of epic. The style of the literature about heroes in Judges is fully traditional, as is much of the Hebrew Bible. Repetition within tales and across the biblical corpus is common, for example, as authors frequently use the same language to convey similar content. Certain key phrases may even be markers of an Israelite ethnic genre comparable to "epic." Possible candidates for such markers of epic are the phrases, *wayĕhî bayyāmîm hāhēm*, literally, "And it was in those days" or "It came to pass in those days," the related *bayyāmîm hāhēm*, "in those days," *wayĕhî bîmê*, "And it was in the days of *X*," and *wayĕhî ʾîš*, "And there was a man."

Wyhy, the so-called *waw* consecutive of the imperfect form of the verb "to be," is used throughout ancient Hebrew narrative to demarcate time (see van der Merwe 1999). In an extremely common use of this term, the narrator provides a specific time frame for the scene or story that follows: for example, "(It was) at that time" (Gen 21:22; 38:1; 1 Kgs 11:29), "(It was) at the end of *x* amount of time" (Gen 8:6; 41:1; Deut 9:11; Judg 11:39; 2 Sam 15:7; 1 Kgs 2:39), or "(It was) on the next day" (Num 17:23; Judg 9:42; 21:4; 1 Sam 11:11; 18:10; 31:8). Less common throughout the narrative portions of the Hebrew Bible is the temporal phrase, "And it was in those days," and the briefer variant, "In those days." These phrases are represented densely in Judges: 17:6; 18:1; 19:1; 20:27, 28; 21:25; and in 1 Sam 3:1; 28:1; LXX 1 Sam 4:1. The context for all of these usages is foundation myth, stories concerning the genesis of the people, often including a war or battle and reference to the career of a hero. The formulaic phrases mark tales of olden times. After such a phrase in Judg 17:6; 18:1; 19:1; 20:27, 28; 1 Sam 28:1; LXX 1 Sam 4:1, the story of a war or battle that took place in the significant past soon follows. Judges 21:25, an inclusio for 17:6 or 19:1, comments on the battles that have just been described. At Judg 20:21 and 1 Sam 3:1, particular heroes are introduced who are significant in a cultural history. Variation upon the phrase "in those days" does seem to frame the sort of content scholars have found in epic; and the phrase is found densely in a specific corpus of similar tales, tales from the days of the early rulers of Israel. There are relatively few uses of these phrases outside Judges–Samuel, and five of these introduce passages that are similar in orientation to those of Judges: Gen 6:4 refers to the presence of the great heroes of old, the Nephilim; Exod 2:11 introduces the bandit career of Moses; Ezek 38:17 refers to old-time prophets; in Neh 6:17 and 13:15, 23, Nehemiah describes his role in his own memoir as a significant feature of the nation's past.

Two additional temporal phrases may signal epic material in the Hebrew Bible. The first phrase, "It was in the days of King *X*," alludes to some aspect of the career of a king. Both Gen 14:1 and Isa 7:1 are preludes to battle accounts, while Esth 1:1 introduces the tale of threat to Jews in diaspora that ends in self-defense, battle, and survival. The reference in Genesis 14 is especially interesting because it places Abraham in a heroic, epic-like setting, quite in contrast to other patriarchal accounts. This mock-heroic tale may suggest that Israelites themselves recognized and adapted an epic genre (Niditch 1993b: 101–2). The second phrase, "There was a man," is found densely in Judges–2 Samuel (see Amit 1984/85 and Judg 13:2; 17:1; 19:1; 1 Sam 1:1; 9:1; 2 Sam 21:20 [1 Chron 20:6]) and introduces a figure who will be part of an important founding myth, often the hero's progenitor (Samson's father, Manoah, in Judg 13:2; Samuel's father in 1 Sam 1:1; Saul's father in 1 Sam 9:1). Elsewhere, the phrase introduces a key player in a series of events in the foundation tale (Judg 17:1; 19:1; 2 Sam 21:20). A close examination of language in Judges in a comparative biblical context thus seems to reveal certain linguistic markers of heroic and perhaps "epic" material.

The authors of tales in Judges also take special pleasure in having characters use riddles, proverbs, and *mĕšālîm*, media of oral performance. Thus Samson propounds a riddle at his wedding in traditional style (Noy 1968; Judg 14:14) and responds to his opponents in proverbial language (v. 18). Gideon calms the Ephraimites, jealous for booty, with a proverb emphasizing their honor—indeed, much in these battle accounts has to do with men's shame and honor (8:2). Enemy kings, facing their own defeat or death, speak in proverbs (Adoni-bezek in 1:7 and Zebah and Zalmunna in 8:21; cf. 1 Kgs 20:11). Jotham employs a *māšāl* to deliver a stinging political critique of the illegitimate ruler Abimelech, who has murdered all of his rivals for power (Judg 9:7–21). Finally, the judge Jephthah offers a case for the justness of his cause in battle with a rhetorically rich speech that draws upon the traditional history of the exodus (11:4–28).

Registers and Redaction

The present use of the term "register" is influenced by the work of Dell Hymes, who defines registers as "major speech styles associated with recurring types of situations" (1989: 440), and by the application of concepts concerning "register" to oral-traditional works by John Foley. Foley describes registers as ways of communicating that are "contextually appropriate signals for institutionalized meanings"; the register is "an expressive code" (1995: 50). As a student of oral-derived literatures, Foley asks, in particular, "To what sort of language do [performers] resort in order to carry on the project of co-creating the work," a work set within a particular cultural context (1995: 49)? The notion of register is helpful as we explore the possible relationships between the varieties of

Hebrew style employed in the Bible and the information or messages that might be conveyed by those styles or by switches in those styles.

[Scholars have long sought to employ linguistic criteria to match examples of Biblical Hebrew with particular historical periods or literary sources in order to explore issues in provenance, authorship, and redaction history] (see, e.g., Japhet 1968; Hurvitz 1982, 2000; Rendsburg 2002; Polzin 1976; and Polak 1998). A careful analysis of syntax and style has led Frank Polak to suggest the existence of a spectrum of registers in Biblical Hebrew that reflects a relative chronology. At one end is the classical style characterized by a high number of short clauses, dominance of finite verb forms, a rarity of subordinate clauses, and a rarity of noun strings. At the other end is late Hebrew with long noun strings and complex sentences "in which a single predicate governs a high number of arguments and subordinate clauses," some of which are achieved via participles and infinitive clauses (1998: 65). In the late style, noun forms are in higher ratio than verb forms, and nominal forms of the verb are more numerous than finite verbs. Between these two ends Polak identifies a somewhat more intricate classical form and a somewhat simpler transitional late form. It is interesting that tales of Samson (Judges 13–16) provide one of his cases for the simplest or purist classical form (1998: 78, 87), while Judges 3–4, 6–9, 11–12, 17–18 exemplify the intricate variety of classical Hebrew (69). Thus tales at the heart of Judges and one narrative complex, which reflects significant influence of the "humanist" voice, belong linguistically and stylistically, in Polak's framework, to early Hebrew.

It would be exciting indeed if Polak's linguistic spectrum unequivocally matched a parallel spectrum in thematic orientation in the narratives of Judges. Unfortunately, such matches are not consistently found. Lines that seem to indicate "late" style are preceded or followed by seemingly classically expressed material, even while the message of the narration seems to be consistent. It is possible that a late writer can and does preserve or compose in "early" style, sometimes writing one or another sentence in a style that reflects his own period. Biblical Hebrew reflects a variety of registers, rooted in various periods and settings, but these registers are not easy to disentangle for redactional purposes in Judges. Edward Greenstein (2002) suggests that a variety of factors, including the anthropological, the discursive, and the psychoanalytical, have to be considered in order to explore the complex connections between language and culture. In this commentary I will suggest that certain seeming divergences from "classical" style may mark the narrative and stylistic choices of authors who use particular registers to capture certain kinds of content. Nevertheless, Polak offers important descriptive tools with which to explore the textural aspects of Judges. He suggests, for example, that his linguistically based spectrum of Hebrew is related to the spectrum between the oral and the written. The classical form, he theorizes, is closer to spoken language, and the late form, the product of a scribal elite. Polak himself suggests a chronological development from oral to written (1998: 60), and he attunes readers to variations in register, some of which are more oral-traditional than others, but his suggestions concerning relative chronology are problematical.

Poetry and Prose, Oral and Written

It is axiomatic to many biblical scholars in search of Israelite epics that such works were originally poetic and orally composed, even if only hints of these qualities remain visible in the corpus of the Hebrew Bible (see, e.g., Cross 1973: 112–13). As James Kugel has noted, however, the line between "poetry" and "prose" is often blurry in Israelite literature (1981: 76–95). Particular cultures will have their own registers of specialized language, quite apart from what a contemporary person might recognize as poetry or prose in English literature. Even within single epics, multiple genres and variations in linguistic style and register are possible (Honko 1998: 27). Thus Judges 5, the Song of Deborah, is characterized by a particular kind of language. Lines are parallel in content and consistent in length, while the language is formulaic and densely repetitive, and refrains are common. Nevertheless, large portions of the narratives of Judges, which modern readers might consider prose, are also presented in highly stylized language. Formulas abound and images are repeated in the parallelistic style seen in more obviously "poetic" works. Thoughts, moreover, are frequently complete at the end of each line so that the tale can be presented in a series of self-contained lines, a trait of traditional-style literature described by Albert Lord (1988: 54; see, e.g., Judg 13:1–25 and on "Format" below). But is this traditional style indicative of oral composition? The style is indicative of oral-style aesthetics and may be rooted in a tradition of extemporaneous oral composition of the kind studied by Lord and Parry, whereby "singers of tales" build compositions by means of formulaic patterns in language and content. Writing was also available, however, at least to certain Israelites, even as the oral tradition flourished.

The very existence of the various writings of the Hebrew Bible in their traditional style serves as proof of the interplay between the oral and the written. Certain pieces may have been orally composed, whereas others may be imitative of oral style. Written works may have been performed orally, while oral works may have been written down by scribes or recreated from memory. Works that existed in writing could be recreated from memory without recourse to scrolls (see Carr 2005: 160–62). Oral works can become quite fixed, a virtual "text," while written works can display the qualities of performance with its variations (Nagy 1996: 69–70). There were, no doubt, oral and written versions of the narratives of Judges, and the relationship between the oral and the written is complex and not possible to unravel (Niditch 1996). While Lauri Honko suggests that "poetry" in our terms is not a necessary criterion of epic, Margaret Beissinger, Jane Tylus, and Susanne Wofford indicate that neither is oral composition (1999: 2–3, 11–12). Questions of poetic style and oral composition are important considerations in exploring Israelite epic-style works such as Judges, but one needs to resist the temptation to oversimplify.

Most scholars, previous and contemporary, agree that the Bible has important connections to oral literature and an oral culture. The argument made by Hermann Gunkel (1966: 1–12, 19, 46–74) and Claus Westermann (1984: 65–66; 1985: 30–50) is that oral versions of biblical narrations found their setting in an early, less sophisticated period in Israelite history. These cultural products were eventually written down in a later period, characterized by greater sophistication, literacy, and a lively scribal culture.

This particular view of the nature of oral literatures and of the relationship between oral and written in Israelite tradition is misguided. Oral literature can be simple or complex and admits of various styles depending upon its function and setting in the culture, courtly or common, rural or urbane, male audience or female audience. Modern students of early and oral literatures have shown that no sharp dichotomy exists between the oral and the written in traditional cultures, nor a simple one-way evolutionary development from orality to literacy, but rather a spectrum in which the oral and written coexist and influence the form and function of one another. Literacy in traditional cultures, moreover, is not to be confused with modern conceptions of literacy.

The writings of the Hebrew Bible reveal economy and repetition, the recurring patterns of language and content, more typical of the oral than the written. This is especially apparent in the book of Judges. There are many oral styles in a traditional culture, as seen in the Israelite case (Niditch 1996: 25–38), some more baroque, some more elegant, and so on. In this commentary I will point to particular traditional styles consistently at work in the book of Judges, but not attempt to grapple with unanswerable questions concerning "origins" in oral composition. Stories of Judges, however, reveal a rich literature that was at home in a world dominated by oral-world assumptions about the workings of traditional narratives. In this oral world, writing was available as a means of composition and preservation. The stories told in Judges are but a fraction of the larger traditional fund—a metonymic snippet of the huge corpus, oral and written, archived or never put in writing, written and then lost, known and then partially or wholly forgotten—that must have existed in the first millennium B.C.E. Awareness of the workings of oral style in the written works of Scripture and acknowledgment of the ways in which pieces of tradition would have existed in variation and multiplicity lead to certain emphases, methodological considerations, and choices in preparing a commentary.

5. Format

Every translator of Scripture must, at the outset, face the question of format. Ancient Hebrew had no commas, no capital letters, no semicolons, and no paragraphs. Contemporary translations of Judges such as the NRSV or JPS Bible generally lay out the literature in prose paragraphs, reserving cola or lines for pieces such as Judges 5 that seem and sound more like "poetry" to contemporary readers. Even the cautious translators of the NRSV occasionally feel the need to employ a format that reflects "visible song," as Katherine O'Brien O'Keeffe calls the continuing presence of oral style in the written works of traditional cultures (1990). These modern translators are guided largely by inner-biblical "headers," the ancient writers' introductory phrases to pieces of tradition. Thus at Num 21:14, after a reference to what is said in the "Book of the Wars of the LORD," the NRSV translators set up a list of place names in cola. But the actual syntax of each of these examples from Num 21:14–15 is no more or less poetic than many portions of Numbers that are set in prose paragraphs.

Concerned to highlight "the spokenness of the Bible," Everett Fox more boldly prints his entire translation of the Pentateuch "in lines resembling blank verse." Influenced by Martin Buber and Franz Rosenzweig, he states that "these 'cola' are based primarily on spoken phrasing. . . . While current scholars, myself included, would not agree with Buber that the text's rhetoric necessarily corresponds to 'breathing,' divisions into lines or cola do facilitate reading aloud and make it possible for the listener to sense the text's rhythm" (1995: xv). But where does each colon end? Fox notes, "Cola do not correspond to the traditional verse divisions found in printed Bibles." They "arise from the experience of reading the Hebrew text aloud and of feeling its spoken rhythms. The specific divisions used in this volume are somewhat arbitrary; each reader will hear the text differently" (xv). Fox's lines sometimes correspond to the translation of Buber-Rosenzweig, but "often not," sometimes to the traditional Jewish punctuation of the Masoretes, but "not always" (xv). The process is thus quite subjective and difficult to imitate.

Another who has wrestled with such issues in format as they relate to the sound, texture, and meaning of Scripture is Phyllis Trible, whose insightful analyses of biblical texts are influenced by rhetorical criticism. Trible, like Fox, sets up texts in cola. The breaks between lines frequently emphasize repetitions in syntax or content (see Trible 1994: 102–3, 151), calling attention to the traditional style of ancient Israelite literature (see, for example, her treatment of Gen 2:4b-7 [1978: 75] and Jonah 1:4 [1994: 131]). Sometimes indentation is used or semicolons or periodization to create subtle shadings that Trible perceives in the ways in which language reflects message or imagery. Trible notes that the process of laying out the text is somewhat subjective (1994: 230–33).

My own approach is influenced by the work of Trible, Polak, and Lord. Lord points out that oral-traditional literatures frequently display a trait of "disenjambement," meaning that the thought is complete at the end of the line, even when the sentence continues. Of South Slavic song he writes, "Very rarely does a thought hang in the air incomplete at the end of a line; usually we could place a period after each verse. The absence of necessary enjambement is a characteristic of oral compositions and is one of the easiest touchstones to apply in testing the orality of a poem. Milman Parry has called it an 'adding style'; the term is apt" (1988: 54). A scholar of sociolinguistics, Dell Hymes, has pointed to a similar phenomenon (1994: 331). I do not seek to prove or test "orality" in the case of Judges, but it is significant in appreciating its texture to note that the work frequently displays an "adding style" with its disenjambed cola. In this commentary I format Judges in lines, as does Fox in his translation of the Torah. Nonindented cola usually have the requirements of a clause, a subject and a verb; they constitute a complete thought or begin a thought. As Polak's work might predict, much of Judges can be arranged well in self-contained cola, indicating the strong presence of classical style.

I use indented lines to mark subordination, such as a clause beginning with "that" or "which" or an infinitival phrase. Sometimes I have indented a long prepositional phrase that creates its own image or thought. Indentation also indicates the presence of a long noun string. The register, as Polak's work would suggest, is less classical in style. Indentation often indicates repetition or a rhetorically meaningful pattern. In this respect the influence of Trible on the format is clear. The length of most cola is between three and six Hebrew words, and I have made an effort to keep the length of lines similar to those of surrounding complete thoughts or clauses that are not indented.

This method of formatting not only pays attention to Trible's emphasis on rhetorical patterning and Fox's interest in the aural qualities of the literature, but also provides some insight into matters of varying register. Some portions of Judges break up easily into cola; others display a good deal of subordination. In the latter instance, the reader must wait quite a while for the thought to be fully completed. Certain registers of traditional style may reflect particular genres. A text such as Judges 5 exemplifies heightened, elegant traditional style, but other portions of Judges display more simple cola, as the author reveals image after image in brief self-contained phrases. See 14:9, 19; 18:3 and compare, for example, my translation of 18:17 with the more integrated English of NRSV. The layout of the translation thus allows for blurring the distinction between prose and poetry, revealing a genre of "poetic prose" that does not fit neatly into modern Western categories, but which seems to characterize the style of so much of biblical literature. In this way, one is better able to pay attention to the texture of Israelite "ethnic genres" (Ben-Amos 1976).

6. Text-Critical Decisions

Text-critical decisions, on a most basic level, affect what scholars deem the texture and text of a work to be. The date of actual, extant manuscripts of Judges in Hebrew and various ancient translations is often quite late, relatively speaking. While in this commentary I make the case that versions of stories in Judges could have been told as early as the late second millennium B.C.E. or the first half of the first millennium B.C.E., no manuscripts of Judges are nearly that early. For example, the Vaticanus Codex, today housed in the Vatican Library and containing most of the Old and New Testaments, dates to the fourth century C.E. Another fairly complete manuscript is the Greek Alexandrinus Codex, which dates to the fifth century and is now housed in the British Library. The variations between Vaticanus (the so-called B text of Judges) and Alexandrinus (the so-called A text) have been of central interest to scholars engaged in text-critical analysis. In addition, an "Old Latin" (OL) version of Judges is believed to reflect a translation into Latin of an earlier "Old Greek" (OG) translation of a Hebrew version that antedates Hebrew traditions underlying Vaticanus and Alexandrinus. An extant Old Latin version of the whole book of Judges, except for the last chapter and a half, is available in the Lyons Manuscript (fifth or sixth century), edited by Ulysse Robert (1900).

The discovery of ancient Hebrew biblical manuscripts in the caves around the Dead Sea provides further valuable information. Several fragments of Judges have been found in manuscripts whose scripts date them to the first century B.C.E. These are 4QJudg[a] (Judg 6:2–6, 11–13), 1QJudg (6:20–22; 8:1 [?]; 9:1–6, 28–31, 40–43, 48–49), 4QJudg[b] (19:5–7; 21:12–25), and XJudg (4:5–6). Some readings in these manuscript fragments not only differ from the MT; they also tally with some of the ancient Greek readings. Others are unique to Qumran.

The variety in the inherited manuscript traditions leads scholars in different directions. An approach that has come to dominate biblical studies suggests there was once, essentially, a single written version of Judges that branched out into different textual traditions (Talmon 1970: 174). In a careful study of the recension history of Judges in the light of the Qumran finds, Julio Trebolle Barrera suggests that Vaticanus (abbreviated Vat, the so-called B text), Alexandrinus (the so-called A text) and group L from which OL branched off, all stem ultimately from an OG translation of a Hebrew text of Egyptian provenance. The MT stems from another version perhaps extant in Palestine. 4QJudg[b] has more in common with the tradition that gave rise to the MT, whereas 4QJudg[a] shares more with the OG translation (1991: 99–100). Ultimately both families of texts go back to one original. An alternate approach associated with the work of Paul Kahle would suggest, to the contrary, that a great plethora of textual traditions—various ways Judges was written down—was eventually homogenized, either under conscious pressure from a politically controlling group who preferred one version and suppressed the rest, or through a less consciously directed effort. Some of the variant texts and their readings managed to survive, revealing a hint of what was once an even greater variety of manuscript traditions (see Talmon 1970: 177–79).

One need not merely speculate about some of the variants that existed in the tradition. Within the MT of Judges, there is evidence of variation that has been embraced rather than edited away. Judges 1 contains, for example, three differing notices about the disposition of Jerusalem (1:7, 8, 21) and two different implied versions of the conquest of Hebron, one involving a leadership role for Judah at v. 10 and another for Caleb at v. 20. Joshua plays the role in Josh 11:21 and Caleb in Josh 15:13–14. Basing his work on the form and content of LXX Josh 24:33b and the Qumran Damascus Document (CD v:1–5), Alexander Rofé has suggested that an earlier version of the book of Judges lacked 1:1–3:11, beginning the narration with the tale of the judge Ehud (1982: 29–32). The existence and circulation of a shorter "Judges" is certainly a possibility.

A work such as Judges no doubt existed in multiple versions, even once its various stories were combined along the lines with which we are now familiar. Oral versions of larger or smaller portions of Judges would have existed side by side with accounts that were written down. Versions preserved by Deuteronomistic-style writers who held to a certain view of history might have differed from versions preserved and told by others in the tradition. Such oral tellings and written portions that may have been preserved in a family archive or the like are all lost. When exploring the preserved and transmitted written manuscript traditions of Judges, one rarely encounters radically different versions; rather, the relatively set content exhibits more subtle variations in terminology and phrasing and differences in relative length.

In this commentary, however, I take the position that even variations in manuscript traditions, which are essentially set in this sense, reflect an oral-world mentality in which different versions exist side by side in the tradition. A model for this phenomenon of mulitiplicity is offered by the Qumran corpus, which contains two editions of Jeremiah, two editions of Exodus, variant editions of Numbers, and two possible editions of Psalms (Ulrich 1993: 75). Scholars point to the richness of "textual plurality" at Qumran (Trebolle Barrera 1993a: 108), where "there were multiple editions of many of the biblical books . . . but the specific textual form was not a consideration" (Ulrich 1993: 92). The attitude is typical of a traditional world in which variant texts are deemed valid and authentic. Similarly, Talmon writes of the "'liberal attitude' towards divergent textual traditions" at Qumran (1964: 97).

In the study of Judges, the reconstruction of the so-called Proto-Lucianic and *Kaige* recensions has been of particular interest. The Proto-Lucianic recension, named after affinities with the fourth-century text of the Christian scholar Lucian, is evidenced in various manuscripts (Trebolle Barrera 1993b: 315–16). Readings shared by these manuscripts show evidence of a first-century B.C.E. translation/ revision of the OG that sought to bring the Greek translation into agreement with a current Hebrew text (McCarter 1986: 77–78). The *Kaige* recension (or Proto-Theodotionic recension) is said to provide another example of the way in which the Greek translation was revised to reflect a Hebrew version, in this case a first-century B.C.E. precursor of the MT. *Kaige* means "and also" (McCarter 1986: 77) or "and indeed" (Boling 41) and is a transitional grammatical element that is one marker of this recension, evidenced in the A and Vat texts of Judges (see Bodine 1980a, 1980b; and Boling 297–300). The Proto-Lucianic and *Kaige* recensions thus provide important evidence for scholars who seek to trace the development of versions of the Hebrew Bible. It is important to emphasize that there is no extant proto-Masoretic manuscript or OG manuscript of part or all of the Hebrew Bible. Rather there are scholarly reconstructions. Scholars make educated decisions about the form of the OG or other versions of the text through an assessment of evidence from various extant manuscripts and seek, in this way, to get back to earlier and purer versions of the various recensions.

The next step common in the scholarly text critical process is to compare recensions to prepare a text of Judges, a best text, according to certain criteria. For example, scholars tend to prefer the shorter reading and the more difficult reading, as long as it makes sense. Some scholars believe it is possible to find the earliest text, or something close to it. Richard D. Nelson's commentary on Joshua is an excellent updated example of such a text-critical approach (1997: 23).

The approach offered in this commentary differs. As a student of the place of manuscripts in largely oral worlds, I am less inclined to reconstruct a whole text, to build it, however judiciously, from the limited number of available manuscripts. Nor will I seek an original or urtext for Judges. I worry about the artificiality of such a process and believe it more true to life to assume that there were always multiple versions of the tradition before the Common Era. One can never know if a reconstructed text ever lived in a community, nor can one recover an original version, if there is such a thing. With a vital interest in "religions as lived," I would like to know that an extant manuscript was meaningful to a group. Variation among manuscript traditions, however, is of lively interest and important to the study of literary and religious tradition, for these various texts may reflect different ways in which communities of Jews and Christians understood the tradition. Scripture was heard in different words, and the medium was important to the message.

Some of the differences between readings make for genuine differences in the plot or in characterization. For example, Achsah in Judg 1:15 emerges somewhat differently as a woman in the various traditions, plucky and less plucky, for the Greek and Latin traditions have Achsah's husband, Othniel, initiate the action, whereas the MT leaves the action to her. The manuscript variants of 1:18 disagree as to whether Judah is successful in battle. At 1:22, MT has Yhwh assist Joseph, whereas OL has the help come from Judah. The traditions differ for 1:22 as to whether the enemy is conscripted into forced labor. It is useful to ask how differences in the texts may reflect the different impression received by particular groups concerning the activities of a Samson or the outcome of a particular battle. Text-critical variations, like contradictions in content within the same manuscript tradition, may mark or effect differences in worldview.

Other differences are more subtle. Variant readings called "synonymous readings" by Shemaryahu Talmon—that is shorter, expanded, or alternate phrases that convey a particular image or piece of content—can be viewed as versions of the same *dābār*, literally, "word," in Person's terms (1998; 2002: 91–97), as oral-style variants of the same essential meaning unit. One might then inquire why an author has preferred one form of the *dābār* to another—matters of aesthetics, taste, message, and thematic emphasis all come into play. Person is building on Milman Parry and Albert Lord's observation that for their informants, epic singers of the former Yugoslavia, a whole phrase was considered a word or unit (see the discussion in Foley 1991: 26 n. 57; 51 n. 22; and, e.g., the variants discussed in ch. 1 in notes u and z).

Some of the variants reflect differing textual traditions as discussed above; the stories were told with certain variations that are still reflected in ancient textual traditions. Other differences have been introduced into the traditions through scribal errors. Sometimes, however, differences in the translations may not be due to differences in the Hebrew *Vorlage* but to translation decisions and creative composition (see Gzella 2003: 19, 26–27, 47).

The attempt to make sense of a difficult reading (which in some cases may have arisen from a simple scribal error) often also leads to creative translations. As James Kugel has suggested about the phenomenon of rabbinic midrash and other modes of Jewish interpretation of Scripture in antiquity, the "ambiguities" or "rough edges" of a text occasion commentary or gloss (1997: 3–5, 18–23, 28–34). Translations may also reflect midrashic techniques that Isaac Heinemann has called "creative philology" (1954: 4–11, 96–107), for example, when the reader takes his cue for meaning from one Hebrew root rather than another or when a root is overliteralized. These ways of reading result in variant traditions, and each variant conveys a set of meanings to a believing community in a process akin to midrash. Hebrew is based on triliteral roots, and such nuances in meaning may be achieved with the shift of a vowel, whether by mistake or in purposeful wordplay. Here one encounters the border between translation and transformational composition in the style of the Jewish targum, a form of translation that allows for gloss and elaboration. See, for example, the treatment of *ṣnḥ* in 1:14 (note o), the variation between *gʾl* and *gll* in 1:15 (note p), the play on *rkb* in 1:19 (note x), and the reading *ʾărām* (Aram, Syria) instead of *ʾādām* at OL for 18:7 (note dd). In a similarly creative mode, the translator may not be working with a variant Hebrew tradition, but has felt it necessary to expand, to gloss, or to fill out the "true" and "full" meaning of the Hebrew, thereby creating an alternate tradition and participating in the compositional process, all allowable in the anonymous oral world of writing, as shown recently by Deborah VanderBilt concerning Anglo-Saxon translations of Latin works (1998: 379). The lengthier version in OL of Ehud's escape and the allusion in OL to Samson's being beaten by captors, which assimilates him to Jesus, may be examples of such techniques of "filling out" and "glossing." All these instances point to the border where translation decisions, textual variants, targum, midrash, inner-biblical variants, and intertextuality meet on oral-world terms.

The focus of this commentary is the MT of Judges read and preserved in close-to-current form by Jews for some one thousand years. I will also consult the Vaticanus manuscript of the LXX with occasional comparisons to Alexandrinus, the Lyons manuscript of the OL, and the extant Qumran fragments for Judges 4, 6, 9, 19, and 21. This commentary does not provide a full apparatus; rather, the notes focus on interesting and significant variations in a number of the traditions. In this regard the version in the OL Lyons manuscript is often most unexpected and rich. In this way I hope not only to open up Judges in a reliable version to readers, but also to give, when appropriate, a sense of some of the varying ways certain pieces of the text were presented and preserved, asking what we can learn from such a comparison.

7. Translation

This is a lively time in biblical translation. Like Everett Fox, who has produced an exciting new translation of the Torah, I am interested in oral and aural aspects of the text in conveying some of the biblical rhythm, syntax, wordplay, and sound. I do not claim that all of the Hebrew Bible was orally composed, though some works possibly were, but suggest that qualities of the oral enliven and infuse the written works of Scripture. Traits such as wordplay on a shared root or upon roots that sound alike, repetition of key terms or formulaic phrases within a piece or across the tradition, and repeated frame language reflect an economic use of language whereby the same language is often preferred to variation for conveying an image or idea. In the Hebrew Bible as in other traditional literatures, webs of meaning and connotation envelop certain terms and phrases, linking one usage with another. John Foley (1991: 13) refers to this variety of traditional usage as a kind of "metonymy" in which the part stands for and invokes the whole (see also Nagy 2003: 16). By attending to root meanings and attempting to use, when possible, the same English term to translate the Hebrew, I hope to highlight rather than hide these qualities of interconnectedness in the tradition.

Oral-related considerations suggest, as Fox noted, that the Hebrew Bible, even in written form, was meant to be heard and spoken; and, like Fox, I have tried to take this spokennness seriously in rendering the Hebrew as closely as possible into English. Fox notes that such literal translations risk a certain "bumpiness." In fact, I have included two translations of Judges, one in the body of the commentary and one in an appendix. The former seeks to aid comprehensibility and readability by converting the Hebrew syntax to a more standard English word order whereby the subject precedes the verb. The version in the appendix, however, retains the Hebrew word order and even more closely conveys the register of the Hebrew. The reader will notice in the appendix, for example, the frequent use of an auxiliary verb to convey the past tense (e.g., "And capture it did Othniel," 1:13), when this construction allows the word order of the Hebrew to make better sense in English. I hope that readers will avail themselves of both translations and enjoy the comparison.

I am also sympathetic to Robert Alter's desire to convey the sense that the Bible uses special and elegant language. The formulicity of the Hebrew Bible, for me, is part of that specialness. The Israelite composers of biblical texts employ, as he notes, "a conventionally delimited language" that is "stylized" and "decorous," using "a limited set of terms again and again, making an aesthetic virtue out of the repetition" (2004: xxv).

Even though Alter emphasizes qualities of the written and literary over the oral, he and I make some similar translation choices. He defends his translation of *waw* as "and," an element that repeats frequently in the Hebrew syntax, but which in modern translations is often finessed to convey a meaning not of conjunction but of subordination (so Lambdin 1971: 108). Alter counters that the *waw* was spoken and heard as repeated, important metrically and syllabically (2004: xxv–xxvii). I tend to agree. My goal throughout is to capture both the meaning and the medium of the Hebrew, paying special attention to its heard qualities and to be as literal and rooted in the Hebrew as possible without sacrificing the economical elegance of the traditional language.

COMMENTARY

Judges 1:1–36
Introduction by Means
of Explicit Ambivalence

1:1　　And it was after the death of Joshua,[a]
　　　　and the descendants of Israel asked of[b] Yhwh, saying,
　　　　"Who will go up for us against[c] the Canaanites, at the beginning,
　　　　　to wage war against them?"
2　　　And Yhwh said,
　　　　"Judah will go up.
　　　　Behold, I have given the land into his hand."[d]
3　　　And Judah said to his brother Simeon,
　　　　"Go up with me into my allotment,[e]
　　　　and let us wage war against the Canaanites,
　　　　and I will come, also I, with you into your allotment."
　　　　And Simeon went up with him.
4　　　And up went Judah,
　　　　and Yhwh gave the Canaanites and the Perizzites into their hand.
　　　　They struck down in Bezek ten thousand men.
5　　　And they encountered Adoni-bezek in Bezek,
　　　　and they waged war against him,
　　　　and they struck down the Canaanites and the Perizzites.
6　　　And Adoni-bezek fled;[f]
　　　　they followed after him;
　　　　they seized him;
　　　　they cut off the large digits of his hands and feet.
7　　　And Adoni-bezek said,
　　　　　"Seventy kings,
　　　　　　the large digits of their hands and feet cut off,
　　　　　used to glean under my table.
　　　　　As I did,
　　　　　　so God has repaid me."
　　　　And they brought him to Jerusalem,
　　　　and he died there.
8　　　And the descendants of Judah waged war against Jerusalem,
　　　　they captured it;
　　　　they struck it down by the mouth of the sword;

and the city, they sent up in fire.[g]

9   And thereafter the descendants of Judah went down
          to wage war against the Canaanites
              dwelling in the hill country, the south, and the lowlands.

10   And Judah went against the Canaanites
          who dwelled in Hebron
          (and the name of Hebron formerly was Kiriath-arba[h])
      and they struck down Sheshai, Ahiman, and Talmai.[i]

11   And they went[j] from there against the dwellers of Debir
          (and the name of Debir formerly was Kiriath-sepher[k]).

12   And Caleb said,
      "He who strikes down Kiriath-sepher and captures it,
          I will give to him Achsah, my daughter, as wife."

13   And capture it did Othniel, son of Kenaz,
          the brother of Caleb (the one younger than he),[l]
      and he gave to him Achsah, his daughter, as a wife.

14   And it was when she came that she urged him[m]
          to ask from her father for a piece of[n] open country.
      And she pounded down[o] from upon the donkey,
      and Caleb said to her,
      "What is with you!?"

15   She said to him,
      "Give to me a blessing;
      for the Negeb (Southland) you have given me,
      but give to me ponds[p] of water."
      And Caleb gave to her[q]
          the upper ponds and the lower ponds.[r]

16   And the descendants of Keni,[s] father-in-law of Moses,
          went up from the City of Palms
              with the descendants of Judah
          into the wilderness of Judah
              that is in the south toward Arad;
      they went and dwelled[t] with the people.

17   And Judah went with Simeon his brother,
      and they struck down the Canaanites who dwelled in Zephath,
      and they devoted it to destruction[u]
      and called the name of the city Hormah (Devoted-to-Destruction).

18   And Judah captured[v] Gaza and its border region
          and Ashkelon and its border region
          and Ekron and its border region.[w]

19   And Yhwh was with Judah,
      and he took possession of the hill country,

        for he could not dispossess the dwellers of the valley
           because chariotry of iron was theirs.[x]

20   And they gave Hebron to Caleb
           as Moses had spoken,
        and he dispossessed from there the three sons of Anak,

21   and the Jebusites dwelling in Jerusalem,
           the descendants of Benjamin did not dispossess.
        And the Jebusites dwell
           with the descendants of Benjamin
           in Jerusalem until this day.

22   And the house of Joseph went up,
           they too, against Bethel,
        and Yhwh[y] was with them.

23   And the house of Joseph went espying[z] in Bethel,
        and the name of the town formerly was Luz.

24   And the guards saw a man going forth from the town,[aa]
        and they said to him,
        "Let us see, I pray you,[bb] the entryway of the town,
        and we will make with you a mercy pact."

25   And he let them see the entryway of the town,
        and they struck down the town by the mouth of the sword,
        but the man and all his family they sent free.

26   And the man went to the land of the Hittites,
        and he built a town and called its name Luz.
        That is its name until this day.

27   And Manasseh did not dispossess Beth-shean[cc] and its suburbs,
           nor Taanach and its suburbs,
           nor the dwellers of Dor and its suburbs,[dd]
           nor the dwellers of Ibleam and its suburbs,
           nor the dwellers of Megiddo and its suburbs,
        and the Canaanites persisted to dwell in this land.

28   And when Israel grew strong,
           they set the Canaanites at forced labor,
        but dispossess they did not dispossess them.

29   And Ephraim did not dispossess
           the Canaanites who dwell in Gezer,
        and the Canaanites dwelled in his midst in Gezer.[ee]

30   Zebulun did not dispossess the dwellers of Kitron[ff]
           nor the dwellers of Nahalol,
        and the Canaanites dwelled in his midst,
        and they became forced labor.

31   Asher did not dispossess the dwellers of Acco,

nor the dwellers of Sidon,
    nor Ahlab, nor Achzib,
    nor Helbah, nor Aphik, nor Rehob.[gg]

32 And the Asherites dwelled in the midst of the Canaanites,
        dwellers of the land,
    for they did not dispossess them.

33 Naphtali did not dispossess the dwellers of Beth-shemesh,
        nor the dwellers of Beth-anath,
    and they dwelled in the midst of the Canaanites,
        dwellers of the land,
    and the dwellers of Beth-shemesh and Beth-anath
        became to them forced labor.

34 And the Amorites pressed
        the descendants of Dan to the hill country,
    for they did not allow them to go down into the valley.

35 And the Amorites persisted to live in Har-heres,[hh]
        in Aijalon, and in Shaalbim,
    and the hand of the house of Joseph grew heavy,
    and they became forced labor.

36 And the border of the Amorites was from Akrabbim (Scorpion-rise),
        from Sela (Rock) and upward.[ii]

a. This phrase is found also in Josh 1:1 concerning the death of Moses. The beginning of the book of Judges thus parallels that of the book of Joshua, and the life story of Joshua parallels that of Moses (cf. Exod 3:5 and Josh 5:15). The phrase and its variants, however, exemplify a widely used formulaic pattern in the biblical corpus that draws attention to the important events or narrative transitions which are to follow. This formulaic marker is found also in Gen 25:11 concerning Abraham, in Lev 16:1 concerning the sons of Aaron, and in 2 Sam 1:1 concerning Saul. See also variants in Gen 50:15; Judg 8:33; 9:55.

b. To "ask" or "inquire of Yhwh" is formulaic and technical language marking the request for a divine oracle. Compare Judg 20:18, 23, 27; 1 Sam 10:22; 22:10; 23:2; 28:6; 30:8; 2 Sam 2:1; 5:19, 23; 1 Chron 14:10, 14. In Israel, as elsewhere in the ancient Near East, the request for an oracle from God is requisite to proceeding to war. In Judges see, for example, 20:18, 23, 27. Note in particular the shared conventional language at 1:1 and 20:18 in which God is asked who should lead in the battle and the response is Judah. For broader ancient Near Eastern parallels see Kang 1989:56–72, 98–107, 215–22.

c. Language of "going up against" is formulaic for military engagement throughout the tradition. See, for example, Judg 6:3; 12:3; 15:10; 18:9; 20:18; 1 Kgs 14:25.

d. A formula indicating divine assistance (cf. Num 21:2, 3; Judg 11:21, 30). See also v. 4.

e. The term *gôrāl* literally means "lot" and is etymologically rooted in a term for stones or pebbles, which were presumably cast in divinatory practices. In biblical texts the term refers to land, service, or responsibility ascertained and apportioned by the throwing of lots. Here, as at Josh 18:11 (see also Josh 19:10), the *gôrāl* is a portion of territory, an inheritance believed to be assigned by divine designation, but see also Judg 20:9, in which the term may refer to a military allotment or enlistment roll.

f. The Hebrew continues use of the *waw* conversive in v. 6, but the quick pace of the narrative is conveyed by semicolons (see also the second and third lines of v. 8). For a discussion of the repetition of "and" as a syntactical device that has aural significance, see the introduction (section 7) to the commentary.

g. The language of battle and destruction evokes the ban (see Deut 13:16; Josh 10:28; 11:11).

h. There is some variation among the manuscripts concerning the place name of Kiriath-arba, or Town-of-Four. The Greek traditions tend to employ terms that sound or read more like Kiriath-sepher, the former name of Debir in MT 1:11.

i. Vat adds after Talmai, "the offspring of Anak," the giant, thereby including a bit more of the mythic genealogy of these heroes as found in Josh 15:13–14 and Judg 1:20, where Caleb, not Judah, is the heroic conqueror of the "three sons of Anak." In another variant, preserved in Josh 11:21, Joshua plays the role. Such variants testify to the oral-world quality of these written texts in which multiplicity is not harmonized away, and in which variants coexist within the tradition (see also Josh 14:14–15).

j. Vat and OL appear to reflect Hebrew *wayyaʿălû*, "and they went up," a minor variant, chosen from the range of traditional language available to describe going to do battle.

k. Vat transliterates the Hebrew Kiriath-sepher, and then translates, "Town/City-of-Document." OL employs the same gloss without transliterating the Hebrew.

l. While the wording of MT is ambiguous concerning Othniel's relationship to Caleb, Vat states that Othniel is Caleb's nephew, while A and OL state the men are brothers. The variant in Josh 15:17 does not mention Othniel's age relative to Kenaz or Caleb, but its syntax with subject and appositive is no more certain in delineating genealogy. Such ambiguity allows for variation.

m. The Greek traditions have the subject of the asking be Othniel, so that the hero initiates the action: "Othniel urged her." MT, both here and in the variant in Josh 15:18, assigns the young woman the more plucky role, and indeed her pleasing verbal aggressiveness in the rest of the verse in Vat and OL seems to tally well with MT's opening characterization.

n. Vat and OL read literally, "a field," without the definite article, whereas MT implies a specific piece of land.

o. The traditions seem to reflect sound-alike variations on the root *ṣnḥ*, an unusual term in Biblical Hebrew that is found also in Judg 4:21 to describe what happens to the tent peg used by Jael to kill Sisera, "and it descended into the ground." The emotional force behind the movement of the peg and a downward direction seem to be implicit in Judg 4 and are reflected in the above translation. Vat and OL, however, have Achsah "grumble" and "cry out" from upon the donkey, perhaps translating the root *ṣrḥ* or *ṣwḥ*.

p. Vat reads the Hebrew root *gll* as *g'l*, "a redemption" of water. This example of minor variation is evidence of the interesting way in which particular readings of a more ordinary or typical phrase, whether caused by scribal error or purposeful wordplay, introduce varied imagery into the traditions. The Greek-receiving audiences of Judg 1:15

(and perhaps but not necessarily the receivers of a Hebrew text behind it) have the image of Achsah's request enriched with notions of covenantal blessing and fertility. Note that OL has Achsah ask for a "blessing" of water.

q. Vat and OL add "according to her heart."

r. OL reads that Caleb gives "a redemption of the upper ponds and a redemption of the lower ponds" (see note p).

s. Vat reads, "the descendants of Jethro, the Kenites," filling out the genealogical information.

t. MT employs a singular verb. Vat omits "went," and OL includes after "Arad" the intriguing variation "and Amalek dwelled with him."

u. OL includes two terms for the destruction, "exterminated and devoted to destruction." While the Hebrew equivalent to the latter term is necessary for the wordplay with Hormah, OL plays on the former term and calls the city "Exterminated," thereby capturing the essence but not the terminology of the *ḥērem* or "ban." This is an excellent example of the literary and compositional phenomenon explored by Raymond Person (1998) under the heading *dābār*. The tradition includes alternate ways of expressing the same idea. Sometimes more than one version of this "word" or speech act appears in a text, forming a kind of synonymous pair (see Talmon 1961). The manuscript traditions concerning the destruction of Zephath offer longer and shorter versions of the annal at v. 17.

v. In a significant variant, Vat, A, and OL have Judah not capturing the three Philistine cities, agreeing with MT at Josh 13:3 and Judg 3:3.

w. Vat and OL add, "Ashdod nor its surrounding areas," including another of the towns of the Philistine Pentapolis (cf. Josh 11:22; 13:3).

x. This formulaic indicator of military inferiority is found also in Josh 17:16, 18 but is applied to Joseph, not Judah. Vat includes a variation on the final phrase, eliminating the chariotry excuse. In Vat Judah is less than successful "because Rechab separates to them." The term for "chariot" (*rekeb*) is taken as a personal name, and the word for "iron" (*barzel*) appears to be read as a form of the verb *bdl*, "to separate." What probably began as a scribal error thus becomes a new bit of narrative content. The resulting multiplicity is within the purview of an oral-world mentality.

y. OL disrupts the common formulaic expression of God's approval and blessing (cf. Gen 21:22; 26:3; Exod 18:19; Deut 21:1; Josh 1:9, 17; Judg 1:19; 6:12; 1 Sam 20:13; 2 Sam 14:17; etc.) by reading not "Yhwh was with them" but "Judah was with them." The role of the human leader is thereby enhanced.

z. The manuscript traditions exhibit interesting minor variations, typical of the sort of multiplicity available to the traditional storyteller in expressing the same essential "word" (see note u). Thus the expanded reading in Vat is, "they encamped and went espying," while OL has, "and the sons of Israel began to fight." All such readings are appropriate to the military setting and the tale of the happy turncoat that follows.

aa. Vat and OL expand the image with "and they seized him."

bb. The phrase translated "I pray you" or "pray" is a common Hebrew particle (*nā'*) indicating entreaty and a degree of respect offered by the speaker hoping to influence the listener's agreement to what he proposes. A certain dignity or civility attaches to the negotiation (see also 4:19; 6:17, 18, 39; 7:3; 8:5; 9:2).

cc. Vat and OL gloss Beth-shean, "which is a city of the Scythians." Throughout 1:27–36 the traditions exhibit variations in the names assigned to places and in the number of towns named. Vat and OL tend to be noticeably more expansive than MT. Still other variations are reflected in the parallel traditions concerning tribal allotments in Josh 17–19. Such variations, no doubt, reflect differing views of geography and ethnography within these ancient traditions.

dd. Vat includes parallel phrases for the suburbs, literally "daughter towns": "nor its daughters nor its outskirts." Notice the similar expansions and/or variations on place names in Vat and OL relating to Dor, Ibleam, and Megiddo. Cf. Josh 17:11–13 and note cc above.

ee. Vat and A add, "and they became forced labor," in a formulaic variation found in MT vv. 28, 30, 33, 35. This more expansionary version emphasizes the power of the conquerors to subdue their enemies if not completely to expel them.

ff. OL substitutes Hebron for Kitron. See note cc. Cf. Josh 19:10–16.

gg. Vat, A, and OL include alternate lists of inhabitants and name variations. Vat, for example, includes, "the dwellers of Dor and the dwellers of Sidon and the dwellers of Delef." See note cc. As in v. 29, Vat adds concerning Acco, "and they became to them forced labor." See note ee and Josh 19:24–31.

hh. Literally, "mountain of the sun." Vat, A, and OL include variations and glosses on Har-heres, some based upon an alternate spelling of *ḥeres* that concludes the word with the *s* sounding letter *śin* rather than *samech*. The former spelling means "pot" or "potsherd." Vat *ostrakōdei* can mean either "a mountain full of potsherds" or "a mountain shaped like a tortoise," and the version elaborates imaginatively: "the Ostrakōdei in which were bears and foxes."

ii. Vat identifies Sela as Petra, while OL suggests the presence of Idumaeans. See note cc and the discussion by Boling (61) of the apparent identification of Amorite with Edomite in some of the traditions.

To make sense of the first chapter of Judges is immediately to come to terms with challenges presented by the book as a whole. If, as some have suggested, Joshua and Judges offer contrasting portrayals of the way in which Israel established itself in the land, the one linear and totalistic, the other a halting series of gains and losses, then ch. 1 might be seen to contribute to the latter depiction. Israelite victories with the help of God dominate in 1:1–18 and 1:22–26, whereas the remainder of the chapter paints a less successful picture of the takeover. Questions then arise concerning the relative historical reliability of material in Judges; a number of scholars find Judges 1 of value in this regard, although caution is advised (see Wright 1946: 107–8; Soggin 26; Gurewicz 1959: 38; and Gray 188–89, 194). In fact, both Joshua and Judges admit of varying views of the so-called period of the conquest. Matching biblical events in the Hebrew Bible with Israelite history is always an uncertain task.

Scholars who are less concerned with historicity than with historiographic orientation often treat the chapter as a polemic. Marc Brettler (1989; 2002: 92–102) finds a pro-Judean orientation, noting that Judah seems to be more successful than the other tribes in Judges 1 (see also Sweeney 1997: 526–27; O'Connell 1996: 3, 7). The view in Judges 1 is often matched with a promonarchic or pro-Davidic orientation that scholars claim to find in the book as a whole (see Brettler 2002: 116). Some find a "late" (Auld 1975: 285) Deuteronomic or Priestly (Burney 1; Van Seters 1983: 338–42) orientation governing the chapter, often with appropriate theological implications about moral decline. (However, see Klein [1988: 29–30], who does not attach the decline to questions of authorship.) Sweeney points in particular to a polemic against Ephraim or the north in the chapter and against Bethel in the book of Judges (1997: 527–28).

One must ask, however, what entity or story is the basis for any suggestions about history or worldview or authorship. Is Judges 1 a whole, a single story in any sense? Is it a set of little stories, a series of annals, a collection of allusions to stories known by sharers of the tradition? Auld treats the chapter as a collection of derivative snippets and commentaries based upon similar material in Joshua joined with the more self-standing narratives about Adoni-bezek, Achsah, and the founding of Luz (1975: 266, 276). Van Seters (1983: 338) and Sweeney (1997: 521) treat the chapter as a whole with a particular polemical tendenz.

The combination of brief battle reports in the third person, punctuated by vignettes related to the battles and their participants, is not easily compared to other material. K. Lawson Younger Jr. (1990: 198; 1994: 208) has drawn comparisons with various ancient Near Eastern battle reports, and yet none of these nonbiblical report texts seems quite comparable to Judges 1, since most of them are first person accounts by kings creating, shaping, and investing their identities in narrations concerning their military successes. Nor do the reports in Judges 1 compare well with the conventionalized battle report studied carefully by David Gunn (1974a). These scenes (1 Sam 4:12–18; 2 Sam 1:1–16) are characterized by formulaic language and have a set narrative format that includes the runner who has witnessed the military encounter, the sentry who reports his coming, the leader behind the lines who receives the report, and the report itself. The topos of the battle report is not represented in Judges 1.

The closest biblical parallel to Judges 1 is the overview of battles and journeys in Numbers 21. Like Judges 1, Numbers 21 is a series of brief annals that reflect richer and fuller traditions about military encounters and their participants. The journeying or directional quality of Numbers 21 (it is a travelogue with battles), the inclusion of proverbial or hymnic material (e.g., Num 21:17–18, 27–30), and the presence of narratives relating to the battle or battle march but not dealing with the fighting per se (Num 21:4–9) relate Numbers 21 to Judges 1.

Questions also arise about the place of Judges 1 in the biblical corpus as it now stands and about its narrative boundaries. Is Judges 1 to be regarded as the introduction to the book and part of that story? Is it rather a bridge between

Joshua and Judges and to be regarded as part of this more extended narrative? Moreover, however one draws the boundaries of Judges 1, one has a somewhat different story. There is a big difference, for example, if the story ends with the boundary of the Amorites at 1:36 or with the scene at Bochim in 2:1–6.

As the Bible now stands, the chapter functions in various narrative trajectories, and one can view its many pieces as separable wholes that may well have circulated independently, in various combinations, formats, and contexts. The book of Joshua preserves examples of such multiplicity and variation, as portions of content found in Judges 1 appear in alternate settings. Compare, for example, Judg 1:19 to Josh 17:16, Judg 1:21 to Josh 15:63, Judg 1:27–28 to Josh 17:12–13, and Judg 1:29 to Josh 16:10.

Judges 1 expresses essential ambivalences regarding Israelite identity, tensions in worldview concerning forms of polity and the nature of political power. As in portions of Joshua, conquest is not totalistic, and the author wrestles with a clash between two sorts of polity, one centralized based on common ties to a leader or state (e.g., Judah in the first half of this chapter) and the other decentralized based on perceived kinship bonds. A more tribal orientation dominates the second half of the chapter. A Judah-led duo gives way to a tribe-by-tribe accounting, and "house of Joseph" in vv. 22–26 gives way to a discussion of Manasseh, Ephraim, and the rest of the tribes. The chapter, in microcosm, reflects concerns that run throughout Judges as a whole and is a thoughtful and mature expression of Israelite self-perception. Like all the tales in Judges, Judges 1 reflects not only the voice of a final composer, the "humanist" voice of post-exilic times, but layers of tradition that often defy certain disentanglement. Judges 1 contains ancient material that may well go back to premonarchic times, but reflects a worldview that is critical and weary of monarchic, centralized leadership and is convinced that human power is unstable and shifting. This voice also differs from that of the theologian, who sees all events in terms of Israel's covenantal faithfulness. That voice appears strongly in the Bochim scene of chapter 2. Stylistically, chapter 1 shows possible evidence of late biblical texture as defined by Frank Polak (1998), especially in the long noun strings at 1:18, 27, and 31. On the other hand, such strings of place names may reflect a particular register employed in a mapping list (cf. Num 21:15). The chapter formats quite well into self-contained cola.

[1–3] The chapter begins with the death of Joshua, a piece of content that might suggest sources, for Joshua seems to be alive in 2:6 and to die again in 2:8. Such an apparent case of "Homer's nodding" is, however, a feature of the preserved written tradition of Israel. Who killed Goliath, David or Elkanah (Gunn 1990: 23)? Why does Samuel not die after his testament scene (1 Sam 12; cf. 1 Sam 25:1)? Bumpiness of this kind is often attributed to an awkward combining of sources. One might suggest rather that such bumpiness is an integral characteristic of a particular episodic style in the Hebrew Scriptures. Such a theory does allow that many pieces of Scripture, in some form, would have had a living context apart from the present arrangement. In Judg 1:1 an author within the tradition employs the death-of-the-leader formula (see note a above) to signal that the following narratives are a significant phase in the life of the people. The reference point of 2:7 is simply different, but the resulting bumpiness is well within the boundaries of biblical style.

The response to the request for an oracle seems to give primacy to Judah. Some therefore suggest a southern or pro-Davidic orientation. It is clear that the composer views Judah as a leader tribe, successful in various exploits, but the chapter may be a comment on the relative homogeneity of the southern population versus the mixed ethnographic composition of northern Israel. The chapter is written from a southern perspective, but not one that is polemically triumphalist.

Judah, the southern tribe, treated as an individual hero, asks his brother Simeon to join him in waging war in a cooperative arrangement. Notice the use of the first person singular in v. 3. The tradition describes the brothers as both sons of Leah, while the present historiographic annal suggests some view of military cooperatives, an image found in subsequent chapters in which components of Israel join in battle against enemies. (See Judg 5 and the discussion of amphictyonic theories.) Lillian Klein suggests that Judah's invitation to Simeon is an initial hint of weak faith or disobedience (1988: 23), for God had said that Judah (himself presumably) should go and engage the enemy (v. 2); but this is to read into the chapter theological messages that do not appear until ch. 2. Were God displeased, things would not go as well for the brothers. Their success, however, is quite resounding.

[4–7] The account of the defeat of Bezek and the capture of its king has occasioned the search for historical data. Adam Zertal, for example, views this annal as possibly describing the way in which "clans of Judah and Simeon moved up from the Jordan Valley to be met at Bezek by Canaanites" (1992: 718). In dealing with material that lacks extrabiblical support such as the defeat of Bezek, one is in a position similar to that of scholars attempting to verify accounts in the *Odyssey* or *Beowulf*. The reliability of the author's use of local color or his representation of the general setting is dependent upon his worldview and upon memory as culturally contoured. Nevertheless, one can say certain things about terminology, content, and implicit point of view.

Canaan and the Canaanites are mentioned in ancient Near Eastern texts dating back to the second millennium B.C.E., for example, in the fourteenth-century B.C.E. Amarna letters. While specifics differ, most descriptions of the territories occupied by Canaanites tally well with the boundaries of Num 34:1–12 and Ezek 47:13–20; 48:1–7, 23–29, as noted by Jo Ann Hackett (1996). The culture of the Canaanites was richly urban by the second millennium B.C.E., and while they used a variety of scripts, they are perhaps best known in history as the "inventors" of the linear alphabet that would give rise to Phoenician, Hebrew, and Aramaic alphabets. Their pantheon of gods, including El, Baal, and Anat, figures in a variety of lively mythological traditions, versions of which were preserved at Ugarit (Hackett 1996: 409–14).

The Perizzites, often paired formulaically with "Canaanites," are found in most of the biblical lists of the pre-Israelite peoples; such lists are recurring traditional-style catalogues or blocks of material that punctuate narrative accounts. The term "Perizzite" may be related etymologically to *pĕrāzî*, "rural country" (see Ishida 1979: 479; Reed 1992: 231; Stager 1988: 225), suggesting that the Perizzites were those who dwelled in unwalled towns, whereas the term "Canaanites" refers to those dwelling in fortified cities (see also Judg 5). Ishida suggests drawing an ethnic distinction between Canaanite, a Semitic group, and Perizzite, a non-Semitic group, perhaps with Hurrian connections (1979: 479). The biblical tradition in Josh 11:3 locates the Perizzites in the hill country of Canaan, while Ishida reads Gen 15:19–21 and Josh 17:15 to imply their presence in the forested region between Judah and Ephraim (1979: 183). The origins of the name of this group and their actual provenance remain difficult to ascertain, along with those of the Hivites and others. Stager derives "Hivite" from the term *hawwôt* for "pastoral encampments" and identifies the Hivites, like the Perizzites, according to "ecological-sociological roots in particular types of rural settlements" (1988: 225). For the biblical writers, all such terms, like "Canaanite" itself, connote the oxymoron "foreign natives," those who will lose power to God's people. The control of Jerusalem by Israelites is frequently treated as key to dating this version of the account, for the city was not secured by the Israelites until the time of David in the tenth century B.C.E.

Bezek has been linked with Khirbet Ibziq, a site northeast of Shechem, although Zertal identifies the site with Khirbet Salhab in the Zebabdeh Valley, a conclusion perhaps overly influenced by the desire to match the biblical account with a likely actual setting (1992: 117–18). The term *bezeq* has been linked to the word for "pebble," hence "rocky place." The account's king of Bezek, Adoni-bezek, literally, "the lord of Bezek," is not mentioned outside the account. Wright (1946: 108) and Burney (5) argue that the king is to be identified with Adoni-zedek of Jerusalem, defeated by Joshua in an alternate account (Josh 10). The two accounts share motifs of place and approximate name, and such variations in a group's war lore are typical of traditional literatures. Matters of identity aside, the story of Adoni-bezek's capture and death in Judges 1 reveals much about the author's orientation. The central theme is that power comes and goes, for the mighty fall. He who inflicts punishment may, with God's will, become the afflicted. The particular treatment of the enemy, described in the narrator's voice and repeated in Adoni-bezek's reminiscence, dehumanizes; he loses his prehensile grip and his ability to walk well in an upright position. So Adoni-bezek had treated his own enemies; they had become doglike, gathering scraps under his table. Now facing the same fate, he identifies with them. The rhythmic proverb, "As I did, so God has repaid me," is less an expression of Israelite or Judahite triumphalism than a warning, colored with pathos, about the vagaries of power.

The quality of the language in vv. 6–7 reinforces its themes: a staccato sense of the battle conveyed in v. 6; repetition in vv. 6–7 to underline the particular war ethos at play—an ethos shared by Adoni-bezek and his enemies; and the concluding proverb, rich in messages about just deserts and the ephemeral nature of power as wielded by flawed human beings.

[**8–15**] This section describes victories of Judah (vv. 8–10), and then concentrates, cameo-style, on interaction between Achsah, Caleb, and Othniel. It points beautifully to the quality of repetition and variation typical of traditional literatures. Verse 8 contains a different version of the disposition of Jerusalem than vv. 7 and 21. Verse 10 provides a leadership role for Judah in the conquest of Hebron, whereas v. 20 features Caleb, who plays the role also in Josh 15:13–14; the role is filled neither by Judah nor by Caleb but by Joshua in Josh 11:21. The story of the conquest and disposition of Debir, involving Othniel, Caleb, and Achsah, is found with slight variations in Judg 1:11–15 and Josh 15:15–19, and the manuscript traditions offer still other interesting variants (see notes above).

Folk traditions about the ancient names of towns are included in the notices about Judah's victories. Kiriath-arba/Hebron, located twenty miles south of Jerusalem, is associated in Genesis with the deaths of Sarah (Gen 23:2) and Isaac (Gen 35:27). Like Kiriath-sepher/Debir (Josh 11:21) and other hill country locations, it is linked to the Anakim, the mythological giants (Gen 6:4; Num 13:33) who frighten the spies sent to survey the land. One tradition suggests that Arba was the greatest warrior of the Anakim (Josh 14:15). Judges 1:10 and 20 include hints to what must have been a richer tradition about other mighty Anak warriors, formulaically referred to as the "three sons of Anak." (See also Josh 15:13–14, which includes a genealogical tradition for Arba, Anak, and the sons of Anak.) Literally "Town of Four," the ancient name for Hebron may refer to four locations: Aner, Eshcol, Mamre, and Hebron (Hamilton 1992: 84).

Described in the Bible as southwest of Hebron in the southern portion of the Judean hill country, Debir/Kiriath-sepher seems to have some relation to writing or scribes or documents, but the nuances of the implicit folk etymology cannot be deciphered with certainty nor can the exact location of the town be determined (see Herion and Manor 1992: 112).

As the annals or tags concerning military encounters are followed in 1:5–7 with the vignette of Adoni-bezek, so the tags concerning Judahite victories in vv. 8–11 are followed by the vignette concerning Achsah. In the traditional pattern that links the fighting of enemies with the exchange of women, both manly pursuits in the bardic traditions of many cultures, Caleb promises his daughter in marriage to the warrior who is able to defeat Kiriath-sepher. In this way, many a traditional chieftain has defeated men and monsters and gained a son-in-law. The link between the hero's difficult task, specified as warrior's art, and the winning or wooing of a wife is found in the Israelite tradition in the tale of David, Saul, Merab, and Michal (see 1 Sam 17:25; 18:17–27).

In the Masoretic tradition for v. 14, Achsah, the bride prize, has her own lively voice and, like Rebekah, Deborah, and Judith, orchestrates or initiates events, urging her husband to seek a gift of land (see Ackerman 1998: 2–3). Implicit in the several traditions is the suggestion that Caleb had tried to deny the couple the watering holes that would make their holdings worthwhile from an agricultural perspective. Indeed, the tradition represented by Vat and OL portrays Achsah as vehement in her protests to her father (see note o), who in all traditions accedes to his daughter's demands and provides her the water rights.

Achsah's leaping from her donkey and offering an angry complaint to her father is reminiscent of the goddess Anat's bullying demands to her father El in the matter of building a house for her brother Baal (*KTU* 1. 3 v 19–34). The motif as found in Judg 1:14 and in the Canaanite tradition portrays the young woman as a plucky, even rebellious, youth who stands up to her father and gets what she wants. Neal Walls (1992: 94) has described Anat as a divine adolescent; some of this quality attaches to Achsah as well. In the context of Judges 1, however, the traditional motif, like the story of Adoni-bezek, becomes a comment on the serendipitous nature of power and on the capacity of unexpected ones to take control. In this case, power is negotiated between men and women, fathers and daughters, and wives and husbands. As elsewhere in Judges, the Israelite author identifies with the female, who is often portrayed as the marginal in Israelite tradition (see Niditch 1993b: 113–17).

[16–21] In line with the theme of fleeting power, this section contains a series of annals concerning less than fully successful battles in the south, a tradition preserved also in portions of Joshua. Certain places and peoples, important in the tradition, are cited.

The Kenites (1:16), one of the many non-Israelite groups encountered by Israel, are associated with Moses by marriage (see 4:11) and with the Midianites as part of a larger political alliance (Stager 1998: 147). Israelite lore includes several references to this group, and as in any folk tradition, details vary and sometimes contradict one another. The name "Kenite" is related by folk etymology both to Cain, brother of Abel (Gen 4:1), and to metalworking (Gen 4:22). For a useful discussion of traditions about the Kenites as they relate to Judges, see Ackerman 1998: 92–96.

The City of Palms is probably Jericho, an ancient city, six miles north of the Dead Sea. Arad is located in southwestern Judah. Zephath, whose actual identity and location are not known, is renamed in a wordplay as "Hormah" (cf. Num 21:3). This is one of the few instances in Judges in which the tradition of the ban is invoked. The enemy is exterminated and their dwelling place razed in fire under the requirement "to devote to destruction." (For a full discussion of this harsh ideology of war and an analysis of relevant biblical texts, see Niditch 1993b: 28–77.)

Gaza or Azah is the southernmost of the Philistine "pentapolis," a set of five cities located on or near the Mediterranean coast. Ashkelon is north of Gaza, Ashdod (Vat, OL) north of Ashkelon, and Ekron northeast of Ashdod. The location of Gath is uncertain.

[18–21] Verse 18 includes a significant textual variant so that MT emphasizes continuing victories for Judah, whereas LXX and OL point to Judah's defeat, as does v. 19 in all the manuscript traditions. Much has been made of a supposed pro-Judean or anti-Ephraimite polemic in ch. 1, based, for example, on the fact that Judah is described as victor in Hebron whereas the hero is Joshua in Josh 11:21. Similarly, the Judahites are a success in Jerusalem in Judg 1:8 whereas Judah fails in Josh 15:63 (see Brettler 1989; O'Connell 1996). However, not only do other characters exchange roles with Judah, even within Judges 1 (see vv. 20, 21), but various Israelite audiences would have received the tradition as preserved in Greek and Latin versions that temper this supposed pro-Judean polemic. Indeed, MT 1:19 refers to Judah's lack of chariotry, whereas Josh 17:16 and 18 attribute the same source of insecurity to Joseph. Judges 1 thus does not evidence the heavy hand of an anti-northern, pro-Judean polemicist.

The reference to the enemies' "chariotry of iron" is an important marker of the narrator's date. Some scholars have suggested that the author imagines wooden Bronze Age chariots fitted with iron plates for durability in the theater of war, and others argue that the iron refers to fittings or clasps. King and Stager suggest the use of iron axles (2001: 189). Robert Drews (1989), however, is critical of previous suggestions, basing his argument on archaeological evidence and the laws of physics. The biblical author, in his view, must be referring either to Assyrian-style chariot wheels made of bronze or to Persian period chariots fitted with cumbersome but fear-inducing iron scythes, both of which are attested. Such a detail says little about the date of the larger contexts and annals to which the detail belongs, but might suggest that whoever presented the annal included imagery from a late monarchic or postmonarchic period. Comparable cases of anachronism are found in Homeric epic (Foley 1993: 10).

Israel's ability to win in the hills and its lack of ability on the plain is mentioned in 1 Kgs 20:23. The Aramaeans make a mistake in believing the vicious rumor about the inability of Yhwh's people to win in the valleys, but the rumor may hold more than a little historical truth. Finkelstein and other archaeologists have read the evidence to suggest that Israel's earliest settlement regions were actually in the central highlands, the hills of Ephraim, and to a lesser extent those of Benjamin and Judah (1988: 81; see also A. Mazar 1992: 350–51). The topographical excuse for failure is remarkably nontheological, and the tone of the account is nontriumphalist, reinforcing the vignettes about the uncertainties of political and military power. In this respect, attitudes in Judges 1 contrast with those of the Deuteronomic-style writer who frames the tales of Judges preserved in chs. 3–16 and with the triumphalist author of the outer portions of Joshua (see introduction, section 3).

The tag concerning the Jebusites (1:21) has been interpreted as evidence that the ancient historian was aware that Jerusalem was not conquered in premonarchic times. Compare the notice concerning the disposition of Jerusalem in v. 8 in which Judah plays the leadership role rather than Benjamin and the conquest is successful. At this point in the chapter, the author leaves the tales of Judah and turns to a tribe-by-tribe accounting of the conquest or lack of conquest.

[22–26] These verses contain the third of the vignettes that punctuate and elaborate the brief annals concerning conquest and disposition of the land. The north (i.e., Joseph) conquers Luz with God's aid, formulaically emphasized. Successful reconnaissance and the assistance of someone from inside the city are marked. The conventional tale of the helpful turncoat always indicates a positive war result for those whom the turncoat encounters (cf. tales of Rahab in Josh 2:1–24 and 6:22–25 and of David in 1 Sam 30:11–15). This tale thus serves as further proof that Judges is not an anti-northern polemic prepared by pro-southern writers. To the contrary, in its current setting, the tale of the founder of Luz acknowledges the way in which power and control fluctuate. The people of the man from Luz are displaced by the descendants of Joseph, and he then goes off to found a city in the land of the Hittites. Within the narrative, the important message is that one Luz is gone and another established. The vision in Judges 1, in contrast to portions of Joshua, is of fluid and shifting power, a theme reinforced by all three vignettes.

In this respect, Judges 1 and the Judges-like material in Joshua 13–17 (e.g., Josh 15:63; 16:10; 17:12, 16) contrast with threads that dominate in the beginning and end of the book of Joshua, such as Josh 21:43–44 and 11:16–23 with their absolute certainty about totally successful conquest. The humanist voice in Judges contrasts with the triumphalism of royalist propagandists writing either during the monarchy or afterward with hopes of royal restoration. This voice also contrasts with the religionist voice that frames chs. 3–16, typical of Deuteronomy, in which all is explained in terms of God's relationship with Israel and its faithfulness to a particular concept of covenant.

Whereas Josh 16:2 seems to suggest that Luz and Bethel are different places, Gen 28:19 and 35:6 equate them as the city bordering Ephraim and Benjamin (see Josh 18:13 and the present context). The remainder of the chapter offers additional geographic locations in which the theme of incomplete conquest is played out.

[27–36] Beth-shean (modern Tell el-Husn), an ancient site between the Jezreel and Jordan valleys, has been occupied by human communities as early as the fifth or fourth millennium B.C.E. (cf. 1 Sam 31:12). Taanach, located five miles southeast of Megiddo, also has a lengthy history of pre-Israelite occupation. Dor, a coastal city mentioned among the conquests in the tradition of Joshua (Josh 11:2; 12:23), served as the center of Solomon's fourth administrative district (1 Kgs 4:11). The Egyptian Tale of Wen-Amon (ca. 1100 B.C.E.) suggests that at some point in the premonarchic period the city was occupied by the Tjeker, one of the Sea Peoples.

Megiddo is an important and well-excavated ancient city of northwestern Israel about twenty miles southeast of modern Haifa (see Aharoni 1972; and Yadin 1970). Gezer (v. 29), another ancient city, is five miles south-southeast of Ramleh (see Dever et al. 1970; Dever 1986). The identity and location of Kitron and Nahalol are uncertain. Acco, a commercially important Canaanite city on the Mediterranean coast, frequently mentioned in extrabiblical sources, has been amply excavated (see Dothan 1992).

Sidon was an ancient Phoenician coastal city located on the eastern Mediterranean (see Katzenstein 1973). The identity of Ahlab is uncertain, as is its relation to Mehebel in a parallel text in Josh 19:29. Achzib, located on the coast of the Mediterranean north of Acco, has been explored archaeologically as far back as the Middle Bronze Age I. Grave sites have been excavated that trace the presence of Canaanite-Sidonian, Israelite, and Syro-Hittite cultural traditions (see Prausnitz 1992: 57–58). Helbah is of uncertain identity, but may be a variant of Ahlab and Mehebel. Biblical tradition locates Aphik and Rehob in Asher (Josh 19:30). Beth-shemesh is located on the northern border of Judah, west of Jerusalem (see Brandfon 1992: 696–98). Beth-anath's location in northern Israel is uncertain.

"Amorite" is a term employed for one of the peoples of Canaan (e.g., Gen 15:19–21; Josh 3:10). While scholars have explored the linguistic, ethnic, and political identity of the Amorites (see Porter 1992), the term is also used synonymously with "Canaanite" as a general designation for the indigenous population of the land, rivals of the occupying Israelites in the biblical founding myth. The identities of Har-heres and Shaalbim are uncertain.

Some scholars view these verses, with their recurring language concerning the various northern tribes' inability to disinherit, as a comment on lost divine favor, a theme consonant with the Deuteronomistic-style thread of the work. Others see continuing proof of the pro-southern orientation of the chapter and the book. Judah, however, is also less than fully successful even in MT v. 19, and the northern tribes, while not disinheriting their enemies, are frequently formulaically described as subjugating their enemies into forced labor. The end of the chapter is thus not a description of consummate defeat, and Israel's superiority over enemies is even more marked in some of the textual traditions, which repeat the formula concerning forced labor more frequently than versions preserved in MT.

These verses do tend to emphasize a tribal concept of Israelite polity rather than a centralized one and acknowledge what was historical reality throughout

Israel's history, <u>the continued significant presence of Canaanite populations in the northern half of the country in particular.</u>

Judges 2:1–23
From "Weeping" to the Death of Joshua

2:1 And a messenger of Yhwh went up
　　　from Gilgal to Bochim,[a]
　　and he said,[b]
　　"I caused you to go up from Egypt
　　and I brought you to the land
　　　that I swore to your ancestors,
　　and I said,
　　'I will not break my covenant with you, forever,
2　　and you will not cut a covenant
　　　with the dwellers of this land.[c]
　　Their altars you will pull down.'
　　But you did not listen to my voice.
　　What is this you have done?[d]
3　　And also I said,
　　'I will not drive them out[e] from before you.
　　And they will be to you a trap,
　　and their gods will be to you a lure.'"
4　　And it was, when the messenger of Yhwh spoke these words
　　　to all of the descendants of Israel,
　　　the people lifted up their voice and wept.
5　　And[f] they called the name of that place Bochim (Weeping),
　　and they sacrificed there to Yhwh.
6　　And Joshua[g] sent the people,
　　and the descendants of Israel went,
　　　each to his inheritance,
　　　to take possession of the land.
7　　And the people served Yhwh
　　　all the days of Joshua
　　　and all the days of the old men
　　　　who prolonged their days beyond Joshua,
　　　　who saw all the great deeds of Yhwh
　　　　　that he did for Israel.
8　　And Joshua, son of Nun, servant of Yhwh, died,
　　　a son of one hundred and ten years.

9   And they buried him within the borders of his inheritance
      in Timnath-heres (Portion of the Sun),
      in the hill country of Ephraim,
        north of Mount Gaash.

10   And also all of that generation was gathered to its ancestors,
    and there arose another generation after them
      who did not know Yhwh,[h]
      and also the deeds that he did for Israel.

11   And the descendants of Israel did evil in the eyes of Yhwh,
    and they served the baals,

12   and they forsook Yhwh, the god of their ancestors,
      who brought them out of the land of Egypt.
    And they went after other gods
      from the gods of the peoples who were round about them,
    and they bowed down to them,
    and they angered Yhwh.

13   And they forsook Yhwh,
    and they served the baal and the ashtarot.

14   And the anger of Yhwh was kindled against Israel,
    and he gave them into the hand of plunderers,
    and they plundered them,
    and he sold them into the hand of their enemies round about,
    and they could no longer stand before their enemies.

15   Every time that they went forth,[i]
      the hand of Yhwh was against them for evil,
        as Yhwh had spoken to them
        and as Yhwh had sworn to them,
    and they were in very sore straits.

16   And Yhwh raised up judges,
    and they[j] delivered them from the hand of their plunderers.

17   But even to their judges they did not listen,[k]
    for they whored after other gods,
    and they bowed down to them.[l]
    They turned quickly from the way
      that their ancestors had walked
        to listen to the commandments of Yhwh.
    They did not do likewise.

18   And when Yhwh raised up for them judges,
      Yhwh would be with the judge,
    and he would deliver them from their enemies
      all the days of the judge;
    for Yhwh would have compassion over their groaning

because of their torturers and oppressors.

19 And it was at the death of the judge
that they would return to go to ruin, worse than their ancestors,
to walk after other gods,
to serve them,
and to bow down to them.
They did not let go of any of their practices or their rough ways.

20 And the anger of Yhwh was kindled against Israel,
and he said,
"Because this nation has crossed my covenant
that I commanded their ancestors,
and did not listen to my voice,

21 for my part, I will not continue
to dispossess one person from before them
from among the nations that Joshua left
when he died[m]

22 in order to test Israel by means of them.
Do they keep to the way of Yhwh, to walk upon it
as their ancestors had kept,
or do they not?"

23 And Yhwh left in place these nations,
not dispossessing them quickly,
for he did not give them into the hand of Joshua.[n]

a. OL and Vat expand the objects of going up to include Bethel, and Bethel and the house of Israel, respectively, more specifically situating "Bochim" in the north.

b. Vat expands, "And he said to them, 'Thus says the Lord,'" employing the formulaic indicator of a formal oracle from God. OL expands more briefly, "And the Lord said to them," accounting for God's first person speech.

c. In all manuscript traditions the language describing God as the savior from Egypt (cf. Exod 20:2) and the covenantal promise as eternal (cf. Gen 17:7) and not to be broken is typical and conventionalized, drawing upon the oral-style recurring idioms of the Israelite tradition. The phrase "break covenant" is typical of traditions associated with Priestly or Deuteronomistically related writers (e.g., Lev 26:15, 44; Deut 31:16, 20; Jer 11:10; 14:21; 31:32; 33:21; Ezek 16:59; 17:15, 16; Zech 11:10). Similarly, OL and Vat include some typically Deuteronomic sentiments and language to parallel the commands in MT concerning altars and relations with the conquered: "nor shall you worship their gods/you will break their carved images" (see Deut 7:2, 5, 16, 25; also Exod 23:24, 33).

d. The question in MT is formulaic in the Israelite tradition to indicate a major breach of proper relations between parties, human and divine or human (Gen 4:10; 12:18; 26:10; 29:25; 31:26; Exod 14:11; Num 23:11; Judg 8:1; 15:11). OL and Vat instead use language of judgment: "because you did these things" (cf. Gen 3:14; 20:10).

e. OL and A expand with language of the ban, "I will not displace the people whom I said to destroy utterly," explaining why the ban was not carried out.

f. OL and A add, "On account of this," an etiological rubric. The etiological folk etymology is a common feature of Israelite founding myths (see Gen 16:14; 22:14; 28:19).

g. OL has God rather than Joshua dismiss the people, continuing the frame of a divinely sent message with which the scene begins.

h. OL has, "did not know Joshua," linking the people's apostasy to the lack of the charismatic leader as in the Deuteronomistic frame of the book. The phrase "did not know *x*" is a formulaic marker of the coming of dangerous new times (cf. Exod 1:8).

i. Vat translates "go forth" as *exeporeuonto* and parallels MT. OL and A, however, read the verb *eporneuon*, "in all the things by which they fornicated," reflecting Hebrew *zānû*, "whored" (cf. 2:17). Thus an inner Greek homophone and a possible influence from v. 17 lead to a variant that nevertheless makes sense in the context.

j. OL and Vat have "Lord" as subject of saving instead of the judges in MT. The Deity thus plays the key role in what may be a theologically motivated reading.

k. OL reads, "They did not listen to his judgment," again emphasizing the relationship with God. The judges are omitted.

l. OL and A include slightly longer variants in describing Israel's apostasy, adding "they incited the Lord to anger."

m. OL omits the phrase "when he died." The syntax and sentence division in the Hebrew are ambiguous between vv. 21 and 22. The lines are enjambed. Verses 21–22 could be translated as one long, intertwining thought.

n. OL reads, "And the Lord handed these nations into the hand of Joshua/Iesu so that he would not quickly destroy them from their [the Israelites'] face. And the Lord put them into the hand of Joshua/Iesu."

Two features are noteworthy in exploring the place of chapter 2 within the corpus of Judges. Its style is characterized by the presence of complex sentence structures, with embedded clauses and much subordination, a trait that Polak (1998) finds in postexilic or Persian period Hebrew. Laying the text out in cola thus reveals considerable enjambment whereby the thought is not completed until a line or two beyond the opening clause. The language, content, and themes of Judges 2, moreover, parallel those of Deuteronomistic writings, emphasizing the idolatry of the natives of the land, the need to separate from these peoples, the tendency to break covenant by consorting with foreigners, and the punishment as defeat that follows. The texture of the passage would seem to indicate a late Deuteronomistic voice. The register is thus quite different from that of ch. 1, which more often than not assumes an epic style, although its date, as preserved, may well be as late or later than that of ch. 2 (see introduction, sections 3 and 4). Structurally, Judges 2 is composed of at least four segments, each of which offers theological explanation for Israel's lack of success in taking possession of the land. All are framed in terms of covenant.

First is the scene at Bochim in which a divine emissary accuses Israel of forging a covenant with the inhabitants of the land and leaving the enemies' altars intact, contrary to God's command. Now Israel will be ensnared (2:1–6). Judges 2:7–10 adumbrates problems to come when Joshua and the people of his generation die and a new generation arises who is ominously said not to know Yhwh or the deeds he did for Israel. Judges 2:11–17 describes the Israelites' fall from covenant faithfulness in strongly Deuteronomic language. Infidelity to God leads to defeat. God raises up judges, but Israel will not listen to them. Judges 2:18–23 describes the recurring Deuteronomistic pattern found throughout the book. Yahweh raises a judge who inspires and delivers the people. The judge dies and Israel backslides. God punishes them with failure in battle; the remaining nations serve as a means of testing Israel's covenant loyalty.

[1–6] The vignette provides a folk etymology, rooted in the word "to cry," for a town said to be located somewhere in the vicinity of Gilgal. Vat and OL associate its location with Bethel, and scholars have suggested that Bochim is to be identified with Bethel. Indeed, Yaira Amit (2000) finds in this identification a polemic against the ancient northern shrine on the part of a pre-Deuteronomistic Judean writer. Divine disapproval is conveyed by a heavenly emissary who delivers an oracle in the style of biblical prophecy. To make a covenant is literally "to cut" it (2:2), an idiom rooted in the sacrificial ritual that reflects and asserts the relationship (e.g., Gen 15:7–12). Notice the parallel constructions in v. 3 by which the sentence of punishment is pronounced upon an unfaithful people.

[7–10] Deuteronomistic in outlook, the style of these verses is characterized by complex sentence structures, built with subordinate and interlocking grammatical units (e.g., vv. 7, 10). Like subsequent judges, Joshua is treated as one who inspires Israel's faithfulness. His death and the passing of his generation lead to the evildoing that follows.

[11–17] In strongly Deuteronomic language, this section details the acts of apostasy committed by Israel (cf. Deut 8:19–20; 11:16–17). Polytheism and idolatry are the rubrics under which Israel's sins fall. "Baal," meaning "master" in Northwest Semitic languages, is the dying and rising hero deity of the Canaanite pantheon, who shares qualities of storm god and warrior with the Israelite Yhwh. Idols are generalized as "baals." "Ashtarot" refers to the Canaanite goddess of fertility and war, Ashtarah (Astarte/Ishtar), associated with Baal (see King and Stager 2001: 349–50), but like the term "baals" is used in general and formulaic accusations concerning Israel's participation in Canaanite religion.

Notice that Israel is described as whoring after other gods (v. 17). Apostasy is a kind of harlotry or adultery; the implicit metaphor equates Israel with God's unfaithful wife, a motif fully developed in Hosea 2, Jeremiah 2, and Ezekiel 16.

[18–23] The essential pattern of Israel's subjugation and groaning, God's raising of a savior-judge, success, the judge's death, and renewed subjugation frames the life stories of the charismatic leaders called judges (chs. 3–16). This framework has been provided by Deuteronomically oriented writers, who are responsible for the theological voice in the work. Writers with the same point of view introduce or conclude accounts concerning the judges Othniel, Ehud, Deborah, Gideon, Jephthah, and Samson (see 3:7–15; 4:1–4; 6:1–10; 8:33–35; 10:6–17; 13:1).

Judges 3:1–31
A Covenantal Introduction and the Judges Othniel, Ehud, and Shamgar

3:1   And these are the nations that Yhwh left in place[a]
           in order to test Israel by means of them—
               all those who had no knowledge
               of all the wars of Canaan.
2   It was only for the sake of the knowledge[b]
           of generations of the descendants of Israel,
           in order to teach them war,
               only because previously[c] they did not have knowledge.
3   The five tyrants[d] of the Philistines and all the Canaanites
           and the Sidonians and the Hivites,
               who dwell in the mountain of Lebanon,
                   from the mountain of Baal-hermon
                       to the entrance of Hamath.
4   They existed[e] to test Israel by means of them
           in order to know whether they would listen
               to the commandments of Yhwh,
                   which he commanded to their ancestors
                       by the hand of Moses.
5   And the descendants of Israel dwelled in the midst of the Canaanite,
           the Hittite, the Amorite, the Perizzite,
           the Hivite, and the Jebusite.
6   And they took their daughters to them for wives,
           and their daughters they gave to their sons,
           and they served their gods.[f]
7   And the descendants of Israel did evil in the eyes of Yhwh,
           and they forgot Yhwh their god,[g]
           and they served the baals and the asherot.[h]
8   And kindled was the anger of Yhwh against Israel,[i]
           and he sold them[j] into the hand of Cushan-rishathaim,
               king of Aram-naharaim,

and the descendants of Israel served Cushan-rishathaim
    for eight years.

9 And the descendants of Israel called out to Yhwh,
and Yhwh raised up a deliverer for the descendants of Israel.
And he delivered them: Othniel, son of Kenaz,
the brother of Caleb (the one younger than he).[k]

10 And there was upon him the spirit of Yhwh,[l]
and he judged Israel,
and he went forth to war,[m]
and Yhwh gave into his hand Cushan-rishathaim,
    king of Aram,
and his hand was strong against Cushan-rishathaim.

11 And quiet was the land for forty years,
and Othniel, son of Kenaz, died.

⌐12 And the descendants of Israel again acted
    to do evil in the eyes of Yhwh,
and Yhwh strengthened Eglon, king of Moab, over Israel
    because they had done evil in the eyes of Yhwh.

13 And he gathered to him the descendants of Ammon and Amalek,
and he went and struck Israel,
and they took possession of the City of Palms.

14 And the descendants of Israel served Eglon, king of Moab,
    for eighteen years.

15 And the descendants of Israel called out to Yhwh,
and Yhwh raised up for them a deliverer,
    Ehud, son of Gera, a Benjaminite,
        a left-handed man.[n]
And the descendants of Israel sent in his hand
    a tribute offering to Eglon, king of Moab.

16 And Ehud made for himself a sword,
and it had two edges,
    a short cubit its length.
And he girded it on under his garment,[o]
    upon his right thigh.

17 And he presented the tribute offering to Eglon, king of Moab.
Eglon was a very fat man.[p]

18 And it was when he finished presenting the tribute offering
    that he sent away the people bearing the tribute offering.

19 And he returned by way of the hewn images
    that were at the circle,
and he said,
"Something secret I have for you, O king,"

and he^q said,
"Silence."
And all those who attended him went away from him.

20   And Ehud came to him,
and he was sitting in the cool upper chamber^r
     that he had,
          alone.
And Ehud said,
"Something from God I have for you."
And he rose up from upon the throne.^s

21   And^t Ehud sent forth his left hand,
and he took the sword from upon his right thigh,
and he drove it into his belly.

22   And the hilt went in^u after the blade,
and the fat closed behind the blade,
for he did not draw out the sword from his belly,
and out he went by the exit way.^v

23   And Ehud went out to the colonnaded portico,^w
and he shut the doors of the upper chamber behind him,
and he bolted them.

24   And he went off.
^xBut his servants came.
They saw and behold, the doors of the upper chamber were bolted.
And they said,
"He must be 'indisposed'^y in the cool room."

25   And they waited until the point of embarrassment,^z
and behold, he did not open the doors of the upper chamber,
and they took the key and opened up,
and behold, their lord was fallen on the ground dead.

26   And Ehud escaped during their tarrying,^aa
and he crossed by the hewn images and
escaped to Seirah.

27   And it was at his coming,^bb
he blasted the shofar in the hill country of Ephraim.
And the descendants of Israel went down with him,
from the hill country,
and he was in front of them.

28   And he said to them,
"Follow after me
because Yhwh has given your enemies, Moab, into your hands."
And they followed after him,
and they captured the fords of the Jordan

over against Moab,
and they let no one cross.

29 And they struck Moab at this time,
about ten thousand men,
all robust, all men of valor,
and not a man escaped.[cc]

30 And humbled was Moab on that day beneath the hand of Israel,
and quiet was the land for eighty years.[dd]

31 And after him, there was Shamgar, son of Anat,
and he struck the Philistines,
six hundred men, with an oxgoad,[ee]
and he also delivered Israel.

a. OL continues its version of 2:23 by having Joshua be the one to leave the nations in place so that "Joshua/Iesu might test Israel." In this tradition, Joshua assumes a heightened role. Does the tradition reflect an ancient author who emphasizes the central leadership of the hero of the wilderness generation, or does a translator, targumic style, implicitly equate the Israelite Joshua with Jesus and thereby enhance his role?

b. Vat and OL omit "knowledge." MT may reflect the residue of a variant for the phrase "to teach them."

c. Vat translates *lĕpānîm* ("previously") as "before them," reading "only those before them did not know these things."

d. "Tyrant" is a Philistine loanword that refers to the rulers of the various petty kingdoms in the ancient Mediterranean.

e. Literally, "they were."

f. The language echoes that of Deut 7:4 and identifies the Deuteronomic-style voice that employs this particular formulaic description of Israel's lack of covenant faithfulness.

g. Formulaic language found in 2:11. The covenantally concerned voice continues.

h. Formulaic language found in 2:13.

i. Formulaic language found in 2:14.

j. Vat and OL have a meaning-neutral variant, "hand over," instead of MT "sold."

k. Vat has Othniel be Caleb's nephew, but OL has Othniel be Caleb's younger brother as in 1:14, an allowable translation of the Hebrew syntax.

l. A formulaic indicator of the charismatic God-sent power that envelops the hero (e.g., Jephthah, 11:29; Samson, 13:25; 14:6, 19; 15:14; Saul, 1 Sam 10:6, 10; 11:6; David, 1 Sam 16:13).

m. Formulaic language of military engagement.

n. Vat and OL have "ambidextrous." This translation of "left-handed" does not carry the nuances of trickster and marginal found in the literal Hebrew, "bound with regard to the right hand."

o. Note that Vat uses a similar sounding translation, *manduan,* for *maddāyw,* and with this term pictures the garment more precisely as a woolen cloak, adding some imagery and texture to the costuming of the hero.

p. Vat and OL translate *bārîʾ* as "subtle, witty, smooth," i.e., not a country hick. The traditions thus emphasize the us/them quality of the story about the success of the unlikely hero. This theme is central to the narrative, to be sure, but by pointing to the social or cultural status of the enemy, Vat and OL have dampened the physical nuances of the character portrayal that are important to the subsequent assassination scene. The king is "well-fed," and his girth creates a visceral metaphor for an aristocratic oppressor.

q. OL expands, "And Eglon, king of Moab," and eliminates "Silence," substituting "for all to go out from his midst." The scene is thus filled out.

r. Vat and OL read a "summer room."

s. Vat and OL add "near him," blocking the scene beautifully.

t. Vat and OL begin, "And it was at the time when he [OL Eglon] rose up.

u. Vat and OL have Ehud be the subject of the act of thrusting in the sword.

v. Vat translates "porch" or "vestibule." The term *paršĕdōnâ,* found only here, has thus been treated as an architectural feature. Others read a reference to "excrement," with a parallel to Exod 29:14 (*pereš*). Halpern's translation (1988b: 36, 38–41) links this unusual term, the phrase for evacuation in v. 24, and the attendants' subsequent embarrassment to suggest that the attendants smell the "dirt" from Eglon's intestinal wound. Barré finds parallels in Akkadian texts with a term meaning "going out" or "escape." With some support from an Akkadian medical treatise, Barré, like Halpern, relates the term to the emptying of the "contents of the bowels," in this case to the place of emptying, the anus (1991: 5–6). See Stager (2003b: 244–45, n. 11) on the rhyme or possible wordplay between *paršĕdōnâ* and *misdĕrônâ* (3:23), two unusual terms perhaps connoting architectural features. My translation suggests an architectural feature for the exit.

w. This verse and the end of v. 22 seem to provide alternate versions of the getaway. The latter, more complex version has Ehud secrete himself on a balcony of sorts until he is able to flee undetected. The term *misdĕrônâ* seems to be from the root *sdr,* "to order," suggesting a row of columns. Noting that some have translated "portico," or "loggia," Stager suggests that the term rooted in "to order" may refer to "aligned beams which frame . . . decorative sunken panels of a room or building." Thus he translates, "a room or unit with coffered ceilings" (2003b: 243). The "order" term leads Vat to a reference to going out by "the arranged ones," perhaps the guards. OL seems to treat the term as a sound-alike architectural space, the *androna,* meaning "men's apartment in a house" or "a passage or corridor."

x. OL adds, "as Ehud was going out," providing a sense of intrigue—they just missed him.

y. This phrase is difficult. The verb may be a form of *nsk,* "to pour," or of *skk,* "to cover." The phrase would then literally read, "to pour out/to cover the feet/legs." The "feet/legs" may refer to feet or to genitals, "feet" being a frequent euphemism in the Hebrew Bible for male and female genitals (see Deut 28:57; Isa 7:20). Vat and some modern translators choose the verb "pour." Vat reads literally, "draining his feet," retaining the euphemism, while modern translators render the phrase "relieving himself," i.e., "urinating." Others read "covering his feet" and suggest the idiom refers to defecation because of the crouching position assumed. So Saul's private activity in a cave is often understood (1 Sam 24:3; BDB 697). Halpern (1988b: 34) prefers this interpretation, which accommodates his interpretation of the scene (see note v), and which may be supported by OL: "Does he not sit on a stool (used for defecation)?"

z. OL glosses *bwš* as "confounded," emphasizing confusion swirling around the assassination events rather than embarrassment.

aa. Vat reads instead, "while they were making a tumult," and OL again contributes a portrait of confusion and bewilderment: "While they ran amok." Vat also adds, "and there was no one who observed him." Similarly, OL has, "and there was no one who gave a thought to him." In these traditions, the story is framed more fully, the motif of the getaway more fully shaped.

bb. Vat adds, "into the land of Israel," while OL has a quite different reading, "and it was that a voice came, and the crowd sounded the shofar." Is the voice Ehud's or a divine pronouncement, or is the OL reflecting an original Hebrew text that included the word *qôl*, which can mean thunder, thus setting the scene as one of tumult and implicit divine intervention?

cc. OL has an alternate expanded reading, "not one of them were saved / nor was there anybody who fled."

dd. Vat and OL complete the tale, "and Ehud judged them until he died."

ee. Whereas MT reads *malmad ĥabbāqār*, literally, "something that disciplines [*lmd*, "to teach"] the ox," OL reads, "six hundred men besides the old men," perhaps reflecting Hebrew *millĕbad hazzāqēn*. A reads, "besides the young bull." One sees here a typical text-critical pattern whereby sound-alike or look-alike words are copied mistakenly from one version and then made sense of. MT and OL are at the beginning and end of the process, whereas A is somewhere in the middle.

The chapter is composed of four parts: (1) 3:1–6, opening explanations for Israel's failure to displace the enemy; (2) 3:7–11, a brief annal concerning Othniel set in a covenantal or Deuteronomic framework; (3) 3:12–30, the traditional tale of Ehud, again covenantally framed; (4) 3:31, the brief annal concerning Shamgar.

The story of Ehud is a beautifully crafted example of the tale of a social bandit, while the opening framework reveals the interests of covenantally oriented preservers of narratives about the judges. The brief annals concerning Othniel and Shamgar raise questions about Israelite historiographic genres and the metonymic quality of traditional literatures. The heavy use of subordination and the complex syntax of sentences, particularly in vv. 1–5, may point to a late biblical date for the opening language of the introduction to Judges 3.

[1–6] Two points of view are at play in these opening verses. The first we recognize from Judges 1, in which the experience of war is seen in human terms, and success or failure is not dependent upon covenant faithfulness. Thus in a traditional-style etiology, the enemies are allowed by God to remain in the land in order to teach the current generation of Israelites the arts of war. This voice, perhaps that of the humanist shaper of Judges, captures well the bardic ideology of war, evidenced in the epic traditions of Judges. Warring is a learned skill, a matter of training. The list of peoples remaining in the land according to v. 3 includes the Philistines, a group who migrated from the Aegean to the Mediterranean coast, west and south of Judah in the twelfth century B.C.E. Judges 3:3 refers to the Philistine pentapolis with its five rulers (see 1:18). Also mentioned are the "Canaanites," here a generic term along with "Amorites" for Israel's competitors in the land (see 1:4–7); the Sidonians, a Phoenician people living on the Mediterranean coast to Israel's northwest; and the Hivites, a group more difficult to locate historically and geographically (see 1:4–7).

Judges 3:3–6 reflects the sort of covenantally oriented author found in ch. 2 and echoes the message of 2:22–23. The remaining nations test Israel's faithfulness, serving both as a temptation to join in the worship of alien gods and as Yhwh's means of punishing his sinful people. The list in 3:5 is a traditional one, found frequently in the tradition (Gen 15:20; Exod 3:8, 17), sometimes expanded, sometimes abbreviated. On Canaanites and Perizzites, see commentary to 1:4–7; on Amorites and Jebusites see 1:27–36.

Note that 3:6 not only speaks in Deuteronomic idiom (Deut 7:3, 4; Exod 34:16) but echoes the primeval story of Gen 6:1–4, where inappropriate marriage to the "other" leads to evil and destruction. There the tale is linked to the Noah account, here to more mundane military defeat. The defeat will be followed by the raising of a savior-judge as the recurring covenantal theme is established.

[7–11] The first verse of this section makes the transition to the recurring framework that encloses many of the tales of the judges and consists of the motifs: evil of people, anger of Yhwh, subjugation as punishment, people's calling out, raising of rescuer. Concerning "baals" and possible female consorts to the Canaanite deity of that name, see 2:13. On the origins and identity of Asherah and connections to Baal and Yhwh, see Judith Hadley 2000: 54–83. The identity of Cushan-rishathaim is unknown, but the second half of his name as preserved plays on the root for "evil," *rš‘*, literally, "evil times two." Such sound plays on the names of enemies, or those whom the writer wishes to mock, are common in the Hebrew Bible (e.g., Mephibosheth, son of Saul whose name incorporates the word for "shame" [2 Sam 4:4]; Nabal, husband of Abigail whose name can mean "foolish" [1 Sam 25:25].). MT locates his city-state, Aram-naharaim, in northern Mesopotamia. Boling attempts to localize this enemy at a more reasonable distance from the land, given what has been reconstructed about the realpolitik of the premonarchic period (81). This effort perhaps expects too much historical verisimilitude from the author.

Othniel is archetypally described as the charismatic military liberator. The *rûaḥ* ("spirit") of Yhwh infuses him, enabling him to fight to victory. Such is the quintessential definition of the judge in Judges. The notice ends with the formulaic indication of years of quiet offered by Othniel's leadership. As Yaira Amit has written (1999: 163), the annal concerning Othniel exhibits intense use of Deuteronomistic formulas. From a literary perspective, the piece functions as a brief paradigm for the career of judge, the theologian's model for the longer episodes to follow. Other traditions concerning Othniel are preserved in Judges 1 and Joshua (see commentary to ch. 1). The narrative weight of Judges 3 is located in the tale of Ehud, which is also introduced by the paradigmatic covenantal frame in vv. 12–15.

[**12–15**] Israel's evil leads to the strengthening of neighboring enemies, the Moabites, Ammonites, and Amalekites, who are under the direction of Eglon, king of Moab, whose name means "young bull" or "calf." The Ammonites, located in north-central Transjordan, were contemporary with early Israel and had a long parallel history. Moab, located to the east of Judah, is known from Assyriological sources and from the Moabite Inscription, a ninth-century B.C.E. text in which the Moabite king Mesha describes his victory over Israel (see Dearman 1989). The Moabite language is closely related to Biblical Hebrew. Indeed, the similarity of Moabite culture to that of Israel motivates the Israelite authors of Judges to demarcate strongly between "us" and "them," the enemy other and the self, all in a process of self-definition (see also 10:6). Associated with Edom in Gen 36:16, the Amalekites are variously located in the Hebrew Bible in Judah and further afield and appear to have been "mobile" if not "nomadic" (see Dearman 1985). They, like Ammon and Moab, serve as iconic enemies in Israelite tradition.

The call of the people to Yhwh leads to the raising of the savior Ehud from the tribe of Benjamin. Benjaminites appear to have a genetic predisposition to left-handedness as seen in the war account of 20:16, a trait that plays upon the name of their tribe and eponymic ancestor meaning "son of the right hand." Halpern has suggested that, like the Spartans, Benjaminites literally bound the right arms of young future warriors to train them to use the left in battle (1988b: 35). Left-handedness is an excellent warrior's weapon against the right-handed majority. In Israelite as in other traditional cultures, the left side is also the symbolic dark side, the marginal, underhanded side of the body as indicated by ritual preferences (see Exod 29:20, 22; Lev 7:32; 8:23, 25; Eccl 10:2). Ehud's lefty status is symbolically appropriate for judges who are often liminal or marginal, in some cultural sense—of illegitimate birth like Jephthah, female like Deborah, or wild and unsocialized like Samson. The left-handedness also allows for the particular deception in this pattern of the trickster.

[**16–30**] Ehud prepares his weapon, as is appropriate for the hero, and hides it under his garment on the right thigh. Presumably the guards would frisk a man on the left, expecting him to draw with the right hand. Taking note of the traditional quality of such narrative "type scenes," as Alter calls them, David Gunn has drawn parallels between Ehud's assassination of Eglon and Joab's murder of his rival Amasa in 2 Sam 20:9–10, where the killer again unexpectedly reaches for his weapon with the left hand and kills with a strike to the abdomen (1974b: 304). As in Judges 4, in the context of guerrilla warfare, an act of deception begins to weave an erotic theme that links the sexual with the aggressive and agonistic. The play on "sex and slaughter," as Emily Vermeule has described it, is found in non-Israelite epic contexts as well (Vermeule 1979:

101–2, 157; Shulman 1986) and is especially important in tales of the judges. Here the short sword worn on the thigh, a male erogenous zone, begins the play, for one hitches a sword at the thigh (Exod 32:27; Song 3:8), but the thigh (or loins) is also the seat of male fertility (Gen 46:26; Exod 1:5), the short blade a phallic image (see also Brettler 1991: 295–96).

Ehud uses the occasion of bringing tribute to the king, the master in this particular feudal relationship of subjugation, to set up a private audience or assignation. As noted by Alter (1981: 41), the word "secret" connotes political intimacy (Jer 37:17; 38:16; 40:15) but also enticement (Deut 13:6 [MT 7]; Job 31:27) and describes David's secret, forbidden union with Bathsheba in 2 Sam 12:12. Thus the play between eroticism and death continues.

Alone with the king, Ehud skewers him through the belly. The term *tqʿ,* "to drive" or "to thrust," is the same terminology used for Ehud's blasting the shofar in a call to combat (3:27) and in Jael's assassination of Sisera. Force and aggression are implicit. The term used for Ehud's ample belly is the same as a term for womb, while the image of the fat closing around the blade is strongly vaginal. As Vermeule has discussed for war imagery in Homeric epic, the defeated soldier is the one who is knocked down, raped, and made the conquered woman (1979: 101). The enemy is unmanned this way, feminized (see Alter 1981: 41; Brettler 1991: 295), and here the enemy is the fat calf Eglon in this battle between strong and weak. Ehud, son of the oppressed Israelites, is victorious within the marginal's war ethic of tricksterism. The weak overpowers the powerful in a favorite biblical theme especially important in Judges. It is uncertain whether such a theme can be linked to Gottwald's theories (1979) about Israelite wars of liberation in the late second millennium B.C.E. Such a theme, however, would have been relevant at other periods in Israel's difficult political history, whether at its emergence as a group or during times of threat.

What Eglon's servants imagine him to be doing in his upper chamber is ambiguous. The colloquialism offered in the translation implies some sort of private bodily function. Suffice it to say that here as in 1 Sam 24:3, the person of power is caught or imagined "with his pants down," continuing the metaphor of feminization of the enemy.

Notice that versions in Vat and OL paint the imagery of Ehud's escape and the confusion of Eglon's retainers more deftly, whether targumically improving on their received Hebrew text via minor additions, alterations, and translation choices, or reflecting a more roundly shaped Hebrew version. For an excellent description of the sort of lock pictured by the author, see Stager 2003b: 241, 244.

The death of the enemy leader, as in various biblical epic accounts, allows for the victory of Israel followed by the formulaic marker of peace for many years, the story of judge Ehud concluding as did that of Othniel.

[31] The annal concerning Shamgar is similar in length and content to the brief notices on judges Tola and Jair in 10:1–5 and on Izban, Elon, and Abdon

in 12:8–15. Although the latter five more clearly share a format, all mention the judge's name, his coming after the last judge, and some aspect of his activity or identity (see the discussion in chs. 10 and 12). Scholarly suggestions of "traditionary erosion," Boling's infelicitous phrase (90), are common with such brief references. It is entirely possible, however, that an ancient composer did have access to longer traditions, but that he did not desire to include them here, the metonymic snippet mentioning the hero, the oxgoad, and his victory being adequate markers of his identity and role.

Much has been made also of the second reference to Shamgar at 5:6. Soggin suggests that he was a Canaanite warrior who sometimes helped the Israelite cause (49). The name "son of Anat" is taken by such scholars to indicate fealty to this important Canaanite goddess (see van Selms 1964: 302), although names are a difficult way to ascertain ethnic identity, as in many multicultural societies. Basing her view on Egyptian parallels, Eva Danielus (1963) suggests that he was a Syrian (perhaps the offspring of an Israelite-Syrian marriage!). Peter Craigie (1972a) has suggested that Shamgar was a professional warrior, a mercenary, hence the association with the Canaanite goddess of war. Others regard "Anat" as a place name. The name Shamgar has also been taken as having Hurrian roots (see Fensham 1961; Danielus 1963).

Shamgar is remembered as a charismatic judge-leader in both Judges 1 and 5. Whatever the intriguing implications of his name, he, like Samson, is a hero capable of wiping out the enemy by unorthodox and single-handed applications of brute strength. That his origins are somewhat obscure, an ethnic mystery, only adds to his mystique as judge. Some of the traditions assigned to Jael in Judges 4–5 may have been assigned to Shamgar in other tellings, thereby explaining the confusion in 5:6 (see below). In similar fashion, David's victory over Goliath, recounted at length in 1 Samuel 17, is much more briefly assigned to one Elhanan in 2 Sam 21:19. Such switches and reassignment of traditions are common in oral-style works.

Judges 4:1–24
Tales of Deborah and Jael, Warrior Women

4:1 And the descendants of Israel again acted
  to do evil in the eyes of Yhwh,[a]
 for Ehud was dead.
2 And Yhwh sold them into the hand of Jabin,
  king of Canaan, who ruled in Hazor,[b]
 and the captain of his army was Sisera,
 and he was dwelling in Harosheth-ha-goiim.[c]

3   And the descendants of Israel called out to Yhwh,^d
     because he had nine hundred chariots of iron,
     and he oppressed the descendants of Israel with force,
          for twenty years.
4   And Deborah, a woman who was a prophet—
          a woman of fire was she—^e
     she was judging Israel at that time.
5   And she would sit under the Palm of Deborah,^f
          between Ramah and Bethel,
          in the hill country of Ephraim,
     and the descendants of Israel would go up to her for judgment.
6   And she sent and called to Barak, son of Abinoam,
          from Kedesh-Naphtali,
     and she said to him,
     "Has Yhwh, god of Israel, not commanded,
          'Go^g and march^h to Mount Tabor
          and take with you ten thousand men,
               from the descendants of Naphtali
               and from the descendants of Zebulun.
7   And I will march to you at the Wadi (Torrent of) Kishon,
          Sisera, captain of the army of Jabin,
          and his chariots and his horde,
     and I will give him into your hand.'"
8   And Barak said to her,
     "If you will go with me, I will go,
     and if you will not go with me, I will not go."ⁱ
9   And she said,
     "Go, I will go with you;
     however, glory for you will not be on the way that you are walking,
     for into the hand of a woman will Yhwh sell Sisera."
     And Deborah rose up,
     and she went with Barak to Kedesh.
10   And Barak called up Zebulun and Naphtali to Kedesh.
     And ten thousand men went up on foot,^j
     and Deborah went up with him.
11   And Heber^k the Kenite had separated from Kayin
          who was from the descendants of Hobab, father-in-law of Moses.
     And he stretched out his tent as far as Elon-bezaanannim,^l
          which is near Kedesh.
12   And they told Sisera
     that Barak, son of Abinoam, had gone up
          to Mount Tabor.

13 And Sisera called out all his chariotry,
    nine hundred chariots of iron,
    and all the people that were with him,
        from Harosheth-ha-goiim to the Wadi Kishon.
14 And Deborah said to Barak,
    "Rise up, because this is the day
        that Yhwh has given Sisera into your hands.
    Is Yhwh not going before you?"
    And Barak went down from Mount Tabor,
        and twenty thousand men after him.
15 And Yhwh caused panic among
    Sisera and all his chariotry,
       and the whole company,
         by the sword's mouth, before Barak.
    And Sisera went down from upon the chariot,
    and he fled on foot.
16 And Barak followed after the chariotry
    and after the company,
       until Harosheth-ha-goiim.
    And the whole company of Sisera fell by the sword's mouth,
    and there did not remain as much as one.
17 And Sisera fled on foot
      to the tent of Jael,
        the wife of Heber the Kenite,[m]
    because there was peace between Jabin, king of Hazor,
       and the house of Heber the Kenite.
18 And out came Jael to meet Sisera,
    and she said to him,
    "Turn aside, my lord,
    turn aside to me.
    Be not afraid."
    So he turned aside to her, to the tent,
    and she hid him with a covering.[n]
19 And he said to her,
    "Give me to drink, I pray you, a bit of water,
    for I am thirsty."
    And she opened a skin bottle of milk,
    and gave him to drink,
    and she hid him.
20 And he said to her,
    "Stand at the opening of the tent,
    and let it be if a person comes,

and asks you and says,
    'Is there here a man?'
you say,
    'There is not.'"

21   And Jael, the wife of Heber, took a tent stake,[o]
    and she put the hammer into her hand,
    and she came to him softly,[p]
    and drove the stake into his temple,
    and pounded it into the ground.
    He had been sleeping,[q]
    he was tired,[r]
    and he died.

22   And behold, Barak was following after Sisera,
    and out went Jael to meet him,
    and she said to him,
    "Come and I will show you the man whom you seek";
    and he came with her,
    and behold, Sisera was fallen, dead,
    and the stake was in his temple.

23   And God humbled on that day Jabin, king of Canaan,
        before the descendants of Israel.

24   And the hand of the descendants of Israel went,
        going harder and harder upon Jabin, king of Canaan,
        until they cut off Jabin, king of Canaan.

a. The formulaic frame recurs (cf. 3:12).

b. Notice the repetition of the language of 3:8.

c. Vat and OL translate *haggôyīm* literally, "of the nations."

d. Notice the language of 3:9, as the conventionalized frame continues.

e. Vat translates, "a woman of Lappidoth," implying place of origin, while OL translates, "wife of Lappidoth," as do many modern translators. The translation above, like that of Ackerman (1998: 38) and many others, is based upon the root meaning of the term with its fiery associations (cf. "torch" in 7:16, 20). Differing translations of the same underlying text thus lead to differing presentations of characterization and story. Is Deborah a kind of Joan of Arc or a more domesticated version of the warrior woman, identified also as wife? If her name does not associate her with a spouse, is she said to be from a particular geographic location or meant to be seen in overtly charismatic terms?

f. OL reads "under a palm," thereby reducing the more cultic image of Deborah as an oracle associated with a sacred tree or space.

g. Vat and OL read *lĕkā* ("to you") rather than *lēk* ("Go").

h. OL translates the verb "sit" or "position yourself," as does NRSV. Vat translates with the nuance of "going."

i. Vat and OL continue, "because I do not know the day in which the Lord will make successful [Vat]/direct [OL] his messenger with me," thereby emphasizing further Barak's need for Deborah's oracular skills on the battlefield.

j. Vat and OL, like NRSV, translate the Hebrew to mean that the men follow Barak, literally in Vat, "went up after his feet," and more colloquially in OL, "after him." Notice the use of technical language for the calling up of troops here and in v. 13 (cf. 7:23, 24; 10:17; 12:1; 1 Sam 10:17; 2 Kgs 3:21).

k. Vat reads Heber as a name, as do most English translations, whereas OL takes the term etymologically, perhaps reading a plural construct and translating "friends of." OL continues with a different text, "and the friends of Cina were kings from the sons of Joab, . . ." but the Latin text itself is problematic here, as noted by Ulysse Robert 1900: 113.

l. Vat appears to be looking for an etymological translation for the place where the oak (Elon) is, employing the root *bṣ'*, "to gain by violence." Similarly, OL translates the place name with a form of *yšn*, "to sleep": "the oak of those who rest [i.e., the dead], which is near Kedesh."

m. Vat reads, "Heber, of the company of Kenaos" (*ḥeber ḥeber haqqênî*), playing on the etymology of the name Heber.

n. The term *śĕmîkâ* is difficult to translate. OL envisions a "skin covering," while Vat translates "covering, wrapper, garment." The Hebrew may be related to the verb *smk*, which in Biblical Hebrew tends to mean "support" or "lean," but which in Akkadian and Arabic has connotations of "cover." One wonders if the text reflects confusion with terms such as *massēkâ* from *nsk*, "to weave," i.e., "woven stuff, covering," and *māsāk*, "covering, screen," from the root *ś/skk*, "to cover, overshadow," or "to weave together." Compare the scene in which a woman hides Jonathan and Ahimaaz at 2 Sam 17:19 by placing a *māsāk* over the well where they have taken refuge.

o. Vat translates *passalon*, "peg" or "stake," a term that has a double meaning of "peg" and "male member."

p. Vat chooses a translation of "softly," *en kryphē*, that invokes nuances of secrecy and clandestine activity.

q. MT juxtaposes the aggression of Jael with the unknowing, sleep state of the exhausted warrior who has been lulled into vulnerability. Vat, however, translates the root for "sleep" (*rdm*) as a state of altered consciousness, as in *tardēmâ*, the state of special sleep in which Abraham experiences a theophany in Gen 15 and the man loses his rib in Gen 2:21. In the case of Judg 4:21, the "sleep" is the altered sleep of death (cf. Jonah 1:5). OL and A seem to read a different root, "convulsed," implying death throes typical of death scenes in Hellenistic historiography: "He convulsed between her knees." The position "between the knees" will appear in 5:27.

r. Vat reflects a different text, reading "was suffused in darkness," whereas OL continues the death scene, "he became cold," i.e., died. Thus the alternate traditions describe Sisera's passage from the living, whereas MT relates that Sisera's weary sleep allowed Jael to strike, paradoxically creating sympathy for the deceived enemy.

This chapter is introduced by the conventionalized covenantal overview that opens the tales of Othniel and Ehud in which Israel's political and military condition is explained in terms of its faithfulness or disloyalty to God. Evildoing leads to defeat, which makes necessary deliverance by a charismatic leader, filled with the spirit of Yhwh. In this case, the activities of the leader, Deborah, and her interactions with her general, Barak, reveal the ways in which judging as wise decision making is perceived as interwoven with oracular and charismatic abilities, all of which are necessary for successful military exploits.

The action in Judges 4 focuses on a battle between Deborah and Barak's forces and the army of Jabin of Canaan. The battle, in turn, frames an exquisite cameo concerning the assassination of the Canaanite general Sisera by a woman, Jael, a tale told a second time in the following chapter. The tale of Jael partakes of the traditional motif of the "iron fist in the velvet glove" and subversively echoes and reverses similar encounters between vulnerable men and strong, resourceful women in the Hebrew Bible. The attitudes of "us versus them," the equation between battle and sex, and gender-related themes are all at play in this passage.

The texture of Judges 4 is quite typical of the book. Neatly divisible clauses predominate, setting a dramatic and rapid pace in the interaction between Sisera and Jael (4:18–22). Somewhat more complex and interlocking lines appear, however, in geographic descriptions (e.g., 4:5, 6, 11; cf. 3:3) and in appositives that serve to describe and delineate characters (4:2, 11, 17). Such variations in texture thus set the scene and beautifully correspond to content.

[1–3] The death of one leader once again results in backsliding by the Israelites and oppression as punishment, as indicated in the formulaic language of the frame (see notes a–d above). Geographic locations and names require some explanation.

Canaan was never a single political entity, but was composed of various city-states. Jabin's title, "king of Canaan," however, provides legendary stature to the defeated enemy in this epic tale. Hazor is an ancient city north of the Sea of Galilee, mentioned also in Joshua (11:11–15; 12:19), which includes an alternate version of the defeat and devastation of Hazor and the forces of Jabin.

The etymology of the name Sisera is uncertain. Soggin looks to Luvian roots (63), while Boling suggests a relation to the Sea Peoples (94). Harosheth-hagoiim is placed by the narrative in the vicinity of the Plain of Esdraelon. The association of the term *ḥărōšet* with wood in Exod 31:5 and 35:33 may suggest various forested or wooded locations, but no consensus has emerged.

The description of the enemy as armed with chariots recurs in Judges and symbolizes Israel's marginal status vis-à-vis various Canaanite and Philistine opponents (see Judg 1:19; 5:28), an important theme of the book and an indicator of worldview. The enemy has chariots, often "chariots of iron," whereas the Israelites do not. In fact, chariots are not used by Israelites until the late eleventh century B.C.E., the time of King David. The "iron" may refer to metal sheathing or plates, reinforcing the wood frame of the horse-drawn, wheeled vehicle, to iron clasps, or to iron axles, but Robert Drews (1989) has offered other explanations (see 1:18–21).

[**4–10**] Deborah is a prophet, that is, one capable of mediating between God and human beings, and is perceived as having gifts of divination and charisma. She is a conduit to God, a vessel for divine communications of various kinds. It is this inspirited, oracular gift that allows her to "judge," leading on and off the battlefield. That she is female and therefore not expected to lead in a military context only enhances the impression of the judge as one raised by God, inspired and unusual, beyond the workaday roles of men and women (see O'Connor 1986: 286). It is for this reason that the common translation "wife of Lappidoth," while possible, seems to miss the point concerning Deborah's charisma. Who better to make decisions regarding battles or other matters of dispute? Thus her countrymen come to her at the site of a special tree, as in the case of Greek oracles, "for judgment." On sacred groves see Stager 2003a: 33–34 and the commentary on 9:1–7. Her wisdom comes from the deity. Her locus, like that of the hero-warrior Barak, is in the north.

Deborah calls up Barak from his home base, Kedesh in Naphtali, the tribal holding to the north/northeast of Manasseh and Ephraim. Kedesh was located in upper Galilee in the hill country of Naphtali (see Josh 19:37; 20:7; 21:32). Deborah mobilizes the troops based upon an oracle from God, and she charges Barak with Yhwh's orders (Judg 4:6–7). He is to take ten thousand troops from his tribe and the neighboring tribe of Zebulun and march from a gathering point at Mount Tabor, in the northeast section of the Plain of Esdraelon, down to the torrent-valley (wadi) of the river Kishon, and there Yhwh will flush out Sisera and his army in order to grant victory to the Israelites. The Israelite force, while declared to be large, as is appropriate for the epic context, is imagined to be a militia, drawn from tribes of a certain area. Such men are ready to answer the call of charismatic leaders, as throughout the book of Judges. They are pictured facing troops of a regular army, led by the commander Sisera.

Barak's declaration that he will go to battle only if accompanied by Deborah (4:8) is not to be interpreted as cowardice; rather, within the context of the worldview of the literature, he is wise to know that victory comes with the presence of God's favorite. Thus Elisha declares concerning the prophet Elijah, who has ascended to his Master in a chariot of fire, "My father, my father, the chariots of Israel and its horsemen" (2 Kgs 2:12); Elijah is worth battalions (Bright 1981: 249; Cross 1973: 226). Barak's words to Deborah in v. 8 enhance her prestige as woman warrior, and her oracle emphasizes a favorite theme of Judges and the larger Hebrew Bible concerning the victory of the unlikely hero. Sisera will be undone by a woman.

[**11–24**] Legendary connections between Israel and the Kenites thread Israelite traditions. Whereas some traditions include the Kenites among formulaic lists of conquered peoples (e.g., Gen 15:19) or mention them as enemies (e.g., 1 Sam

27:10), others suggest a positive relationship through affinal kinship or military neutrality (Judg 1:16; 4:11; 1 Sam 15:6). See commentary at 1:16.

Benjamin Mazar (1965) has proposed that Sisera flees to the tent of Jael because she and her husband belong to an aristocratic priestly Kenite family and that the tent, suggestively located by oaks, which frequently mark sacred spaces in the Hebrew Bible, is a sort of sanctuary for the fleeing warrior. Its location near Kedesh also informs Mazar's theory; Kedesh is listed as a city of refuge in Josh 20:7. The identification between Hobab and Jethro, names applied to the father-in-law of Moses, is also a piece of Mazar's argument, given that Jethro is associated with priestly status, albeit as a Midianite. (See also Cross 1973: 201; and Ackerman 1998: 93–101, who extend Mazar's work.)

The overall message of the story contrasts marginals with well-armed enemies and Jael, the tent dweller, with Sisera, the urbane charioteer, and thus would seem to argue somewhat against a special priestly status for Jael. She appears rather as a twist on the traditional motif of the woman who hides the soldiers, found in stories of Rahab (Josh 2) and the woman who hides Jonathan and Ahimaaz (2 Sam 17:17–20; see further discussion under Judg 5).

After the defeat of his forces as predicted by Deborah (4:14), Sisera leaves his chariot behind and flees on foot. Barak finishes off his adversaries, and his victory is described in terms invoking the ban (v. 16); not one enemy remains. Verse 17 explains why, within the contours of the story, Sisera heads to Jael's tent. His destination has to do with a political connection between Jael's husband and Sisera's king. As in the tale of Abigail, David, and Nabal, implicit is a world of small independent chieftains or sheikhs who pledge loyalty to one or another overlord. As with Abigail, Jael's loyalty turns out to be other than her husband's, and her sympathies are with the winning side, that is, the one blessed by Yhwh. As in the tale of Abigail, the woman offers food, encouraging words, and succor, but here the offer of womanly help is a ruse. The supposed sympathizer does not assist Sisera or hide him from his enemies, but uses her allure and his trust to destroy him. Thus the "helper" turns out to be an assassin in an artful transformation of "the woman who hides and saves" into the motif of "the iron fist in the velvet glove."

The interaction between Sisera and Jael is characterized by the mix of sex and slaughter discussed in connection with the assassination of Ehud. Here, however, the ravisher is herself a woman! Jael lures Sisera to her tent with language to calm fear (v. 18); she covers him and slakes his thirst. She offers him milk to drink whereas he had asked only for water, acting like a solicitous mother, as Robert Alter has noted. Images of mother blend into images of lover as she "comes to him softly" (see Alter 1985: 48–49). So Ruth comes to Boaz at the threshing floor in one of the Bible's most erotic scenes. Soft approach is followed by what Alter rightly deems the phallic thrust of the tent stake (1985: 43–49). The root *tqᶜ* is also found in the assassination of Eglon (3:21). The MT version of the scene contrasts Jael's aggression with poor Sisera's vulnerability. He was tired and had been lulled to sleep by a woman warrior, disguised as a would-be lover or mother. Expectations about her own soft side as a woman make her deadly. The Israelite writer identifies with the power of the feminine. She who is expected to be weak turns the male warrior into the woman raped, a theme drawn much more overtly in the version in 5:27. So Israel, lacking chariotry and relying on a war plan of tricksterism, gains the upper hand, and with God's help turns out to be stronger than the enemy. Guerrilla warrior that she is, Jael greets Barak with an announcement that she has the man whom he seeks. The tale ends with formulaic indications of relief from enemies, but is reiterated in the exquisite composition preserved in Judges 5.

Judges 5:1–31
The Song of Deborah

5:1 And Deborah sang[a]
   and Barak, son of Abinoam,
      on that day, saying,
2 "When the flowing locks flowed in Israel,[b]
   when the people freely offered themselves,[c]
bless Yhwh.[d]
3 Listen, kings!
Lend an ear, potentates!
I to Yhwh, I will sing.
I will make music for Yhwh, god of Israel.[e]
4 Yhwh, at your going forth from Seir,
   at your marching from the open country of Edom,
      the earth shook,
      even[f] the skies spouted,[g]
      even the dark clouds spouted water.
5 The mountains streamed[h] before Yhwh—
      this is Sinai—[i]
   before Yhwh, god of Israel.[j]
6 In the days of Shamgar, son of Anat,
   in the days of Jael,
high roads[k] came to a halt,[l]
and walkers on pathways
   walked on back roads.[m]
7 Ways of life in the unwalled towns[n] came to a halt.
In Israel they came to a halt

      until I arose, Deborah,
      until I arose, a mother in Israel.[o]

8   When they choose[p] new gods,
      then war[q] is in the gates.
     Shield was not seen, upon my oath,[r] nor spear
      in the forty thousand in Israel.

9   My heart is with the commanders[s] of Israel
      who freely offer themselves[t] among the people.
     Bless Yhwh![u]

10   Riders on tawny donkey mares,
      those who dwell near Midian,[v]
      those who walk on the way,
     tell one another!

11   With the sound of tambourines[w] between watering holes,[x]
      there they recount the justice-bringing acts of Yhwh,
        just acts for those in his unwalled towns[y] in Israel.
     Then the people of Yhwh subdue[z] the gated cities.

12   Awake, awake, Deborah!
     Awake, awake, tell a lyric tale.[aa]
     Rise up, Barak.
     Capture your captives, son of Abinoam![bb]

13   Then a survivor subdues[cc] the chieftains.
     The people of Israel subdue for me[dd] the mighty.

14   From Ephraim—their root is in Amalek.[ee]
     Behind you, Benjamin,[ff] with your people.
     From Machir the commanders[gg] go down[hh]
     and from Zebulun they march to the baton of the muster officer.[ii]

15   And the princes of[jj] Issachar are with Deborah.
     And Issachar, support of[kk] Barak,
      in the valley was sent on foot.[ll]
     In the divisions of Reuben,
      great are the stout of[mm] heart.

16   Verily[nn] you dwell between the settlements[oo]
      to hear the whistling for the flocks.
     Concerning the divisions in Reuben,
      great are the stout of heart.[pp]

17   Gilead in Transjordan plies his tent,[qq]
     and Dan, verily, he resides[rr] in ships.
     Asher dwells on the shore of the sea
     and on its promontories,[ss] he plies his tent.

18   Zebulun is a people whose soul taunts Death,[tt]
     and Naphtali on the heights of the open country.[uu]

19   Kings came; they waged war.
       Then the kings of Canaan waged war
            in Taanach at the waters of Megiddo.[vv]
       Plunder[ww] of silver they did not take.
20   From the heavens the stars waged war.
       From their orbits,[xx] they fought with Sisera.
21   The Torrent of Kishon swept them away,
            the torrent of primordial times,[yy]
            the Torrent of Kishon.
       You will tread down the life force of the strong.[zz]
22   Then hammer did the horse hooves,[aaa]
            the stampeding, stampeding[bbb] of their stallions.
23   Curse Meroz, says the messenger of Yhwh.
       Curse a cursing upon her indwellers,[ccc]
       because they did not come to the aid of Yhwh,
            to the aid of Yhwh among the mighty.
24   More blessed than women is Jael,[ddd]
            the wife of Heber, the Kenite,
       more than tent-dwelling women is she blessed.
25   Water he asked for,
       milk she gave,
            in a basin fit for chieftains,
       she brought near curds of cream.[eee]
26   Her hand[fff] she sent[ggg] for the tent stake,
            her right hand for the workman's hammer,
       and she hammered Sisera.
       She destroyed[hhh] his head.
       She shattered, she pierced his temple.
27   Between her legs, he knelt, he fell, he lay.
       Between her legs, he knelt, he fell.
       Where he knelt, there he fell, despoiled.[iii]
28   Through the window she looked down.
       The mother of Sisera wailed from behind the latticework.[jjj]
       'Why does his chariotry delay to come?[kkk]
       Why do the clatterings[lll] of his chariots tarry?'
29   The wise women among her ladies answer.[mmm]
       Yea, she returns her words to herself.
30   'Are they not finding, dividing spoil?
       A wench, two wenches[nnn] for each man.
       Spoil of dyed stuff for Sisera,
            spoil of dyed stuff,
            embroidered dyestuff,

> doubly embroidered stuff
> for my neck, spoil.'°°°

31   Thus may all your enemies perish, Yhwh,
      and those who love him, be like the going forth of the sun in his strength."
      And quiet was the land for forty years.

a. The feminine singular verb in the MT agrees with the first noun, as in Num 12:1 and Gen 33:7.

b. The opening phrase of the poem has been variously translated. The root *prʿ* most literally means "let go, let loose" (BDB 828, III). Soggin moves from "let go" to "burst forth" or "liberate" and translates the phrase, "Because in Israel the people have regained liberty" (84). Boling, working somewhat more closely with the root meaning and influenced, perhaps, by biblical usages that refer to free, unbound, or disheveled hair, translates: "When they cast off restraint in Israel" (107), although he expresses sympathy for Craigie's translation, "When in Israel men were dedicated unconditionally." The latter (1968: 399) links *prʿ* with the Arabic *faraġa*, "used in the sense of volunteering for war." In this way, the first colon parallels the second that describes Israel's "presenting themselves" for war (see Rabin 1955: 125–34). Janzen pays special attention to biblical usages of *prʿ* that do not deal specifically with hair and concludes that the "liberation" implicit in the root has to do with "disregard, or flouting of and rebellion against structures and constraints claimed (rightly or wrongly) to be foundational to true and life-giving order" (1989: 405). He translates, "When the rebels cast off restraint in Israel," and sets the line in a socio-historical context of rebellion against oppressors (403–4, 405).

Support for hair-related translations of the term *prʿ* is found at Deut 32:42, although here too translation is difficult. As in many places in Scripture, e.g., Num 6:9, here the head is used metonymically to refer to hair. The head and the root *prʿ* refer to locks of hair in a lengthy, unbound, or disheveled state (see also Num 6:5 and Ezek 44:20). In Num 5:18 *prʿ* serves as a verb for the act of letting hair loose rather than the loose, free, long hair itself, and again the head refers to the hair. Taken as a group these various passages do seem to support a hair-related interpretation of *prʿ*, with the implication for Judg 5:1 and Deut 32:42 that in ancient Israel as elsewhere in the wider ancient Near Eastern and Mediterranean world, the young warrior was frequently pictured as wild-haired or long-haired, the hair possibly relating to his warrior's prowess and power.

The ancient translations reflected in A, OL, somewhat like BDB (828 I), choose, "When rulers ruled in Israel," emphasizing the quality of standing out of the crowd or sticking out (like unbound hair, the root's most frequent association in the Hebrew Bible), while Vat either reflects a quite different Hebrew text or understands *prʿ* here as in LXX Num 5:18 to mean "uncover" rather than "dishevel": "A revelation was revealed in Israel." The translation adopted here conveys the repetition in the root *prʿ* with its notions of freedom, of being loose. The f of the English "flow" evokes the *f/p* sound of Hebrew *biprōaʿ pěrāʿôt*.

c. The hair relates to vowing and sacrifice, once one links long hair to Nazirite status in the old-time religion of Judges. Hence a hair-related meaning beautifully parallels *hitnaddēb*, "offering oneself up," employed in the second colon (see Exod 35:29; 36:3; Lev 22:18; Num 15:3). To present for war is to become a freewill offering in a sacrificial sense.

Vat and OL read *akousiasthēnai* rather than the equivalent to *ndb, hekousiasthēnai,* resulting in "when the people had sinned through ignorance" (Vat) and "in the stubbornness of the people" (OL). A misreading of an earlier translation of Hebrew *ndb* thus leads to an interesting image that plays on the recurring theme of Israel's backsliding.

d. Notice traditional style repetition between v. 2 and v. 9.

e. The verse is built of formulaic expressions. The synonymous pairs "listen/lend an ear," "kings/potentates," "sing/make music," "Yhwh/god of Israel," which are found in chains of parallel items elsewhere in the tradition, are made a part of common formula patterns. The first of the two patterns is "listen term + source of power (natural, figure of state, cosmic)," the second is "a term for song or praise + 'to the Deity.'" For the former see Deut 32:1; Isa 1:2; the chain in Jer 13:15; and the variants in Isa 49:1; Mic 1:2; 3:1. For the latter see Exod 15:1; the variants in Pss. 57: 9 (MT 10); 68:4 (MT 5); 105:2, 138:1; and the chain in 27:5 (MT 6).

f. Dahood related the term *gam,* "even, also," to an ancient Ugaritic word for thunder (1968: 14).

g. The root *ntp* means literally "drip" or "drop." See Ps 68:8 (MT 9); Song 5:5; Joel 3:18 (MT 4:18); Mic 2:11. For the second image, OL reads that heaven "was in an uproar" or "disturbed," an approriate variant in the scene of cosmogonic activity.

h. Vat and OL read the root *zll,* "to shake," as in Isa 64:1, 3 (MT 63:19; 64:2). This image picks up on the earthquake of v. 4, whereas the above choice from the root *nzl,* "to flow," follows from the water imagery of that verse (so also Moore 140–41). Either vocalization and the translations that follow are fully traditional.

i. OL omits the gloss in MT and Vat that identifies the mountain as Sinai.

j. Judges 5:4–5 contains traditional and formulaic material. Note the formula "God + motion verb and locus of origin" and compare Ps 68:7–8 (MT 8–9); see also Deut 33:2–3. Coogan (1978: 162) lists vocabulary and idiomatic speech shared with Ps 68 but treats them as deliberate allusions rather than the use of traditional, oral-derived compositional techniques (see also Blenkinsopp 1961: 67–68; Albright 1950–1951: 20; Cross 1973: 100–101). Notice also the internal chant-like repetition ("from before Yhwh") and see notes l, o, s, z, pp, ccc, iii.

k. The term can be vocalized to mean "caravans" rather than the roads themselves. So Coogan 1978: 147; Moore 114; and Schloen 1993: 22.

l. The root *ḥdl* most commonly means "to stop," as reflected in translations by Vat, Craigie (1972b: 350), and Coogan (1978: 147), but Boling prefers an alternate meaning, "to grow plump" (109). The root meaning chosen greatly affects the sociological and political portrayal that one finds behind the poem. Are the Israelites successful bandits profiting in the chaos, or do all suffer in a period of social and economic depression? OL reflects an alternate text: "Kings ceased/withdrew." J. David Schloen translates "to hold back" and sets the image in the context of a socioeconomic situation involving caravan trade in the Early Iron Age (1993: 28, 35). On the poet's use of repetition in a traditional-style economy of language (*ḥdl* in vv. 6, 7), see the introduction to Judg 5.

m. OL reads, "they [the kings] walked on [literally] crooked ways," possibly emphasizing a moral dimension as well as geography (see Ps 125:5). This orientation again suits the theme of backsliding.

n. The term *pĕrāzôn* has been variously translated. Vat and OL translate "the powerful," continuing the OL image of kings ceasing in v. 6. In this vein, Soggin (82) translates,

"The leading class was inactive," and Boling, "The warriors grew plump" (see note l). The above translation, "ways of life in the unwalled towns," is derived from the term *pěrāzâ,* meaning "open region, hamlet" (BDB 826), found in Ezek 38:11; Zech 2:8, lengthened with the ancient adjectival ending (see Hess 1999: 152; Albright 1968: 48, n. 101); cf. "warriors," so Coogan 1978: 147; and Craigie 1972b: 350.

o. Vat and OL have the third person, "Until Deborah arose." MT, with the first person usage, thus emphasizes authorship by the heroine and connotes a strong sense of her own role. Note the repetitive, refrain-like style in both sets of lines in v. 7, as is common throughout the poem.

p. The Hebrew connotes habitual action, literally, "When one chooses." Vat reads a plural: "They chose for themselves new gods," and OL, "They chose new gods."

q. The root *lḥm* would seem to have battle connotations, but is not the usual word for war. As vocalized in MT, *leḥem* means "bread." Boling (110) reads *lāḥămû,* "they fought." Vat reads, "When they fought the cities of the rulers." OL translates, "Just as barley bread."

r. An oath formula, the line literally reads, "Shield, if it was seen." The implication is, "I swear, there wasn't one," or "May I be cursed if there was one."

s. Vat and OL translate with the "law" nuance of the root *ḥqq,* but within the context reference to the head warriors is preferable, a translation that is also possible within the root (i.e., those who make the rules in war). Note that this term reappears in vv. 14, 15, and 16 (as emended; see below) with the economy of vocabulary typical of this traditional-style poem.

t. Notice the same language in v. 2 that equates volunteering for war with ritual sacrifice. OL and A contain the variant, "the powerful of the people."

u. See note d.

v. Following the association between Midian and Sisera in Ps 83:9 (MT 10), the translation reads the verse quite literally. So Coogan 1978: 148. It is of course possible that Ps 83 contains an intertextual reference to this hymn. See also the city Middin in Josh 15:61. Others have translated with the nuance of judgment contained in the root *dyn* (Boling 110, after David Noel Freedman, Vat). A third possibility followed by Moore (148) is to derive from the term *mad* as in Judg 3:16 (garment), hence "cloths," "saddle cloths," or "carpets." See also Ps 133:2. OL provides a variant reading for the entire bicolon, omitting the donkeys: "Those who go up on chariots, sitting amid the clattering sounds."

w. The term translated "tambourines" is a difficult one. Some find a connection to *ḥiṣṣîm,* "arrows" or "archers," while others root their translation in *ḥṣh,* "to divide." Soggin, for example, suggests, "Louder than the cry of those who distribute water near the drinking places." *DCH* translates "strike up a tune" (3:296; so also Vat), while others suggest that clanging sounds lie behind an onomatopoeic root (see Coogan 1978: 148); Boling (102) translates "cymbals"; Na'im Dehan (2000) suggests "the clanging of water jars"; also see Albright 1922: 81–82, n. 4. *Ḥṣṣ* can mean gravel, i.e., divided stones. Could the text suggest a percussion instrument involving pebbles, as found in many traditional cultures? Kittel suggests *mḥṣṣrym,* "clarion," as in 2 Chron 5:13 and elsewhere in Chronicles. OL reads, "Voices striking instruments."

x. OL reads, "in the midst of feasters," painting a festive scene.

y. OL and A read a root meaning "strong" or "strengthen." Vat reads, "O Lord, increase justice-acts in Israel." For my translation see note n. Notice the refrain style.

z. The verb (root *yrd*) as vocalized means "go down" (so Boling; Soggin; Coogan 1978: 148; Vat, OL), but can be rooted in *rdh* ("have dominion") or *rdd* ("beat down, subdue"), the translation chosen here and in v. 13, as the use of a limited set of vocabulary continues. Stager treats *yrd* as military language, "marching down (to battle) against," and suggests a meaning of the root shared with that of vv. 13 and 14 (1988: 226; see 1:9). Stager's translation requires a flexible use of prepositions in vv. 11 and 13, but is a real possibility.

aa. Literally, "Speak or say a song." The phrase "awake, awake" is used in calls to arms as in the call to the divine warrior (Isa 51:9) and to the sword, a metonymic evocation of his power at Zech 13:7.

bb. The repetitive style in this verse is typical of the song. OL includes an interesting variant.

> Rise up, Deborah,
> and arouse a thousand, thousands with the people.
> Rise up,
> speak with a song in power.
> Rise up, Barak,
> and Deborah, strengthen Barak.
> Take your human booty, son of Abinoam.

While MT (equivalent to Vat in this verse) appeals more aesthetically and suits the style of the larger song, with its recurring, almost chant-like refrains, this variant too is a rousing charge to the leaders, appropriate to the context and traditional in its imagery and language.

cc. Vat reads *yrd* ("go down") as do Coogan (1978: 148, n. 35) and Boling (11). OL has a different reading for the first colon: "Then his strength is magnified." The second colon can find rough equivalence in some form of the literal words of the Hebrew: "O Lord, humiliate [bring down] those stronger than I."

dd. Vat reads, "for him," rather than "for me."

ee. Vat reads "root" as a verb, "Ephraim has rooted them out in Amalek," while OL appears to read "Amalek" as *ʿēmeq*, "valley."

ff. As noted by Coogan (1978: 164), this phrase is a war cry found also in Hos 5:8. Perhaps it means, "Heads up!"

gg. Vat and OL base their reading not on *ḥqq* ("inscribe, decree") but on *ḥqr* ("to search out, investigate"). See below on "stout of heart" in vv. 15, 16. The manuscript traditions oscillate in their reading of the root, with significance for the meaning of the verses. The present translation reads *ḥqq* with implications of law, obligation, or resolve. See notes s and mm (cf. Halpern, 1983: 386; and Cross 1998: 53–56).

hh. Cf. notes z and cc. Here I vocalize with *yrd*, "to go down." This term plays on the homophonic stems in vv. 11 and 13.

ii. *Šēbeṭ* ("staff" or "baton") can also mean "tribe," while the term translated "muster officer" literally means "one who counts, enumerator, scribe." Vat attempts to translate literally, "with the staff of the narrative of the scribe." OL, however, has "From Zebulun the Lord fights for me with the powerful."

jj. A construct form with the preposition, which as noted by Coogan (1978: 149, n. 41) is found elsewhere in the tradition.

kk. The translation is based upon the root *kwn/knn* ("to be firm, stable, established").

ll. Vat is equivalent to MT in the first colon of v. 15, but continues, "and Barak. So Barak in the valleys sent in his feet." An alternate text may have presented itself to the Greek translator or he may have used common sense and some literalism to convey a difficult Hebrew equivalent. He seems to have no repetition of Issachar in the second colon, takes *kēn* to mean "thus," and vocalizes *šlḥ* ("sent") in the Qal perfect. OL provides a more distant variant: "In Shechem from the tribe of Issachar with Deborah, he/she sent his/her foot soldiers in the valleys."

mm. From the root *ḥqq*, with the nuance of resolve. See notes s and gg. OL does not include this refrain. Vat seems to read *ḥqr*, as in MT v. 16, "searchings." These two variants lead to quite different readings. Is Reuben filled with self-doubt or are his warriors filled with bravery—hence my translation "stout of heart," a refrain in vv. 15, 16.

nn. Most modern translators choose "why," like their ancient counterparts, Vat and OL, which grapple in various ways with the rest of the verse. Cross suggests, however, that *lmh* is best read not as "why," as is most common in Biblical Hebrew, but as an example of the "emphatic *lamed* extended by *-ma,* known from Ugaritic" (1973: 235, n. 74) and so translates "Indeed." Cross's suggestion inspires Halpern's translation (1983: 383) and is later developed by Cross himself (1998: 54–55, n. 7). The many discussions seeking to explain why Reuben, Gilead, Dan, and Asher supposedly hold back from the fighting (Stager 1989) and the somewhat forced translations that accompany them thus become unnecessary (cf. Zobel 1965: 62–63). See commentary below on the catalogue of fighters.

oo. The root *špt* has been used to describe setting a pot on fire (2 Kgs 4:38). This unusual term is used in a catalogue concerning Issachar in Gen 49:14. There Issachar, the hero tribe, is described as crouching between the settlements. See Coogan 1978: 164; cf. Craigie 1977: 41–43 for an alternate suggestion.

pp. MT reads the root *ḥqr*, "searchings (of heart)" (so Vat and OL). Given the refraining style of the poem, it seems likely that the same phrase appears here as in v. 15. See note mm above.

qq. Comparisons might be drawn with Gen 49:13; 16:12; Deut 33:18–19. A traditional catalogue formula "tribe + location + tenting/residing" characterizes the references from Genesis and those concerning Gilead, Dan, and Asher in Judg 5:17, while the example from Deuteronomy applies alternate catalogue material to Zebulun. These descriptive formulas are the building blocks of tradition. Note that Gen 16:12 has generally been mistranslated to create a forced and negative portrait of Ishmael, but the verse really refers to his whereabouts and occupation, as is typical in this formula pattern. Catalogue material can be found in various contexts: war roster, genealogy, testament form, and birth narrative (see Coogan 1978: 162–63 for an alternate approach to this material).

rr. Noting that the root *gwr* may refer to a temporary status as a resident alien, Stager suggests that the Danites "serve as clients on ships" (1989: 63–64).

ss. From the root *prṣ* ("burst through"), hence the place that juts out into a body of water. Vat and OL translate "outlets."

tt. The translation assumes the vocalization *māwet*, the noun, rather than the infinitive *mût*, "to die." For the syntax "reproach + infinitive," see 2 Chron 32:17. As in the Canaanite epic of Baal and Anat, Death is personified as an enemy warrior.

uu. OL reads, "The Nephtalim came onto the height of the open country," employing the verb with which MT and Vat begin v. 19. Stager (1989: 55) suggests that the phrase "heights of the open country" actually refers to the hillside terraced farming in which agriculturalist Israelite settlers would have engaged in the Early Iron Age.

vv. OL reflects an alternate reading, "They dwelt at the waters," and omits the reference to Megiddo.

ww. Vat translates "plunder" as "gift/booty," whereas the tradition behind OL captures the avaricious nuance of Hebrew *beṣaᶜ*, translating "the avariciousness for silver."

xx. The root *sll* means literally "cast up, lift up," as in a highway (see, e.g., Isa 11:16; 33:8; Joel 2:8; Judg 20:31, 32, 45), hence the notion of "orbit," a "heavenly highway." OL translates, "from their order." Vat translates, "from their paths."

yy. MT reflects a version of the word for antiquity, usually *qadmâ*. Coogan (1978: 150, n. 48) emends to *qdmm*, "ancient," translating the phrase, "that ancient wadi." See Boling (113), who repoints to read, "overwhelmed them," following Cross and Freedman 1975: 29, 35. Vat reads "the ancients." Notice the refrain quality of the language in the first three cola of the verse.

zz. Vat provides a slightly variant reading: "My powerful soul will trample him." Differences in the reading may result from creative syntactic decisions on the part of the translator. OL reads, "The rivers of Kishon threw them out / My foot trampled them / My soul is powerful." This is good epic material evocative of passages such as Exod 15:9.

aaa. OL land Vat read, "The hooves of a horse are cut off [OL]/fettered [Vat]."

bbb. The verb has the connotation of rushing, hence Vat, "His powerful ones (*ʔabîrāyw*) hastened in haste." OL, "My foot will assuage them regarding the injustice of his folly," presents a different reading.

ccc. Notice the repetition in vocabulary and syntax, typical of the poem. Vat translates, "Everyone who dwells in it is accursed." OL reflects an expanded execration and some variation in syntax, within the framework of the same roots or vocabulary.

> Let them see pain;
> let them see curses.
> The angel of the Lord cursed those who dwell in it,
> because they were not found to help,
> the Lord our helper,
> the Lord among the powerful fighters.

ddd. One might also translate, "Blessed among women."

eee. In elegant but telegraphic phrases, the interaction is described between seductive assassin and assassinated dupe. OL presents an alternate version.

> He asked for water from her.
> She gave milk to him
> in a basin of water.
> She offered butter
> to the prince.

As is frequently the case, the plot remains the same with the same essential action motifs, but the aesthetics change slightly.

fff. Vat specifies "left hand."

ggg. Or "Her hand reached."

hhh. Vat employs the same verb for "destroyed" and "pierced," and may reflect a Hebrew text that is dense in the sort of repetitions of key words seen throughout.

iii. For a full discussion of translation choices made in this verse, see Niditch 1989: 47–51. OL reads the end of the verse: "he slept under her feet. Trembling, the miserable one fell." MT exhibits internal repetition in the style of incantation, as noted by Alter 1983: 630.

jjj. Vat translates "arrow hole," specifically imaging the architecture a certain way.

kkk. Vat reads literally, "Why is his chariot embarrassed to come?"

lll. Or "hoofbeats."

mmm. OL continues, "the wisdom of her virtue will respond to him."

nnn. Literally, "a womb, two wombs." Moore translates "wench," which captures the abusive tone used in reference to enemy women by would-be members of the conquering side (173; see also Alter 1983: 633).

ooo. Judges 5:28–30 continues repetitions in syntax and vocabulary typical of the economic traditional style. OL provides a significantly different version of v. 30 that describes the defeat of Sisera.

A beautiful and moving example of the traditional type of the woman's victory song, the "Song of Deborah" may be one of the most ancient works of the Hebrew Bible. As in Exodus 15, the divine warrior displays his military power and prowess on behalf of the people Israel; but in contrast to that victory song, here human heroes play an even greater role on their own behalf, as divine intervention alternates with human initiative. Central in the victory are women warriors: Deborah the poet-prophet, charismatic leader, and "mother in Israel"; Jael, a guerrilla warrior and archetypal seducer-killer who exemplifies the folk motif of the iron first in the velvet glove. The author, whether male or female, assumes the voice and perspective of a woman, visualizing not only female Israelite victors but also the women of the Canaanite enemy, waiting for their heroes to return from battle, successful.

Much has been written about the poem's possible links to the ancient history of Israel. Does the social reality pictured by the song reflect an actual period in the history of Israel or provide information about origins? Was there, as Martin Noth suggested (1930), an early Israelite amphictyony in premonarchic times? Why might some tribes have participated in the battle and not others (Stager 1989)? Why would Sisera flee to Jael's tent and what is the significance of this locus (B. Mazar 1965: 301; Halpern 1983: 379–401; Ackerman 1998: 96–98)? What does the song suggest about links to Kenites, a group mentioned elsewhere in Scripture (Cross 1973: 201; Ackerman 1998: 93–109)? These questions are framed by larger issues: Why does an Israelite author portray the battle a certain way? What are his/her notions of Israel's founding myth? Does the portrayal help to identify his/her life setting and religion? As in the cases of the *Iliad* or the *Song of Roland*, it may well be that the artistic rendering is rooted in actual wars and battles. The telling, however, is shaped along the conventionalized patterns of Israelite traditional narrative and the cultural patterns of the group's myth.

In Judges 5 temporal battle and victory have cosmic participants and consequences. The battle, also described in a less poetically stylized narrative texture in ch. 4, juxtaposes divine and human action, historical allusion and metahistory, in a slice of Israelite epic-style literature. The long lens of world-defining battle alternates, however, with effective close-up shots: for example, beautifully articulated details about the homelands of the warriors in the catalogue of vv. 14–18 and a cameo from the battle itself, rich in motifs of eroticism and death, as the fleeing enemy general Sisera is lured to safety and then murdered by Jael. With imaginative brilliance, the author juxtaposes the scene of assassination with a portrait of the enemy's mother, waiting for his return in her home beyond the battle. All of this is presented in the conventionalized but richly elaborated medium of traditional language, content, and structure.

The style of the song is characterized by parallel constructions typical of the most poetic of Israelite literature, with oral-style variation upon formulaic expressions and phrases, the use of an economical or limited vocabulary, and frequent chant-like refrains. Scholars have explored matters of prosody in the composition, seeking better to understand its genre and the conventionalized aesthetics behind the work, engaging in lively debates concerning matters of metrics, stress, syllabification, stanza structure, syntax, and the definition of Hebrew poetry itself. Such matters, of course, all affect translation and the way in which one understands the cultural medium to convey the message. Coogan (1978), for example, points to the dense variety of repetition in the song, to line length, and to stanza structure. Blenkinsopp (1961) explores "ballad" form. O'Connor (1980) provides an extensive review of issues concerning scholarly approaches to Israelite poetry, including a thoughtful discussion of often neglected matters of musicality and orality, offering his own linguistically grounded approach. Cross and Freedman (1975) draw insightful comparisons with Ugaritic epic literature. Kugel (1981) creatively raises new issues about parallelism and blurs the line between prose and poetry with sensitivity to what Israelites thought concerning the genres of their literature. Geller (1979) employs the modern field of linguistics to explore the aesthetics and meanings created by the parallel constructions of early Hebrew compositions, including Judges 5.

An abiding interest in the oral-traditional qualities of Judges 5 informs both the brief notes above and the commentary below. The reader will notice that indentation of lines often marks the repetition in language and the metonymic, purposeful, partial repetitions typical of ancient Hebrew verse. Indentation thus points to the parallel constructions of a particular classical, oral-traditional style, rather than to the subordination and list-like appositives seen occasionally in previous chapters, indicating a change in register. The traditional bardic style in Judges 5 is appropriate to the traditional themes and motifs that build this epic battle account.

The song reveals a repetitive thematic structure:

Introduction: 5:1–3
  Divine warrior's march/cosmogonic myth: 5:4–5
    Historical setting; human heroes and enemies: 5:6–13
      Catalogue of Israelite warriors: 5:14–18
  Battle/mythic allusions: 5:19–22
  Human heroes: 5:23–30
Conclusion: 5:31

[**1–3**] The opening rubric attributes the song to Barak and Deborah, but the verb "sing" is feminine singular (see note a) and the ongoing, controlling creative voice, first person feminine singular; the singer alludes to herself (v. 7). The opening context is quite self-consciously oral-traditional and musical with its parallel cola.

Long hair is associated with vow and sacrifice here as in the tradition of the Nazirite vow in Numbers 6 (see Margalith 1986a; cf. Niditch 1990: 613). An important symbolic complex in ancient Israel associates the male warrior's power, sacral status, and free unbound hair (see notes b and c).

[**4–5**] Yhwh, the storm god, is pictured in his march to battle, setting out from his mountain camp. The motif is found also in Num 10:35; Deut 33:2; Hab 3:3; and Ps 68:8–9 (MT 9–10). Particularly interesting is the association between Seir, Edom, and Sinai, a formulaic set of locations that sometimes includes or substitutes other place elements such as Paran (Deut 33:2) or Teman and Paran (Hab 3:3). The preponderance of named locations leads Cross (1973: 86) and others to see the origins for this mythic complex and perhaps for Yahwism itself in the mountainous regions to Israel's southeast.

Yhwh has the capacity to transform nature and holds power over the waters (cf. Ps 77:16–19 [MT 17–20]). The refrain "from before Yhwh" evidences the particular economical style found throughout the song.

[**6–7**] On the judge Shamgar see 3:31. The song alludes to dark, bandit-ridden days in which villages are at risk and travelers hesitate to use the main routes for fear of attack. Such a picture tallies with historians' views of the political and economic uncertainties of the Late Bronze Age. Deborah is the savior in these difficult times. The human leader is thus juxtaposed with the divine hero of vv. 4–5. These are marginal times in which a woman can lead the men (Hackett 1985).

[**8–9**] The first bicolon of v. 8 may be a proverb. Note the topic/comment structure (see Dundes 1981). The saying is rooted in mythological notions about the relationship between divine and human events. When Marduk rules the roost, Babylon ascends, as described in the Mesopotamian creation account *Enuma elish*. In this context, the proverb comments on the new times inaugurated by Deborah's great success and suits the song's larger thematic framework in which divine and human action alternate.

The second bicolon is an oath formula that places the singer at the battle and emphasizes the marginal status of Israelite warriors who are not armed properly with shield or spear. The victory is therefore all the greater, the power of the divine warrior the more apparent.

At v. 9 the poet continues to involve herself in the events with the use of the first person. The refrain of v. 2 is repeated: "who freely offered themselves. / Bless Yhwh."

[**10–13**] If the above translation of vv. 10–13 is correct, these lines are some of the few in ancient Hebrew literature that set a context for oral performance. At communal gathering places, the song is delivered and composed, accompanied by musical instrumentation. The tellers purport to report events even as they create impressions and shape memories. (On memory and history see Hendel 2001.)

Judges 5:11 and 13, like vv. 6–7, suggest that the Israelite warriors are the military and political underdogs. Aided by the might of the divine warrior, those whose origins are in unfortified villages are able to defeat those who control gated cities. The survivors defeat the chieftains; Israel vanquishes the mighty. A clear contrast is drawn between the Israelites and the powerful enemy. (See also Stager 1988: 224–25; 1989: 54–55.)

Verse 12 is a charge to the leaders, Deborah and Barak, as the song emphasizes human warriors and their victories. The very language in 5:11–12 links human and divine warriors.

[**14–18**] This section is a traditional-style catalogue of the Israelite forces, to be compared with *Iliad* 3.160–244. Whereas in Judg 4:6 only Naphtali and Zebulun participate in the battle, here ten tribes are mentioned: Benjamin, centrally located between Jerusalem and Bethel; Machir, which is to be identified with Manasseh (see Stager 1989: 53) in central Palestine; Ephraim, whose association with Amalek is not based on ancient geographic situations that are known to us (the Bible places Amalekites, who often appear as consummate enemies of Israel, in disparate locations); Issachar, perhaps also in the central hill country (see Gal 1982: 79–86); Zebulun and Naphtali from further north in Galilee; Reuben, herders whose locus is less certain (see Stager 1988: 227); Gilead, which is to be identified with Gad from east Jordan (see Num 32:1); Asher, on or nearby the coastal plain (see Finkelstein 1988: 97, citing the survey by Rafi Frankel); and Dan, whose location is uncertain but who is associated with seafaring.

The author has the audience picture a confederation consisting of these tribal groups and Meroz (v. 23), who does not heed the call to arms. As in chs. 19–21, for example, the groups gather together for mutual support in war. On traditions of ten versus twelve tribes see Stager 1989: 53.

The catalogue listing the members of this confederation is a traditional topos found several times in ancient Hebrew literature in genealogies, testaments, or other forms. Constituted by brief notices about heroes or groups, which sometimes appear separately—in the annunciation form, for example—the catalogue serves a critical cultural function in asserting group identity. It says essentially, this is how we are constituted, who our ancestor heroes are. Here is a slice of our history as we understand it, "a charter" (Michalowski 1983). In Judges 5 various groups are described, where they dwell, what their occupations are, and how brave they are.

[**19–22**] Discussions of vv. 19–21 have tended to concentrate either on questions of historical verisimilitude or on historical archaeological reconstruction. Could Sisera have run the many kilometers to Jael's tent from one of these locations (see B. Mazar 1965; Halpern 1983; Ackerman 1998: 97–98)? Are conditions in Taanach or Megiddo in the Late Bronze Age consistent with settlement or conquest patterns implicit in Judges 5 (see Albright 1936; Aharoni 1970)?

In exploring worldview one must ask more centrally what place the constellation of Taanach, Megiddo, and Kishon holds in the symbolic and mythological complexes of Israelite tradition. How do Israelites reveal themselves in these artistic lines, their foundation history, their relation to the land, and their identity? Could these three sites function as special, even sacred, spaces? Ackerman and B. Mazar begin to approach some of these issues in attempts to identify Jael's oak as a sacred, priestly location, although the evidence is perhaps too sparse for their assertions (see Ackerman 1998: 93; B. Mazar 1965).

It does seem possible that Taanach and Megiddo, two strategically and economically important cities overlooking the Esdraelon Plain and facing the flood-prone river Kishon about equidistantly, create with the river an important conceptual space that both defines the region and emphasizes the power of the deity in the water. Yhwh is after all the one who causes skies to spout and mountains to stream (vv. 4–5). Kishon is described as the "torrent of primordial times." Notions of world creation, fertility, and destructive power are all included. Like the Red Sea, the Kishon waters sweep away the enemy (see Craigie 1977: 33–34 on additional references to the wider ancient Near Eastern traditions of the storm god). The battle has cosmic dimensions as the stars, Yhwh's foot soldiers, fight (again see Craigie 1977: 34–37 for possible Ugaritic nuances). Human and meta-human adversaries collide and cooperate, and the primordial Kishon, as personified, alternates with the sound of stampeding horses; the sights and sounds of battle encompass both.

[**23**] The composer makes the transition back to a discussion of human warriors, opening with a curse directed against one ally who did not participate.

Of the named Meroz we know nothing. Curses in the ancient Near East, as in other traditional cultures, are powerful vehicles having the capacity to bring themselves about. Threats of curses against those who might break promised terms are therefore common in political agreements (cf. Deut 27–28). The cursed Meroz contrasts with the blessed Jael. At v. 24 the composer introduces the subject of the cameo scene that follows.

[24–31] One thread of scholarship attempts to trace the Kenite connections of Jael, some suggesting that she is a Kenite priestess, her tent a sacred locus where the fleeing general seeks refuge and protection (see note s to ch. 1 and the commentary to 4:11–24). The interest of the composer, as in ch. 4, seems to be in the traditional motif of the iron first in the velvet glove. The language is of eroticism and death and describes motherly or loverlike nurturing that masks murderous intentions. He asks for water, but she gives him milk, rich curds fit for a prince. Even as she offers the food to him, the poet's language swoops into another motion, as Jael reaches for the hammer and stake with which to impale the man. The overt violence of v. 26 is followed by the double entendres of v. 27 in which images of defeated warrior play upon those of would-be lover.

The legs or feet are euphemistic language for the genitals (see, e.g., Deut 28:57; Judg 3:24; 1 Sam 24:3; Isa 7:20; see also Ezek 16:25 for an erotic description of Israel as harlot). Thus the enemy lies at her feet (as in the translations by Boling 104; and Lindars 1983: 171) but is also between her legs (see also Alter 1983: 635). Similarly, he sinks or kneels and falls like a casualty of war (see Ps 20:8 [MT 9]), but the term "kneel" is also used in the sexually charged imagery of Job 31:10. If Job has committed adultery, he declares himself worthy of just deserts: "My wife will 'grind' for another [another sexual euphemism; see Isa 47:2], / Upon her will kneel others." The term "lay" also refers both to death, that is, lying or sleeping with the ancestors (see 1 Kgs 1:21; 2 Kgs 14:22; and Ezek 32:21, 29 for death in a war context); and to sex, usually illicit sex, to sleeping with a forbidden person (see, e.g., Gen 19:32, 34, 35 [Lot and his daughters]; Gen 34:2, 7 [the rape of Dinah]; 2 Sam 13:11, 14 [the rape of Tamar]). Finally, the term *šādûd* ("deal violently with, despoiled, devastated") describes the destruction of sites and enemies in war (Isa 15:1; 23:1; Jer 47:4), but is used in the sense of raped or despoiled in the erotic imagery of Jer 4:30 in which Israel is described as an unfaithful wife. The double entendre thus continues. Such equations between sex and death are, as Emily Vermeule has shown, common in classical Greek epic (1979: 101–2; 157–58), but are found in classical South Asian literature as well (see Shulman 1986). The defeated enemy becomes the woman who is raped, the victor her rapist. Here, ironically, it is a woman who is in the position of rapist, the enemy male general her victim.

Perhaps most exquisite in the song is the way in which the composer juxtaposes the cameo of the victorious Jael with the image of Sisera's own mother waiting for his return with her ladies. The identity of the woman, enigmatically introduced at the beginning of v. 28 by the feminine pronoun, is revealed in the next colon. Her aristocratic pose, looking out the lattice-work window, is, as Susan Ackerman (1993) has shown, the conventionalized portrait of the queen mother or woman of status. The motif serves again to emphasize a contrast between the mighty and the weak, the urban and the rural, Canaanite and Israelite, a theme that recurs in the book of Judges. So in the song itself the mighty contrast with the survivors, the inhabitants of unwalled villages with those who live behind gates. It is a particular self-image of the underdog that Israelite authors savor in various guises. What is so special here, however, is the composer's capacity to identify with the enemy, to assume the voice of the Canaanite women much as Homer assumes that of the Trojan women. The author leads us to sympathize with them, even while rejoicing in the defeat of Israel's enemies, as in v. 31. Sisera's mother tries to convince herself that all is well and is encouraged by her ladies in waiting. Her thoughts about the captured booty are descriptively rich. Indeed, she makes reference to women booty (v. 30), employing a root that literally means "womb." The woman who anxiously waits for the return of the hero who has already died is another traditional epic motif (see McCarthy 2002). The reader knows, whereas she does not, that Sisera, her son, has been made into woman booty in the tent of Jael—he has been defeated by a woman warrior.

Judges 6:1–40
The Call of Gideon

6:1   And the descendants of Israel did evil in the eyes of Yhwh,[a]
        and Yhwh gave them into the hands of Midian
           for seven years.[b]

2   And strong was the hand of Midian upon Israel.
      Because of Midian, the descendants of Israel made use for themselves
        of river gorges[c] that were in the mountains,
          caves, and hidden strongholds.[d]

3   And it was if Israel sowed seed,
        Midian and Amalek and the Easterners would go up,
        and go up against it.[e]

4   And they would encamp against them,
      and they would ruin the produce of the land[f]
        until the vicinity[g] of Gaza,

and there did not remain a source of livelihood[h] in Israel,
    even a sheep, even an ox, or even a donkey.
5   For they and their cattle would go up,
    and their tents would come as many as locusts,[i]
    and to them and their camels[j] there was no number,
    and they came against the land to ruin it.
6   And Israel was laid very low because of Midian,
    and the descendants of Israel called out to Yhwh.[k]
7   And it was when the descendants of Israel called out to Yhwh,
        because of Midian,
8   that Yhwh sent a man who was a prophet
            to the descendants of Israel,
    and he said to them,
    "Thus says Yhwh, god of Israel,
    'I brought you up from Egypt
    and brought you out from the domain of slaves,
9   and I saved you from the hand of Egypt,
        and from the hand of all your oppressors,
    and I drove them out from before you,
    and I gave to you their land.'
10 And I said to them,
    'I am Yhwh, your god.
    Do not reverence[l] the gods of the Amorites
        in whose land you live,'
    and you did not listen to my voice."[m]
11 And the messenger of Yhwh went
    and he sat under the oak
        that was in Ophrah
        that belonged to Joash the Abiezerite,
    and Gideon, his son, was beating out wheat in the winepress,
        to hide it from Midian.[n]
12 And the messenger of Yhwh appeared to him,
    and he said to him,
    "Yhwh is with you, mighty man of valor."
13 And Gideon said to him,
    "With all due respect, my lord,
    if Yhwh is with us,
        why have we encountered all this?
    And where are all the wonderful acts
        that our ancestors told us about, saying,
            'Has not Yhwh brought us up from Egypt?'

And now Yhwh has forsaken us
and he has given us into the hand of Midian."
14 And Yhwh[o] turned to him,
and he said,
"Go in this your strength,
and you will deliver Israel from the hand of Midian.
Have I not sent you?"[p]
15 And he said to him,
"With due respect, my lord,
by what means will I deliver Israel?
Behold, my family group is the lowliest in Manasseh,[q]
and I am the youngest in my extended household."[r]
16 And Yhwh[s] said to him,
"Because I will be with you,[t]
and you will strike down Midian
as if they were one man."
17 And he said to him,
"If, I pray you, I have found favor in your eyes,
make for me a sign
that you are the one speaking with me.[u]
18 Don't, I pray you, depart from here
until I come to you.
And I will bring my offering,
and I will set it before you."
And he said,
"I will sit still
until you return."
19 And Gideon came,
and he prepared a she-goat kid,
and matzo cakes of an ephah's measure of flour.
The meat he put in a basket,
and the broth he put in a pot,
and he brought them out to him,
to under the oak,
and he approached.[v]
20 And the messenger of God said to him,
"Take the meat and the matzos,
and set them on this rock,
and the broth, pour out";
and he did so.
21 And the messenger of Yhwh sent forth
the end of the staff that was in his hand,

and he touched the meat and the matzos,
and the fire went up from the stone,
and it consumed the meat and the matzos.
And the messenger of Yhwh went out of his sight.

22 And Gideon saw that a messenger of Yhwh was he,
and Gideon said,
"Alas, my Lord Yhwh,
for I have seen the messenger of Yhwh, face-to-face."

23 And Yhwh said to him,
"Peace to you.
Do not be afraid.
You will not die."

24 And Gideon built there an altar to Yhwh,
and he called it, "Yhwh is peace."
Until this day, it is still at Ophrah of the Abiezerites.

25 And it was on that night,
and Yhwh said to him,
"Take the steer of the head of cattle[w] that belongs to your father,
    the second steer, seven years old,
and tear down the altar of the baal that belongs to your father,
and the asherah[x] that is next to it cut down.

26 And build an altar to Yhwh your God,
    on top of this stronghold in the row,[y]
and take the second steer,
and raise up a burnt offering
    with the wood of the asherah that you cut down."

27 And Gideon took ten men from his servants,
and he did as Yhwh spoke to him.
And it was because he feared the household of his father
    and the men of the town
        too much to do it by day,
    that he did it by night.

28 And the men of the town rose early in the morning,
and behold, the altar of the baal was broken down,
and the asherah that was next to it was cut down,
and the second steer was being raised up in sacrifice
    upon the altar that had been built.[z]

29 And each person said to his neighbor,
"Who did this thing?"
And they searched and sought out,
and they said,[aa] "Gideon, son of Joash, did this thing."

30 And the men of the town said to Joash,

"Bring out your son and he will die
because he broke down the altar of the baal
and because he cut down the asherah that was next to it."

31 And Joash[bb] said to all who stood against him,
"Will you contend for the baal?
Will you deliver him?
Whoever contends with him,
    let him die by morning.
If he is a god,
    he will contend for himself
    because someone broke down his altar."

32 And they called him on that day Jerubbaal, saying,
"Let the baal contend with him
because he broke down his altar."

33 And all of Midian and Amalek and the Easterners gathered together
and they crossed over and made camp in the Valley of Jezreel.

34 And the spirit of Yhwh clothed[cc] Gideon,
and he blasted the shofar,
and Abiezer was called out after him.[dd]

35 And he sent messengers into all Manasseh,
and they too were called out after him,[ee]
and he sent messengers into Asher, and Zebulun, and Naphtali,
and they went up to meet them.

36 And Gideon said to God,
"If you have a deliverer for Israel by my hand
    as you spoke,

37   behold, I am placing the woolen fleece on the threshing floor.
If there is dew on the fleece alone,
    and on the whole ground, dryness,
        I will know that you are delivering Israel by my hand,
            as you spoke."

38 And it was thus,
and he rose early the next morning,[ff]
and he pressed down the fleece,
and he squeezed dew from the fleece,
    a bowlful of water.

39 And said Gideon to God,
"Let not your anger burn against me,
but let me speak, just one more time.
May I test, I pray you, just once more with the fleece.
Let it be dry on the fleece alone,
and on the ground let there be dew."

40	And God did thus on that night,
and it was dry on the fleece alone,
and on all the ground there was dew.

a. The formulaic language of the theologian's voice recurs (cf. 2:11; 3:7, 12; 4:1).

b. The chronological rubric is a frequent part of the framework, whether indicating years of oppression or of relief (cf. 3:11, 14; 4:3; 5:31).

c. The root *nhr* may derive from "river" or from the more unusual verb "to shine, beam." I translate to convey the image of places in the mountains hollowed out by water (so BDB 626). Vat translates, "holes."

d. The root of this term, which is frequently used to mean "stronghold," as in Jer 48:41 and Isa 33:16, may be *ṣûd* ("to hunt"), from which are derived terms for hunting instruments such as the net. A forest hideaway is perhaps imagined.

e. Vat has "the sons of the East would go up with them," while 4QJudg[a] omits the phrase. The root *ʿlh* ("to go up") has military connotations.

f. Vat reads "their fruits," while OL reads "boundaries," *gĕbûl*, rather than "produce," *yĕbûl*.

g. MT literally reads "your entrance," but cf. Gen 10:19.

h. The term, from the root "to live," might be translated "preservation of life" or "sustenance" (see Gen 45:5; Judg 17:10).

i. This bicolon is awkwardly constructed in the Hebrew, likely due to a process of transmission, but the imagery is comprehensible as the text now stands. The image of the invading enemy as numerous as locusts is common (see, e.g., Judg 7:12 [the same formula]; Joel 1:4; Nah 3:15).

j. 4QJudg[a] and OL omit the reference to camels.

k. Formulaic language of address to God, requesting succor (cf. Exod 14:10; Num 20:10; Josh 24:7). The same verb is used in "calling up" the various tribal allies in preparation for war. Vat begins v. 7 with the second colon and omits v. 7 ("And it was . . . Yhwh"), avoiding some repetition.

l. Literally, "fear."

m. Judges 6:6–10 is not found in 4QJudg[a], which follows the end of v. 6 with v. 11. Like the opening verses of ch. 2, these verses formulaically invoke the language of Deuteronomy. Judges 6:7–8 includes interlocking subordinate clauses, evocative of a late style of Hebrew. The message of covenantal disloyalty, delivered by a prophet, and the formulaic medium point to the theologian's voice. This particular shaping of the Gideon story is not in the tradition preserved at Qumran, which follows without interruption the dominant recurring pattern in Judges of oppression, calling out to Yahweh, sending of help. Trebolle Barrera (1989: 238, 245) has suggested on the basis of this variation that 4QJudg[a] reflects an earlier and shorter form of Judges than that of MT or LXX. Tov (2001: 135–36) and Ulrich (1999: 105–6) agree with Trebolle Barrera's conclusions, but Fernández Marcos (2003: 1–16) is not convinced that the data are sufficient to support this hypothesis. Verse 7 is not in Vat.

n. Notice more of the enjambed, subordinating style.

o. Vat and OL have "messenger of the Lord," a divine emissary in contrast to the bolder assertion or uncovering of God's actual presence.

p. Vat has "Behold, I have sent you." The commission language in either version is formulaic (see Exod 3:12 concerning Moses).

q. OL reads, "thousands are diminished in Manasseh," literalizing the word for "family group" or "clan," a grouping of a thousand people, and taking the "poor, lowly" term as a verbal root.

r. Literally, "house of my father."

s. Vat has "messenger of the Lord." See note o above.

t. The language of the hero's initiation, accompanied by a divine helper's promise, echoes that of God to Moses in Exod 3:12. See also Gen 26:3; 31:3; Exod 4:12, 15; Deut 31:23; Josh 1:5; 3:7; 2 Sam 7:9; 1 Chron 17:8. Vat reads, "the Lord will be with you," again distancing God's participation in the encounter.

u. Vat and OL omit the phrase about the sign and read instead, "and you will do for me everything you say, do not depart," continuing as in v. 18 MT.

v. OL reads that Gideon brought the offerings to the messenger, whereas Vat reads that Gideon himself drew near, as in the present translation.

w. This somewhat unusual phrase that includes two words for the bull is translated "the calf of a bull" by Vat, whereas OL reads a variant, "the fed/fatted calf" (see Rudman 2000).

x. Notice the ways in which the ancient translators treat the "asherah." Vat and OL have "sacred grove."

y. A difficult phrase to translate. OL transliterates the term *mā῾ôz*, which is derived from ῾*wz* ("take or seek refuge") or from ῾*zz* ("strong"). The translation "in the row" is rooted in ῾*rk*, "to arrange" or "set in order." Vat and OL, like NRSV, translate "in proper order."

z. Notice the internal repetition in vv. 25–28, as the passage exhibits considerable economy of language in the traditional style.

aa. Vat reads, "they knew or learned."

bb. In Vat the subject is Gideon himself. In MT the hero thus appears younger, reliant on his father for defense.

cc. A reading preserved in Vat is "empowered" (*enedynamōsen*), whereas OL reads "clothed" (*induit*) with MT and A (*enedysen*). Inner-Greek look-alike/sound-similar verbs have thus led to variants in the tradition, both of which make sense.

dd. An interesting inner-Greek variation appears in Vat, due to the sound-alike Greek verbs for "fear," *ephobēthē* (Vat), and "call," *eboēsen* (A). Vat thus reads "and Abiezer was feared after him." OL reads ᵓ*aḥărāyw* ("after him") as sound-similar ᵓ*eḥāyw* ("his brother"): "he called Abiezer his brother."

ee. Vat does not have the phrase "and they too . . . after him." OL reads Qal rather than Niphal, "he called, he himself, after them." The MT is a bit awkward, and the above translation reads the Niphal verb as plural in meaning.

ff. OL can have the nuance, "kept vigil until the morning," a nicely enhanced image in the tale.

Tales of the hero Gideon richly partake of traditional topoi, linking him with Moses and Joshua on one side of the biblical chronology and Saul and David on the other. Gideon's origins, like those of Saul and David, are in an agricultural or pastoral setting. Like Moses and other biblical heroes, he experiences God in a theophany, and the divine presence is confirmed by fire (see Gen 15:17; Exod 3:2–6; Judg 13:19–23). Like Joshua, Moses, and others called by God, he receives a charge and signs as confirmation of his future success, interacting with a divine messenger or intermediary. Even his attempt to refuse the call marks him as the quintessential biblical hero (cf. Exod 3:11; 4:10). On the level of texture, the story cycle is characterized by traditional-style internal repetition of key terms and phrases, by the use of formulas seen elsewhere in the book and the wider tradition, and by the presence of traditional literary forms such as the proverb. The chapter divides easily into self-contained thoughts, although enjambement and subordinating structures are also found intermittently, as throughout Judges. Subordinate clauses present rhetorical questions to Yhwh's messenger in 6:13 and create the conditional request to Yhwh in 6:17. Subordination thus performs a rhetorical function, reflecting the speaker's hesitation and uncertainty in his interaction with a divine being. Subordination at vv. 7–8 also marks the presentation of background information. Register thus reflects content.

Introduced with the recurring frame that describes Israel's rise and fall in covenantal terms (vv. 1–7), the cycle of stories about Gideon, like tales of Ehud, Deborah, and the other judges, describes Israel's oppression, in this case by Midianite enemies, Israel's resistance, and the underdogs' victory with the help of a protective God. Chapter 6 describes the initiation of the hero in a theophany that shares much with the encounter between Samson's parents and a divine messenger. The initiation is followed by Gideon's bold act of subversion. This act leads to his gaining a new heroic name and is followed by "the sign of the fleece," the divinely sent sign—another traditional motif in the biography of biblical heroes.

[1–10] The opening verses of the Gideon cycle partake of theologically charged formulas and covenantal concerns, associated with Deuteronomistic writers. This conventionalized language also typifies ch. 2 and the framing language that introduces the careers of many of the judges. The pattern of faithlessness, decline and defeat, crying out to God, and rescue is present; in the story of Gideon, however, portions of the "frame" or introduction are specific to the narrative, for the nature of the oppression emphasizes the agricultural concerns and setting of the cycle (vv. 1–4). Israel tries to hide its produce from Midianite enemies who would destroy it.

The Israelite tradition evidences genuine ambivalence and self-contradiction in attitudes expressed toward Israel's southeastern neighbor in northwestern Arabia. Moses is described as having close, positive, in-marrying relations with Midianites, while other passages describe them as enemies (Num 22:1–7) and seducers (Num 25:1–7, 16–18; 31:1–12). In the cycle of stories about Joseph, they are identified with Ishmaelites (see also Judg 8:24). In the tale of Gideon, they play the role of Israel's oppressor. Lawrence Stager has suggested that the portrayal of "benign relations" between the Midianites and Moses' group reflects the sociohistorical situation before 1100 B.C.E., whereas Judges 6 reflects a time "when the camel-riding and -raiding Midianites had become archenemies of the Israelites" (1998: 143).

In response to Israel's complaint, God sends a prophet who explains the reason for Israel's difficulties. They have not responded to God's saving acts in Egypt with full covenantal loyalty, but have been seduced by the gods of those they have conquered. This interaction is typical of the themes of the book of Deuteronomy and of scenes in the prophetic and Deuteronomistic literatures. The delivery of God's message through an intermediary leads to Gideon's call as God's hero, for after his condemnation of Israel's past behavior, the prophet awaits Gideon to announce his people's deliverance.

[11–24] The divine being, like the "three men" in Genesis 18 or the dangerous "man" encountered by Jacob at the river Jabbok in Genesis 34 or the "man" who announces the birth of Samson in Judges 13, is anthropomorphized, but MT wavers between the divine and humanlike identities of the messenger, calling the speaker "Yhwh" in vv. 14 and 16. He appears in a sacred space, "the oak that was in Ophrah," in Gideon's ancestral home. Gideon, like Saul in a later generation, is engaged in farmer's work at this time of crisis. Due to the oppressive political circumstances, Gideon not only beats out the wheat but also has to hide it from destructive enemies.

The interaction between Gideon and the messenger is reminiscent of several traditional theophanies, in particular those of Abraham and Moses: the divine being addresses the hero with assurances of God's favor; the hero takes issue with the messenger's rosy version of God's devotion; the hero is called to action in the service of his people; he attempts humbly to refuse the commission (cf. Exod 3:11; Jer 1:6; 1 Sam 9:21); and he asks for and receives a sign (cf. Gen 15:8; Exod 4:1; also Exod 3:12–13). The presence of God is confirmed by a fiery consumption of an offering; God is symbolized by the fire here as in Gen 15:17; Exod 3:2; and Judg 13:19–20. The content is fully traditional, while the language is formulaic in references to the escape from Egypt (Judg 6:13; cf. 11:13, 16; 1 Sam 8:8; 10:18; 15:2; 2 Sam 7:6; Neh 9:18), in the commission language (v. 14, "Have I not sent you"; cf. Exod 3:12; Ezek 3:6), in the divine expression of favor ("I will be with you," v. 16; and cf. Gen 26:3; 31:3; 2 Sam 7:9), and in Gideon's response (v. 22; cf. the link with Moses in Num 12:8). Language in this section is also internally repetitive (vv. 13, 15, 20, 21) and reveals significant parallelism in the style of traditional Israelite narration.

Gideon's complaint that Yhwh is not acting as in the great days of the past when he rescued the Israelites from slavery in Egypt is typical of Israel's national laments (cf. Pss 74; 77:7–20 [MT 8–21]). The way in which the hero takes issue with the messenger is reminiscent of Abraham's interaction with the deity in Gen 15:2.

The realization that he has been in God's presence, followed by the setting up of an altar to Yhwh and the naming of the place, equates Gideon with the patriarchs (e.g., Gen 12:7, 8; 13:18; 26:23–25). Gideon's altar building, like theirs, serves to mark the place as belonging to Yhwh and his people, an important theme in these tales of political and territorial rivalry.

[25–32] God speaks to his hero again, charging him to commit a daring act of subversion under the cover of night. He is to destroy the altar of Baal, the Canaanite storm god, the quintessential icon of the "other" in the Yahwistic assertion of Israelite identity apart from the other populations of the land. The very similarity of Baal's mythology to that of Yhwh, and of Canaanite cultures to that of Israel, makes the need to create distinction all the more urgent. Asherah is both goddess and icon, associated with Baal and with Yhwh (see 3:7). The sacred pole or asherah, which is also to be cut down, symbolizes the deity's indwelling presence (see McCarter 1987: 148–49). In a dismissive and purposely demeaning treatment of a symbol that the author regards as pagan, foreign, and "other," the wood from the pole will serve as kindling at an altar of Yhwh that Gideon is to substitute (cf. Isa 44:15–17). Note that he is told to sacrifice his father's steer, symbolizing the movement in the story from the everyday agrarian setting to a martial context. So too Saul sacrifices his father's oxen to call out the members of a military league (1 Sam 11:7). The narrator emphasizes the covert nature of the operation, the danger involved, for Gideon is challenging the gods and the very worldview of those around him. He is engaging in a form of uncivil disobedience. The searching out and seeking in v. 29 may refer to an investigation by technical means of an oracle. Gideon's father defends him against the locals, and Joash's challenge is incorporated into Gideon's new name, "Let the baal contend with him." The terminology of disputation is technical language appropriate to legal settings and enhances the quality of contest in the scene (see Wright 1965). The interaction emphasizes the weakness of Baal and suggests the sort of contest motif found in Moses' challenge to Pharaoh and in Elijah's challenge to the priests of Baal. Gideon, the farmer's son, is now transformed into a charismatic leader, "clothed" with the spirit of Yhwh. Name changes frequently accompany such transformations, for example, Abram to Abraham and Sarai to Sarah (Gen 17:5–6, 15–16), Joseph to Zaphenath-paneah (Gen 41:45), and Jacob to Israel (Gen 32:28). Ironically, the enemy of Baal bears a Baal-related name (cf. Merib-baal in 1 Chron 8:34; Esh-baal in 1 Chron 8:33; and Boling 135, n. 32)

[33–40] The epic account continues with the gathering of enemy forces. Now the "Easterners" include Amalek as well as Midian. Israel's enemies, like Israel itself (see v. 35), are pictured frequently as a league of allies. On Amalek, see notes at 3:13 and 5:14. The fertile Valley of Jezreel, located between Galilee and Samaria, was important strategically, a crossing ground for armies and traders.

Gideon is pictured as a charismatic leader infused with the divine spirit. In the pattern of the judges and later Saul, Gideon calls up the tribal militias to join him in battle. The language of "calling out" is technical and formulaic terminology for the gathering of troops (cf. 4:11; 1 Sam 14:20). The same verb is used to describe appeals to the divine warrior (see Judg 3:9, 15; 6:6, 7; 10:10; 1 Sam 12:8).

Gideon, one of the most pleasingly insecure of the biblical heroes, requests another sign; and once God allows the fleece miraculously to be filled with dew while the ground is dry, he requests that God reverse the sign so that the fleece remains dry while the ground is covered with dew. God complies. Signs are frequent motifs in covenantal theophanies and may serve as responses to the hero's doubt, as in Gen 9:13–17; 15:17; and Exod 4:2–9. The nighttime setting enhances the mystery of the events. God's control of nature is typical of the deity, while the repetitiveness of the language further marks this scene as fully traditional.

Judges 7:1–25
The Battle with Midian

7:1　 And Jerubbaal, that is, Gideon, rose up early,[a]
　　　　　and all the people who were with him,
　　　and they encamped by the spring of Harod,[b]
　　　and the camp of Midian[c] was to the north of him,
　　　　　down from the hill of Hammoreh[d] in the valley.
2　　　And Yhwh said to Gideon,
　　　"Too many are the people with you
　　　　　to allow me to give Midian into their hands,[e]
　　　　　lest Israel glorify itself at my expense saying,
　　　　　　　'My hand has delivered me.'
3　　　And now, call, I pray you, in the ears of the people, saying,
　　　'Whoever is afraid and trembling, let him return
　　　and let him fly away[f] from the mountain of Gilead.'"
　　　And there returned from the people twenty-two thousand,
　　　and ten thousand remained.
4　　　And Yhwh said to Gideon,
　　　"Still the people are too many.
　　　Bring them down to the water,
　　　and I will smelt away[g] some from you there,
　　　and so it will be[h]: those about whom I say to you,
　　　　　'This one will go with you,'
　　　　　he will go,
　　　and about whom I say to you,
　　　　　'This one will not go with you,'

he will not go."[i]

5 And he brought the people down to the water.
And Yhwh said to Gideon,
"Everyone who laps with his tongue from the water,
  as a dog would lap,
    place him to one side,[j]
and everyone who kneels on his knees to drink. . . ."[k]

6 And the number of lappers
    (their hands to their mouths)[l]
  was three hundred men,
and all the rest of the people
  kneeled on their knees to drink water.

7 And Yhwh said to Gideon,
"With the three hundred men who lapped, I will deliver you,
and I will give Midian into your hand.
And as for all the people, let each man go back to his place."

8 And the people took provision in hand,[m]
    and their trumpets,
and every (other) Israelite man he sent off,
    each man to his tent.
And the three hundred men he retained,[n]
and the camp of Midian was below him in the valley.

9 And it was on that night,
and Yhwh said to him,
"Arise, go down[o] to the encampment,
because I have given it into your hand.

10 And if you are afraid to go down,[p]
    go down, you and Puah, your lad,[q] to the encampment.

11 And listen to what they say,
and afterward, your hands will be strengthened,
and you will go down against the encampment."
And he and Puah, his lad, went down,
    to the edge of the battle arrays[r] that were in the camp.

12 And Midian and Amalek and all the Easterners[s]
    lay[t] in the valley as many as locusts,
and to their camels there was no numbering,
    as many as the sands that are on the shore of the sea.[u]

13 And Gideon went,
and behold, a man was telling his companion a dream,
and he said,
"Behold, a dream I dreamed,[v]
and behold, a round barley bread
    was turning over and over in the encampment of Midian,

and it came to the tent and struck it and it fell.
It upturned it, and the tent fell down."[w]

14   And his companion answered and he said,
"This is none other than the sword of Gideon,
        son of Joash, man of Israel.
God has given into his hand
        Midian and all the encampment."

15   And it was when Gideon heard
        the telling of the dream and its breakdown,[x]
            he bowed down.
And he returned to the camp of Israel,
and he said,
"Arise, because Yhwh has given into your hand,
        the camp of Midian."

16   And he divided the three hundred men into three units,[y]
and he gave trumpets into the hand of all,
        and empty jars, and torches in the jars.

17   And he said to them,
"Me you will see, and likewise you shall do,
and behold, I am going to the edge of the encampment,[z]
and let it be, as I do, likewise you shall do.[aa]

18   And when I and all who are with me blow on the trumpet,
        then you blow on the trumpets, also you,
            around the whole encampment,
        and say, 'For Yhwh and for Gideon.'"[bb]

19   And Gideon went, and the hundred men who were with him,
        to the edge of the encampment, at the beginning of the middle watch.
Indeed, they had just posted the guards.[cc]
And they blasted the trumpets
and shattered the jars[dd] that were in their hands.

20   And the three units blasted on the trumpets,
and they broke the jars,[ee]
and they held in their left hand the torches,
and in their right hand the trumpets to blast,
and they called out,
"A sword for Yhwh and for Gideon."

21   And each man stood in his place, around the encampment,
and the whole camp ran,
and they raised the alarm and fled.

22   And they blasted the three hundred trumpets,[ff]
and Yhwh set the sword of each man against his neighbor,
        and against the whole company,

and the company fled, until Beth-shittah, toward Zererah
until the edge of Abel-meholah until Tabbath.
23 And the men of Israel were called out, from Naphtali,
and from Asher, and from all Manasseh,
and they followed after Midian.
24 And Gideon sent messengers
in all the hill country of Ephraim, saying,
"Go down to meet Midian,
and capture them against the waters,
until Beth-barah^{gg} and the Jordan."
And called out was every man of Ephraim,
and they captured the waters
until Beth-barah and the Jordan.
25 And they captured the two chieftains of Midian,
Oreb and Zeeb,
and they killed Oreb at the Rock of Oreb,
and Zeeb they killed at the Winevat of Zeeb,
and they followed after Midian,
and the heads of Oreb and Zeeb they brought to Gideon,
across the Jordan.

a. Vat conveys the Hebrew root with a verb meaning "lie awake before dawn," and OL has the first person but translates the verb similarly, "In the dawn I was vigilant." Both of these phrases create a mood of expectation, filling out the simpler Hebrew, which refers more to action than to psychological state. See 6:38.

b. The root has to do with "trembling."

c. OL adds "and Amalek."

d. Literally, perhaps "the early rain." Cf. Joel 2:23.

e. OL reads, "the people are great, and I will hand Midian into their hands," thereby omitting any sense of the deity's insecurity. That desire for self-promotion is typical of the charismatic warrior gods of the ancient Near East and elsewhere.

f. Instead of the unusual term that seems to refer to the motion of a bird, OL reads "go down." Vat reads "depart." Perhaps MT reflects confusion with the similar word for "refine" or "smelt" in v. 4.

g. Vat reads, "clear out," a different verb than in v. 3 and one that in the passive can mean "to be refined" or "purified." OL reads, "test them to you there." MT uses a term for "refine" (*srp*), frequently found in late biblical literature to describe God's weeding out of evildoers. See Jer 6:29; Zech 13:9; Mal 3:2; Dan 12:10.

h. OL concludes briefly, "whoever I say to you, he will not go."

i. Notice the traditional style within the verse and throughout the passage in which limited vocabulary and recurring phrases predominate.

j. Literally, "place him by himself."

k. MT, like Vat, trails off with the implicit "on the other side" or "in his own group," unstated or lost. A and OL include the parallel second phrase. This little text-critical variant raises a number of interesting issues for the student of ancient manuscript traditions and translations. Are the translators behind A and OL providing a gloss necessary to understand the scene, or do they actually have a Hebrew manuscript that completes the line this way? Are MT and Vat defective, or is the end of the thought obvious and not necessary to spell out?

l. This phrase, translated literally by Vat "in their hands to their mouths," may be dislocated from the end of the verse. The larger group kneels and cups the water in their hands. OL omits the phrase and has "who lapped with their tongue like a dog," repeating the image of v. 5 in good traditional style.

m. Vat translates with the word order, "And they took the provisions of the people in their hand."

n. The root meaning of *ḥzq* is "to be strong"; thus Vat translates, "he strengthened." A double entendre may be implicit, implying Gideon's retention of the men and his strengthening them.

o. OL reads, "go down quickly against."

p. That is, "Go militarily."

q. Literally "young man," but frequently used in a more technical military context. The status of "squire," "aide-de-camp," or "young recruit" is implicit. MacDonald (1976) suggests that the term translated as "lad" refers to a male of aristocratic standing who is often pictured in service to an aristocrat of higher status. He may be a young man but need not be. Contexts in Judges tend to suggest the youthfulness of the "lad," but see 17:7–8.

r. A term rooted in multiples of five/fifty.

s. OL translates *qedem* ("east"), which literally means "opposite," as "enemy."

t. Literally, "fell."

u. This idiom, literally, "like *x* with regard to multitude," is used twice in this verse and in 6:5.

v. Notice the formulaic language to introduce or allude to a dream (cf. Gen 37:5–10; 40:5–9; 41:11–15; 42:9; Dan 2:1).

w. OL reads more concisely, "It came to the tent of Midian, and it struck it, and the tent fell."

x. A word for "interpretation" rooted in the verb "to break." The interpreter has cracked the code. Vat employs the same word for "interpretation" found in Gen 40:12.

y. Literally, "heads."

z. OL adds, "as the watch begins."

aa. Notice the repetition in vocabulary and syntax in vv. 16–20 and throughout the chapter as a whole.

bb. OL reads, "say to the Lord, 'Behold Gideon,'" thereby reducing the impression that God and Gideon are military partners.

cc. Note the same Hebrew root as in the term for "watch."

dd. OL: "They crushed the jars" (omitting "that were in their hands"); Vat reads, "They rattled the jars."

ee. OL reads more expansively, "threw the jars of their hands and two battle lines were turned to them."

ff. OL deepens the scene by adding, "and the camp of Midian and Amalek and all the enemy men feared."

gg. OL reads, "Bethel."

The outcome of the battle depends not upon Israelite expertise, but upon the prowess and goodwill of the divine warrior, protector of Israel. The fewer the number of human soldiers, the greater the victory of God. Like the exodus, the battle with the Midianites has to do with a manifestation of God's glory. Thus Yhwh demands that Gideon reduce the size of his fighting force, the episode of the "lappers" being an idiosyncratic means to achieve that end. The battle and Gideon's own career are framed by an encouraging divinatory experience, while the battle suggests a ritualized view of holy war. In this case, tribes called to participate are Naphtali, Asher, Manasseh, and Ephraim. The battle is narrated in traditional economical style. Lines break up easily into full clauses, which predominate.

[1–8] Events surrounding the honing down of Gideon's fighting force portray the battle as belonging to divinely controlled holy war. Gideon's close connection with his patron deity has already been made clear, for God sends him a messenger and miraculous signs and communicates directly with the hero. Now the deity commands that Gideon take fewer men to battle, for the victory is about the power of the divine warrior himself. This passage echoes aspects of various miracle accounts in which God subdues enemies (e.g., Exod 17:8–13; Josh 6:20; 10:12–13; 1 Sam 7:9–11; 2 Kgs 7:5–7; 19:35–37; 2 Chron 20:1–30). The deity demands the sort of reduction in forces pictured by Deuteronomy 20. The question, in v. 4, is a variation on Deut 20:8. The exaggerated numbers describe a reduction in twenty-two thousand soldiers; the remaining ten thousand are still too many. A kind of water trial that distinguishes "lappers" from "kneelers" leaves Gideon with a small force of three hundred. Is the implication that those who lap like dogs will fight like wild creatures, or is the test more arbitrary? In any case, God is now pictured satisfied that no one will confuse miraculous victory with mere human prowess. The deity conducts every aspect of the battle and even directs Gideon to receive an additional sign of his success, a kind of confidence-building oracle.

[9–14] Sent to the outskirts of the enemies' camp by God to receive another confirming sign, Gideon and his squire find themselves in a divinatory setting, receiving revelation. Throughout the ancient Near East, dreams were regarded as having future-telling relevance. Uncontrollable and serendipitous, entering the mind when it is suspended in sleep, dreams were considered divinely sent interventions in the realm of the mortals. Within the biblical tradition, examples are richly provided by the cycle of stories about Joseph, who has divinatory dreams and the ability, with God's help, to interpret the dreams of others. (For a full discussion of the dream in an ancient Near Eastern context see Niditch 1980: 1–19.) In this passage, the symbolic dream is combined with another sort of divinatory technique, the random overhearing of a statement by a passerby that can be understood as relevant to the listener's current situation. In Greek tradition, such a form of unintentional prophecy is called the *klēdōn* (see, e.g.,

Odyssey 18.117; 20.120). Gideon has a double divinatory experience, for he hears the dream report of a passerby and another's interpretation of it; what the interpreter says applies specifically and overtly to him. A rolling loaf of bread that upends a tent is interpreted to mean that Gideon will be victorious, rolling over his enemies. The tent clearly represents enemy troops and bivouac. The term for "bread" is identical to the root for another word "to make war," so perhaps in accordance with traditional dream interpretation, word association is assumed. Throughout the Near East, word association, like idea association, is a common divinatory technique.

[15–25] The remainder of the chapter describes Gideon's final preparations for battle and his great victory. The tactics of shouting and trumpet blasting, reminiscent of the battle of Jericho in Joshua 6, and the use of torches and jar smashing are suggestive of ritual action and miracle accounts. Such are the tactics of bandit warriors, and richly invoke the flavor of ancient battle narratives, similar to battle scenes of the *Iliad* in which trickery, luck, and divine favor sometimes figure more prominently than skill and weaponry. Notice the economy of language in vv. 16, 18, 19, and 20, as materials are handed out and directions are given and carried out. The battle cry at vv. 18 and 20 juxtaposes the divine and human heroes.

The location of places mentioned in v. 22 is uncertain, but Boling suggests locations for Beth-shittah and Zererah in the Jordan Valley and for Tabbath in eastern Gilead (148).

Verses 23–25 suggest the calling out of members of the military league. As discussed in the introduction, section 2, scholars have become suspicious of details of Martin Noth's thesis concerning a twelve-tribe Israelite amphictyony. Nevertheless, it does seem likely that Israelite groups from various areas, some of whom had their own particular histories in relation to the land, would unify for military action and consider themselves related by bonds of kinship as well as by shared military and political interests. The enemy kings are captured and executed at their home bases, and their heads are brought to the hero Gideon.

Judges 8:1–35
Inner-Group Tensions, the Rejection of Kingship, and a Hero's Burial

8:1 And the men of Ephraim said to him,
      "What is this thing you have done to us:[a]
          not to call us
              when you went to wage war against Midian?"

And they contended with him forcefully.[b]

2   And he said to them,
"What have I done now compared to you?
Are not the gleanings of Ephraim better
    than the vintage of Abiezer?

3   Yhwh gave the chieftains of Midian into your hands,
    Oreb and Zeeb,
and what have I been able to do compared to you?"
Then their temper[c] abated from against him
    when he spoke this thing.[d]

4   And Gideon went toward the Jordan,
    crossing was he,
and the three hundred men who were with him
    were exhausted and in pursuit.[e]

5   And he said to the men of Succoth,
"Give, I pray you, round loaves of bread
    to the people who follow in my footsteps,
        because they are exhausted,
and I am following after Zebah and Zalmunna,
    kings of Midian."

6   And the chieftains of Succoth said,
"Is the palm[f] of Zebah and Zalmunna now in your hands
    that we should give to your army bread?"

7   And said Gideon,
"Therefore, when Yhwh gives Zebah and Zalmunna into my hand,
    I will thresh your flesh
        with the thorns of the wilderness and with briars."

8   And he went up from there to Penuel,
and spoke to them like this,
and the men of Penuel answered him
    as the men of Succoth had answered.

9   And he said also to the men of Penuel, saying,
"When I return in peace,
    I will break down this tower."

10   And Zebah and Zalmunna were in Karkor,
and their company[g] was with them,
    around fifteen thousand men,
        all who remained
            from all the company of the Easterners,
    for those who had fallen
        were one hundred and twenty thousand sword-drawing men.

11   And Gideon went up on the way of the tent dwellers,[h]

east of Nobah and Jogbehah,
and he struck the encampment,
for the camp was unsuspecting.[i]

12   And Zebah and Zalmunna fled,
and he followed after them,
and he captured the two kings of Midian,
          Zebah and Zalmunna,
and all the camp he made tremble.[j]

13   And Gideon, son of Joash, returned from the war scene,
          at the ascent of Heres.[k]

14   And he captured a lad[l] from the men of Succoth,
and he questioned him,
and he wrote down for him the chieftains of Succoth and its elders,
          seventy-seven men.

15   And he went to the men of Succoth and said,
"Here are Zebah and Zalmunna,
          about whom you reproached me saying,
          'Is the palm[m] of Zebah and Zalmunna now in your hands
              that we should give bread to your exhausted men?'"

16   And he took the elders[n] of the town,
          and wilderness thorns and briars,
and he "educated"[o] the men of Succoth with them.

17   And the tower of Penuel he broke down,
and he killed the men of the city.

18   And he said to Zebah and Zalmunna,
"Where[p] are the men whom you killed in Tabor?"
And they said, "As you are, so were they.
Each one had the form of the sons of a king."

19   And he said,
"My brothers, the sons of my mother, they were.
[q] As Yhwh lives, had you left them alive,
          I would not kill you."

20   And he said to Jether his eldest,
"Rise and kill them."
But the lad could not draw his sword,
because he was afraid
because he was still a lad.

21   And said Zebah and Zalmunna,
"You rise yourself,
and strike us down,
for as is the man, so his strength."
And rise did Gideon,

and he killed Zebah and Zalmunna,
and he took the crescents
    that were on the neck of their camels.

22   And the men of Israel said to Gideon,
"Rule over us, you and also your son,
    and also the son of your son,
because you delivered us from the hand of Midian."

23   And Gideon said to them,
"I will not rule over you
and my son will not rule over you.
Yhwh will rule over you."

24   And Gideon said to them,
"Let me ask you an asking.
Give to me, each man, an earring of his booty."
(For earrings of gold they had
because they were Ishmaelites.)

25   And they said,
"Give we will surely give."
And they[r] spread out the mantle,
and they threw there, each man, an[s] earring of his booty.

26   And the weight of the earrings of gold for which he asked was
    one thousand seven hundred gold-weight,
        apart from the crescents and the pendants
        and the clothing of purple
            that was upon the kings of Midian,
        and apart from the neck pendants
            that were on the necks of their camels.

27   And Gideon made it into an ephod,
and he stationed it in his town, in Ophrah,
and all Israel whored after it,
and it was to Gideon and his family a lure.

28   And humbled was Midian before the descendants of Israel,
and they did not continue to lift their heads,
and quiet was the land for forty years in the days of Gideon.

29   And Jerubbaal, son of Joash, went,
and he dwelled in his homestead.

30   And Gideon had seventy sons,
    the issue of his loins,
for many wives had he.

31   And his concubine who was in Shechem bore him, also she, a son,[t]
and he[u] set his name as Abimelech.

32   And Gideon, son of Joash, died at a good old age,[v]

and he was buried in the burial place of Joash, his father,
in Ophrah of the Abiezerites.

33   And it was when Gideon died
that the descendants of Israel returned
to whoring after the baals,
and they set up for themselves Baal-berith (of the covenant) as a god.

34   And the descendants of Israel did not remember Yhwh their god,
who saved them from the hand of all their enemies round about.

35   And they did not do acts of fealty
toward the house of Jerubbaal Gideon
in accord with all the good that he had done for Israel.

a. Formulaic accusation of wrongdoing. See, e.g., Gen 12:18; 20:9; 26:10; 29:25; Exod 14:11; Num 23:11; Judg 15:11.

b. Literally, "with strength."

c. Literally, "spirit" or "wind."

d. The colon is economical in vocabulary, literally, "spoke this speaking."

e. The manuscript traditions evidence typical variation. Vat: "were hungry and pursuing"; A: "fainthearted [probably a translation of "tired/exhausted" as in MT] and hungry"; OL: "weak [also probably reflecting Hebrew "tired/exhausted"] and hungry." The simplest sensible combination is probably "tired and hungry," and one might suggest that *rdp*, "to pursue," is a corruption of *r'b*, "to be hungry." On the other hand, the various images have been understood by receiving communities and operate as variants. There may have been versions that had only the term for "tired." *Rdp* enters under influence of the following verse, and some of the ancient translators/writers "correct" it to "hungry."

f. OL reads the variant "head."

g. Literally, "camp."

h. Vat reads literally, "those who tent in tents."

i. MT reads literally, "trusting." OL reads, "the camp was in a place that they trusted."

j. Vat reads, "all the camp he got rid of," while OL and A read, "he upset," "put into disarray," perhaps reading with MT, literally, "he caused to tremble/quake."

k. *Ḥeres* is literally "the sun," that is, the east. OL reads "from the rise of the sea."

l. "Lad" is here technical language for a young functionary in the military, a squire or aide. See 7:7, 11 and MacDonald 1976.

m. OL includes the variant, "head." See v. 6.

n. OL expands slightly with "leaders and elders."

o. MT literally reads, "made to know" or "taught." Gideon teaches them a lesson and makes a public spectacle of them. Vat and OL reflect the same verb found in v. 7 ("thresh"), a verb that in the imperfect *waw* conversive (*wayyādōš*) sounds like MT *wayyōdaʿ*. Has the more difficult reading in MT crept in through scribal error or is the easier reading an attempt to make sense of the less common image? Is each a variant? Each version works well enough and reflects the oral-style variation that characterizes the manuscript traditions.

p. OL reads, "Who and what kind were . . . ," questions more precisely suited to the response.

q. OL provides the introduction, "And he swore to them," framing the form of the adjuration.

r. Vat reads, "he spread out his mantle"; OL reads, "Gideon spread out his mantle." Both make better sense of the scene than MT.

s. OL has the slightly more expansive and descriptive, "golden earring."

t. OL reads, "he had concubines in Shechem," an explanatory gloss.

u. Vat and OL have the concubine name the son. Perhaps in these versions, his name, meaning "My father is king," reflects her ambitions for a dynasty.

v. Literally, "well hoary headed." Vat omits "at a good old age" and reads, "died in his city."

Encounters with enemies and allies are portrayed in bardic dimensions, typical of the epic literatures of other cultures. Enemy warriors are shown to relate to one another with a degree of respect for their counterpart's prowess and within a code of reciprocity, and relations within the group—in this case Israel—are often characterized by friction regarding distribution of war spoils and other matters.

Chapter 8 also features important attitudes to kingship. Some have argued that Gideon is a less than perfect leader because of his iconic ephod, described Deuteronomistically as a "lure" or "snare," and that the portrayal of this judge contributes to the message that a king would be a better leader. A close examination, however, reveals that those behind the Gideon cycle are far from enthusiastic monarchists, that Gideon is portrayed as a great hero, and that minor ambivalences about the nature of the hero and major ambivalences about the best form of polity are typical of Judges and the tradition as a whole.

As in Judges 6 and 7, the style is traditionally economical. A shift in register characterizes some of the dialogue as lines enjamb (e.g., 8:1, 6, 15). Interlocking phrases are also found in descriptions at vv. 10 and 26. The halting style provides a good sense of the significant dimensions of the defeat of the enemy (v. 10) and the large amount of booty contributed (v. 26). The medium thus suits the message.

[1–3] The opening of ch. 8 portrays the sort of tensions that arise concerning the distribution of war spoils within decentralized political and military structures. Such disputes are frequent motifs in the bardic-style literary traditions about war. One might draw comparisons, for example, with tales of Achilles and Menelaus. Participants in battle fight with hopes of obtaining a piece of the victory spoils, and the Ephraimites complain that they were not called up sufficiently early in order to partake fully in the conquered goods and the glory. Gideon, able leader that he is, diffuses their anger by use of a proverbial saying.

Set in the syntax of a rhetorical question, the form of the proverb exhibits the typical pattern "*x* better than *y*," as found in Prov 22:1 and Eccl 7:1 (for international examples see Fontaine 1982: 64; Dundes 1981: 54). The author portrays a typical setting for the deploying of a proverb, or *māšāl* in Hebrew. This brief speech act draws a comparison between a present situation or event and some metaphorically relevant motif, scene, or story that reduces tension or resentment in an interaction between groups or individuals who are protective of their status. The proverb deflects anger and prevents overt confrontation or violence. In a self-effacing way, Gideon graciously compliments the Ephraimites for their superior valor and accomplishments. He states obliquely through the saying and then overtly in its interpretation that the Ephraimites have, after all, captured the greatest prize of battle, enemy leaders. This accomplishment makes his own conquests pale by comparison. Thus the "gleanings" gathered by Ephraim, the grapes merely left behind after the harvest, are better than the "vintage," that is, the best that Gideon of the clan of Abiezer could accomplish. Hearing what they want to hear about themselves, they depart, anger abated, and the disagreement does not lead to blows.

[5–17] The geographic setting for subsequent scenes includes Karkor (v. 10), a place in the mountains of eastern Gilead whose exact location is unknown; the ascent of Heres (v. 13), "the sun," an intriguing name for an uncertain location that has been variously translated and emended; and Succoth, which seems to be located near the eastern bank of the Jordan River. Neither this site nor Penuel can be located with certainty, the identification of Succoth with Tell Deir Alla having now been challenged by archaeological evidence (see Baly 1985: 996–97; Boling 155).

This passage is reminiscent of David's encounter with Nabal during his bandit phase. He asks for provisions and hospitality from those who hold the local power, making clear that he operates on their behalf, and is rudely rebuffed. In this case, the chieftains of Succoth and the men of Penuel take on the Nabal role. The response of the leaders of Succoth is a taunt, suggesting in other words, as does a later hero (1 Kgs 20:11), that those who are about to put on armor should not brag like those who have just taken it off. They are not convinced that Gideon and his forces can capture the Midianite kings. For his part, Gideon makes an oath that he will punish them appropriately upon his successful return. He does accomplish his mission and punishes them as promised. The recurring language emphasizes the message of just deserts. Gideon repeats the refusal of the leaders of Succoth (vv. 6, 15) with the addition of the word "exhausted." Gideon implies that the elders knew how needy his troops were and that they nevertheless refused to help, acting in a most mean-spirited fashion.

The young man's ability to write down the list of leaders for Gideon (8:14) has been taken as evidence of a modern-style literacy in ancient Israel. Even a lad has scribal skills. The term *naʿar*, however, is to be understood more technically as a military aide, as seen above. The cooperation of one from a hostile camp is an omen of the successful mission to come, as in the tale of the happy turncoat discussed in ch. 1.

[**18–21**] The interaction between Gideon and his royal captives richly evokes a heroic ethos of war (see Niditch 1993b: 90–105), in which respect is expressed between combatants and in which it is considered proper for men of equal skill and training to confront one another. One recalls Goliath's resentment at being paired for combat with the young, inexperienced David (1 Sam 17:43) or the general Abner's reluctance to kill the younger brother of Joab, his enemy counterpart, when the lad, Asahel, pursues him (2 Sam 2:21–22). Nuances of just war are also present. Some sort of code applies among warriors.

The Midianites describe their Israelite enemies in admirable terms, "sons of a king," like Gideon their captor (v. 18). As in the *Song of Roland*, warriors speak admiringly of their counterparts in battle. Gideon declares that those whom the Midianites had killed were his brothers, maternal kin, thus emphasizing the kinship-based networks that undergird group identity and the composition of the actual armies mustered. He also declares that had the Midianites spared his brothers, he would spare them, again invoking a kind of warrior's code.

His eldest son Jether, who is still a "lad," a young soldier, possibly his aide-de-camp, does not have the nerve to slay the kings; and, with a proverb, the kings ask Gideon himself to do the job, as befits their mutual status. Again, the proverb serves as powerful oblique speech. In this case, the noble enemies are portrayed as negotiating their own execution. The bardic concern for their status as heroes, deserving of enemies' respect and a heroic death, thus ends the scene.

[**22–33**] This passage is important for exploring attitudes to kingship in Judges. In no uncertain terms, the hero rejects dynastic monarchy, for Yhwh is king (8:23). Some scholars interpret the subsequent scene as proof of Gideon's failings as a leader.

Intriguing details in Judges 7:4 associate Midianites with Ishmaelites (see commentary on 6:1–10) and the latter with earrings. Frank Zimmerman implies that the enemy is generalized as the exotic "other," dripping with jewels (1952: 113–114). As in the escape from Egypt, the oppressors' jewelry becomes Israelite booty (Exod 12:35–36), available for later use. Gideon's request for gold earrings and his fashioning an icon out of the precious metal parallels the episode of the golden calf. Here, as in Exodus 32, the passage is probably at its root an etiology for an icon, founded by a hero of old. The ephod, usually a special garment worn by the priest, in this case seems to be some sort of statuary. Other passages suggest a divinatory device (1 Sam 23:6–12; see Miller 2000: 165–66). Verse 27 casts the episode as an example of apostasy; Exodus 32 has been so shaped as well. All great biblical heroes have their flaws and make errors. Moses hits the rock (Num 20:11) and Aaron is accomplice in the episode of the golden calf (Exod 32:2–5). The way in which the author concludes the chapter, however, strongly argues against the view that Gideon is a failed leader whose shortcomings point to the need for a monarchy. After the brief comment concerning the ephod (v. 27), the positive message and tone about Gideon's success as a leader quickly resumes.

The enemy has been subdued, and the land has rest, as does Gideon. He sires seventy sons, a sign of divine blessing. One son, Abimelech, introduced in v. 31, will emerge as the villain of Judges 9. Implicit is a contrast between the good leader, Gideon, and his son Abimelech, who would be recognized by receivers of the tradition as an evildoer. The introduction of the name suffices as the narrator prepares for the traditional pattern of good father/evil son, as found in tales of Aaron (Lev 10:1–2), Eli (1 Sam 2:12–17, 22), and Samuel (1 Sam 8:3). Gideon has refused kingship, whereas his son, ironically named "My Father Is King," will ambitiously and murderously pursue it. Gideon himself lives to a ripe old age and is buried in the ancestral tomb, a hero fully deserving of God's favor and blessed with the interment of a good man.

The frame of the theologian picks up at v. 33 with the death of the good leader and the people's renewed apostasy. The condemnatory language of "whoring after," frequently used by prophetic (Jer 2:20; Ezek 16:30; 23:3; Hos 2:5 [MT 7]) and other biblical authors (Exod 34:16; Lev 17:7; 20:5) plays on the metaphor of Israel as unfaithful wife. While this theme is found in Hosea (eighth century B.C.E.), it is especially popular, trenchant language in the exilic and postexilic period. Judges 8:35 emphasizes the contrast between Gideon's good works and the people's lack of loyalty, setting the scene for the story of Abimelech.

Judges 9:1–57
The Rise and Fall of Abimelech, the Would-be King

9:1   And Abimelech, son of Jerubbaal, went to Shechem
            to the kin[a] of his mother,
        and he spoke to them and to all the clan members
            of the extended household of his mother, saying,
2   "Speak, I pray you, in the ears of all the lords of Shechem.[b]
        'What is better for you,
            if seventy men rule over you,
                all the sons of Jerubbaal,[c]
            or if one man rules over you?'
        And remember that your bone and flesh am I."
3   And the kin of his mother spoke concerning him
            in the ears of all the lords of[d] Shechem,
                all these words.

And their hearts stretched after Abimelech,
for they said, "Our kin he is."

4   And they gave him seventy pieces of silver
        from the house of Baal-berith (of the Covenant);
     and Abimelech hired with them[e]
        worthless and reckless[f] men,
     and they went after him.

5   And he came to his father's extended household at Ophrah,
     and he killed his brothers, the sons of Jerubbaal,[g]
        seventy men on one stone,
     but there remained Jotham, son of Jerubbaal, the youngest,
     for he hid himself.

6   And gathered were all the lords of[h] Shechem
        and all of Beth-millo,
     and they went and kinged Abimelech as king[i]
        at the oak of the standing stone[j] that was in Shechem.

7   And they told Jotham,
     and he went and stood on the top of Mount Gerizim,
     and he lifted his voice,
     and he called and said to them,
     "Listen to me, lords of[k] Shechem,
     and listen to you will God.

8   To go went the trees[l]
        to anoint over them a king,
     and they said to the olive tree,
        'Be king over us.'

9   And the olive tree said to them,
     'Would I halt producing my luxuriant oil,
        which, by me,[m] they honor gods and men,
     and go sway over the trees?'

10   And the trees said to the fig tree,
        'Come you, be queen over us.'

11   And the fig tree said to them,
     'Would I halt producing my sweetness
        and my good fruit
     and go sway over the trees?'

12   And the trees said to the vine,
        'Come you, be queen over us.'

13   And the vine said to them,
     'Would I halt producing my new wine
        that makes gods and men[n] rejoice
     and go sway over the trees?'

14 And all the trees said to the bramble,
  'Come you, be king over us.'
15 And the bramble said to the trees,
'If in truth you are anointing me
  to be king over you,
come, seek refuge in my shade;[o]
but if not, may a fire go forth from the bramble
and consume all the cedars of Lebanon.'
16 And now, if you have acted in truth and integrity
  when you kinged Abimelech,
and if you did good things for Jerubbaal and his extended household,
and if in accordance to his dealings with his hands,
  [p] you have done for him
17   (in that my father waged war for you
  and risked his life to the limit,
  and saved you from the hand of the Midianites.
18   And you have risen up against the household of my father today,
  and you have killed his sons,
    seventy men on one stone,
  and you have kinged Abimelech, son of his concubine,
    over the lords of Shechem,
  for your kin is he).
19 But if you have acted with Jerubbaal[q] in truth and integrity,
  and with his extended household this day,
rejoice in Abimelech,[r]
and let him rejoice, also he, in you.
20 And if not, may fire go forth from Abimelech,
and let it consume the lords of Shechem and Beth-millo,
and may fire go forth from the lords of[s] Shechem
  and from Beth-millo,
and let it consume Abimelech."
21 And Jotham escaped,
and he fled and went to Beer,[t]
and he dwelled there
  because of Abimelech his brother.
22 And Abimelech became chief over Israel three years.
23 And God sent an evil spirit
  between Abimelech and the lords of Shechem,
and the lords of Shechem dealt treacherously with Abimelech,
24   in order that the violence toward
    the seventy sons of Jerubbaal, and their blood,
      be put upon Abimelech, their brother,
        who killed them,

and upon the lords of Shechem
who made his hands strong
to kill his brothers.

25 And the lords of Shechem set ambushes for him
    on the tops of the mountains,
and they robbed[u] all who would cross them on the way,
and it was told to[v] Abimelech.

26 And Gaal, son of Ebed, and his kin came,
and they crossed over to Shechem,
and the lords of Shechem trusted in him.

27 And they went out into the open country,
and they gathered grapes from their vineyards,
and they trod down
and made thanksgiving praises,
and they came to the house of their god,[w]
and they ate, and drank, and cursed[x] Abimelech.

28 And Gaal, son of Ebed, said,
"Who is Abimelech
and who is[y] Shechem that we should serve him?
Did not the son of Jerubbaal and Zebul his deputy
    serve[z] the men of Hamor, father of Shechem,
and why should we serve him?

29 Would that someone give this people into my hand,[aa]
and I would remove[bb] Abimelech."
And he said[cc] to Abimelech,
"Make many your army and go forth!"[dd]

30 And Zebul, chieftain of the city, listened
    to the words of Gaal, son of Ebed,
and he became angry.[ee]

31 And he sent messengers to Abimelech in Torma,[ff] saying,
"Behold, Gaal, son of Ebed, and his kin have been coming to Shechem,
and behold, they are making the city an enemy[gg] against you.

32 And now, arise tonight,
    you and the people who are with you,
and set an ambush in the open country.

33 And when it is in the morning,
    when the sun rises,[hh]
you rise early and make a raid[ii] on the city;
and behold, he and the people who are with him will go forth against you,
and do to him as your hand finds."[jj]

34 And Abimelech rose up
    and all the people who were with him in the night,
and they set an ambush for Shechem, four units.[kk]

35 [ll] And go did Gaal, son of Ebed,
and he stood at the entrance of the gate of the city.
And Abimelech rose up, and the people who were with him,
from the ambush site.
36 And Gaal saw the people,
and he said to Zebul,
"Behold, the people are coming down from the tops of the mountains."
And Zebul said to him,
"The shadow of the mountains you see as men."
37 And Gaal spoke again some more
and he said,
"Behold, the people are coming down from Tabbur-erez,[mm]
and one unit is coming from the way of Elon-meonenim."[nn]
38 And Zebul said to him,
"Where oh where[oo] is your mouthiness as you said,
'Who is[pp] Abimelech that we should serve him?'
Is this not the people that you despised?
Go out, I pray you, now,
and wage war against him."
39 And Gaal went forth before the lords of Shechem,
and he waged war against Abimelech.
40 And Abimelech followed after him,
and he fled from before him,
and many fell, pierced through,
against the entranceway of the gate.[qq]
41 And Abimelech dwelled in Arumah,
and Zebul drove out Gaal and his kin
from dwelling in Shechem.
42 And it was the next day,
and the people went forth to the open country,
and they told Abimelech.
43 And he took the people
and divided them into three units,
and they set an ambush in the open country.
And he saw,
and behold, the people going forth from the city,
and he rose up against them,
and he struck them down.
44 And Abimelech and the units that were with him made a raid,
and they took a stand at the entranceway of the gate of the city,
and two units made a raid[rr] on all who were in the open country,
and they struck them down.

45   And Abimelech waged war against the city, all that day,
and he captured the city,
and the people who were in it he killed,
and he broke down the city,
and he sowed it with salt.

46   And all the lords of the Tower of Shechem heard,
and they went to the hideout[ss] of the house of El[tt]-berith (of the Covenant).

47   And it was told to Abimelech
      that gathered together
          were all the lords of the Tower of Shechem.

48   And go up did Abimelech to Mount Zalmon,
      he and all the people who were with him,
and Abimelech took the axes in his hand,
and he cut tree brush and lifted it,
and placed it on his shoulder,
and he said to the people who were with him,
"What you see me do,
      quickly, do as I do."[uu]

49   And all the people, each man, also cut brushwood,
and they went after Abimelech,
and they put them against the hideout,
and they kindled with them the hideout in fire,
and all the people of the Tower of Shechem also died,
      about a thousand men and women.

50   And Abimelech went to Thebez,
and he encamped in Thebez, and captured it.

51   And a strong tower was in the midst of the city,
and there fled all the men and women
      and all the lords of the city,
and they closed it up behind them,
and they went up to the roof of the tower.

52   And Abimelech came up to the tower,
and waged war against it,
and he approached the entranceway of the tower,
      to burn it with fire.

53   And one woman threw down an upper millstone
      on the head of Abimelech,
and she crushed his skull.

54   And he called quickly to the lad who carried his gear,
and he said to him,
"Draw your sword and kill me,
lest they say of me,

'A woman killed him.'"
And his lad pierced him through,
and he died.

55 And the men of Israel saw
that Abimelech was dead,
and each man went back to his place.

56 And God returned the evil of Abimelech
that he did to his father,
to kill seventy of his kin.

57 And all the evil of the men of Shechem
God returned upon their heads,
and there came upon them
the curse of Jotham, son of Jerubbaal.

a. Literally, "brothers."

b. Vat reads, "men of Shechem" here and throughout, perhaps avoiding mention of the term *baʿal*, literally, "master, lord," that is also the name of the Canaanite deity. OL reads, "men of Shechem, saying."

c. OL reads, "Gideon," rather than "Jerubbaal" (see note b).

d. Vat and OL read, "men of" (see note b).

e. Vat translates, "and Abimelech hired for himself."

f. Vat reads, "cowardly." OL reads or translates, "fearless." The traditions thus provide minor variants, "synonymous readings" in Talmon's terms (1961).

g. OL reads, "Gideon" (see note b). MT employs "Jerubbaal" as does Vat in this instance.

h. Vat reads, "men of" (see note b). OL translates *baʿălê* as "princes."

i. Vat and MT have the "king" root, whereas OL has "anoint," a minor variant, typical of traditional-style versions.

j. Vat includes two variants for *mṣb*, one rooted in "to find" (*mṣʾ*) and the other in "to stand" as in "pillar" or "standing stone" (from the root *nṣb*). Vat reads, "by the found oak tree of the standing (stone)." OL reads, "under the dense oak tree that was in Shechem." A reads, "under the oak tree of the standing in Shechem." Each provides a slightly different image.

k. Vat and OL read, "men of," avoiding the *baʿal* term, as throughout.

l. The rhythmical opening phrase of the *māšāl* that employs an infinitive absolute, literally, "to go did go," is captured in Vat by "the trees going went" and by OL, "going out the trees went out."

m. Vat reads, "by which men glorify God," with a more overtly religious overtone than that of MT. OL translates literally, "which the Lord and men glorified in me."

n. The traditions indicate discomfort with the language that describes wine as gladdening the hearts of "gods" and men. Vat translates the term *ʾĕlōhîm* as "God," while OL reads "the joyfulness that God and men glorified." A has similarly "the joyfulness that is from the God of men." The variation has theological significance.

o. Vat reads, "Come stand under. . . ." OL reads, "Come enter under my protection." These are both typical variants expressing the same essential idea. See Talmon (1961) and Person (1998) on equivalent parallels.

p. OL adds, "just as he did to you. . . ."

q. OL reads, "Yeruboam," again avoiding the *ba'al* term.

r. OL reads, "may you be blessed and may you feast from Abimelech and may he feast from you," a variant or a translational gloss that includes the notion of eating.

s. Vat reads, "men of," and OL reads, "princes of," again avoiding the term for "lord," *ba'al*.

t. OL has a slightly expanded version of Jotham's departure.

u. Cf. 21:23, where the term is translated "stole." OL implies the making of a group of rebels: "and they called upon all those who were passing through them on the way."

v. Vat reads, "to the king Abimelech," emphasizing the status he takes upon himself.

w. OL reads, "their gods," which is possible within the Hebrew and portrays the enemy as polytheists.

x. Vat reads the sound-alike Greek verb for "said" instead of "drank," so that the scene becomes through this scribal error, "they ate and said and cursed."

y. Vat reads, "son of Shechem."

z. Vat reads, "his deputy, his servant with the men." OL omits the serve word altogether to read, "Was not the son of Gideon and Zebul his deputy among the men of Hamor . . . ?"

aa. The adjuration formula pattern literally reads, "Who would . . ." (see also 2 Sam 15:4 and 23:15).

bb. OL reads, "stand up against/oppose."

cc. OL reads more ambiguously, "It was said to him." Vat reads, "I will say to him." 1QJudg reads, "They said to Abimelech." The nuance thus differs in each tradition. Gaal is the clear antagonist in MT and Vat, although the latter has him picturing his own taunt.

dd. The saying is in the nature of a taunt in MT, directed to Abimelech by his challenger.

ee. OL, Vat, and 1QJudg read, "very angry."

ff. Vat reads, "secretly." This variant allows for nuances of conspiracy and counterconspiracy and for a sense of besiegement. OL reads "with gifts," *bitrûmôt*, either an attempted translation of the place name Torma, as is frequent in the Greek and Latin traditions, or a reflection of a genuinely different Hebrew text. In either case, the received text becomes richer in bardic nuances that emphasize the relationship between allies symbolized and effected by items of exchange. Cf. the place name in v. 41, *ba'rûmâ*, "in Arumah."

gg. Vat and OL read "besiege" from the root *ṣwr*. MT and 1QJudg may be translated this way, but Boling (178) and Soggin (186) suggest a transitive meaning of the root: "alienating the city" or "stirring up the city" (cf. Deut 2:9, 19; Esth 8:11).

hh. The Hebrew has two different roots translated "rise" in v. 33, and a third root in v. 34.

ii. Vat has, "stretch out against the city," in the sense of "make a line/military formation." OL reads more briefly, "When the sun has arisen, enter into the city."

jj. One might translate, "whatever seems good to you" or "as you see fit." For this idiom see 1 Sam 10:7; 25:8.

kk. OL reads, "and they sat in the field against Shechem in four groups."

ll. OL begins, "And it became morning," with a slightly expanded setting of the scene.

mm. Tabbur-eretz means "navel of the earth"; thus BDB (371) explains "mountainous country of Israel, highest part, central, prominent." Vat and OL read more expansively and mythologically, "coming down along the sea [reading *min-hayyām,* "from the sea," rather than *mē'îm*, "from"], being from [Vat]/from the joining of [OL] the navel of the earth," thus literalizing and translating the place name.

nn. Literally, "the oak of the diviners." The root may be onomatopoeic from the "nasal twang" (BDB 778) that diviners emit in trances. See Deut 18:10; Mic 5:12 (MT 11); Isa 2:6; 57:3. Cf. Judg 9:6 for another sacred tree.

oo. OL and Vat employ one term for "where," lacking the rhythmic quality of the tradition in MT.

pp. OL repeats "who is" as in the double "where" at the opening of the questioning taunt in MT.

qq. 1QJudg reads, "up to the entranceway of the gate of the city" (cf. 9:35). OL reads, "up to the gate of the city." Vat agrees with MT as translated above. All of the above are typical minor variants.

rr. Vat and OL read, "two units were spread out." Vat employs the same verb found in v. 33.

ss. A difficult term that seems to be rooted in "dig, cleave, rend open." Stager suggests "rockcut tunnel, . . . an ambulatory inside the walls" (2003a: 32). BDB (863) translates, "underground chamber." Vat seems to suggest a "meeting place." Some sort of hideout is implicit.

tt. OL has the variant "Baal." The Shechemites are Baal worshipers. Cf. 8:33; 9:4.

uu. A formula for instructions in ambush making. Cf. 7:17.

The career of Gideon's son Abimelech is an important lesson in political ethics and provides insight into the ways in which Israelites wrestled with critical issues of leadership and polity. It has often been suggested that the book of Judges projects an image of a period of national failure and political chaos, making necessary the establishment of the monarchy. In this commentary I make the case that Judges provides a more complex, ambivalent, and self-critical portrait of the monarchy and of preceding experiments in statehood. The judges belong to the "old days," before there were kings in Israel, but these early leaders are portrayed as clever, brave, inspired, charismatic, and flawed. They are heroic, engaging figures, and none of them is a king. Gideon, in fact, rejects kingship outright, declaring that Yhwh is the only king (8:23); and the story of Abimelech's illegal, murderous coup, undertaken to establish himself as a king, is surely a negative portrayal of Judges' one experiment in Israelite kingship. Jotham's parable about the trees, delivered in a traditional literary form, the *māšāl*, criticizes monarchy in general while condemning this manifestation of kingship in particular. The curse of Jotham predicts and assures the downfall of the would-be king, whose lack of fealty to the house of Gideon is mirrored in his subjects' capricious lack of loyalty to him. He subdues the rebels only to be killed by a woman—the ignoble and shameful end to a would-be man of power, in the bardic, epic-like traditions of Judges.

Like the narratives about Gideon, the tale of Abimelech evidences traditional style. Notice, in particular, repetition in the parable. Most verses break into cola that are complete thoughts and whole clauses, but there is subordination at 9:16–18, following the conditional "if" (cf. 6:13, 17), and at 9:24. Both instances in ch. 9 provide significant background asides that emphasize Abimelech's evildoing in contrast with his father's uprightness and the reason for the son's downfall (cf. 8:35; 9:15). The change in register calls attention to these important pieces of content.

[1–6] This section underscores the tension between two forms of polity, one decentralized and the other centralized (see especially v. 2). The sides drawn in this conspiracy are nevertheless based in clan and kin (vv. 2–3). Even this would-be monarchy is not a state in the modern sense in which all citizens of various origins share loyalty to one ruler. (On terms in v. 1 for "clan," literally, "family," and "extended household," "literally, "father's house," see King and Stager 2001: 39–40.)

Abimelech's name has an ironic connotation. As Soggin (166–67) and Boling (163) point out, its pattern is typical of a Northwest Semitic ruler's name, meaning "My father is king," and implies descent for the ruler from a divine king of kings or proper inheritance of a previous human king's mantle. In this case, Abimelech is neither. He does not serve with divine blessing, and his father chose not to be king, believing God to be the only true king. Abimelech does not inherit power but seizes it.

Shechem, an ancient and venerable northern Israelite city located about forty miles north of Jerusalem, is the scene of Joshua's covenant renewal in Joshua 24, an important foundational passage perhaps reflecting an annual cultic festival that predates the monarchy. This city predates Israelite occupation and continues to be associated with Canaanite custom and tradition thereafter. (See references to the temple in vv. 4, 27, 46–47, 49; and Stager 2003a.)

The language for Abimelech's cohorts at v. 4 connotes utter disdain (cf. 11:3 and 2 Sam 6:20), while Abimelech himself is portrayed as consummately illegitimate, a murderer killing all rivals on the paternal side of his family (v. 5). This passage contributes to an understanding of ancient Israelite political ethics; it is a window into the worldview of the presenters of these traditions. Implicit is the notion that leadership requires legitimacy rooted in divine selection, as well as a sort of contract between the ruler and the ruled (see the parable). The murder of rivals is not presented as a legitimate means of taking power; might does not make right in the thread of thought found in the tale of Abimelech's rise and fall.

The *millô* (v. 6) is an earthen structure, an artificial hill supported by walls, upon which buildings or a building, literally, the "house of *millô*," could be built. (On such Bronze Age buildings in Shechem, see Wright 1965: 80–102.) The coronation takes place at a sacred spot, a raised hill where a temple may be built, by a sacred tree connoting oracular activity. The tree is next to a "standing stone" or pillar symbolizing divine presence. See above on Deborah's oak

(4:4–10). (On the association of sacred trees, sacred pillars, and altars at Shechem, see Stager 2003a: 33–35; and cf. Gen 12:6; 33:19–20.)

[7–15] One brother has escaped the hand of Abimelech and is pictured going atop Mount Gerizim to accuse Abimelech publicly of evildoing. His accusation is cast in the form of the *māšāl*. In Deuteronomy 27 Mount Gerizim and Mount Ebal are ritual loci for the performance of stylized blessings and curses that proclaim the terms of God's covenantal relationship with Israel. Mountain peaks that are literally above the fray and closer to heaven itself are settings for politically important speech and social critique. The *māšāl* is a traditional literary form found throughout the Hebrew Bible. Rooted in the verb meaning "to be similar," the *māšāl* is "a form of oblique and artful communication (a saying, an icon, a narrative, a symbolic action, or another form) that sets up an analogy between the communication and the real-life settings of the listeners" (Niditch 1993a: 86). The *māšāl* is often a vehicle to express worldview and expose serious social or political tensions. Frequently it is an indirect means by which a person of lower status confronts one with power over him or her (e.g., 2 Sam 12:1–15; 14:1–20). As in other cultures, this one ethnic genre includes what we might consider a range of different literary forms, sayings, parables, fables, oracles, and so on (for a list of biblical examples, see Niditch 1993a: 67–91; and above on Judg 8:2). In Judges 9 the analogy is drawn between Abimelech's usurpation of power with the support of the Shechemites and the tale of the trees' search for a ruler. The style is fully traditional with repeating frame language: the offer of kingship and the individual tree's refusal. The folk motif concerning the status of the trees is found elsewhere in the world's folklore as revealed by Stith Thompson's compendious, indexed collection of folk motifs (1995–1958). Motif J411.7, "the laurel and the olive tree scorn the thornbush as umpire in their dispute as to who is more useful," is related as is the more general J461.1, "the belly and the members," in which the parts of a body debate about which part is worthy of leadership. In Jotham's parable, the various examples of vegetation insist that they are too important and worthwhile to be king. The olive with its "luxuriant oil," the fig with its sweet fruit, and the vine with its new wine all refuse to be king. Only the useless bramble accepts. The *māšāl* is a comment on the unworthiness of monarchs in general and of Abimelech in particular.

The bramble's words at the end of the *māšāl* also relate to issues in social contract. The bramble says that if the trees truly want him to be king, appointing him "in truth," then he will welcome them, but if not, then the relationship will end in violent dissolution. The Israelite author may be suggesting that monarchy is a necessary evil and that many kings are useless, but the political arrangement, flawed as it is, has a chance to work only when both parties enter into the agreement in good faith. Jotham's interpretation and application of the *māšāl* continues this line of thought and directs a stinging critique at Abimelech's coup and his kingship.

[16–21] Jotham makes clear that the supporters of Abimelech have paid back Gideon with evil, even though he "risked his life to the limit" as their savior. The violence of the mass killing that eliminated a lineage is emphasized in the image of killing seventy men on one stone (9:5, 18) in a kind of slaughter reserved for animals (see 1 Sam 14:33–35). They have clearly not acted "in truth and integrity" (Judg 9:19), and the fiery curse of the bramble will fall upon them and the ignoble son of Gideon's concubine.

[22–57] The theme of just deserts begins with the formulaic indicator of divine displeasure. Yhwh "sends an evil spirit" to break up the alliance between Abimelech and the lords of Shechem. Similarly, by means of an "evil spirit," God begins a pattern leading to the hero Saul's fall at 1 Sam 16:14. Such a spirit is real in a world in which curses and blessings have physical power and in which the "other" world may intervene in the affairs of human beings. The notion of an evil spirit also captures the psychoanalytical aspect of moods that may sour and relationships that may self-destruct without overt cause or motivation. The deity is behind all events, and the theme of political injustice is strongly articulated in Jotham's *māšāl* (v. 24). Vengeance will be undertaken and justice will prevail.

The lords of Shechem become bandit rebels, engaging in ambush and piracy (9:25). A new leader arises for these forces, Gaal, son of Ebed, a name that evokes negative connotations, "to abhor, loathe" and "slave" (see Boling 176). Verse 27 pictures the conspirators reveling in a prebattle banquet scene, filled with drinking, cursing of the enemy, and taunts (v. 28). Within their bold taunt a new character is introduced, Zebul, a name meaning "lofty, exalted." The followers of Gaal suggest that Abimelech, the son of Gideon, and his officer were once in an inferior vassal-type relationship to the rulers of Shechem. As expressed in MT, the words to Abimelech are a challenge to arms, if he dares. The taunting tone continues. Zebul, Abimelech's ally, sends warning to him and advises a course of action to counter his enemies (vv. 31–33). Abimelech follows Zebul's strategy. Notice the recurring language of ambush and raiding in the warring style of bandits.

In vv. 36–38 Zebul appears to be embedded in the camp of Gaal, a traitor in his midst, in the style of Hushai during the rebellion of Absalom. Hushai appears to advise the rebel son, whereas he is really the agent of David (2 Sam 17:5–16). Similarly, Zebul tries to distract Gaal and give the forces of Abimelech more time to approach for battle. A trickster, Zebul tells Gaal that the enemy troops he thinks he sees are just shadows. Then in v. 38 Zebul reveals his true loyalties, quoting Gaal's taunt back at him, daring him to confront the forces he so disdained. Gaal and his forces are defeated and driven out from Shechem. The battle account appears to be complete, but the reader knows that there must be more to the larger story, for the vengeance upon Abimelech is yet to be taken. The victory over Gaal only delays his fall.

Judges 9:42 may reveal one way in which the events described in vv. 22–25 continued in some renditions of the story, minus the Gaal episode, for the line "it was told to Abimelech" or "they told Abimelech" seems to be a hook found in vv. 25 and 42. There is a similar phenomenon in 1 Kgs 19:9 and 13. Biblical writers sometimes introduce such narrative resumptions or plot alternatives through the repetition of key language. The tradition would have included various scenes and battle stories concerning Abimelech and his enemies. Writers could provide shorter or longer versions of the tradition with fewer or more episodes, and employ a repeated phrase to resume the now expanded account.

In the open country and the city, Abimelech confronts his enemies, Shechemites who have turned against him. He destroys one group of enemies, the people of the Tower of Shechem, perhaps a temple fortress, by trapping them in their hideout, which he sets ablaze. (On the archaeological identification and history of this site, see Stager 2003a: 26–35, 66–69.) Next, he confronts his enemies in Thebez, a town near Shechem, which also contained a fortified tower like those of Shechem and Penuel (see 8:9, 17). The people of Thebez flee to the tower, but Abimelech besieges it with fire, and ironically, just as it seems he is to emerge victorious from his battle, "one woman" fatally wounds him by throwing down a millstone that crushes his skull.

The millstone is not pictured to be a massive ox-drawn piece of equipment but a modest handheld stone, lethal when dropped from a height (see Herr and Boyd 2002). Abimelech knows that his death is an ignoble one. Like Sisera (Judg 4–5), he has been bested by a woman wielding a domestic tool. He asks his aide to kill him quickly with the sword lest the world say his death was by the hand of a woman. Similar is Saul's request of his aide that he be killed lest the uncircumcised enemy be the ones to finish him off and "make sport" of him. Themes of shame and honor emerge in these bardic tales of war (1 Sam 31:4). Abimelech's death is thus remembered as unbefitting a hero. The bloodguilt for the murder of the sons of Gideon is repaid.

Judges 10:1–18
The Judges Tola and Jair,
and Israel's Subsequent Decline

10:1 And there arose after Abimelech,
>to deliver Israel,
>>Tola, son of Puah, son of Dodo,[a]
>>a man of Issachar,

and he dwelled in Shamir
  in the hill country of Ephraim.

2 And he judged Israel twenty-three years,
and he died and was buried in Shamir.

3 And there arose after him Jair the Gileadite,
and he judged Israel twenty-two years.

4 And there were to him thirty[b] sons,
  who rode on thirty donkeys,
and there were to them thirty villages,
them they call the villages of Jair,
  —until this day—
    which are in the land of Gilead.

5 And Jair died,
and he was buried in Kamon.

6 And the descendants of Israel again acted
  to do evil in the eyes of Yhwh,
and they served the baals and the ashtarot,
  and the gods of Aram,[c] and the gods of Sidon,
  and the gods of Moab, and the gods of the descendants of Ammon,
  and the gods of the Philistines,[d]
and they forsook Yhwh
and did not serve him.

7 And kindled was the anger of Yhwh against Israel,
and he sold them into the hand of the Philistines
  and into the hand of the descendants of Ammon.

8 And they shattered and crushed the descendants of Israel,
  in that year—for eighteen years—
    all the descendants of Israel
      who were in Transjordan
        in the land of the Amorites,
          which is in Gilead.

9 And the descendants of Ammon crossed the Jordan
  to wage war also with Judah and Benjamin
    and with the house of Ephraim,
and there were very dire straits for Israel.[e]

10 And the descendants of Israel called out to Yhwh saying,
"We have sinned against you,
for we have forsaken our god
and have served the baals."

11 And Yhwh said to the descendants of Israel,
"Did not (I deliver you) from[f] Egypt and from the Amorites
  and from the descendants of Ammon and from the Philistines?

12   And the Sidonians, and Amalek, and Maon oppressed you,
      and you called out to me,
      and I delivered you from their hands.
13   But you have forsaken me,
      and have served other gods.
      Therefore I will not act again to deliver you.
14   Go and call to the gods[g] whom you have chosen.
      Let them deliver you in the time of your dire straits."
15   And the descendants of Israel said to Yhwh,
      "We have sinned.
      Do with us whatever seems good in your eyes,
      but save us, I pray you, this day."
16   And they removed the foreign gods from their midst,
      and they served Yhwh,
      and his soul was cut to the quick over the trouble of Israel.[h]
17   And the descendants of Ammon were called to arms,
      and they encamped in Gilead,
      and gathered were the descendants of Israel,
      and they encamped at Mizpah.[i]
18   And said the people, the chiefs of Gilead,
          each man to his companion,
      "Whoever is the man who begins to wage war
          against the descendants of Ammon,
          he will be head of all those who dwell in Gilead."

a. Vat reads the name etymologically as "his uncle," while OL offers an alternate expanded epithet, "son of Ful, son of Charreon, his uncle."

b. Vat reads "thirty-two" throughout v. 4, a typical minor variation.

c. Vat reads, "Arad." OL reads, "Syria," citing the same location as MT.

d. OL consistently translates "Philistines" as "foreigners," depicting this group, as does Judges, as the "other" par excellence. Judges 10:6–7 evidences the formulaic language that unifies and frames tales of the judges (cf. 2:11–14; 3:12; 4:1–2; 6:1; 13:1). Notice the lengthy noun string typical of Late Biblical Hebrew.

e. Vat uses the same verb, *thlibō*, that carries nuances of oppression in the Vat version of the first verb of v. 8.

f. OL omits "from" so that the lengthy list of peoples is the subject of "oppress." Vat agrees more closely with MT but after the list of enemies has "those who oppressed you," implying that Israel called to God from those places. A comparison with comparable formulaic speech in 6:8–9 suggests that the word "deliver" is missing from MT. Notice, as in v. 6, the list-like set of objects: "Amorites, descendants of Ammon," etc.

g. OL omits "gods," perhaps thereby omitting the theological implications of suggesting that other gods exist, however inferior.

h. OL has, "and they served the Lord God alone and they were disheartened in the labor [a literal translation of the word translated "trouble" above] of Israel." OL thus does not reflect the more emotional, empathetic, and perhaps guilty deity represented in MT. Cf. language of covenant renewal in Josh 24:23.

i. The line includes formulaic language of battle preparation (cf. 4:10; 6:35; 7:23–24). Vat translates the place name "lookout place" from the root *sph.*

Judges 10 is an interesting and transitional chapter that begins with brief notices about two judges, Tola and Jair, and ends with a segue to the career of Jephthah. Between the opening and closing is a richly Deuteronomic-style rendition of the conventional pattern of apostasy and rehabilitation within the literary form of the lawsuit. Israel again acts in an evil way by worshiping foreign deities; God's anger follows with Israel's oppression as punishment. The people complain to God and repent. Rescue is anticipated in the role of a deliverer.

The brief annals of judges, like those of Judges 12, are different in framework, length, and content from the longer tales that surround them. For example, here as in chapter 12, the annals appear not to have "rounded out" the years of the judges' reigns (see the excellent discussion by Hackett 1998: 181–82; 185–87). Are references to Tola and Jair insertions taken from an alternate source concerning the judges to which similar material in ch. 12 belonged? Do the brief notices suggest that some of the traditions about judges were less well preserved than others? Or are they, rather, metonymic references to fuller traditions, familiar to an Israelite audience, cited here in brief for particular reasons of context or for specific compositional and thematic purposes?

The noun string in 10:6 and the subordinated constructions at 10:8 suggest a late register but also serve thematic purposes. Verse 6 emphasizes the indiscriminate apostasy of the people who serve so many deities, and v. 8 is another of the many pieces of geographic information in Judges that are presented in subordinating and list-like constructions (cf. 11:13, 22, 26, 29).

[**1–5**] The introductory frame in v. 1 is shared with comparable material in 12:8–15. The pattern of content in this little literary form is: allusion to the previous leader followed by the name of the new deliverer, his genealogical background or tribal/geographic origins, number of years that he judged, his death and place of burial (cf. vv. 1–2 concerning Tola and 12:11–12, 15 concerning Elon and Abdon). Additional information is offered in some of the annals concerning his offspring and their patrimonies, marriages, or mounts (v. 4 concerning Jair, and 12:8–9, 13–14 concerning Ibzan and Abdon, respectively). The mention of numerous sons, marriages contracted (Ibzan), donkeys on which the judges' sons rode (Jair, Abdon), and the villages named after the patriarch (Jair) are details that point to status and wealth in a traditional culture. These are the sort of stock details that characterize tales of heroes, their cultures' "big men." The conventionalized language in which these details are expressed further underscores the traditional nature of the material. Such annals may be examples of the highly stylized, breath-saving devices used in oral composition by tellers of tales who are preparing for the next big episode as they compose aloud. Perhaps this written work imitates oral accounts in this regard. For a possible inner-biblical comparison see some of the brief annals concerning individual members of David's band of warriors (2 Sam 23:8–39) and Judg 3:31 concerning Shamgar. Also relevant in this regard are Gregory Nagy's suggestions concerning "expansion" and "compression" (2003: 76) and the "even and uneven weighting" of certain episodes in traditional-style narratives (1996: 77–79). He theorizes that not only the goals of the narrator but also the expectation, interests, and demands of the receiving audience affect the weighting and relative length of pieces of content.

The places associated with the leaders of 10:1–5 are difficult to identify and locate with certainty. Shamir is perhaps to be identified with Samaria (see Boling 187); villages of Jair are placed in Gilead (1 Kgs 4:13) or Bashan (Josh 13:30); Gilead is the mountainous area in Transjordan from the river Arnon to the river Yarmuk; Boling associates Kamon with Qamm "on the Jordan-Irbid road" (188).

[6–9] This section commences with essential motifs of the lawsuit form: Israel is accused of evil; the deity responds with anger and punishment. Worship of "baals and ashtarot" are formulaic accusations of apostasy in the covenantally rich threads attributed to the voice of the theologian in, for example, 2:11, 13, and throughout ch. 6, the initiation of Gideon. The equally generic reference to gods of various peoples is interesting on grounds of style and content.

Overall language is formulaic ("serving [other gods]"; "kindled was the anger") echoing Deuteronomy and its offspring in Judges, which I have attributed to the voice of the "theologian" (see introduction, section 3). Some verses stand out as examples of a late biblical style. Judges 10:6 is characterized by noun strings. Syntax is repeated, as in traditional-style literatures, but cola are strings of nouns rather than clauses. Paul Hanson has pointed to this "prosaic" style as a marker of late material in Second Isaiah (1975: 59, 104–5). Similarly, v. 8 is characterized by the intensive use of subordinate clauses. The thought is not completed within a brief colon but phrases intertwine with subordinate phrases until the thought's completion. The point of view of the Deuteronomic-style theologian is thus here preserved in a late biblical register.

The list of sources of alien deities is especially interesting from the point of view of voice and history. Reminiscent of the list of indigenous nations (Exod 3:8; Deut 7:1; Josh 3:10; 9:1; 24:11; Judg 3:5), the nations whose gods tempt the Israelites in v. 6 are a veritable "who's who" of Israel's enemies in the book of Judges and the larger tradition. The links between these groups and the historical setting of late-second-millennium B.C.E., premonarchic Israel, a period assumed by the author, are difficult to make (see Hackett 1998: 201–6). Aram or Syria, to the northeast of Israel, was a significant political player in the late second and early first millennium B.C.E., rising to empire status in the ninth century. Even in the Hebrew Bible, its importance as rival is associated with the monarchy in Israel rather than a previous period. Thus although the reference in Judg 3:10, like that of 10:6, implies that the nation-state, Aram, is an early enemy, it is in fact an important later rival. Moab and Ammon probably existed among the various Canaanite ethnic groups in the Early Iron Age, but as Hackett notes, they probably lacked the sophisticated state-like status attributed to them by biblical writers (1998: 204–5; see also Judg 3:13). Moab is pictured as Ehud's opponent with its king, Eglon. Ammon is said to be the enemy who confronts the leader, Jephthah. The Ammonites too are said to have a king and are pictured engaging in diplomatic exchange and counterexchange with the Israelite leader. The Philistines were genuine competitors to early Israel, having arrived to the southern coast of the Mediterranean in the twelfth century B.C.E. One of the "Sea Peoples," the Philistines originated in the Aegean; their migration was occasioned by the collapse of Mycenaean civilization at the close of the Late Bronze Age. They figure prominently in the tales of Samson. Sidon, a Phoenician city mentioned as early as the fourteenth century B.C.E., in the Amarna correspondence, was probably an active participant in the economic and political competition of the period before as well as during the Israelite monarchy, for as Hackett notes, "both the Homeric epics and the Bible refer to Phoenicians as 'Sidonians'" (1998: 206).

The reference to these nations in Judges 10 invokes the larger tradition of tales of judges, and the references to the gods of Sidon and of the Philistines, in particular, seem appropriate to the historical setting drawn by the writer. Like the lists of seven or six enemy nations, however, such a catalogue serves an important and wider symbolic function. The writer seeks to identify his people Israel and its God over against cultural enemies with whom much is shared in terms of language, worldview, and geography. An excellent example is provided by Moab. As we know from the Moabite Stone (ninth century B.C.E.), Israel's language and its very theology are extremely similar to those of the Moabites (Dearman 1989). The Moabite writer describes how his god Chemosh punished his people for their sin, making them suffer militarily and politically at the hand of Israel. Having forgiven them, Chemosh allows the Moabites victory against Israel. For their part, the Moabites devote their enemies to destruction as vowed to Chemosh, killing men, women, and children. War views and worldviews thus parallel those of the Israelite writers of the Bible. The enemies list is necessary to distinguish "us" from "them." A comparable process of self-definition emerges in the tales of Samson and the Philistines. They are "the enemy" not because they are so different from Israel, as the writers would have us believe, but because they are regarded as so similar to Israel, sharing many of the same beliefs and aspirations.

[**10–16**] The conventionalized pattern of motifs and language continues (cf. 3:15; 4:3; 6:6). The confession frequently precedes requests for God's intervention on behalf of Israel (cf. Dan 9, Ezra 9, Neh 9, and the language in 1 Sam 12:10).

As in Judg 6:8–10, Yhwh recites the quintessential proofs of his covenant faithfulness, a loyalty not reciprocated by Israel. The list of enemies in vv. 11–12 is somewhat different from that of v. 6. The great enemy Egypt is added to the list, as are Amalek and Maon. Boling (192–93) links Maon to Midian, Gideon's chief opponent. Amalek, while mentioned as an ally of Moab and Ammon against Ehud in 3:13, has a lengthy biblical trajectory as a quintessential enemy of Israel (see Exod 17:8; Num 14:45; 24:20; Deut 25:17–19).

Emotional and interactive in tone, these verses emphasize the covenantal relationship between Yhwh and Israel and are similar in orientation to comparable prophetic oracles. While language of accusation, judgment, and confession are quite formulaic, the "conversation" between the deity and the people in vv. 11–15 adds a personal tone, found, for example, in the patriarchs' various debates and dealings with God. The deity's words smack of wounded feelings and resentments at v. 14. The people react with desperation and guilt at v. 15 (cf. 10:10 and 2 Sam 12:10) and seek to remedy the situation (10:1; cf. Josh 24:23). The deity's response of forgiveness in v. 16 includes the unusual, emotive, and anthropomorphic phrase, "his soul was cut to the quick."

[**17–18**] The chapter closes with the call to arms. Forgiven by the deity, the people can now face their enemy with some hope of success, but they need a leader. The search for the warrior hero is accompanied by the promise of reward as elsewhere in this bardic tradition. Saul offers his daughter's hand in marriage to the warrior who will defeat Goliath (1 Sam 17:25), while the chiefs of Gilead offer rulership and status. Similar promises and honors are conferred upon Marduk before his battle with Tiamat in the Babylonian creation account (*ANET* 60–72). The reward will be reaped by Jephthah, the next successful social bandit in the line of biblical judges.

Judges 11:1–40
Jephthah, Epic Hero

11:1   And Jephthah the Gileadite was a mighty man of valor,
         and he was the son of a whore woman,
         and Gilead begat Jephthah.

2   And the wife of Gilead bore to him sons,[a]
         and the sons of the wife[b] grew up,
         and they drove away Jephthah,
         and said they to him,

"You will not share inheritance with our paternal household,
for the son of another woman you are."[c]

3   And Jephthah fled from before his brothers,
and he dwelled in the land of Tob (Goodland),
and worthless[d] men gathered around Jephthah,
and they went forth with him.

4   And it was after a time,
the descendants of Ammon waged war with Israel.[e]

5   And when the descendants of Ammon waged war with Israel,[f]
the elders of Gilead went to take Jephthah back from the land of Tob.

6   And they said to Jephthah,
"Come and be to us chief,[g]
and let us wage war against the descendants of Ammon."

7   And said Jephthah to the elders of Gilead,
"Did you not treat me as an enemy,
and drive me out from my paternal household,
and why do you come to me now
when you are in dire straits?"

8   And the elders of Gilead said to Jephthah,
"Even so,[h] now we have returned to you.
Go with us
and wage war against the descendants of Ammon,
and you will be to us the head[i] of all who dwell in Gilead."

9   And Jephthah said to the elders of Gilead,
"If you are bringing me back
to wage war against the descendants of Ammon,
and if Yhwh gives them over to me,
I will be to you a headman."

10   And the elders of Gilead said to Jephthah,
"May Yhwh be the 'listener'[j] between us
if we do not do according to your word."[k]

11   And Jephthah went with the elders of Gilead,
and the people set him over them as headman and chief,
and Jephthah spoke all his terms
before Yhwh in Mizpah.

12   And Jephthah sent messengers
to the king of the descendants of Ammon saying,
"What is between me and you[l]
that you have come to me to wage war against my land?"

13   And the king of the descendants of Ammon said
to the messengers of Jephthah,
"Indeed, Israel took my land

when he came up from Egypt,
    from the Arnon until the Jabbok and until the Jordan.
And now, return it in peace.'"[m]

14   And again Jephthah sent messengers[n]
    to the king of the descendants of Ammon,
15   and he said to him,
"Thus says Jephthah:
Israel did not take the land of Moab
    and the land of the descendants of Ammon.
16   Rather, in their going up from Egypt,
    Israel went in the wilderness until the Red Sea,
and they came toward Kadesh.
17   And Israel sent messengers
    to the king of Edom saying,
'Let me cross, pray, over your land,'
but the king of Edom would not listen;
and also to the king of Moab they sent,
but he was not willing,
and Israel stayed in Kadesh.
18   And they made their way in the wilderness,
and they went around the land of Edom,
    and the land of Moab,
and they came to the sunrise side of the land of Moab,
and they encamped across the Arnon,[o]
and they did not go within the boundary of Moab,
for the Arnon is the boundary of Moab.
19   And Israel sent messengers to Sihon,
    king of the Amorites, king of Heshbon,
and said to him Israel,
'Let us cross, pray, over your land, to our destination.'
20   And Sihon did not trust Israel
    to cross over his boundary,
and Sihon gathered all his people,
and they encamped in Jahaz
and waged war against Israel.
21   And Yhwh, god of Israel, gave over
    Sihon and all his people,
        into the hand of Israel.
And he struck him,
and Israel took possession
    of all the land of the Amorites
        who were dwelling in that land.

22 And they took possession of all the boundary of the Amorites,[p]
    from the Arnon to the Jabbok[q]
    and from the wilderness to the Jordan.
23 And now Yhwh, God of Israel,
    has dispossessed the Amorites
        for the sake of his people Israel,
    and you would take possession of us!
24 Is it not the case that whatever Chemosh your god dispossesses for you,
    it you should possess,
    and all that Yhwh our god dispossesses for our sake,
        it we should possess?
25 And now, are you good and better than Balak son of Zippor,
    king of Moab?
    Did he quarrel a quarrel with Israel?
    Did he wage a war against them?
26 While Israel dwelled in Heshbon and its suburbs,
    and in Aroer and its suburbs,
    and in all the towns that are next to the Arnon,[r]
        for three hundred years,
    why did you not engage in recovery[s] in that time?
27 And I, I have not sinned against you,
    but you are doing me wrong
        to wage war against me.
    Let Yhwh the judge judge today[t]
        between the descendants of Israel
            and between the descendants of Ammon."
28 And the king of the descendants of Ammon would not listen
    to the words of Jephthah
        that he had sent to him.
29 And there was upon Jephthah the spirit of Yhwh,[u]
    and he crossed over to Gilead and to Manasseh,
    and he crossed to Mizpah of Gilead,
    and from Mizpah of Gilead
        he crossed over to the descendants of Ammon.
30 And Jephthah vowed a vow to Yhwh and he said,[v]
    "If give you give the descendants of Ammon into my hand,
31   and it will be: the emerging thing that emerges[w]
        from the doors of my house to meet me,
            upon my returning in peace
                from the descendants of Ammon,
        shall be for Yhwh,
    and I shall offer it up as a whole burnt offering."

32   And Jephthah crossed over to the descendants of Ammon,
        to wage war against them,
    and Yhwh gave them into his hand.

33   And he struck them from Aroer until the vicinity of Minnith,
        twenty towns,
        and until Abel-keramim (Greenland of the Vineyards),
            a very great striking,
    and the descendants of Ammon were humbled
        before the descendants of Israel.

34   And Jephthah went to Mizpah, to his home base.
    And behold, his daughter was coming forth
        to greet him with timbrels and whirling dances.
    And only she was the one.[x]
    No others did he have but her,
        son or daughter.

35   And it was[y] when he saw her,
        he tore his garment,
    and he said,
    "Alas, my daughter.
    Causing me to kneel, you have knelt me down.
    You have become (enmeshed) in my troubles.[z]
    And I have opened my mouth to Yhwh,
    and I cannot turn back."

36   And she said to him,
    "My father, you have opened your mouth to Yhwh.
    Do according to what came forth from your mouth,
    now that Yhwh has done for you
        acts of vengeance upon your enemies,
            upon the descendants of Ammon."

37   And she said to her father,
    "Let this thing be done[aa] for me.
    Allow me two months,
    and I will go,
    and I will go down into the mountains,
    and I will cry over my maidenhood,[bb]
        myself and my companions."

38   And he said, "Go."
    And he sent her for two months.
    And she went, she and her companions,
    and she cried over her maidenhood upon the mountains.

39   And it was at the end of two months,
    and she returned to her father,

and he did to her the vow that he had vowed.

And she had never known a man.

And it became a rule in Israel:

40   From year to year,

the daughters of Israel would go[cc]

to tell[dd] of the daughter of Jephthah the Gileadite,

four days each year.

a. OL omits "wife . . . sons" and includes a traditional-style expansion of the tale that has much in common with the story of Sarah, Abraham, and Hagar in Gen 21: "And the wife said to her husband, 'Throw these from my face.'" Could Gilead have had several illegitimate children in other versions?

b. OL reads, "husband."

c. OL uses the phrase "fornicating woman." Vat reads, "courtesan" (*hetairas*), a term that sounds like the Greek word for "other" (*heteras*). Cf. the play between *zānâ* ("harlot") and *zārâ* ("strange woman") that appears in Proverbs and its manuscript traditions. Do OL and Vat reflect an underlying Hebrew text different from MT, a conscious play on words in the Greek, or an accepted cultural gloss whereby "other woman" has sexual connotations? All the possibilities are within the realm of the traditional.

d. Literally, "empty," as in Vat. OL reads, "Thieves gathered to him and they dwelt with him," an alternate image of the social bandit.

e. Notice the repetition of the formulaic language of military engagement in vv. 4, 5, 8, 12, 32, 33 (cf. ch. 1).

f. The clause "when . . . Israel," which repeats the end of v. 4, is omitted in Vat.

g. The term for "chief" used here and in v. 11 is an unusual one, perhaps derived from the root "to cut off," from which comes a word for "end" (*qṣh*). Is the leader one who separates one matter from another, that is, one who decides?

h. Hebrew *lākēn* frequently means "Therefore." Here the phrase operates in a different connective fashion.

i. Notice the recurring language of leadership.

j. Literally, "the one who listens," Yhwh is pictured as the witness to a vow, a legally binding transaction.

k. Cf. 1 Sam 24:16 and the language of law. OL reads, "The Lord is he who will hear among us that we do according to your word."

l. Formulaic language, indicating dispute or "repudiation" (so BDB 553). Literally, "What is there to me and to you." See also contexts in 2 Sam 16:10; 19:23; 1 Kgs 17:18; 2 Kgs 3:13. Cf. Josh 22:24.

m. Vat adds, "And I will go."

n. OL adds, "And the messengers returned to Jephthah." The message delivered in the following verses recounts an oft-told tale in the Hebrew Bible concerning the postexodus route and encounters of the Israelites. Variants are found in Num 20–21 and Deut 2 (see also Josh 12:1–5). The versions share formulaic language (e.g., "let us cross," Judg 11:17, 19; Num 20:17, 21; Deut 2:27) and exhibit variation in language and content.

o. OL reads, "in Transjordan," i.e., across the Jordan.

p. Vat and OL omit, "And they took possession . . . Amorites."

q. OL adds, "up to the boundary of the sons of Ammon."

r. Vat and OL read, "Jordan." Notice variations among the rivers cited throughout.

s. The term for "recovery" is from the root translated elsewhere literally as "to save."

t. OL turns the preceding section into an oracle with the formula, "The Lord says who judges today. . . ."

u. Formulaic language for the descent of the divinely sent charisma that is the source of the warrior's prowess and other forms of leadership (3:10; 13:25; 14:6, 19; 15:14; Num 24:2; 1 Sam 10:6, 10; 11:6; 16:13).

v. The formulaic language of vow making as in Gen 28:20; Deut 23:22. See, in particular, the war vow in Num 21:2.

w. Vat and OL translate to indicate that the "emerging one" is a person.

x. A and OL add "his beloved," influenced by the other child sacrifice in Gen 22:2 and perhaps by early Christian interpretations of that scene.

y. OL adds "immediately," increasing the drama of the scene.

z. Vat employs the same verb, in poetic economy, throughout the verse: "troubling me, you have troubled me and you are in my troubles." OL reads, "you have entangled me/tripped me up and have become deprived (of life) before my eyes" (i.e., "taken from before my eyes"). MT reads literally, "you are in my troubles."

aa. Vat reads, "Let my father do this thing."

bb. Vat translates "youth/maidenhood," emphasizing the age aspect of the word, literally, "virgin." OL translates "virginalia," "things appropriate to a girl of marriageable age."

cc. Notice repetition of the term "to go" in vv. 37–40.

dd. Vat reads or glosses in translation, "to bewail/sing a dirge," and OL reads, "to utter cries of lament," emphasizing an additional aspect of the girls' ritual action.

A complex hero-judge, Jephthah is portrayed in this chapter as a social bandit who begins his career as an outcast. He is a politically savvy negotiator who makes a case for a just war, and a tragic hero who loses his daughter because of a war-vowed sacrifice to God. Themes of kinship, gender, leadership, and group unity/disunity inform the tales of Jephthah, a collection that is very much at home in the corpus of Judges and that points to foundational and defining issues in Israelite worldview.

Disenjambed, whole clauses shape the texture of ch. 11. As seen earlier, however, geographic descriptions, place lists or itineraries, are in a register rich in strings of nouns or sets of prepositional phrases and their objects (cf. 11:13, 22, 26, 29 and, e.g., 1:18, 27, 31; 10:8). Also notable are the complex constructions in 11:30–31, 40. Verses 30–31 feature conditional syntax (cf. 6:13, 17 and 9:17–18) in which the speaker, Jephthah, describes a future situation, and v. 40 describes a perpetual custom. Such rhetoric in both cases is designed to slow down the readerly process and thereby highlight the central content, namely, the vow that leads to the sacrifice of the daughter and the yearly ritual occasioned by her sacrifice. The reader, speaker, or listener is purposefully made to pause over these pieces of content.

[**1–11**] Jephthah is described in the warrior idiom as "a man of valor." His personal history, like that of many biblical heroes, traces a pattern from early rejection and low status to leadership. Rivalry between brothers is a theme of Jephthah's life, as it is in the careers of Cain and Abel, Ishmael and Isaac, Jacob and Esau, David and his brothers, and David's sons. The success of the unlikely son, be he the youngest or the one unlikely to inherit for some other reason, is a traditional folk motif rooted in the reality of patrilineal cultures. The theme serves to reinforce a message about the serendipitous power of the deity to select whom he will and is a symbolic counterbalance to controlling social structures and institutions.

As the outcast son of a harlot, banished by his paternal kin, Jephthah becomes a "primitive rebel." Like David, Abimelech, and Jeroboam, he gathers around himself a band of military ruffians, men outside the institutional power base. The image of the hero surrounded by the outcasts of society is typical of the careers of successful bandit heroes (cf. Abimelech, 9:4; the displaced Danites, 18:25; and Jeroboam, 2 Chron 13:6 7).

When the Ammonites threaten, Jephthah's skills as a warrior bandit are newly appreciated by his kin in Gilead, and he is welcomed back as a savior. As in the tales of Abimelech (ch. 9) and the civil war of chs. 19–21, power is intimately related to matters of kinship, as variously defined, whether the connection leads to cooperation or to conflict.

[**12–28**] Gilead, meaning "rugged," "of hill country/mountain range" (BDB 166), was the forest-filled area in Transjordan between the Arnon and Yarmuk rivers. While foundation myths that purport to relate Israel's earliest history assign control of this land to "Amorites," it was apparently later under the control of or claimed by Ammon, hence the dispute in ch. 11. Some commentators, such as Boling, have examined 11:12–28 to uncover historical matters of territorial import, while others, such as Soggin, have been more concerned with redactional questions involving the pericope itself and its relationship to variants in Numbers 21–22 and Deuteronomy 2. These verses provide another example of traditional lore. Jephthah's words allude to the encounter with Balak in Numbers 22–24 that includes the fanciful and poetically rich tale of the internationally recognized prophet Balaam, hired to curse the Israelites. The interaction between Sihon and Moses, appearing several times in the biblical corpus, points to critical concerns: questions about divine right to the land and the desire to demarcate ancient boundaries; reflections upon Israel's relationships with neighboring peoples; and the desire to portray the people Israel as good international citizens. Especially interesting is the spin that each context gives the story, thereby revealing particular composers' interests and points of view.

In Num 21:23 and Judg 11:19, Sihon himself refuses to let Israel "cross over" and then mounts an assault. In Deuteronomy 2 the Lord has hardened Sihon's heart, causing him to refuse passage to the Israelites. This version emphasizes divine control and draws implicit comparisons between Sihon and the pharaoh of the exodus. Deuteronomy 2 emphasizes kinship among Israel's neighbors. The people are ordered not to engage Edom, Moab, or Ammon in battle because the first was Jacob's brother and the last two were the sons of Lot, promised land by the deity. Accounts in Judges and Numbers are more coolly political. In the versions in Numbers 20 and Judg 11:17, Edom is formulaically asked for safe passage but refuses. In the version at Num 20:20–21, a more antagonistic Edom not only refuses Israel safe passage but prepares an attack so that the Israelites turn away. This aggressiveness is nowhere to be found in Deuteronomy 2. Indeed, Moses' speech in Deut 2:29 suggests that Esau did let Israel pass and that Sihon should follow suit. In Deuteronomy kinship among those whom Israelites regard as sharing their foundation myths, divine control, and Israel's success in God's plan are emphasized. Versions in Judges 11 and Numbers 20, by contrast, cast the enemy strongly in terms of "us versus them," as befits tales of epic warriors.

Jephthah's words to the king of Ammon include some culturally informative details. Chemosh is treated as the national god of Ammon, although he is most centrally the national deity of the Moabites. The passage seems to conflate Moabite and Ammonite in this detail, as in the larger historical overview. The comment on Chemosh suggests the belief that such gods do exist. They may succeed in battle on behalf of their nations, a situation described by an actual Moabite king in an inscription of the ninth century B.C.E., commemorating the victory of Chemosh for his people, from a Moabite perspective (see Dearman 1989). The passage also makes reference to a particular time frame, counting three hundred years of occupation since the days of Moses.

Sites that figure in this section include Tob or "Goodland" (11:3, 5), a Syrian town (cf. 2 Sam 10:6–8); Heshbon (11:26), a town east of the Jordan River; and Aroer (v. 26), perhaps meaning "crest of a mountain" or "juniper." Aroer frequently refers to a fortress on the northern rim of the Arnon River, a site that has led archaeologists to some evidence for the Late Bronze Age, but the location mentioned in v. 33 and Josh 13:25 may refer to a different site south of Amman, not yet excavated (see Mattingly 1992a). The river Arnon, sometimes coupled with formulaic partners, the Jabbok and/or the Jordan (11:22), is an important marker of the territorial borders in Israelite tradition. See Num 21:13–14, 28; 22:36; Deut 2:24, 36.

The exchange between Jephthah and the king of Ammon reflects a particular attitude to war. Jephthah's insistence that Israel is no aggressor, fighting only when provoked, suggests the concern with just cause. Similarly, Jephthah points to Israel's long-term, unchallenged possession of the disputed land as proof of ownership. Right is on his side. Victory in war, moreover, entitles the victor to conquered land and reflects the power of the victor's deity.

The eloquent, traditional style of Jephthah's speech with its formulaic renditions of history, rhetorical questions, recurring language, and emphatic flourishes ("And I . . . ," 11:27) contributes to Jephthah's characterization as a capable leader who knows his rights and defends his people. The language and literary form, moreover, are informed by juridical language and motifs such as the opening question in v. 12, the disclaimer at v. 27, and the reference to Yhwh as adjudicator in v. 27. Exchanges involve the sending of emissaries and waiting for responses in a formal diplomatic exchange.

Some scholars consider this very positive portrayal to be at odds with the subsequent tale of a man who makes a rash oath; in fact, the two parts of ch. 11 are consistent. The tale of Jephthah's daughter, poignant and troubling, has to do with keeping one's word in a culture of vow making and covenants. The important social and political relationship is between the men, that is, Jephthah and the male deity, and it models such relationships between human men in which women serve as valuable exchange items and mediators.

[**29–40**] "The spirit of Yhwh" (11:29), powerful, empowering, dangerous, and difficult to control, endows the hero with the charisma to defeat his enemics and confront other challenges; it is a criterion of various kinds of leadership roles including judgeship, prophetic status, and kingship. In Judges and in the cases of Jephthah and Samson, the descent of the spirit prepares the hero for battle (see 3:10 concerning Othniel, and 13:25; 14:6, 19; 15:14 concerning Samson).

The vow (11:30) is another piece of preparation for war. As in Num 21:2–3, the warrior promises a sacrifice of some sort to God in exchange for victory in battle. The war ideology of the ban by which whole populations and towns are destroyed as a "whole burnt offering" to Yhwh (see Deut 13:16) is integrally related to an ideology of sacrifice. The deity receives the best of the spoil, and no spoil is more valuable than human spoil (see Niditch 1993b: 28–55; and cf. Josh 7; 1 Sam 15; and 1 Kgs 20:35–43). Much has been written in recent decades about the possibility that human sacrifice was practiced in ancient Israel (see Mosca 1975; J. Day 1989; Levenson 1993; Niditch 1993b: 46–49; and polemics in Lev 18:21; 20:2–5; Deut 12:31; 18:10; Jer 7:30–31; 19:5). The authors of Genesis 22 and this passage understand that all life is God's to bestow or take back. Later in the tradition, martyrdom comes to be understood as efficacious because on some level God accepts human sacrifice. Implicit in the war vows in Num 21:2–3 and Judg 11:30 are threads in this deep mythological understanding of the way life works.

As in some tellings of the European tale "Beauty and the Beast," the object to be offered in exchange for the protagonist's success or release is left dramatically ambiguous: "whatever you first see upon returning home." The reader/listener, steeped in the tradition, knows that the daughter will emerge, but such knowledge only increases the pathos and the anticipation. The specific location of sites, Minnith and Abel-keramim ("Greenland of the Vineyards"), mentioned in v. 33, is uncertain (see Boling 208).

The role of women as musical celebrants of their men's victory is a common biblical motif as in the traditions of the "songs" of Miriam and Deborah. See the scene at 2 Sam 18:6–7. The case has been made that Jephthah should have or must have known who would greet him. He is thus either a rash fool or a conscious practitioner of human sacrifice, like the Moabite king of 2 Kgs 3:26–27. Others suggest that Jephthah blames his victim for his troubles, viewing v. 35 as an accusation. The narrative itself contains no such value judgment. Jephthah, a hero caught up in the agonistic divine spirit, makes a not untypical war vow, one that he fully comprehends on a mundane and tragic level only in the wake of war. The vow obligates Jephthah and his daughter, who is portrayed as accepting her role in a world controlled by men, to a particular course of action. In the hands of a different biblical author, such vows can be abrogated (see concerning Saul and Jonathan at 1 Sam 14:45). The daughter must be sacrificed because this tale is really about a special sort of sacrifice.

As beautifully explored by Peggy Day (1989), the foundation myth in ch. 11 has an important social function and is presented as the motivation for a women's ritual in ancient Israel, one mentioned nowhere else in the Bible. Like C. F. Burney (334), Day draws useful comparisons with Greek traditions concerning Iphigeneia and Kore-Persephone. Comparison with tales such as "Beauty and the Beast" is again relevant. Set in a warring context, the tale of Jephthah's daughter has wider significance for the rites of passage experienced by all young women of marriageable age in traditional cultures. On some level, the woman is to be sacrificed to the "Beast," the male to whom she is given in exchange by her own men, father or brothers. Her "sacrifice" confirms the relationship between these men. In Judges the males involved in exchange are the deity and the hero.

Day notes that the term often translated "virgin," here "maiden," sometimes refers in Hebrew and cognate languages to a woman who has not yet "known" a man, a physical virgin, but always to a nubile woman, a youth, who has not yet taken on responsibilities of wife and mother (see also Walls 1992: 77–79). Age and place in the life cycle are the critical factors. The women in the ritual are mourning the end of their old status as daughters while preparing for their new status with the full range of female adult responsibilities. Life passages such as these are marked in the myths and rituals of many cultures. The range of European tales describing women snatched from home and kept in a tower ("Rapunzel"), or falling into a death-like sleep ("Sleeping Beauty" and "Snow White") all underline the critical passage in the lives of women. The sleep, the stay in the tower, and the temporary death all symbolize the "liminal phase" in such passages that effect transformation (Turner 1969).

Thus a tale of war that helps to shape Israelite concepts of their foundation in the land also becomes the origin myth that establishes a life-shaping ritual for young women and their families. This "return to beginnings," to borrow a phrase from Mircea Eliade, has to do with the formation of critical relationships between men, formed by the giving up of daughters, a process that supports androcentric social structures. The tale, however, like "Beauty and the Beast" and the other European folktales about girls in passage, allows one to empathize with the young heroine and with her father. The tale might also be read from the woman's perspective. The daughter, although unnamed, speaks her mind and creates her own ritual, albeit fully within the contours of a particular patriarchal system that she is portrayed as supporting.

Judges 12:1–15
Internecine Strife and Brief Annals of Ibzan, Elon, and Abdon

12:1 And the men of Ephraim[a] were called out
and they crossed northward,
and they said to Jephthah,
"Why did you cross to wage war with the descendants of Ammon,
and us you did not call to go with you?
Your home base we will burn upon you with fire."

2 And Jephthah said to them,
"I was a man involved in an egregious dispute,[b]
myself, my people, and the descendants of Ammon,
and I called out to you,[c]
and you did not deliver me from their hand.

3 And I saw that you were not acting as deliverer,[d]
and I put my life in my palm,[e]
and I crossed over to the descendants of Ammon,
and Yhwh gave them into my hand.
And why have you come up to me[f]
this day to wage war against me?"

4 And Jephthah gathered all the men of Gilead,
and Jephthah waged war against Ephraim,
and the men of Gilead struck down Ephraim,
for they said, "Fugitives of Ephraim are you, Gilead,
in the midst of Ephraim, in the midst of Manasseh."[g]

5 And Gilead captured the fords of the Jordan against Ephraim.
And when the fugitives of Ephraim would say,
"Let me cross,"

the men of Gilead would say to him,
"An Ephraimite are you?"
And he would say, "No."

6   And they would say to him,
"Say, pray, 'shibboleth,'"[h]
and he would say "sibboleth."
And he could not accomplish[i] to say it thus,
and they would seize him and slaughter him
    at the fords of the Jordan.
And from Ephraim fell at that time
    forty-two thousand.

7   And Jephthah judged Israel for six years,[j]
and Jephthah the Gileadite died,
and he was buried in the towns of Gilead.[k]

8   And Ibzan from Bethlehem judged Israel after him.

9   And there were to him thirty sons.
And thirty daughters he sent outside,
and thirty daughters he brought in for his sons from outside.
And he judged Israel for seven years.

10   And Ibzan died,
and he was buried in Bethlehem.

11   And after him, Elon the Zebulunite judged Israel,
and he judged Israel for ten years.

12   And Elon the Zebulunite died,
and he was buried in Aijalon in the land of Zebulun.[l]

13   And judge Israel after him did Abdon,
    son of Hillel the Pirathonite.

14   And there were to him forty sons and thirty grandsons
    who rode on seventy donkeys.
And he judged Israel for eight years.

15   And Abdon died,
    son of Hillel the Pirathonite,
and he was buried in Pirathon in the land of Ephraim,
    in the hill country of the Amalekites.

a. Vat reads, "cried out." OL begins with the variant, "The sons of Ephraim gathered together, and they went." The term in MT, literally, "to call out," is technical language for battle muster, as at 10:17.

b. Literally, "a man of quarreling/contention." The language of lawsuit is here applied to the political dispute that leads to war. The same root is used in the tale of Gideon to describe the hero's quarrel with Baal and provides the folk etymology for Gideon's new name (6:31–32).

Vat reads, "I was a fighter," which may imply a different Hebrew term, or it may be a gloss on "man of quarreling." OL includes a variant, "I was an opponent, and my people (also), and the sons of Ammon humiliated me exceedingly."

c. A variant of the term translated "called out" in v. 1. The language is formulaic for calling out troops of a military alliance (see 10:17).

d. OL omits "And I saw . . . deliverer."

e. English equivalent: "I took my life in my own hands."

f. Formulaic language for entrance into war, as in ch. 1 and throughout.

g. OL omits "For they said . . . Manasseh."

h. Vat translates literally, "ear of corn." The term may also mean "flowing waters."

i. The term in MT, from the root meaning "to be established," is difficult to translate smoothly and literally. Vat reads, "He could not succeed to speak thus." OL reads, "Give us a sign, and their ways of speaking did not agree."

j. Vat reads, "sixty years."

k. OL and Vat read, "in his city, in Gilead."

l. OL reads, "And Elon the Zebulunite died in Elim, and they buried him in Zebulun."

Judges 12 is composed of two parts. Verses 1–7 describe a dispute between the Gileadites and the Ephraimites that follows the battle with Ammon. This example of inner-Israelite strife highlights the weaknesses of epic models of leadership and polity and points to the ethnographic differences between two groups of Israelites. It continues the portrayal of Jephthah as a local chieftain who defends his power against other Israelite groups who would challenge him. Verses 8–15 are a brief catalogue of judges, a set of annals comparable in style, language, and content to the list in ch. 10 (see commentary on 10:1–5).

In terms of style, self-contained lines, often full clauses, allow for the chapter to be arranged nicely in cola. Language of going to war, battle, and victory is formulaic and found throughout the book.

[1–7] The Ephraimites accuse Jephthah of not including them in the battle with Ammon, presumably thereby denying them a share of booty. True to character, Jephthah claims justice is on his side: he had called them to battle but they did not respond. The account of the defeat of Ammon in ch. 11, as written, does not include mention of such a call. Is Jephthah portrayed as lying or is a call to arms assumed to be that which the leader does in such a decentralized political system? In any event, the conflict between his men and the Ephraimites points to the weaknesses of such a confederation and the difficulty of maintaining group unity. In a similar situation with Ephraimites, Gideon skillfully averts a skirmish with fellow Israelites (see 8:1–3). Here the two sides come to blows.

Judges 12:4 appears to include an accusation or taunt hurled at the Gileadites by the Ephraimites. The taunt questions the status of the Gileadites and suggests an identity as outsiders or refugees, not "original" to the area. Such accusations are common in ethnic disputes between groups who share or vie for the same resources.

For their part, the Gileadites identify the Ephraimites as speaking an alien dialect, unable to pronounce *sh* properly in their view. Various historical linguistic suggestions have been offered to explain the dialectical difference between pronunciations of the word beginning with *š/s* (see Speiser 1967).

Linguistic variation is a critical marker of difference in the story of the tower of Babel (Gen 11:7–9). Similarly, biblical prophets describe the enemy as people "of obscure speech and difficult language" (Ezek 3:5, 6) or of speaking "a language you do not know" (Jer 5:15). One who is regarded as strange and not to be trusted speaks in "an alien tongue" (Isa 28:11). Judges 12:6 is one of the few places in the Hebrew Bible in which the author consciously distinguishes between accents or dialects. Such differences are of great enthnographic significance and further testify to Israelite awareness concerning the "mixed multitude" that constituted the people. Some of the deepest animus is reserved for fellow Israelites in the book of Judges.

[**8–15**] The language, contents, literary form, and possible context of these brief annals about judges are discussed in 10:1–3, which appears to share a genre with the material in 12:7–15. Of note in v. 9 is the emphasis on the exchange of women, a theme important to the larger book (e.g., Achsah, Jephthah's daughter, the stolen wives of ch. 21). The judge's capacity to arrange for such exchanges on a large scale testifies to his status. The contrast between bringing women in from outside and sending women outside suggests exogamous arrangements, but it is unclear how far "outside" the group the author implies. As in 10:1–3, the judges' reigns last various, relatively short lengths of time in contrast to the lengthy, rounded out periods of rulership mentioned for other judges. Hackett perceives this difference to be an indicator of separate sources (1998: 184). As for all judges, the peaceful patrilocal burial betokens the end of a respected career.

Judges 13:1–25
The Birth Story of Samson, Superhero

13:1   And the descendants of Israel again acted
      to do evil in the eyes of Yhwh.
   And Yhwh gave them into the hands of the Philistines
      for forty years.[a]

2   And there was a certain man from Zorah[b]
      from the clan of the Danites,
  and his name was Manoah.
  And his woman[c] was barren,
  and she had not given birth.[d]

3   And the messenger of Yhwh appeared to the woman,
     and he said to her,
     "Behold, you are barren
     and have not given birth,
     but you are pregnant,[e]
     and will give birth to a son.
4   And now, keep on your guard, pray,
     and do not drink wine or strong drink,
     and do not eat anything unclean,[f]
5   for behold, you are pregnant,
     and will give birth to a son,[g]
     and a razor will not go up upon his head,
     for the lad will be a *Nazir* to God from the womb,[h]
     and he will begin to deliver Israel
          from the hand of the Philistines."[i]
6   And the woman went,
     and she said to her man, saying,
     "A man of God came to me,
     and his appearance was like the appearance of the messenger of God,
          exceedingly awe-inspiring.
     I did not ask where he was from,[j]
     and his name he did not tell me.
7   And he said to me,
     'Behold, you are pregnant[k]
     and will give birth to a son,
     and now do not drink wine or strong drink,
     and do not eat anything unclean,
     for the lad will be a *Nazir* of God,[l]
          from the womb until the day of his death.' "
8   And Manoah made supplication to Yhwh,
     and said, "Please,[m] Lord,
     the man of God whom you sent,
          may he come, pray, again to us, and teach us
               what we should do for the lad to be born."
9   And God listened to the voice of Manoah,
     and the messenger of God again went to the woman.
     And she was sitting in the open country,
     and Manoah her man was not with her.
10   And the woman hurried,
     and she ran and told her man,
     and she said to him,
     "Behold, appeared to me the man

who came today to me."

11   And Manoah rose and went after his woman,
      and he went to the man,
      and he said to him,
      "Are you the man who spoke to the woman?"
      And he said, "I am."

12   And said Manoah,
      "Now, should your words come to be,
           what will be the rule[n] of the lad and his deeds?"

13   And the messenger of Yhwh said to Manoah,
      "Of everything that I said to the woman she shall keep guard.

14   Of everything that comes from the vine of wine she shall not eat,
      and wine and strong drink she shall not drink,
      and all unclean things she shall not eat.
      All that I command her she shall keep."

15   And Manoah said to the messenger of Yhwh,
      "Let us, pray, detain you,
      and make ready before you a she-goat kid."

16   And the messenger of Yhwh said to Manoah,
      "If you would detain me, I will not eat your bread,
      and if you would make a burnt offering, send it up to Yhwh,"
      for Manoah did not know
           that a messenger of Yhwh was he.

17   And Manoah said to the messenger of Yhwh,
      "What is your name,
           so that, if your words come to be, we may honor you?"

18   And the messenger of Yhwh said to him,
      "Why do you ask concerning my name,
      for it is wonderful."

19   And Manoah took the she-goat kid and the grain offering,
      and he raised (them) upon the rock to Yhwh—
           he who makes things wondrous[o]—
      and Manoah and his wife were watching.

20   And it was as the flame arose from upon the altar skyward,
           that the messenger of Yhwh went upward in the flame of the altar,
      and Manoah and his woman were watching,
      and they fell on their faces to the ground.

21   And the messenger of Yhwh did not again act
           to appear to Manoah and his woman.
      Then Manoah knew
           that a messenger of Yhwh was he.

22   And Manoah said to his woman,

> "Die, we will surely die,
> for God we have seen."

23   And his woman said to him.
> "If Yhwh desired to kill us,
>> he would not have taken from our hands
>>> a burnt offering and a grain offering,
>> and would not have shown us all this,
>> and now he would not have had us hear things such as these."

24   And the woman gave birth to a son,
> and she called his name Samson,[p]
> and the lad grew up,
> and Yhwh blessed him.[q]

25   And the spirit of Yhwh began to impel him,[r]
> in the encampment of Dan
>> between Zorah and Eshtaol.

a. Cf. 10:6 for comparable formulaic language typical of the voice of the theologian. OL commonly translates "Philistines" as foreigners. See 10:6 and 13:5.

b. The phrase "There was a man" is found densely in Judges–2 Samuel (Judg 13:2; 17:1; 19:1; 1 Sam 1:1; 9:1; 2 Sam 21:20 [1 Chron 20:6]) and introduces a figure who will be part of an important founding myth, often the hero's progenitor (Samson's father, Manoah, in Judg 13:2; Samuel's father in 1 Sam 1:1; Saul's father in 1 Sam 9:1), other times the key player in a series of events in the foundation tale (Judg 17:1; 19:1; 2 Sam 21:20). See Amit 1984/85.

c. The term could be translated "wife," but the most basic root meaning is offered here.

d. Information about the woman's condition is repeated in traditional style in vv. 3, 5, and 7.

e. Vat reads, "You will conceive a son," omitting the verb "give birth" in the next line. Similar language is employed in the annunciation in Luke 1:31.

f. See vv. 7 and 14 for traditional-style repetition of the messenger's instructions.

g. Vat translates in the present tense as above: "And behold, you have in your womb and you will bear a son." Luke 1:31 reads, "You will conceive in your womb and you will bear a son." OL reads future tense.

h. Notice the repetition of this important piece of information in v. 7.

i. See 13:1 on "Philistines."

j. OL reads, "I was asking him where he came from," a typical question to pose to a mysterious traveling stranger, one that elicits a long and fictive story from the divine helpers in Tob 5:5 and *Odyssey* 1.169–70. MT and Vat, however, frame the tale with a sense of fear and awe as the woman keeps her questions to herself. A small detail, the presence or absence of the negative, thus lends a different nuance to the narrative.

k. Vat reads in the present, "You are pregnant." OL reads the future tense, "You will conceive."

l. Vat translates *nāzîr* as "a holy one of God." The term has the nuance of consecration, dedication, and separation. Cf. Luke 1:35. OL reads *nazareos*, the term that is found in the Latin translation of Matt 2:23 concerning Jesus.

m. Vat literalizes the idiom *bî*, "in me." OL makes sense of the phrase to convey the nuance, "let him come to me," creating the gender-conscious impression that the husband demands that the visitor deal with him.

n. The term translated "rule" employs the same root as the word "judge." One might translate, "his judgment" or "his manner."

o. Vat reads from the root *plh*, "and he separated to do" or "went apart."

p. The root "sun" with an ancient adjectival ending: "Sunny One, Sun Child."

q. OL reads, "And the Lord blessed the son and he grew up," a minor variant.

r. Or "move him," literally, from the root "to do, make."

The brief theologian's frame in v. 1 is followed by one of the Bible's many "annunciation" scenes, instances in which the deity interacts directly with women concerning their children's future (Hagar: Gen 16; 21:8–21; Sarah: 18:9–15; Rebekah: 25:22–23). The relationship between the divine being and the woman is defined by themes of fertility and generation; such matters are critical to the foundation and future of the people. The expressed barrenness of the wife of Manoah foreshadows the birth of a hero as in the cases of Sarah (Gen 18), Rebekah (25:21–28), Rachel (29:31), and Hannah (1 Sam 1:2). A form of theophany, the annunciation often includes: the news for the woman, delivered by the deity or his emissary; particular instructions and information about the boy; an offering of sacrifice; the allusion to a divine name or identity; a miraculous passage revealing or sealing the importance of the event; and an expression of awe or fear on the part of those who experience the visitation. Judges 6:11–24 provides a close parallel to the theophany in ch. 13.

The style of the chapter is economically repetitive and the text easy to lay out in self-contained cola, with little subordination and no lengthy noun strings. The author does frequently begin a thought with a conditional phrase, lengthening the completion of the thought and leading to the creation of drama and anticipation in this theophanic scene (see, e.g., vv. 12, 17, 23; and cf. 6:13, 17; 9:16–18; and 11:30–31). Overall, Judges 13 is richly traditional in style and content, leading Polak (1998) to suggest that this and other tales of Samson are excellent examples of classical Hebrew that he regards as rooted in the oral end of the linguistic spectrum.

[1–2] The covenantal theme concerning Israel's unfaithfulness requires a mere verse, as the text quickly moves to the cycle of tales concerning the hero Samson. It is often remarked that the woman bears no name, and yet she is central to the action. Some scholars, such as Esther Fuchs (1985), find propaganda in favor of male dominance in biblical annunciations, suggesting they reinforce stereotypical female roles and make it seem as if women approve of them. There is no doubt that an androcentric culture governs such stories and that the author has great interest in the background of the male hero. Nevertheless, within the admittedly limiting contours of this culture, Manoah's wife is shown to be worthy of divine information, more worthy than her dolt of a husband. As in many traditional cultures, the empowerment of women takes place within the system and is imagined within stereotypical roles.

[3–5] The messenger is not described in this first allusion. His words not only reveal that the woman has conceived and will bear a son but also instruct her to create a Nazirite environment for the fetus in the womb. She is not to imbibe intoxicants or eat nonkosher food. As a sign of his special, sacred, and charismatic status, the child is never to have his hair cut. The avoidance of alcoholic beverages, created by a cultural process and so important to social interaction, and the prohibition concerning haircutting imply an immersion into the nature side of a nature/culture dichotomy. To be holy on some level is to be apart from the social and cultural. The contrast between nature and culture is at play in the larger cycle of stories about Samson, although one must be careful not to overdraw this contrast. The very definition of the "natural" is rooted in culture, as is the act of prohibiting one sort of food and allowing others.

Numbers 6 describes in priestly detail the ritual passage involved in the voluntary assumption of Nazirite status by means of a vow. The voluntary Nazirite vows to avoid wine and grape products, to eschew contact with the dead, and to allow the hair to grow freely. The priestly version of Nazirite status, available to both women and men, is a late democratizing form of nonhereditary and temporary holiness; no charisma is involved. Samson's status, like that attributed to Samuel (1 Sam 1:11, 22), another great warrior hero who was the son of a barren women, is, however, a sign of divine favor, a boon from God to certain male heroes who manifest prophetic and other forms of charismatic leadership (see also Kaufmann 142). Thus Amos 2:11–12 has the deity declare: "And I raised up from among your sons some to be prophets / and from among your young men some to be *nĕzirîm*." As in Numbers 6, Samson's form of holiness is nonhereditary in contrast to priestly leadership; it is potentially explosive and differs from the tamed version of the phenomenon described in Numbers 6.

The Nazirite status of Samson, which emphasizes a God-sent charisma, aligns him with other judges of the tradition. He is not an unusual judge if one realizes that "to judge" in Judges is not to sit soberly at court. Judges make decisions based upon divine inspiration. They command respect as leaders because of the perception that the spirit of God is within them, and their battle prowess sometimes places them on the outer borders of sanity. Samson takes his place among the book's other "primitive rebels" and "social bandits" who break the laws of the establishment to help the oppressed (see introduction, section 1, and Hobsbawm 1969: 13–29; Niditch 1990: 621–24). Samson is a more solitary and explosive social bandit than Gideon or Ehud, a type Hobsbawm calls "the avenger" (1969: 50), but nevertheless he is in the spectrum of judgeship implicitly defined in Judges.

Long hair appears to have been an attribute of epic warriors in the Hebrew Bible. David's son Absalom is portrayed taking pride in his thick, heavy locks, and the poetic allusion in Judg 5:2 may refer to the warriors' long hair (cf. Mobley 1997: 228–33). The hair plays a significant role in the story of Samson's rise and fall and is introduced at the outset of the story cycle. Like circumcision (see 14:3), the hairdo is a body trait that serves to mark and define a person's identity as a member of one group or another or as a special individual within one's own society. In tales of Samson, the Nazirite status, which has special connotations in an ancient Israelite culture of heroes, provides a particular Israelite expression of folk motifs such as "magic strength resides in hair" (Thompson Motif D1831; see also F531.1.6.13; G221.1) and the "life token" (E761), which is often related to a trait of false invulnerability. The hero is protected by a necklace or a cross or his long hair, but the destruction of the item leads to his downfall. As Hobsbawm has noted, the "social bandit" is frequently betrayed (1969: 42). For Samson, betrayal will involve the secret about his hair (see also Thompson Motif K975, "secret of strength treacherously discovered," and Thompson type 590). As warrior hero, Samson will deliver Israel from its enemies, a key role of the biblical judge.

It is important to explore briefly the identity of the particular enemy of the Samson cycle, the Philistines. The Philistines were one of several "Sea Peoples" who migrated from their homelands in the Aegean to settle on the southeast coast of the Mediterranean in the early twelfth century B.C.E. They continued to control the coastal area for the next six hundred years, and their major cities, Ashdod, Ashkelon, Ekron, Gaza, and Gath, all figure in biblical narratives (see on 1:18 above). Archaeological evidence clearly identifies and distinguishes this group both from the Israelites and from other contemporary Canaanite neighbors in terms of building design, food preferences, pottery style, clothing, and hair customs (see Bloch-Smith 2003: 412–25; Stager 1998: 153, 159–65). Iron Age I Philistine pottery shares much in design with Mycenaean material with its decorative painted creatures (for example, birds and feather-helmeted warriors) and complex painted geometric shapes, whereas Israelite/Canaanite pottery was much plainer. The Philistines raised hogs and ate pork, the bones of which have not been found in Israelite/Canaanite sites. Philistines are portrayed in Near Eastern art of the period, moreover, as clean-shaven, whereas Israelites and Syrians have beards. It is clear that the Israelites considered the Philistines to be uncircumcised, but concerning this we have no extrabiblical evidence. Indeed, certain other Sea Peoples are said to be circumcised in an important Egyptian source, the great Karnak inscription of Merenptah (see Bloch-Smith 2003: 415).

Lawrence Stager suggests that the Samson account may reflect a genuine Iron Age I situation in which Israelites and Philistines "interact along the boundaries shared by two distinctive cultures, Semitic and early Greek" (1998: 154). The Philistine expansion into the highland region of the Israelites leads to serious confrontation and war. The Israelite king David successfully repels the Philistines, who retreat to the coastal areas by the mid-tenth century B.C.E. "Philistine regions" or "Ashdod" are mentioned in later biblical sources concerning sporadic conflicts and tensions (e.g., Joel 3:4–8 [MT 4:4–8]; Neh 4:1; 13:23–24; see Machinist 2000: 57). It is clear, then, that the Philistines would have been an appropriate enemy in premonarchic times in the region where Samson's life is set, but they also might have been understood as enemies in subsequent renditions of the Samson cycle, during the monarchy and beyond. As Peter Machinist notes, "The Philistines are not simply memories from older tradition, but still existent, in some historical form, through the post-Exilic period of Achaemenid Persian domination" (2000: 57). Machinist suggests, however, that the Philistines retain identity as a quintessential "other" not because of later disputes, but precisely because of their antagonistic presence in the land at the time "when Israel became an organized society" (2000: 69), that is, genuinely early in Israel's history. The beardless Philistines are less hairy than Israelites, and certainly less hairy than the *Nazir* Samson. Hair becomes an important way in which the Israelite author reflects upon Israelite identity and culturally demarcates his people from the uncircumcised "other." That the enemy is Philistine makes Samson's never cutting his hair especially important.

[**6–14**] The insight of Manoah's wife emerges in her interaction with her husband and in the divine messenger's preference to deal with her (see Exum 1983: 39; Amit 1984/85: 388–89). The woman recognizes immediately that the messenger is no mere mortal (v. 6), whereas the husband treats him as a holy human being (vv. 8, 17). The woman's repetition of the instructions (v. 7) emphasizes the importance of Samson's "separated" status. Note that Manoah's prayer to God to receive additional confirmation results in the messenger's appearing again not to him but to the woman (v. 9). Manoah then follows after his wife to greet the stranger (v. 11), reversing the expected order of status in a patriarchal culture. In response to Manoah's inquiries (v. 12), the messenger alludes to his conversation with the woman—to what only she and he know—and omits reference to the important detail concerning the hair and the term *Nazir.* While this third version of the instructions, like the other two, emphasizes Samson's special status from the womb, it also serves to portray Manoah as outside the loop. God and women deal with matters of birth and the hero-son's future, as in other biblical annunciations.

The repeated request for confirmation is not unlike the request for signs by an insecure Moses (Exod 3:11; 4:1) or Gideon (Judg 6:36–40; 7:9–15). In this context, however, the request motif serves to contrast an insecure, unknowing man with a calm and wise woman. Comparisons might be drawn with Deborah and Barak (ch. 4). A skillful contributor to the tradition creatively employs a familiar motif to draw out particular themes—in this case the woman's centrality to her son's career—and to shape particular dynamics between characters.

James Kugel (2003) has pointed to the many guises in which the deity appears in the Hebrew Bible (e.g., angels, one man, three men) and to the significant ambiguities of these many portrayals for understanding Israelite views of the role and nature of the divinity. Israelite writers allowed for the deity's complex demeanor and ways. At Judges 13 the being appears in human form but projects an awe-inspiring aura. This status, obvious to the woman but not to her husband, emerges in the following scene.

[15–23] This scene and 6:19–23 share a traditional pattern. Like Gideon, Manoah wishes to make an offering in the guest's honor. For a comparable scene of hospitality offered to "three men" who are manifestations of the deity, see Gen 18:4–8. In ancient Israelite culture, meat eating usually follows sacrifice in which the appropriate portion of the animal is sent upward to the deity in the fire. In a sense, sacrifice and the banquet that follows offer an opportunity for humans to share a meal with the deity while the human beings who eat together form a community and also reinforce their relationship.

The special sacred identity of the visitor emerges as he refuses his host's food (Judg 13:16) and resists revealing his name (v. 18), enigmatically describing it as "wonderful." Jacob's theophanic experience at the river Jabbok (Gen 32:22–32 [MT 23–33]) includes a similar demur on the part of the divine being; ambiguity surrounds his name in response to the same question asked at Judg 13:17 (see Gen 32:29 [MT 30]). To know the deity's name is to hold power; it is used only sparingly and points to the status granted Abraham and Moses at key covenant revelations (Gen 15:7; Exod 3:13–14; 6:2).

As the couple watches, the altar's flame—fire often being a symbol of the deity's power (Gen 15:17; Exod 3:1–6; Judg 6:19–23)—takes the messenger with it skyward. No mere holy person is he. Verse 21 concludes the theophanic interaction: the messenger does not appear again (cf. 13:3, 10). Fear expressed by those who have experienced a divine being is not unusual (Gen 28:17; 32:29 [MT 30]; Judg 6:22), but as in the case of the man's request for confirmation of the prophecy, a common traditional motif serves to contrast the down-to-earth good sense of the woman, who understands the significance of the events, with the timidity and ignorance of the man. She knows that acceptance of the offering and the news brought by the messenger mark the experience as fortuitous.

[24–25] The story closes with the birth of the boy, who is named by his mother, another sign of her status in a patrilineal world. He is to be a servant of Yhwh, blessed by the deity and impelled by his divine spirit. Alter (1990) has pointed to the importance of this word "impel" in the rest of the cycle (see below). Samson's activity is located in the traditional "original" location of Dan (cf. chs. 17–18) to the east of the Philistine cities.

Judges 14:1–15:20
Samson and Marriage with the Philistines

14:1   And Samson went down[a] to Timnah,
    and he saw a woman in Timnah
      from the daughters of the Philistines.[b]

2   And he went up and told his father and his mother,[c]
    and he said,
    "A woman I saw in Timnah
      from the daughters of the Philistines,[d]
    and now take her for me as a wife."[e]

3   And his father and his mother said to him,
    "Is there not among the daughters of your kin[f]
      and in all our people[g] a woman
         that you must go take a woman
           from the Philistines, the uncircumcised?"[h]
    And Samson said to his father,
    "Take her for me,
      because she is right in my eyes."

4   And his father and his mother did not know
      that it was from Yhwh,
    for he was seeking an opportunity[i] against the Philistines,[j]
    and at this time the Philistines were ruling Israel.

5   And Samson went down, and his father and his mother, to Timnah,
    and they[k] went to the vineyards of Timnah,
    and behold, a whelp of the lions roaring to meet him.

6   And the spirit of Yhwh rushed upon him,
    and he tore it in two like the tearing of a kid,
    and nothing was there in his hand,
    and he did not tell his father and his mother
      what he had done.

7   And he[l] went down and spoke to the woman,
    and she was right in the eyes of Samson.[m]

8   And he returned after some days to take her,
    and he turned to see the fallen body of the lion,
    and behold, a swarm of bees
      in the carcass of the lion,[n] and honey.[o]

9   And he scraped it out into his palms,
    and he walked along, walking and eating,
    and he went[p]
    to his father and to his mother,

and he gave to them and they ate,
and he did not tell them
   that from the carcass of the lion
    he had scraped the honey.

10   And his father went down to the woman,
and Samson made there a feast,
for thus the young men would do.

11   And it was when they saw him,^q
they took thirty companions,^r
and they were with him.

12   And Samson said to them,
"Let me, pray, riddle you a riddle.
If tell you tell it to me
   within the seven days of the feast,
and you find out,
   I will give to you thirty linen garments
    and thirty changes of clothing.

13   And if you are not able to tell me,
   you will give to me thirty linen garments
    and thirty changes of clothing."
And they said to him,
"Riddle your riddle and let us listen."

14   And he said to them,
"From the eater came forth eats,
and from the strong came forth sweets."^s
And they could not tell the riddle for three days.

15   And it was on the seventh day,
and they said to the woman of Samson,
"Seduce^t your man,
and let him tell us^u the riddle,
lest we burn you and the household of your father with fire.
Was it to dispossess us that you called us together or not?"

16   And the woman of Samson wept over him,
and she said,
"You only hate me and do not love me.
The riddle you have riddled to my kinfolk,
but me you have not told."^v
And he said to her,
"Behold, my father and my mother I have not told,
and you shall I tell?"

17   And she wept over him for the seven days
   that they had for the party,

and it was on the seventh day that he told her
because she pressed him.
And she told the riddle to her own folk.

18 And the men of the town said to him on the seventh day,
  before the setting[w] of the sun,
"What is sweeter than honey,
and what is stronger than the lion?"[x]
And he said to them,
"If you had not plowed with my heifer,
  you would not have found out my riddle."

19 And the spirit of Yhwh rushed upon him,
and he went down to Ashkelon,
and he struck from among them thirty men.
And he took their gear,[y]
and he gave the clothing to the tellers of the riddle.
And his anger[z] was kindled,
and he went up to his father's household.

20 And the woman of Samson was for his companion,
  who had served as companion to him.

15:1 And it was after some days, in the harvest of the wheat,
and Samson visited his woman with a she-goat kid.
And he said,
"I would go to my woman in the chamber,"
but her father would not give him permission to go.

2 And her father said,
"Say I said, surely hate, you hate her,
and I gave her to your companion.
Is not her younger sister better than she?
Let her, pray, be for you in place of her."

3 And Samson said to them,
"I am clean from guilt this time[aa] as regards the Philistines,[bb]
for I am going to do with them mischief."[cc]

4 And Samson went,
and he captured three hundred foxes,[dd]
and he took torches,
and he turned tail to tail,
and he put one torch
  between two tails, in the middle.[ee]

5 And he caused fire to burn in the torches,
and he sent (them) among the standing grain of the Philistines,
and he caused to burn from stacks to standing grain
  and to vineyards, olive groves.[ff]

6   And the Philistines said,
    "Who did this?"
    And they said, "Samson, son-in-law of the Timnite,
    because he took his woman,
    and he gave her to his companion."
    And up went the Philistines
    and they burnt her and her father[gg] with fire.

7   And Samson said to them,
    "If you do something like this,
        surely I will take vengeance upon you,
    and afterward I will stop."[hh]

8   And he struck them leg upon thigh,
        a great striking.
    And he went down and dwelled in the cleft of the Rock of Etam.

9   And the Philistines went up,
    and they encamped in Judah,
    and they spread abroad in Lehi.[ii]

10 And the men of Judah said,
    "Why have you come up[jj] upon us?"
    And they said, "To bind Samson we have come up,
        to do to him as he did to us."

11 And down went three thousand men from Judah,
        to the cleft of the Rock of Etam,
    and they said to Samson,
    "Do you not know that the Philistines are ruling over us,
    and what is this you have done to us?"[kk]
    And he said to them,
    "As they did to me so I did to them."[ll]

12 And they said to him,
    "To bind you we have come down,
        to give you into the hand of the Philistines."
    And Samson said to them,
    "Swear to me, lest you assail[mm] me."

13 And they said to him saying,
    "No, for to bind we will bind you,
    and we will give you into their hands,
    but kill we will not kill you."
    And they bound him with two new ropes,
    and they brought him up from the rock.

14 He came to Lehi,[nn]
    and the Philistines raised a war cry to meet him.
    And the spirit of Yhwh[oo] rushed upon him

and the ropes that were on his arms were
    like flax that was burning in fire,
and the bindings melted from upon his hands.

15   And he found the fresh jawbone of a donkey,[pp]
and he sent his hand,
and he took it and struck with it a thousand men.

16   And Samson said,
"With the jawbone of a donkey
    a heap, two heaps,[qq]
with the jawbone of a donkey,
    I struck one thousand men."

17   And when he finished speaking,
he threw the jawbone from his hand,
and he called the place Ramoth-Lehi ("Height[rr] of the Jawbone").

18   And he was very thirsty,[ss]
and he called to Yhwh, and said,
"You gave into the hand of your servant
    this great deliverance,[tt]
and now I will die of thirst,
and I will fall into the hand of the uncircumcised."

19   And God split the hollow that is in Lehi,
and water came forth from it,
and he drank, and his spirit returned,
and he lived.
For this reason, he called its name En-hakkore ("Well of One Who Calls"),[uu]
    which is in Lehi to this day.

20   And he judged Israel
    in the days of the Philistines[vv]
        for twenty years.

a. Language of directions, up and down, frame the tale in chs. 14–15. See 14:2, 5, 7, 10, 19; 15:6, 8, 9, 10, 11, 12, 13.

b. Vat and OL read "foreigners" for "Philistines," as is common throughout the book. OL adds at the end, "and she was pleasing in his sight"; cf. v. 3.

c. Notice the recurring emphasis on the parents through language of mother and father (vv. 3, 4, 5, 6, 9, 10, 19). The language reveals this to be a tale about kin and nonkin, endogamy versus exogamy.

d. OL reads, "foreigners." See note b.

e. As in the tale of Samson's mother and throughout the Hebrew Bible, the term for wife literally means "woman" and is the same word used in v. 1. Notice that the language of marriage is the language of acquisition (see vv. 2, 3, 8, 15, 16, 20).

f. Literally, "brothers."

g. MT and Vat read, "my people." OL reads, "our people."

h. Vat and OL read, "foreigners." OL omits "uncircumcised."

i. Vat reads, "vengeance." OL reads, "return," in the sense of retribution or payback.

j. For both references to Philistines in this verse, see note b.

k. Vat and OL read, "and he went," enhancing the secrecy of the scene.

l. Vat and OL read, "they," implying that the parents make arrangements (see v. 2).

m. Cf. v. 3 for traditional repetition.

n. OL reads, "a honeycomb of bees was in the mouth of the lion," and Vat reads, "a gathering of bees was in the mouth of the lion." Both translations provide more specific detail than MT. Are these variations due to a different *Vorlage* or a way in which translators take liberties to enliven a scene?

o. OL omits "and honey."

p. The Hebrew literally reads, "walked," a term used densely in this verse, creating a sense of movement.

q. OL reads the similar sounding root *yrʾ* (to fear): "It was since they feared him." OL thus implies that the Philistines plant some of their own kin in the wedding party to keep control of the situation, whereas MT and Vat assume an expected ritual pattern at exogamous wedding encounters.

r. OL continues, "they brought to him thirty companions." The Latin verb may carry the nuance of pressure, an appropriate continuation of OL (see note q).

s. OL abbreviates the riddle: "From the eater came forth sweetness." In the Hebrew, the words do not rhyme but create rhythm by means of alliteration of the *m* sound, by repetition of language ("from," "eat," "came forth"), and by similar line length of the two cola of the riddle.

t. The root is related to the word "to open up." The woman pries open her man psychologically and sexually (see commentary).

u. OL and Vat read, "let him announce to you."

v. OL includes the variation, "You hated me. You proposed a riddle to my countrymen. Why did you not tell it to me?"

w. Vat reads, "rising of the sun."

x. Again notice the plays on *m* sounds and the comparable length of cola. The answer to a riddle looks like a riddle.

y. The root may derive from the meaning "to draw off" and refers to that which is stripped off a defeated enemy (see 2 Sam 2:21), but an alternate meaning of the root is "equip for war." Vat reads "cloaks." OL reads more briefly, "He took their clothing and gave to. . . ."

z. Vat reads, "and Samson was very angry."

aa. Notice the recurrence of the root *pʿm* (15:3; 16:15, 18, 20, 28) and see 13:25 and Alter (1990).

bb. OL and Vat read "foreigners" for Philistine in this chapter and throughout the book.

cc. Literally, "bad" or "harm."

dd. There is some debate about the species of tailed animal pictured here. Margalith suggests that a cross-cultural confusion between the local "jackal" and the Greek "fox" underlies the legend of the "torch tails" (1985).

ee. The traditions evidence some variation as translators try to make sense of this odd scene. Vat adds, "and he bound."

ff. Cf. Exod 23:11.

gg. OL reads, "and her father's household."

hh. Samson speaks in the formulaic language of oath taking. One might begin the last two cola, "I swear that. . . ." The literal translation reflects an idiom meaning, "I will not stop until I take vengeance. . . ." OL reads, "if you do in this way, I will not forgive you but I will take vengeance from each of you, and then I will stop."

ii. Literally, "Jawbone." The narrator places the evocative name of the location before the explanatory tale with its folk etymology.

jj. Language of military engagement, as in ch. 1 and frequently in Judges.

kk. Formulaic accusation of wrongdoing (e.g., Gen 12:18; 20:9).

ll. Notice the parallel in language between charge and countercharge (see v. 10).

mm. The word translated "assail" has the basic root meaning "encounter." One may meet with hostility or with kindness. Vat translates, "meet," while OL incorporates both nuances, "that you will not kill me and hand me into their hands, lest you meet me."

nn. Vat and OL translate, "Jawbone."

oo. See 14:9 for formulaic language for Samson's experience of divine charisma before battle.

pp. OL reads, "great jawbone." Vat reads, "jawbone of a donkey thrown away" (literally, "spread abroad").

qq. MT plays on the root *ḥmr*, "donkey" or "ass" and also "heap." Vat and OL play on an alternate meaning, "to cover/smear over," as metaphorically meaning "destroy" in the Greek and thereby read "with the jawbone of a donkey, I will destroy them [Vat]/you [OL]."

rr. Vat translates the root *rwm* "lifting up," by *Anairesis,* which can alsdo mean "slaying/destruction." In a kind of targumic process, OL takes one side of the Greek play on words and reads, "The Killing of the Jawbone."

ss. OL adds, "even up to death."

tt. Vat reads, "You were pleased with this great deliverance by the hand of your servant."

uu. Vat and OL do not include Samson's foundational role as the one who names the place. Instead they read the passive. Vat reads, "Because of this, its name is called, 'The Well of One Who Calls Out'"; and OL reads, "Because of this, its name is called, 'The Invocation of the Jawbone.'"

vv. OL omits "in the days of the Philistines."

The tales of Samson are characterized by recurring language, motifs, and patterns of content. Repeatedly, Samson makes overtures to foreign women (Timnite, harlot, Delilah), performs superhuman feats (killing the lion with his bare hands, killing the Ashkelonites, jawbone killing, lifting the city gates, destroying the house of Dagon), and is associated with symbols of fertility (honey, water). He participates in and is countered by trickery (Samson's riddle, the Philistines' stealing the answer to the riddle, his feigning capture, his deceiving Delilah, and Delilah's treachery). He is involved in vengeance and countervengeance (Samson torches Philistine crops, they burn the Timnites; Samson kills Philistines, they capture and blind him; he takes vengeance by killing thousands of them). He frequently withdraws (to his parents, to the "cleft," finally to death itself). Various patterns and themes in the tales of Samson have also been explored by Crenshaw (1978: 20, 52–57, 64–98), Alter (1990: 48–51), and Exum (1981).

The recurring events of the cycle of tales about Samson emphasize certain messages and trace dramatic developments in the life of the hero, although each of these episodes could have circulated on its own as a well-known piece of the larger tradition. Narrative threads emphasized in the cycle include: the up/down movement of the romance, framing tales of the hero on the drift; the us/them theme in which oppressed Israelites face ruling Philistines; the related contrast between exogamy and endogamy (see Crenshaw 1978: 78–81) that serves to color outsiders as enemies; and the contrasts between social and antisocial and nature and culture (see Gunkel 1913: 39–44, 51; Humbert 1919: 159), which portray Samson as a special kind of superhero, the "social bandit" (see introduction, section 1, and Hobsbawm 1969).

Like Achsah (ch. 1), Jephthah's daughter (ch. 11), and the women in the troubling tale of civil war (chs. 19–21), women in Samson's adventures serve as commodities of exchange, the mediating doorways linking or separating groups of men. In Samson's case, exchange goes awry and women are sources of deception, betrayal, and destabilization rather than sources of stability and union. The clear message is not to create social connections with the hated enemy (see Crenshaw 1978: 78–81).

Throughout, Yhwh finds "an opportunity against the Philistines," and Samson as a charismatic holy man, wearing the long hair of the *Nazir,* serves the purposes of the deity (Exum 1983: 44–45; Crenshaw 1978: 135). Stories about Samson reveal the patriotic, heroic, and foundational messages of Israelite authors, as he confronts the Philistine establishment and defeats them.

Some scholars have treated Samson as a foolish dolt, an antihero, or a poor leader, who makes the cries for a king in 1 Samuel 8 seem appropriate (see, for example, Amit 1999: 266–67). Others treat him psychoanalytically as one with a sexual addiction (e.g., Alter 1990), or a man who has a problem with women and intimacy (Bal 1984: 355–56). Samson is a complex, epic-style hero who would be incomplete without flaws. His dangerous womanizing and his hubris, like his clever use of sayings and riddles and his Herculean acts of strength, all mark him as an Israelite version of an international character type who appears in a range of heroic or "epic" traditions (see Bynum 1990: 64–70). He is a worthy judge; the judge is to be understood, however, not as a seated and robed adjudicator of justice, but rather as an action hero. Stories of Samson may well be as old as Israel's origins and at least reflect the writers' desire to depict early times as fraught with struggle against oppressive overlords, a theme found throughout the book and one central to Mendenhall's and Gottwald's reconstructions of Israelite origins. Tales of Samson as preserved in the Hebrew Bible, however, would have continued to appeal during the nationalist experiments with monarchy and statehood—he is after all a great hero—and during Israel's postmonarchic history as well. The humanist compiler/author of Judges would have appreciated the ways in which Samson's tales deal with the vagaries of power. The frame of the covenantally oriented theological voice is very muted in tales of Samson (see 13:1), but a fundamental religious dimension is nevertheless at play. Samson's power comes from God, his success is elicited by prayer (Exum 1983: 39–43), and the deity never completely deserts him, in spite of his weaknesses and failings. This sort of religious dimension is pan-Israelite, typically biblical, and offers no sure indication of provenance or author.

The texture of chs. 14–15 is traditional. Overall, the tales format well into disenjambed cola.

[**14:1–9**] The setting for much of the interaction with the Philistines in chs. 14–15 is Timnah, located on the border of Judah near Philistine lands (see Josh 15:10; 19:43). Like Prov 2:16; 5:20; 7:5; 22:14; 23:27, the tales of Samson draw a clear distinction between "us" and "them," based upon suitability for marriage relations. Samson's attraction to inappropriate, foreign women is central, as well, to the characterization of the hero and frames subsequent stories of betrayal and battle, defeat and victory. The narrator begins with an interaction between the rebellious son and the loving parents. The repeated phrase "daughter of the Philistines" underscores the Timnite woman's foreign status. Samson's parents, both mother and father, are pictured as offering Samson advice and guidance, urging him to marry among "kinfolk," their own "people." The Philistines are described as "uncircumcised." As shown by Elizabeth Bloch-Smith (2003), circumcision appears to have been one of the key cultural self-identifiers in ancient Israel. As in the examples of beard length, hairdo, clothing, and diet, the physical adornment, treatment, or alteration of the body is a way of wearing one's culture, of carving identity into male persons (see Eilberg-Schwartz 1990).

The parents do not realize that the very compulsion of their son to mate with a daughter of "the uncircumcised" serves a larger divine purpose, to make war against the Philistines, Israel's political oppressors and cultural competitors. As in the tale of Samson's conception in ch. 13, a certain mystery surrounds the hero, an aura of the divinely sent and humanly uncontrollable. In 14:15 the author portrays the process by which exogamous relations are formed. The parents and son go to the girl's town to begin to formalize the match. Out of their sight, Samson encounters a young, wild lion. Lions would have been commonplace in the forested ecosystem of ancient Israel.

That Samson kills the lion with his bare hands testifies to his heroic status and places him on the natural end of the nature/culture continuum. Like Strong John in European tradition (Thompson type 650A), Samson is an "unruly hero" (Thompson Motif L114.3). Honey, which serendipitously appears in the lion's carcass, is a symbol of fertility in many cultures and an appropriate food eaten on the way to form marriage relations (see Bynum 1978: 42–51, 58–64). It can be found in the wild, is produced by insects in some process unknown to ancient writers, and has a sweet revivifying capacity, a source of instant energy for the weary traveler or the warrior (see 1 Sam 14:29). It is, as Claude Lévi-Strauss has discussed, a betwixt-and-between substance, neither animal nor vegetable, neither liquid nor solid (1973: 17–47). As one jousting between cultures, the superhero, alien even to his own people, is an appropriate finder and eater of honey. That this honey comes from the body of a dead lion is all the more miraculous and beyond the ordinary. (On possible connections to Greek myths concerning Aristaeus, see Margalith 1986a: 227–29.) Honey continues to be an important motif in the marriage matters that follow. The secrecy surrounding the kill (v. 6) and the finding of the honey (v. 9; see repetition of "he did not tell") is an important continuing theme of ch. 14 and subsequent scenes. Secrecy allows for deception and trickery, underscoring Samson's character as a loner and his group's alienation from the Philistines.

[**10–14**] The phrase, "For thus would do the young men," suggests that the groom's feast is part of the marriage ritual. The encounter between in-marrying groups is continued with the attachment of thirty Philistine "companions" to the groom. This piece of the ritual process, like the riddling contest, would seem to be a means of defining opposing groups while having them interact, the goal in actual marriage events: to create a new sense of community and union. In this case, of course, the results are the opposite.

"Let me riddle you a riddle" is a formulaic opener of the contest (on the ludic, gaming aspect of the encounter see Camp and Fontaine 1990: 135). The root *ḥwd* and the related term *ḥîdâ*, translated "riddle," are mentioned several times in the Hebrew Bible and suggest the existence of an Israelite "ethnic genre" (Ben-Amos 1976). The context in Judges 14–15 suggests that at least one variety of *ḥîdâ* suits the structural definition of the international genre of the riddle offered by Alan Dundes and Robert Georges, "a traditional verbal expression which contains one or more descriptive elements . . . ; the referent of the elements is to be guessed" (1975: 99). A wider look at biblical contexts for this root suggests parallels with the *māšāl* (see Ezek 17:2; Hab 2:6; Prov 1:6; Ps 49:4 [MT 5]). The *māšāl* is "a form of oblique and artful communication that sets up an analogy between the communication and the real-life settings of the listeners" (see Niditch 1993a: 86; and Judg 9:10). This form thus includes not only sayings but also what we might call parables, oracles, paradigms, and taunts. As with the *māšāl*, a term rooted in the meaning "to be like," the key to the *ḥîdâ* is the comparison drawn between the verbal play and the "referent," but the comparison is hidden. The root *ḥwd* may have to do with "turning aside," "avoiding"; thus to propound a "riddle" is to purposely misdirect, to obfuscate.

In Num 12:8 *ḥîdōt* are contrasted with the way in which the Deity communicates with Moses, "face-to-face," "up front" or "in view." The Queen of Sheba "tests" Solomon via *ḥîdōt*, emphasizing the unrevealed aspect of the riddle, the playful, contest quality (1 Kgs 10:1). In Ps 49:4 (MT 5), the play aspect is emphasized in another way: "I will open my riddle with a lyre." Perhaps implicit is the association between the playing of musical instruments and the prying open of prophetic, hidden knowledge (see 1 Sam 10:5; 2 Kgs 3:15; 1 Chron 25:1). *Ḥîdâ* is also used in parallelism with the word *mĕlîṣâ*, from the root meaning "to scorn" (Prov 1:6; Hab 2:6). Presumably, one scorns or derides by making an example of someone. Nuances of interpretation or indirect speech also may be implicit in the root of *mĕlîṣâ*. The riddle, cloaked in mystery and requiring interpretation, appropriately accompanies the wedding situation in which groups come together who are suspicious of one another, in which husband and wife are barely acquainted, and in which a major rite of passage is about to take place. The exogamous match between Samson and the Timnite is fraught with distrust, while the theme of secrecy runs throughout the tales of Samson, as noted by Crenshaw (1978: 21–26, 149–51).

The riddling contest involves a wager and is a typical part of marriage ceremonies (Noy 1968; Burns 1976). Like other symbolic means of safely acting out the potentially difficult relations between in-marrying groups (see Radcliffe-Brown 1965: 106–7), the riddling contest is meant to point to "social disparity" and to "intensify tension" (Pepicello and Green 1984: 124; see also Camp and Fontaine 1990: 134) within ritual contours so that what emerge are "communicative bonds between participants" (Pepicello and Green 1984: 125). Playing the game is supposed to make for genuine "companions." Even though the riddler has the power in the play initially (Pepicello and Green 1984: 128), he is to accept his rivals' solving his riddle graciously, as they are to accept a failure to solve it. In the tales of Samson no such amicable resolution occurs.

The literary form of Samson's riddle has been nicely explored by Camp and Fontaine (1990). Like Nel (1985) and Crenshaw (1978: 112–20), they note that an obvious answer exists for the riddle that serves to misdirect the Philistines: love or sex. Camp and Fontaine provide a visceral interpretation of the "love solution" involving oral sex and bodily fluids (1990: 141–42). Only Samson knows the bizarre "true" solution rooted in his own adventures.

[15–20] The threat to Samson's wife emphasizes the impossibility of unions with the Philistines from the writer's perspective. Upon penalty of her death and the death of her family, she is coerced into betraying her husband. The description of the way in which she seduces Samson anticipates the scene with Delilah in ch. 16 and recalls Jael's seduction of Sisera in chs. 4–5. All three women employ feminine wiles to subdue, defeat, and betray the enemy. To be sure, the Timnite's dilemma evokes pathos; she is forced into betrayal by the

Philistines. Her actions and interactions convey realistically a sense of bitter, local, ethnic tensions.

The response to the riddle (14:18), offered in the form of a question right before the deadline, is another riddle; and one of its solutions, as in the case of Samson's riddle, is love or passion (Song 8:6). Samson's response to the Philistines is also rooted in erotic verbal play. "Plowing with my heifer" suggests that the Philistines have used his woman, worked her over. They have had their way with her. To pry open the woman to expose Samson's secret is to cuckold her husband, for those in control of the woman have the power.

Unlucky Ashkelonites, inhabitants of one of the five cities of the Philistine pentapolis (see Judg 1:18; Josh 13:3), are killed by Samson and mined for their gear, booty for in-laws who had won the riddle wager by forcing his wife into finding his secret and betraying it. After Samson absents himself, the Philistines marry the woman off to one of their own, a member of the wedding party, one of the so-called companions (Judg 14:11). Again, the authority to give the woman reflects political and social power as well and leads to further confrontation and violence.

[15:1–8] Samson attempts to reinitiate the process of marital exchange. He comes at a time ripe with conjugal possibilities, the fertile harvest (see Ruth 3), and he brings a gift, a tender goat.

The interaction between the girl's father and Samson is similar to the way in which other biblical fathers-in-law play fast and loose with the objects of the young men's interest, for example, Saul and David (1 Sam 18:17–29) and Laban and Jacob (Gen 29:15–30). In traditional cultures, the exchange of a woman is a matter of power relations between men, a contest for relative status. Fathers of brides-to-be are thus portrayed imposing tests before the marriage is sanctioned, for example, Saul's demand for one hundred Philistine foreskins (1 Sam 18:24), or refusing for one reason or another to proceed with the original deal concerning the match. Thus David is promised Merab, but she is given to another, and he has to win the younger daughter Michal (1 Sam 18:19). Jacob is given the elder Leah instead of the desired Rachel, and he has to pay seven more years of labor for the younger girl whom he loves (Gen 29:23–27). Like Saul, the Timnite father-in-law offers Samson the girl's younger sister as substitute. His attempt to appease Samson treats his daughters as commodities: "Is not her sister better than she?" The alternate bride is not accepted good-naturedly by the superhero. He prepares countervengeance.

Once again, Samson uses animals in an irregular fashion as weapons against the Philistines. Scholars have searched Mediterranean folklore for comparable tales involving foxtails and fire, and the closest parallels appear to be Ovid's description of the Festival of Ceres in which foxes are sent into fields with "firebrands tied to their tales," and Livy's allusion to the way in which Hannibal frightened Roman troops by sending oxen "into their fields with firebrands tied to their horns" (Gaster 1981: 2:435). Specific borrowings are usually impossible to prove, for such tales are local versions of common motifs (e.g., Thompson Motif K2351, "animals help in military victory").

Fire is a recurring destructive force in the tales of Samson, a source of vengeance and countervengeance suited to the heated tensions between Philistines and Israelites and to the explosiveness of Samson's personality (14:6). A force of nature, Samson's wild animals, with torches for tails, wreak havoc among the Philistines' planted groves and vineyards, their rows of grain, the products of their agricultural economy. The Philistines respond with their own fire, burning to death the Timnite family who had brought Samson among them. Notice how they refer to Samson as "son-in-law of the Timnite." Samson strikes the Philistines again and then, as in 14:19, absents himself. The author appears to situate the Rock of Etam near Zorah, but it has not been identified archaeologically with certainty. The cavelike image of Samson's dwelling in the cleft of the rock, however, furthers the portrayal of Samson as loner.

[**9 20**] Samson has become a lightning rod for Philistine aggression, and the Judahites agree to try to contain him. An avenging wildman is a difficult sort of hero to deal with, even for the community he champions. He is too uncontrollable, too explosive. It is also true that Israelite writers understand the tendency of an oppressed group to "love their chains" or to prefer them to overt revolt. See, for example, the way in which the Israelites turn against Moses when he seeks to liberate them (Exod 2:14; 5:21).

The Judahites thus serve as mediators between the Philistines and Samson. As is often the case for those caught within ethnic violence, they just desire some degree of peace. Notice the way in which Samson's excuse for acting violently echoes that of the Philistines in a quintessential expression of what David Little (1995: 3–9) calls "the pathology of violence": "to do to them as he did to us." The Judahites negotiate with the hero (15:12–13), promising merely to restrain him and hand him over. They take an oath not to kill Samson, for although he is a superhero, he is not immortal. The "new ropes" used by them anticipate the scene with Delilah (16:11–12), as does Samson's capacity to extricate himself (16:9). The ropes melt as if in fire. Again, the image of burning captures the intensity of Samson's actions and testifies to the divine spirit that operates within him, for Yhwh is a god of fire.

The array of irregular weapons drawn from nature and employed by Samson, the bare hands and foxtails, continues with the jawbone of a donkey. Like traditional figures such as Strong John (Thompson type 650A), the hero kills a huge number of people with an unlikely weapon (see Thompson Motif F614.2: "hero uproots tree and uses as weapon").

Once again Samson speaks in verbal play. His victory taunt (15:16) plays on the root *ḥmr*, pointing to the heaps of dead. Vat and OL play on a different root meaning "to smear," showing the elasticity of some Hebrew words and the various double meanings they can occasion. Like many biblical heroes, Samson punctuates his divinely inspired experience with the naming of a place (cf. Gen 16:14, Hagar; 28:19, Jacob). In this case, the naming plays on the name that the place is assumed to have earlier in the story, Lehi ("Jawbone"), one perhaps rooted in the topography of the area.

The hero's capacity to obtain water from a rock, often with the aid of a divine helper, is an international folk motif. One thinks of Moses in the biblical tradition. Like Esau, who declares to his brother that he will die without food (Gen 25:30–34), Samson is expansive and demanding, exaggerating for effect. He wants to address immediate needs and desires and treats the deity with familiarity. What good are his victories if he dies of thirst? The Philistines, as in ch. 14, are described by lack of circumcision, the physical trait that distinguishes them from the Israelites. And so the deity makes water gush forth for his favorite. Here Yhwh is a master of nature as throughout the Hebrew Bible; the origin of springs by miraculous means or divine intervention is a common international motif (see Thompson Motif A940–941).

The chapter concludes with a reminder that Samson was a judge. We have explored throughout the boundary where the judge meets the "social bandit" and the "epic hero." The epic hero is often the tragic hero, as seen in the tale of Samson and Delilah that follows.

Judges 16:1–31
The Female "Other," Delilah, and Death

16:1 And Samson walked to Gaza,
　　　and there he saw a whore woman,
　　　and he went[a] to her.
2 To the Gazites it was told,[b] saying,
　　　"Samson has come here."
　　　And they formed a circle and lay in wait for him all the night
　　　　　at the gate of the city.
　　　And they kept themselves quiet all the night, saying,
　　　"Until the light of morning, and we will kill him."
3 And Samson slept until the middle of the night,
　　　and he arose in the middle of the night,
　　　and he seized the doors of the gate of the city
　　　　　and the two doorposts,[c]
　　　and he pulled them up with the bar,
　　　and he put (them) on his shoulders,

and he took them up to the head of the hill
    that was in front of Hebron.
4   And it was after this
    that he loved a woman in the Valley of Sorek,[d]
    and her name was Delilah.[e]
5   And went up to her did the lords of the Philistines,[f]
    and they said to her,
    "Seduce him[g]
    and see by what means is his great strength,
    and by what means we may have power over[h] him,
    and we will bind him to humble[i] him,
    and we will give to you, each man,
        one thousand one hundred in silver."
6   And Delilah said to Samson,
    "Tell me, pray, by what means is your great strength,
    and by what means may you be bound in order to humble you."[j]
7   And Samson said to her,
    "If they bind me with[k] seven fresh[l] gut cords
    .that have not been dried out,[m]
    I will become weak,
    and I will be like any human being."[n]
8   And the lords of the Philistines brought up to her
        seven fresh gut cords
            that had not been dried out,
    and she bound him with them.[o]
9   The ambushers waited for her[p] in the inner chamber,
    and she said to him,
    "Philistines are upon you, Samson."
    And he tore the gut cords
        as a twisted thread of tow is torn[q] at the very scent of fire,
    and his strength source was not known.
10   And Delilah said to Samson,
    "Behold, you have mocked me,[r]
    and you have spoken to me lies.
    Now tell me by what means you may be bound."
11   And he said to her,
    "If bind they would bind me with new ropes,
        with which work has not been done,
    I will become weak,
    and I will be like any human being."
12   And Delilah took[s] new ropes,
    and she bound him with them,[t]

and she[u] said to him,
"Philistines are upon you, Samson."
And the ambushers were staying in the inner chamber;[v]
and he tore them from upon his arms like a thread.

13   And said Delilah to Samson,
"Until now you have mocked me,
and you have spoken to me lies.
Tell me by what means may you be bound!"
And he said to her,
"If you weave the seven plaits[w] of my head
      with the loom stuff."[x]

14   [y] And she thrust with the pin,
and she said to him,
"Philistines are upon you, Samson."
And he awoke from his sleep,
and he pulled out the pin of the loom and the loom stuff.

15   And she said to him,
"How can you say, 'I love you'?
And your heart is not with me.
This is three times you have mocked me,
and you have not told me
      by what means is your strength great."

16   And it was because she pressed him[z]
      with her words day in and day out,
and she urged him,[aa]
his soul was cut short to death.

17   And he told her all his heart,
and he said to her,
"A razor has not come upon my head,
because a *Nazir*[bb] of God I have been
      from the womb of my mother.[cc]
If I am shaven,
      then my strength will turn away from me,
and I will become weak,
and I will be like every human being."[dd]

18   And Delilah saw
      that he told her his whole heart,
and she sent and she called to the lords of the Philistines saying,
"Go up this time,[ee]
for he has told me all his heart."[ff]
And up to her went the lords of the Philistines,
and they brought up the silver in their hands.

19   And she made him sleep on her knees.[gg]
      And she called the man,[hh]
      and she shaved off the seven plaits of his head,
      and she began to humble him,[ii]
      and his strength turned away from him.

20   And she said,
      "Philistines are upon you, Samson."
      And he awoke from his sleep,
      and he said,
      "I will go forth like the other times[jj] and be shaken free,"[kk]
      but he did not know that Yhwh had turned away from him.

21   And the Philistines seized him,
      and they gouged out his eyes,
      and they brought him down to Gaza,
      and they bound him with bronze[ll] shackles,
      and he became one who grinds[mm] in the prison house.

22   And the hairs of his head began to grow
          after he was shaven.

23   And the lords of the Philistines gathered
          to sacrifice[nn] a great sacrifice
              to Dagon their god and to joy,[oo]
      and they said,
      "Given has our god into our hands,
      Samson our enemy."[pp]

24   And the people saw him,
      and they praised their god,
      for they said,
      "Our god has given into our hands
          our enemy and the devastator of our land
              who made many our fatally wounded."[qq]

25   And it was when their heart was merry,[rr]
      they said, "Call Samson,[ss]
      and let him sport[tt] before us."
      And they called Samson from the prison house,
      and he sported before them,[uu]
      and they stood him between the pillars.[vv]

26   And said Samson to the lad who held his hand,
      "Allow me[ww] to touch the pillars
          upon which the house is set,
      and I will lean upon them."[xx]

27   And the house was full of men and women,
      and there were all the lords of the Philistines,

and on the roof were about three thousand men and women,
   those watching the sporting of Samson.

28   And Samson called to Yhwh,
      and he said, "My Lord, Yhwh,
      remember me, pray, and strengthen me, pray,
         just this one time,[yy] O God,
      and I will take vengeance in a single vengeance
         for my two eyes, on the Philistines."

29   And grasp did Samson the two pillars of the central portion
         upon which the house was set,
      and he leaned upon them,
         one in his right hand and one in his left.

30   And Samson said,
      "May my soul[zz] die with the Philistines";
      and he stretched out[aaa] with his strength,
      and fall did the house upon the lords,
         and upon all the people who were within;
      and the dead whom he made die in his death
         were more than he made die in his life.

31   And down went his brothers and all his father's extended household,
      and they lifted him and went up,
      and they buried him between Zorah and Eshtaol
         in the sepulchre of Manoah, his father.[bbb]
      And he had judged Israel for twenty years.

a. The word for "go" or "come" may have sexual overtones. See discussion of 4:21.

b. The translation follows Vat and OL. MT reads as if it were an announcement, "To the Gazites, saying. . . ."

c. Vat reads, "with its two standing posts. . . ." OL is more summative: "he took the doors of the gate of the city and the two posts with the bar, and he put them on his shoulders."

d. The Hebrew word for "valley" may also mean "torrent" or "wadi" rather than the topographic feature carved out by the water. OL thus reads "river." The same Hebrew text can thus through translation choices lead to a different image or setting, "by the river." Boling translates "Vineyard Valley" (245, 248); *śōrēq* is "a choice species of vine" (BDB 977), perhaps rooted in the term for "red tinge" (see Isa 5:12 and Jer 2:21).

e. Various suggestions have been offered for the meaning of the name Delilah. One possibility, "loose hair," would relate both to Samson's status as *Nazir* and to Delilah's undoing the "plaits of his hair." A second possibility is "small, slight." A charming name for a young girl, the name would also serve to evoke Samson the superman's conquest by a woman. A third possibility, a play on the word for "night," suggests mystery and surreptitiousness. For Exum (1992), the last possibility may suggest a battle between day (Samson/sun) and night.

f. OL and Vat translate "foreigners" throughout the chapter, as in previous chapters. See 16:8, 9, 12, 14, 18, 20, 21, 23, 27, 28, 30.

g. See 14:15. OL reads, "trick him."

h. Literally, "be able over," or "prevail over."

i. The Piel form of the root, literally, "to be bowed down, afflicted," expresses various forms of oppression, as in the treatment of Hagar (Gen 16:6) and the enslavement of the Israelites (Exod 1:11, 12), but also has a strongly sexual nuance, meaning rape in Gen 34:2; Deut 22:24, 29; Judg 19:24; 20:5; 2 Sam 13:12, 14, 22, 32. Cf. the discussion of Judg 5:27.

j. Notice the repetition between the words of the Philistines and Delilah's (vv. 5, 6) and the repetition that frames the encounter between Samson and Delilah (see, e.g., vv. 6, 10, 13, 15).

k. Notice the repeating frame in vv. 7, 11, 13, 17.

l. The word for "fresh" or "moist" sounds like the word for "jawbone" in 15:15 and the place of the jawbone slaughter (15:14, 16).

m. Vat translates another connotation of the root meaning "to be dry," "to ruin." The same Hebrew thus lends itself to different nuances.

n. Literally, "like one of humankind."

o. Notice the internal repetition typical of traditional literature (see vv. 6–8, 11–13).

p. OL omits "waited for her," literally, "sat still/stayed for her," and reads, "the ambushers were in. . . ." Cf. v. 12.

q. Vat reads, "as if one would tear away. . . ." OL reads, "as a rope is split when it gets wind of fire." Cf. v. 12 and 15:14.

r. The term includes nuances of "deception, trifling with" (see BDB 1068).

s. OL adds, "in that night," enhancing the setting.

t. Vat adds, "and the ambushers came out from the chamber" and omits the penultimate colon of the verse. The scene thus differs slightly from MT, in which the ambushers remain hidden longer and Delilah is responsible for all the interaction with Samson. See note u.

u. OL reads, "they." Vat reads, "and she said," omitting "to him."

v. See the reuse of language from v. 9 in addition to the recurring frame (see vv. 14, 20).

w. Vat describes the locks or plaits as dreadlocks, literally, "ropes," thus linking the hair to the rawhide cords and the new ropes in the first two false revelations.

x. Both Vat and OL have longer texts finishing off in formulaic ways the shorter MT in tune with vv. 7, 11, 17. Traditional text critics might write of haplography in MT v. 13, but it is also possible that the writer in the MT tradition leaves the rest unstated because it is metonymically understood, whereas the translators, or the Hebrew traditions they are translating, prefer to say it all. One resists choosing in this way "a better" or "original" text in order to acknowledge variation in the traditions, differing aesthetic and storytelling preferences, and the possibility that the translator himself provides expected continuations of the scene within a traditional medium. Vat thus reads, "If you weave the seven ropes of my head with the warp, and you hammer the peg into the wall, I will be weak like one of men." OL reads, "If you take apart the seven locks of my head and you lay the warp of a web and you lay bare my hairs in it as if the web is covered over, I will become weak." Vat imagines pinning the dreadlocks to the wall, whereas OL imagines taking apart Samson's plaits and rearranging them in a pattern, perhaps like woven cloth. All three images suggest taming or controlling the hair through weaving, pinning, or reconfiguration.

y. Vat continues the image of v. 13 with the variant: "And it was while he was sleeping, and Delilah took the seven locks of his head and she wove in the warp and she pegged with a peg into the wall, and she said, 'Foreigners are upon you, Samson.' And he was awakened from his sleep, and he took out the peg of the woven thing from the wall."

OL reads, "And Delilah made him sleep and she took apart the seven hairs of his head with fear, and she went out in the length of the room, and she fixed it in pins and she said to him, 'Foreigners are upon you, Samson.' And he rose up from his sleep, and he plucked out the pins with the loom and the 'division' [of his hair?] and his strength was not known."

z. OL reads, "tricked him with words the whole night," a variant. OL uses the same verb for trickery in 16:5.

a. Vat reads, "she hemmed him in," perhaps conveying the notion of "pressing." OL translates, "and she was vexing to him."

bb. Vat translates, "holy one of God," conveying the meaning of *Nazir.* OL reads *nazareus* as in 13:7. See note l there.

cc. Cf. the language at 13:5 and 7 for traditional-style repetition.

dd. Cf. 16:7, 11, and 13 for the recurring frame.

ee. Notice repetition of the root p^cm, "this time" (see 15:3, n. aa; Alter 1990). Vat reads or translates "again" and OL omits.

ff. Notice the repetition of the phrase from v. 17.

gg. The position carries sexual nuances. See also Gen 30:3 for associations between the knees and childbearing.

hh. OL has the more specific variant "barber."

ii. OL reads, "he began to be humiliated." For the sexual nuance see note i.

jj. Notice the use of the root p^cm once again. OL reads, "I will go and do what is necessary."

kk. OL continues, "and I will shake myself." Notice that the root for "shake" has the same letters as the root used for a young, inexperienced man (n^cr). Is a wordplay implied suggesting Samson's naiveté about the source of his strength? He should know better.

ll. OL omits "bronze." Notice that the word for bronze or copper also seems to have some sort of sexual connotation in Ezek 16:36 (see BDB 639), a suggestive wordplay that works well with the following image of a "grinder." Notice also that the filthy pot filled with woman's uncleanness, Ezekiel's visceral and misogynistic metaphor for Israel's sin (Ezek 24:1–13), is made of copper (24:11). The red-orange color suggests a woman's genitals or menstrual fluids.

mm. "To grind" implies the domesticated subservient status of a woman or a beast, but as noted by the rabbis and modern scholars, "to grind" also has sexual connotations. See Isa 47:2; Job 31:10.

nn. OL reads, "gathered to sacrifice to their gods and to make great sacrifice to Dagon their god."

oo. Vat and OL read, "to be joyful."

pp. The taunting ditty has a rhyming quality.

qq. Rhyming upon the first person plural suffix continues.

rr. Literally, "good."

ss. Vat adds, "from the prison house."

tt. OL reads, "dance," picturing Samson to perform like a captured dancing bear. The Greek of Vat may be translated as "play/sport" or "dance." OL adopts one over another of the connotations of the Greek translation, thereby creating a different image. The sporting term (literally, "laugh") may have sexual connotations. Cf. Gen 26:8; 2 Sam 6:5, 21–22; 1 Chron 15:29.

uu. Vat adds, "and they beat him," invoking images of Jesus (Crenshaw 1978: 139–41). OL reads, "from the prison house, and they derided him." Samson does not sport nor do they beat.

vv. OL reads, "between the two pillars upon which the house was based" (cf. v. 26).

ww. Literally, "let me rest and let me touch."

xx. OL adds, "and the boy did so," filling out the imagery here as at the end of v. 25.

yy. Again note the use of the word $p^c m$.

zz. That is, the life force.

aaa. Vat and OL seem to imagine somewhat different motions. Vat has Samson lift up the pillars, and OL has him pull them toward himself.

bbb. Formulaic language for the death and burial of the good leader. See, for example, Gideon at 8:32 and the brief annals in 10:1–5 and 12:8–15.

In ch. 16 the trickster hero Samson first deceives the enemy, displaying his superhuman strength, and then, in turn, is himself tricked. The motif of the seductive and dangerous foreign woman finds quintessential expression in the character of Delilah. Samson's capture, however, has less to do with her capacity to deceive than with Samson's own hubris. He makes the mistake of assuming that he is invincible, with or without his hair, the divine source of his power. As in the case of Sisera and many epic heroes (see Vermeule 1979: 101–2, 157, 171), Samson's defeat is described in terms of his feminization (notes i, gg, ii, ll, mm, tt). The loss of his hair is part of this imagery (see below), but the hair grows back. The hero, although blinded and enslaved, recovers strength and makes peace with the patron deity who gave him miraculous power. In a great apotheosis, Samson destroys his Philistine enemies, dying a heroic death. Deservedly, he is buried in the paternal sepulchre.

The style of the tale of Samson and Delilah is one of the most fully traditional in the book with its recurring frames and variation upon repetitions for narrative emphasis (cf. 16:9, 12, 14, 20; see also vv. 11, 12, 13, 15; vv. 17, 18; and vv. 5, 6, 10, 13, 15). Cola are easy to arrange in disenjambed units.

[1–3] Samson's brief encounter with a harlot in the Philistine city of Gaza/Azah (see 1:18) contributes to his portrayal as a womanizer and underscores the ways in which experiences with foreign females lead to confrontations with Philistines, trickery, and countertrickery. Sexual relations are a very basic form of social intercourse, a means of transforming and socializing heroes such as Enkidu in the Mesopotamian Epic of Gilgamesh (cf. Mobley 1997:

229). As in the case of the abortive marriage to the Timnite woman in chs. 14–15, the union with the harlot leads not to a degree of socialization but to discord. The message in ethnography is clear: no social relations with the Philistines succeed. Nor is Samson, the loner and the avenger, able to establish a lasting conjugal relationship. In many ways, he embodies the antisocial.

The Gazites, like vultures, are pictured circling around in preparation for an ambush at dawn. Samson, however, surprises them, escaping in the night. His violent seizure of the city gates and the way in which he carries them off evoke comparisons with Paul Bunyan and other folk heroes who perform acts requiring prodigious and superhuman strength (cf. Thompson Motif F614.2). Samson moves the gates from a Philistine to an Israelite locus (see 1:10 on Hebron), connoting a removal of power and status.

[4–21] The third woman in Samson's completion of a traditional triad is Delilah, and the setting is Sorek, which Boling (248) and others have identified as Wadi es-Sarar, located approximately thirteen miles southwest of Jerusalem. The area is thus appropriate for interactions with Philistines. As Mieke Bal has observed, the relationship with Delilah is described as one of greater emotional involvement than the previous two (1984). Samson "loves" Delilah. Is Samson but a fool for love?

Bal treats the recurring scenes, Delilah's request for disclosure, Samson's deception, her betrayal, his escape/capture, as tracing the pattern of Samson's emotional development (1984: 360). In a feminist psychoanalytical approach, Bal explores the link between love and surrender (356, 362). To love maturely, she suggests romantically, is to surrender fully. This surrender is to become infant-like and trusting; Bal describes Samson's condition—bald and asleep on a woman's lap—as a return to infancy (365).

With irony, Bal alludes to Delilah's "therapeutic activity." Samson matures with Delilah, overcoming his fear of women, but in the end rids himself of his twin "passions," fear and attraction (the quintessential male psychological dilemma) "by getting rid of women altogether" (372). His death is a rebirth, but a "womanless rebirth" as he emerges from the great thighlike pillars of the temple (367). Bal's analysis of the tales of Samson might be compared to Joseph Campbell's astute psychoanalytical study of patterns of the hero. For Campbell, as for Bal, the hero's death is a dramatic rebirth and symbol of transformation.

Whether or not one is fully convinced by Bal's particular approach to Samson, it does allow for exploring the depth of his characterization. Samson is no buffoon, nor is he a less than human "feral creature" (Bynum 1990: 63). Like Hercules and other great superheroes of tradition, Samson is a complex character, beloved by a deity, capable of grand and clever acts of deception, artful in his use of language, and able to perform superhuman feats. He is susceptible to women's attractions and to the delusion that his great power is self-generated. By succumbing to Delilah, he takes his place with Odysseus and other epic heroes who should keep key aspects of their identities to themselves. Instead, they boast by word or by action.

Delilah might be considered the Philistines' Jael, even though, less heroically, Delilah betrays Samson for money (16:5). In this respect, Bal compares her to the prostitute of Gaza (1984: 357–58).

The "feminization" of the hero commences in 16:6 with a question followed by the first of three false revelations, similarly framed. Gut cords are a natural binding, made of animal material. Each revelation comes closer to "culture" and closer to the truth (Niditch 1990: 615–16). The fire motif continues as the bindings fall from his hands in a metaphor of fire (cf. 15:14).

That Samson hears Delilah call upon the Philistines repeatedly (vv. 9, 12, 14, 20) strikes many commentators as proof of his folly. Similar comments are frequently made about folk characters such as Snow White. How could she possibly be seduced by the witch's deception a third time? On the one hand, folktale heroes and heroines always engage in these patterns of repetition. In traditional literatures, the repetitions create thematic emphasis, shape characterization, and build tension, for those within the tradition know where the stories are headed. It is the process of getting there that counts. In Samson's case, each instance of the frame and the line about the Philistines draws an essential contrast between "us" and "them," while showing Samson growing bolder and bolder, convinced finally that his power is unassailable, hair or no hair. Alter (1990: 50) suggests with insight that Samson is addicted to taking chances. One might also read vv. 9 and 12 to suggest that the Philistines remain hidden in the inner chamber while Delilah refers to them, waiting to see how the hero will react. Perhaps Samson does not believe that Delilah has actually betrayed him and thinks that she is merely testing the veracity of his admission, which adds to the pathos of the account.

The second exchange involves ropes (16:11), a somewhat more culture intensive product, having undergone some process whereby fiber is cultivated, harvested, treated, and woven. The ropes are new and unused but not raw. Samson's seeming submission to these recurring acts of tying suggests subversive play in an erotic context.

Samson's reference to taming his hair in the third exchange (16:13) moves more closely to the true source of his strength. Weaving is "typically women's work" in ancient Near Eastern village culture, a cottage craft undertaken at home (King and Stager 2001: 152–58). Thus talk of looms suggests a metaphoric link between the conspiratorial webs and designs of women such as Delilah and an actual feature of women's material culture. Samson's instructions to Delilah and her actions in v. 14 tally with what is known about the logistics of weaving in ancient Israel (see King and Stager 2001: 157). This is the first time the audience has heard that Samson wears his hair in seven plaits. The various manuscript traditions picture the hairdo somewhat differently (see notes w, x, y). The term for plaits, rooted in a verb meaning "to pass through," suggests a form of hair treatment that involves care and skill (cf. Mobley 1997: 224).

Delilah's nagging, like that of the Timnite wife, is conveyed with a visceral term implying physical pressure (16:16). The quality of exaggeration is implicit in the narrator's description of Samson's discomfort, as in Samson's complaint to Yhwh in 15:18.

The tale comes full circle as Samson's revelation to Delilah (16:17) echoes the divine messenger's repeated instructions to his mother in ch. 13. The long, never-cut hair is shaved by the forbidden razor, a manmade tool. The symbolism of long hair and shaved hair is important to tales of Samson. Imagery here and in ch. 13 suggests a border in Israelite thought where heroic warrior status and holy status meet in the symbolism of long hair (see also Kaufmann 131–32, 241) while pointing to the significance of hair for differentiating Israelite from Philistine.

Hair is a part of the body, alive, and yet it can easily be separated from the body without pain. It regenerates, changes texture and color over time, and can be purposefully manipulated, arranged or disarranged. As such, hair, so pliable and so open to various treatments and styles, has served and continues to serve human beings as a consummate means of symbolic self-definition and a source of group identity. The way in which hair is worn may connote insider or outsider status, cultural identity or countercultural challenge, member of the establishment or rebel, old or young, and male or female.

Some scholars have attempted to find universal meanings in hair customs, for example, in the significance of short or shaven hair versus long hair, but as Gananath Obeyesekere has shown, the interpretation of the meaning of hair in a traditional narrative or a life setting is a complex matter having to do with the nature and history of particular cultures and societies, personal experience, and a more universal set of psychogenic, almost Jungian, responses (1981; see also Leach 1967 for cautions about oversimplifying the meanings of hair). Thus Samson's hair may be interpreted on various levels.

On one level, wild long hair connotes freedom, tied or cropped hair a more socially bound condition. Even such a seeming universal must be approached with caution. There may, for example, be cultures in which everyone wears their hair long whether married or not, young or old. In such cases, short hair might convey the meaning, "not one of us." For tales of Samson, however, the suggestion that long hair connotes freedom from certain kinds of constraint works beautifully within the contours of the story. Samson has been a force of nature rather than a member of society; with hair shorn, he becomes a prisoner, literally bound to do the Philistines' bidding. From a Freudian perspective haircutting is often associated with castration, with a loss of male power, and this is a connotation that also seemed to be at work in ancient Israel. Like Samson, men who lose half their beards to enemy razors, as in 2 Sam 10:4, are unmanned.

Bal has pointed to Samson's childlike position (16:19), bald and asleep on a woman's knees (1984: 365). Hair loss is associated with the feminization of the defeated warrior, a theme we have seen throughout tales of judges, expressed through various images and key terms. Saul Olyan (1998) has explored the way in which haircutting and shaving connote "transformation" in ancient Israelite literature; clearly, Samson's loss of hair leads to a critical passage in his career as does its regrowth. Finally, an important inner Israelite meaning of the hair has to do with Samson's Nazirite status as discussed in ch. 13. To be holy to God from birth, a charismatic warrior called by the deity, involves leaving the hair uncut and other lifestyle requirements such as the avoidance of wine. To be dedicated to God is, on some level, to cling to the natural end of a nature/culture continuum, but of course the very act of wearing the hair a certain way is culturally conditioned. The plaits, in particular, imply a cultural activity. The very symbolization of freedom is to conform to certain rules.

The final line of 16:20 is very important to the interpretation of Samson's hubris. He does not believe that God would turn away from him or that the symbolic hair matters. That v. 20 repeats the frame found in vv. 9, 12, and 14 with this variation contributes to the drama of the story.

[21–31] Judges 16:21 extends the imagery that describes turning the hero into a woman (see notes ll, mm, and tt). The image of grinding is especially important. As indicated by Job 31:10 and Isa 47:2–3, "grinding" is a euphemism for sexual intercourse. The defeated enemy is the one who performs sexually for the winners. The metaphor linking sex and military or political power is potent and clear (see Niditch 1993b: 114–17). Karel van der Toorn has noted that enemy prisoners are depicted in Akkadian visual sources as marching into exile carrying mortars and pestles, the object being to reduce enemies "to a state of complete effeminacy" (1986: 252, n. 9).

Verse 22 adumbrates the plot reversal to come: Samson's hair is growing and with it his strength. Samson's hair is now truly loose and wild, in a natural state. The Philistines are pictured "fiddling while Rome burns." Their singsong taunts allude to Samson's power, a power that is returning to him. The reader knows that vengeance is at hand. These verses emphasize the religious dimension of the contest between Israelite and Philistine with mention of the god Dagon and allusion to sacrifices in praise of him.

The sexual nuances of "sporting" (16:25) continue the theme of the feminization of the hero (see note tt). Tension builds as the reader knows what is about to happen, while the Philistines rejoice in their ignorance. For his part, Samson describes vengeance in personal terms. The hero wants recompense for his two eyes. Notice the importance of prayers in the climax of the tale (Exum 1983: 39–43).

Samson's death is presented as heroic, his burial noble. He kills thousands of the enemy in fulfillment of God's plan and in the liberation of his people. His family and lineage unite to collect his remains, and he is buried in his father's sepulchre. This image of Samson in death confirms that the author seeks to portray him positively. The rejoinder (see 15:20) that he had "judged" for twenty years seals the positive image of Samson as leader and hero.

Judges 17:1–18:31
Micah's House Shrine
and the Founding of Dan

17:1   [a] And there was a man
            from the hill country of Ephraim,
        and his name was Micaiah.[b]

2   And he said to his mother,
        "The one thousand and one hundred in silver
            that were taken from you[c]
                and (about which) you uttered a curse,[d]
                and also you mentioned it in my ears,
            behold, the silver is with me.
            I took it."[e]
        And his mother said,
        "Blessed be my son to Yhwh."

3   And he returned one thousand and one hundred in silver to his mother.
        And his mother said,
        "To be holy, I have made holy the silver to Yhwh,
            from my hand to my son
                to make a hewn icon and a cast icon,
            and now I return it to you."[f]

4   And he returned the[g] silver to his mother,
        and his mother took two hundred in silver,
        and she gave it to the smelter,
        and he made it into a hewn icon and a cast icon,
        and it was in the house of Micaiah.

5   And the man Micah had a house of God,[h]
        and he made an ephod and teraphim,[i]
        and he consecrated[j] one of his sons,
        and he became for him a priest.

6   In those days, there was no king in Israel.
        A man would do what was right in his eyes.[k]

7   And there was a lad from Bethlehem of Judah,[1]
        from the clan of Judah,
    and he was a Levite,[m]
    and he sojourned there.
8   And the man went from the town,
        from Bethlehem of Judah,
            to sojourn wherever he would find,
    and he[n] came to the hills of Ephraim
        until the household of Micah
            to make his way.[o]
9   And Micah said to him,
    "From where do you come?"
    And he said to him,
    "A Levite I am
        from Bethlehem in Judah,
    and I am going to sojourn wherever I might find."[p]
10 And Micah said to him,
    "Dwell with me,
    and be to me a father and a priest,
    and I will give to you ten pieces of silver for the days
        and an estimate[q] for clothing and your sustenance."[r]
    And the Levite went.[s]
11 And the Levite was willing to dwell with the man,
    and the lad became to him like one of his sons.
12 And Micah consecrated the Levite,
    and the lad became to him a priest,
    and he was in the household of Micah.
13 And Micah said,
    "Now I know that Yhwh will make it go well with me,
    because I have the Levite as a priest."[t]
18:1 In those days, there was no king in Israel,[u]
    and in those days, the tribe of Dan was seeking for itself
        an inheritance to dwell in,
    for there had not fallen to him
        until that day
            an inheritance in the midst of the tribes of Israel.[v]
2   And the descendants of Dan sent
        from their clan[w] five men,
        from the whole of them,[x] valiant men,
            from Zorah and from Eshtaol,
                to spy out the land and to search it;
    and they said to them,

"Go, search out the land."
And they went to the hill country of Ephraim,
    until the house of Micah,
and they spent the night.[y]
3   They were with the household of Micah,
and they recognized the voice[z] of the Levite lad,
and they turned there,
and they said to him,
"Who brought you here,
and what are you doing in this (place),[aa]
and what is for you here?"
4   And he said to them,
"Thus and such Micah did for me,
and he hired me,
and I became for him a priest."
5   And they said to him,
"Inquire, pray, of God,
for we would know,
will our way lead to success,
    the one upon which we are walking?"
6   And the priest said to them,
"Go in peace.
Before Yhwh is your way
    upon which you walk."
7   And the five men walked,
and they went to Laish,
and they saw the people who were in her midst
        living in trust after the custom of the Sidonians,
        quiet and trusting,
        and not plotting a thing in the land,[bb]
        possessing restraint;[cc]
and far were they from the Sidonians,
and they did not have dealings with any human.[dd]
8   And they[ee] went to their kin at Zorah and Eshtaol,
and their kin said to them,[ff]
"What (do) you (think)?"[gg]
9   And they said,
"Rise up and let us go up against them,
for we have seen the land,
and behold, it is very good,[hh]
and you are being silent!
Do not be sluggish to set out to go

to possess the land.[ii]

10 And when you go,
   you will come to a trusting people,[jj]
   and the land is wide-handed,[kk]
   for God has given into your hands
      a place where there is no lack
         of anything on earth."[ll]

11 And the clan of the Danites traveled from there,
   from Zorah and from Eshtaol,
      six hundred men,
         girded with the instruments of war.

12 And they went up and they encamped
      in Kiriath-jearim (Town of Forests) in Judah.
   For this reason,
      they have called that place Mahaneh-dan ("Encampment of Dan")
         until this day.
   Behold, it is at the back of Kiriath-jearim.

13 And they crossed over from there to the hill country of Ephraim,
   and they came to the house of Micah.

14 And the five men answered,
      the ones who had been going to spy out the land of Laish,
   and they said to their kinfolk,
   "Did you know that there are in these houses
      an ephod and teraphim, and a hewn icon and a cast icon?
   And now, know what you will do."

15 And they turned here,
   and came to the house of the Levite lad,
      at the household of Micah,
   and they inquired of him as to his well-being.

16 And six hundred men
      girded with instruments of war
         were standing at the entrance of the gate
   who were from the descendants of Dan.

17 And up went the five men,
      the ones who had been going to spy out the land;
   they came there;[mm]
   they took the hewn icon and the ephod
      and the teraphim and the cast icon,
   and the priest was standing at the entrance of the gate,
      and the six hundred men,
         girded with the instruments of war.

18 And these came to the house of Micah,[nn]

and they took the hewn icon and the ephod,
   and the teraphim and the cast icon,
and the priest said to them,
"What are you doing?"

19 And they said to him, "Be silent.
Put your hand on your mouth,
and go with us,
and be to us a father and a priest.
Is it better your being priest to the household of one man
   or your being priest to a tribe and clan in Israel?"

20 And the priest felt good at heart,
and he took the ephod and the teraphim and the hewn icon,[oo]
and he went in the midst of the people.

21 And they turned and went,
and they put the children
   and the cattle and the riches[pp]
      in front of them.

22 They went a distance from the household of Micah,
and the men who were among the households
   that were with the household of Micah
      were called out,
and they overtook the descendants of Dan.

23 And they called to the descendants of Dan,
and they turned their faces,
and they said to Micah,
"What's with you[qq] that you called to arms?"

24 And he said,
"My gods that I made you have taken
   and the priest,
and you have gone off,
and what do I have left,
and what is this that you say to me,
'What's with you?'"

25 And the descendants of Dan said to him,
"You better not make your voice heard among us,
lest bitter-souled men strike you down,
and you[rr] will gather up your soul and the souls of your household."[ss]

26 And the descendants of Dan went on their way,
and Micah saw that they were stronger than he,
and he turned and returned to his household.

27 And they took what Micah had made,
   and the priest that he had had,

and they went to Laish,
  against a people quiet and trusting,[tt]
and they struck them by the mouth of the sword,
and the town they burned with fire.[uu]

28   And there was no savior,
  for far away it was from Sidon,
  and they had no dealings[vv] with any human,
  and it was in the valley that belongs to Beth-rehob,
  and they built up the town,
  and they dwelled[ww] in it.

29   And they called the name of the town Dan
  in the name of Dan their ancestor[xx]
    who was born to Israel,
  but Laish was the name of the town at first.

30   And the descendants of Dan raised up for themselves the hewn icon,
  and Jonathan, son of Gershom, son of Moses,[yy]
    he and his sons, became priests to the tribe of the Danites,
      until the day of the exile of the land.

31   And they set up for themselves the hewn icon of Micah
    that he made,
      all the days that the house of God was in Shiloh.

a. In a style similar to the annalistic language found elsewhere in the book (see 3:31; 10:1–3; and 12:8–15), OL presents a longer version of the opening of this chapter that includes the description of a judge unknown in MT or Vat: "And there arose after him Asemada the son of Annan, and he slaughtered of the foreigners six hundred men, besides the animals, and the Lord made Israel safe."

b. The language is formulaic, typical of phrases that introduce protagonists and the foundation stories in which they take part (cf. Amit 1984/85, 13:2, note b, and see introduction, section 4. The names Micaiah and Micah are variants, the later being an abbreviated form).

c. Vat reads, "that you took for yourself." OL reads, "that you took." Both traditions seem to soften the embezzlement theme, but work less well with the reference to the curse that follows. Note the formulaic amount of silver (cf. 16:5).

d. Vat reads, "and you cursed me," and OL reads, "and you swore."

e. The style of this verse is one of heavy enjambement. The implications of the main and opening clause are not revealed until the next to last phrase of the sentence. The complicated sentence structure may explain confusion in the traditions about the subject of the "taking."

f. Again notice the enjambed style. OL reads, "from my hand through myself to make it a hewn icon and a cast icon, and in time I will return it to you."

g. OL reads, "He returned that silver to his mother." There is potential confusion in the passing of the silver from son to mother, to son, and back to the mother. Who is commissioning the icons, the son (v. 3) or the mother herself (v. 4)? Verse 4 is composed of neatly self-contained phrases differing stylistically from the rendition in vv. 2–3. Perhaps this summative and slightly alternate version of the events is in a different narrator's register.

h. Vat reads, "The house of Micaiah was to him a house of God." OL omits "to him," the language of possession, thus reading awkwardly, "the man Micah was a house of God."

i. Verse 5 includes terms for divinatory paraphernalia that are difficult to translate. On the ephod, see commentary on 8:27. The teraphim appear to have been small statues or figurines that may have had significance for rituals or beliefs involving the ancestors. See Gen 31:19.

j. Literally, "filled the hand of." Cf. Exod 28:41; 29:9, 29, 33, 35; Num 3:3; 1 Kgs 13:33. The translator behind OL does not quite understand the idiom or literalizes on purpose: "he made a hand of one of his sons."

k. This description of the era or an abbreviation of the description is found several times in the last five chapters of Judges. See 18:1; 19:1; 21:25. An important internal marker, the full phrase forms an inclusio here and at 21:25, while the partial repetition at 18:1 and 19:1 creates transitions and frameworks for the stories that follow.

l. Cf. 17:1 and see introduction, section 4, for a discussion of the relationship between this formulaic introductory narrative language and a possible epic genre.

m. OL omits "and he was a Levite."

n. Vat and MT read "he" whereas OL reads "the lad" (cf. "man" in the first colon of v. 8). Although these are minor variations, they serve as a reminder that the term translated "lad" need not refer to a youth but may refer to aristocratic status, subordinate to that of a lord, king, or chieftain. See MacDonald 1976.

o. Notice again the enjambed quality of narration.

p. Notice the internal repetition from v. 8.

q. Vat reads, "ten pieces of silver per day and a garment of clothing." OL translates the term ʿrk (literally, "order") in terms of equivalence, perhaps "and its equivalent in garments."

r. Literally, "living." BDB (313) translates "preservation of life."

s. OL has a variant final colon: "And he compelled him."

t. OL reads, "the Lord has done well with me because he made for me a Levite as a priest." Is the translator dealing with the same *Vorlage* but translating in a way that makes it seem as if the priest is an appreciated blessing but not the source of future well-being?

u. See 17:6.

v. As in 17:2–3, 8, and 18:2, the grammatical structures intertwine. The completion of the thought comes late in the syntax.

w. Literally, "family." See 1:25.

x. Literally, "from the ends" (i.e., "the whole"). Vat omits the phrase, "from the whole of them."

y. OL and A read, "rested there." Is the Greek translator providing nuance in his translation of the more specific term "lodge" or do the *Vorlage* traditions use different words, manifesting minor variations of the same *dābār* (see introduction, section 6)?

z. Vat translates more generally "the sound." Do they hear his accent?

aa. Cf. Gen 38:21, 22; Exod 24:14; 1 Sam 1:26; 9:11.

bb. The root of the verb translated "plotting" means "to complete, be at an end," thus "determined" in a bad sense. See 1 Sam 20:7. Vat reads, "there was no perverting or dishonoring of discourse in the land," expanding slightly and choosing the translation "word" rather than "thing" for *dābār*, thereby drawing an implicit contrast with social intercourse in the Greek cities. OL reads, "they were not able to speak a word."

cc. Vat paints an ideal economic picture, reading the root meanings (or sound) of terms found in MT to refer to the peaceful quality of inheritance in Laish: "no heir of the treasure oppressing." There is thus plenty for all and no tension between generations. OL omits the phrase translated "possessing restraint."

dd. With a variation in one letter, OL reads, *ʾărām,* "Aram," rather than *ʾādām,* "human." This scribal variation thus leads to a different image and makes perfectly good sense. They have no dealings with Syria.

ee. Vat and OL read the variant, "and the five men," a more specific rendering of the subject.

ff. Vat and OL read, "and they said to their brethren," omitting "to them." The subject is the five men rather than the kin. OL continues with traditional-style repetition of v. 7: "because we entered and we went around the land of Geshem, and we saw a people dwelling in it in trust just like the Sidonians and a far way from Sidon, and there was no correspondence between them and Syria."

gg. Vat reads, "Why are you sitting?" The five men urge action. OL omits the final colon as I have arranged the verse.

hh. The language evokes the recurring phrase associated with the version of the creation preserved in Gen 1:4, 10, 13, 18, 21, 25 (see also Exod 2:1).

ii. Omitting "do not be sluggish," OL reads, "and you, you will be silent, lest you enter to possess the land. In your entrance. . . ." See notes ll and nn.

jj. OL omits this line.

kk. Cf. Gen 34:21. The idiom conveys spaciousness and fullness.

ll. Vat agrees with MT, but OL continues from v. 9, "you will enter a land, having an outstretched hand [notice the overliteralizing of the idiom] because the Lord has given to us a place where there is not from nothing of all the deeds which are upon the land." Perhaps this difficult-to-understand overliteralization of the Hebrew attempts to capture the isolation of the Laishians.

mm. Vat has a briefer text for v. 17: "And the five men, the ones who had gone up to spy out the land, went up." It omits "they came there . . . war." The taking of the paraphernalia is repeated in MT v. 18.

nn. Vat reads "and these came there into the house of Micah, and the priest was standing." The remainder of the verse agrees with MT (see Vat 18:17).

oo. Vat includes the molten or cast icon as well (cf. 18:14, 17, 18).

pp. Vat reads, "children, and possession, and the burden," literally, "the heaviness," in an overliteralization of the root *kbd,* translated "riches" above. The second object, "possession," can be traced to an overliteralization of the Hebrew term for cattle rooted in the verb "to acquire," and the third, "burden," to the root *kbd,* literally, "heavy," from which is derived a common word for "glory." OL thus reads, "they set the course of action and the glorious possessions."

qq. Formulaic language that suggests an accusation of wrongdoing (cf. 1:14).

rr. Vat reads, "they."

ss. That is, you will die. The life force will be taken from you and your supporters.

tt. OL has the variant, "resting and silent."

uu. Formulaic language of war in the Hebrew Bible, in particular the ban (Num 21:24; Deut 13:6, 16; Josh 6:21; 8:24; 10:28; Judg 1:8, 25).

vv. Literally, "thing, matter, word" (see 18:7). Vat and OL translate "word/speech," choosing one of the meanings.

ww. Vat includes a variant term for dwelling, literally "tenting."

xx. Literally, "father."

yy. In some manuscripts of MT, the letter *nun* is found raised and apparently inserted between the letters *mem* and *shin* to turn the name "Moses" into "Manasseh." This variation offers a fascinating indication of the way in which a scribe could revise a text. Vat reads, "Manasseh." OL reads, "Moses."

Judges 17–18 is a classic foundation myth, dealing with the conquest of land and the establishment of a tribal holding for Dan. Whereas tales of the judges in chs. 3–16 offer a defensive posture in their justification for war—Israel is oppressed and seeks relief—this tale is characterized by an aggressive, conqueror's demeanor that might be called hegemonist. Israelites, desirous of land, defeat an admittedly innocent group and take their land simply because they want it and they are able to do so. The ideology of expediency (see Niditch 1993b: 123–33) operates as one is made to see the workings of realpolitik in the ancient world. In chs. 17–18, as in the vignettes in ch. 1 and the tale of civil war in chs. 19–21, themes concerning the transience of power are especially strong. One group falls and another rises. Such are the ways of power. No covenantal ideology frames the acts of violence, justifying who wins and who loses or why, and the role of the deity, arbiter of war, while always implicit might be seen as muted. It is in this context that we read, "In those days there was no king . . . ," a phrase or rubric that appears first in 17:6 and, in part or in whole, three more times in chs. 17–21. This line is not, as some have suggested, an indictment of early times of chaos, but an accepting commentary on a romantic, battle-ridden, foundation period in the history of the nation. The phrase is a reflection on the nature of power itself. The rubric also frames, in a neutral way, various forms of religious activity that would be considered highly irregular by Deuteronomic-style writers: the ad hoc priesthood whose founder begins his career as a retainer for a wealthy chieftain; the peculiar way in which various iconic objects are funded and created; and the very use of paraphernalia such as an ephod, condemned in the tale of Gideon by the voice of the theologian but here associated, at least in some manuscript traditions, with the genealogy of Gershom, son of Moses. The tale in chs. 17–18 serves ultimately as founding myth for an ancient and valued cultic center. In these tales can be heard the voice of the humanist.

While the majority of verses divide easily into self-contained cola, the tales are punctuated by several examples of intricate enjambement. These cases find parallels elsewhere in Judges, and in each case the texture suits the content: 17:2–3 beautifully reflects the halting quality of speech, uttered by a guilty son, and provides background information (cf. the dialogue at 8:1, 6, 15); 18:2 also opens the narrative account, setting up the situation in a style that unfolds slowly (cf. 6:7–8; 9:17, 24 on "background"); 17:8 and 18:10–11 provide descriptive geographic or travel information (cf. 3:3; 4:5, 6, 11); and 18:30 preserves an etiology with genealogical significance that sums up the account (cf. 11:40).

[**17:1–6**] Like 8:22–27 and the lengthy accounts of God's orders to Moses in the "wilderness" period (e.g., Exod 24–28), Judg 17:1–6 includes a tale concerning the origins of religious paraphernalia. Some have suggested that the account of the golden calf, as preserved in Exodus 32, once performed a similar cultural function, namely to explain the origins of the bull icon that represented the presence of the deity at some ancient cultic centers in Israel (Cross 1973: 198–200). The origins of the two icons of ch. 17, one hewn and the other poured or cast, are rooted in a story of apparent embezzlement. The son has taken money in silver from his mother. She takes her case to God via a curse, and the son confesses his crime and returns the silver to her. The reconciliation of mother and son and the rehabilitation of the family thief are consummated and celebrated with the commissioning of religious objects out of the stolen loot. The son, called Micaiah or Micah, variations on the same name, then adds to these icons other sacred objects, an ephod and teraphim, and establishes a house sanctuary at which one of his sons serves as ad hoc priest.

The hewn and cast objects are not idols but iconic representations that allow worshipers to focus upon the deity and upon his/her qualities. The icon symbolizes the indwelling presence of the deity. On the form and function of the religious objects mentioned in Judges 17–18, see Miller 2000: 56, 165–66. Drawing comparisons with the silver-plated bronze calf found at Ashkelon, Lawrence Stager has suggested that the terms translated above as "a hewn icon and a cast icon" are actually one object, a figurine carved of wood or made of bronze upon which has been placed a silver coating or foil (2006: 405). All of the sacred objects mentioned seem to be statuaries of some kind; the ephod and teraphim are associated elsewhere with divination (see 8:27 above). It is certainly true that dominant threads in the Hebrew Bible are iconoclastic or aniconic, rejecting such representations as alien or idolatrous worship—even if the representations are meant to connote Yhwh and not Baal or another deity. Hence in Exod 20:4, within the Decalogue, is a clear order not to produce such representations; the condemnation of iconic objects dominates various passages such as the tales of Jeroboam, the first northern king (1 Kgs 12:25–14:17). Jeroboam is accused of idolatry by the Deuteronomistic narrator, but reading between the lines suggests that Jeroboam himself was providing his people not representations of a foreign deity but ancient portrayals of Yhwh as the bull of Jacob. The narrator of Judges 17–18 is aware of the iconoclastic bent of the tradition and probably accepts it as fully valid, but the phrase at 17:6 is far from an overt, zealous condemnation of the kind found elsewhere in the Hebrew Bible. Rather, he notes that these were early times, before the monarchy, when religious expression had not yet become uniform or orthodox. Indeed, the same could be said of tales in Genesis in which the patriarchs build various altars in various sacred locations. Such scenes also portray a religious world that precedes the centralization enjoined by the author of Deuteronomy 12. The saying in Judg 17:6 is thus not a condemnation, anticipating the need for the monarchy, but an indication that in the old days things were different. Such is the message of foundation myth.

[7–13] The wandering Levite from Judah finds employment at Micah's house shrine. Having a genuine Levite serve in the shrine is deemed to be preferable to the ad hoc arrangement with Micah's own son. The passage beautifully portrays relationships in terms of kin. The priest, not having a set hereditary homestead of his own in the style of the Levites, becomes a member of Micah's family, a retainer attached to a home shrine. Micah's declaration at v. 13 suggests that Levites are wandering holy men who bring good luck with them. They are quintessential mediators between God and humans, have divinatory abilities, and are quite a catch for the repentant son, con man, and cult founder.

[18:1–12] The tale of Micah, the house shrine, and the Levite continues with a foundation tale concerning the tribe of Dan. As in Numbers 13, Joshua 2, and Judg 1:23, would-be conquerors send out reconnaissance troops. They are given lodging in Micah's household in accordance with customs of hospitality. The phrase in 18:3, "they recognized the voice of the Levite lad," perhaps suggests that they recognize his southern accent. One is reminded of the dialectical variations in the pronunciation of the letter *shin* in 12:6. The warriors ask the Levite how he came to be at Micah's. They make use of his skills as diviner and ask formulaically for him to make inquiry of the Lord. The news for them is positive, and they continue on their exploratory journey.

Reconnaissance activities lead the team of five men to the town of Laish. The people of the town are described as nonaggressive and peaceful. The set of national characteristics listed by the author strikes the modern reader as most positive: trusting, quiet, nonconspiratorial, and restrained. The Laishians live "after the custom of the Sidonians," the inhabitants of an ancient Phoenician city-state located on the coast of the Mediterranean, nowadays the coastline of Lebanon. While Laishians are said to be culturally, perhaps ethnically, related to the Sidonians, the inhabitants of Laish live far from them and, indeed, live in isolation from other peoples as well.

The kinfolk of the reconnaissance troops are pictured dwelling at Zorah and Eshtaol (17:2, 11), locations associated with Samson, whose father Manoah is a Danite from Zorah. The tale purports to describe a northward migration of the

Danites. In Judges 5 Dan is associated via traditional language with seafaring (see Stager 1988, 1989 on the livelihood of the Danites), an activity less suited to an inland northern location such as Laish/Dan than to the "area bordering the Sharon and Philistine plains" and the accessibility of "the Sea Peoples' merchant vessels" (Boling 112).

The language of cosmogony is found in v. 9: "behold it is very good" (see Niditch 1996: 18–19). This formulaic phrase, employed in Genesis 1 (see note hh), evokes language of Israelite foundation myth. Laish is described as a kind of paradise with the felicitous imagery of "wide-handedness." They lack nothing. This image contrasts with that of the warrior culture of the Danites who seek to conquer others' land and others' possessions. The Danites are repeatedly described as a force "girded with instruments of war" (18:4, 17).

[13–26] An important thread of the Danite foundation myth builds on the tale of Micah's house shrine. The advance force let their allies, their kin, know about the shrine and its iconic and divinatory paraphernalia. They come to Micah's household and help themselves to these items and to the holy man as well. Micah protests, to no avail, for they are stronger than he and might makes right in their ideology of war. They describe themselves as "bitter-souled men" (18:25). These are people who have nothing to lose, brigands, bandits. One thinks of Abimelech's militia of "worthless and reckless men" (9:4) and the "worthless men" whom Jephthah gathers to himself. The vengeance of Gideon against the elders of Succoth (Judg 8) and David's threats against Nabal also come to mind (1 Sam 25:13, 21–22). These bitter-souled men are pictured as marginal, aggressive fighters hardened by living on the lam, by the very impermanence and vulnerability of their situation, and by the ambivalence of their status.

[27–29] The description of the conquest of Laish again sharply contrasts the peacefulness of the original inhabitants with the violent killing and destruction by the usurpers, whose activities invoke language reminiscent of the ban. The isolation of the Laishians is emphasized. Laish, conquered, is renamed Dan.

As modern ethicists, we can condemn the unjust war of conquest. Even the biblical narrator, who offers no overt condemnation and seems to accept that conquest is the way of the world, repeatedly mentions the Laishians' way of life in the most idyllic terms. The "bitter-souled" Danites are merciless, cutthroat, and self-serving. God does not condemn them, however, nor does the voice of the theologian. On one level, the story as narrated seems to say that foundation comes in violence; new nations are built on the ruins of the old. Yet a tone of wistful regret emerges in the contrast drawn by the narrator between the people "quiet and trusting" and the language of the ban. The reference to the ban-like war here is not infused with the tone of self-righteous justification found in the conquest accounts of Deuteronomy and Joshua. This tone in vv. 27–29 points rather to the humanist voice suggested as responsible for the final form of Judges and especially for the inclusion of chs. 1 and 17–21.

[**30–31**] The concluding verses of ch. 18 include intriguing and somewhat confusing material. The Levite lad is named in v. 30, and in some manuscript traditions is provided an illustrious genealogy in the line of Moses. Some manuscripts of MT, however, have introduced confusion into the reading "Moses" by including a raised *nun* that "corrects" the name Moses to Manasseh, a name associated with opprobrium in the Deuteronomistic History (2 Kgs 23:12). Are the Danites said to claim a priesthood that descends from the northern tribe of Manasseh, or, more likely, are they said to claim a priestly heritage in the line of Moses himself, through his son Gershom? The latter, more illustrious ancestry would no doubt have appealed to those who worshiped at an ancient northern shrine. One can understand political and theological reasons for the insertion of the *nun* by Judean, southern, pro-Davidic writers who would not want any shrine in the north, which was regarded as renegade by certain voices in the Hebrew Bible, to have the status of Mosaic origins.

Many scholars thus suggest that the Danite foundation tale, with its icons of suspicious origins, is a Judean critique of apostate northerners and their shrines, a critique that further contributes to the message concerning the need for a Davidic king who would centralize and purify worship. The supposedly tainted origin of the shrine provides moral justification for the destruction of Dan and the northern kingdom by the Assyrians, who act as God's tools of vengeance (see Soggin 277–78). For speculation concerning a later anti-Samaritan bias reflected in the reading with *nun*, see Weitzman 1999.

The present translation, however, reads "Moses." Some traditions present and understand this tale as an important foundation myth. The priest's descent from the venerable Moses undermines the interpretation that views the tale of the Danites as propaganda against the north, as does the uncritical neutrality of the narrator. He may feel sorry for the people of Laish and consider the Danites to be pirates, but he presents the tale of the great old shrine as he understands it, ending his account with the etiological comments about the length of time that the "Mushite" priesthood, i.e. a priesthood claiming descent from Moses, served at the northern shrine and when that shrine existed.

Scholars generally suggest that the phrase "until the day of the exile of the land" refers to the conquest of the northern kingdom by the Assyrians in 721 B.C.E. with its attendant exile of the elite. It is interesting, however, that the vocabulary for "exile" and the phrase "exile of the . . ." is overwhelmingly found in postexilic sources. Amos, the eighth-century B.C.E. prophet, does use this term to refer to the sin of Gaza and Tyre, who exile neighboring peoples in a type of war behavior that he condemns (1:6, 9). Amos also uses the root to describe the doom threatened by the Assyrian invasion (5:5; 6:7; 7:11, 17). Passages in 2 Kings use the root to refer to the exile of the north (2 Kgs 17:6; 18:11). The vast majority of the usages, however, are in clearly late material: Ezekiel, Jeremiah, Zechariah, Esther, Ezra, Nehemiah, 1 Chronicles, and 2 Kgs 24:11,

15. Thus the language of exile may well point to the postexilic date of the contributor to the tradition who presents the tale in Judges 17–18.

As implied by Kittel's suggestions for emendation, the reference to Shiloh at the conclusion is perhaps odd. The whole tale has been about the foundation of Dan, its shrine, and its priesthood. Why now use the presence of the house of God at Shiloh as a chronological marker? Frank Cross has suggested that Shiloh and Dan were both ancient Mushite shrines (1973: 197–98). Perhaps the author believed that God's tenting was in Shiloh (hence the stories about Eli, Samuel's service, and the tabernacle) and that the altar at Dan, another holy site, was best dated by reference to the more important and more famous location.

Judges 19:1–30
The Rape and Murder
of the Levite's Concubine

19:1   And it was in those days,
and there was no king in Israel.
And there was a Levite man
    living in the recesses[a] of the hill country of Ephraim,
and he took for himself a concubine woman
    from Bethlehem of Judah.
2   And his concubine "played the whore"[b] against him,
and she went from him to the house of her father,
    to Bethlehem of Judah,
and she was there four months of days.
3   And her husband rose up,
and he went[c] after her
    to speak upon her heart,
    to bring her back.[d]
And his lad was with him and a pair of donkeys.
And she brought him to the house of her father,[e]
and the father of the lass saw him,
and he rejoiced to meet him.
4   And his father-in-law laid hold of him,
    father of the lass,
and he dwelled with him three days,
and they ate, and drank, and spent the night there.[f]
5   And it was on the fourth day,
and they rose up early in the morning,

and he arose to go.
And the father of the lass said to his son-in-law,
"Sustain your heart with a morsel of bread,
and afterward you may go."

6   And they sat and they ate,
         the two of them together,
     and they drank.
     And the father of the lass said to the man,
     "Be willing, pray, and spend the night,
     and may your heart be glad."[g]

7   And the man rose up to go,
     and his father-in-law urged him,
     and he stayed and spent the night there.[h]

8   And he rose up early in the morning,
         on the fifth day to go,
     and the father of the lass said,
     "Sustain, pray, your heart."
     And they tarried until the stretching forth of the day,[i]
     and the two of them ate.

9   And the man arose to go,
         he, and his concubine, and his lad.
     And his father-in-law said to him,
         the father of the lass,
     "Behold, pray, the day is withdrawing to become evening.
     Stay, pray, the night.
     Behold, the declining of the day.
     Stay the night here,
     and let your heart be glad,
     and you will rise up early tomorrow to be on your way,
     and go to your home."

10   And the man was not willing to stay the night,
     and he arose and went,
     and he came up to Jebus,
         that is, Jerusalem,
     and with him was the pair of saddled[j] donkeys,
     and his concubine was with him.

11   They were at Jebus,
     and the day was mostly gone,
     and the lad said to his lord,
     "Let us turn
         into this city of the Jebusites,
     and spend the night there."

12 And say to him did his lord,
    "We will not turn into a foreign[k] town
        that does not belong to the descendants of Israel,
    but we will go to Gibeah."

13 And he said to his lad,
    "Come and let us draw near to one of the places,
    and let us spend the night in Gibeah or Ramah."

14 And they crossed over and went,
    and the sun went down upon them nearby Gibeah
        that belonged to Benjamin.

15 And they turned there to go to spend the night in Gibeah,
    and he went and sat in the plaza of the town,
    and there was no man gathering them
        into the house to spend the night.[l]

16 And behold, an old man came from his work,
        from the field in the evening.
    And the man was from the hill country of Ephraim,
    and he resided in Gibeah,
    but the men of the place were descendants of Benjamin.

17 And he raised his eyes,
    and he saw the wayfaring man in the plaza of the town,
    and the old man said,
    "Where are you going,
    and from where do you come?"

18 And he said to him,
    "We are crossing over from Bethlehem of Judah
        to the recesses[m] of the hill country of Ephraim.
    I am from there,
    and I had gone to Bethlehem of Judah,
    and with the house of Yhwh[n] I walk,
    and there is no man gathering us into his house.

19 And even straw, even fodder there is for our donkeys,
    and even bread and wine there is for me,
        for your maidservant, and for the lad.
    With your servants there is lacking not a thing."

20 And the old man said,
    "Peace to you.
    Only let all you lack be upon me,
    only in the plaza do not spend the night."

21 And he brought him to his house,
    and he gave provender to the donkeys,
    and they washed their feet,

and they ate and drank.

22   And they were making glad their heart,
and behold, the men of the town,
    worthless men,
       surrounded the house.
They were beating violently on the door,
and they said to the man,
    the old master of the household, saying,
"Bring out the man who came to your house,
and we would know° him."

23   And out to them went the man, master of the household,
and he said to them,
"Don't, my brothers,
don't do evil, I pray you,
    given that this man has come to my house.
Do not do this wanton folly.

24   Behold, my maiden daughter and his concubine.
I will bring them out, I pray you,
and you humiliate them,
and do to them what is good in your eyes,
but to this man
    do not do this deed of wanton folly."

25   And the men were not willing to listen to him,
and the man took hold of his concubine,
and he forced (her)ᵖ to go out to them outside,
and they knew her, q
and they abused her all the night until morning,
and they sent her away at the rise of dawn.

26   And the woman went at the turning of the morning,
and she fell at the entrance of the house of the man,
    where her lord was until the light (of day).

27   And her lord arose in the morning,
and he opened the doors of the house,
and he went forth to go on his way,
and behold, the woman his concubine was fallen
    at the entrance of the house,
and her hands were on the threshold.

28   And he said to her
"Get up, let's go."
But there was no answerer.ʳ
And he took her on the donkey,
and arise did the man,

and he went home.

29 And he went to his house,
and he took the knife,[s]
and he lay hold of his concubine,
and he cut her in pieces, limb by limb,[t]
  into twelve cut pieces,
and he sent her[u] into all the territory[v] of Israel.

30 And it was that all who saw it said,
"There has not been done nor been seen anything like this,
  from the day of the going up of the descendants of Israel
    from the land of Egypt[w]
      until this day.
'Set yourselves upon it,
take counsel and speak."

a. Vat overliteralizes by translating, "the thighbone," the inner recess of the upper leg.

b. Vat reads, "went from him," that is, left him. Note that the Greek verb *poreuō*, "to go," is similar to the verb *porneuō*, "to fornicate" or "play the whore," as translated above. OL and A read, "was angry with him." Alternate manuscripts thus provide a quite different nuance to her behavior. See commentary.

c. Vat employs the same term used for her action in leaving in v. 2.

d. OL reads, "so that he might reconcile her to him and lead her back." It is difficult to know whether OL reflects a different text or a sensitive, somewhat free translation that seeks the meaning of the Hebrew, "speak to her heart."

e. OL reads, "He went up to her house." The greeting and initial interaction is thus between the men.

f. The language of eating and drinking, spending the night, rising to go, the number of days, the invitation to tarry and rejoice are formulaic markers of hospitality in vv. 4–9, a unifying pattern of repeated language broken in v. 10. See commentary.

g. More briefly, OL has the father say, "Stay and be with me."

h. OL reads in a more summary fashion as in v. 6: "and he compelled him and he remained there."

i. OL reads, "heart with a morsel of bread, and he [literally] made him different [perhaps "diverted his attention" or "changed his mind"] until the day passed. . . ." Notice the anthropomorphizing of the day here and in v. 9.

j. Vat translates, "loaded down" or "packed up." OL reads with some variation, "and they set up/equipped a pair of donkeys and his lad, and he struck the donkeys and he took his concubine with him," painting the picture more fully.

k. OL omits "foreign," whereas MT doubly emphasizes the contrast between Israelite and non-Israelite.

l. OL reads, "no one to refresh them," thereby capturing the essence of the needs of travelers on a hot dusty day.

m. Here and throughout Vat literalizes the term, colorfully translating "recesses" as "the thighbone."

n. The intriguing phrase in the MT implying a search for a fellow Israelite seems to define identity in theological terms. The version is less loaded in Vat/OL: "I am going/returning to my house."

o. Know sexually, as in Gen 4:1, 17, 25; 24:16; 38:26; 1 Sam 1:19.

p. In MT the pronoun "her" is not stated but is understood. OL reads more fully, "threw her to them outside."

q. OL adds, "and they humiliated her," employing a verb connoting "rape," the term used in v. 24.

r. Vat reads, "and she did not answer because she was dead." OL reads, "She did not hear him but she was dead." Vat and OL thus are more explicit about the woman's condition, but MT is the more powerful in its implicitness and brevity.

s. Vat and OL view the cutting utensil as a "sword."

t. The language of cutting literally "by the bones" is used in contexts of animal sacrifice. 1 Samuel 11:7 provides the closest parallel for the cutting and sending of animal pieces in calling the league to military action. See also Exod 29:17; Lev 1:6, 12; 8:20; 1 Kgs 18:23, 33.

u. Vat reads, "these." OL reads more graphically, "her limbs."

v. Literally, "border."

w. OL continues with repetition of the people's reaction earlier in the verse, "and he commanded the men through whom he sent, saying, 'You will say this to every man of Israel. If this has been done according to this deed from the day of the coming up of the sons of Israel from Egypt until to this day, place yourselves according to this thinking and word.'"

Judges 19 provides the first installment in a cycle of interconnected stories in chs. 19–21. Shocking and yet familiar to readers of the great epic traditions of the world, this story cycle is filled with tales of violence and re-creation: violence against visitors contrary to ancient rules of hospitality, violence against women, the violence and mayhem of civil war, the undoing and reconstitution of the people Israel, and the decimation and rehabilitation of the tribe of Benjamin. Judges 19 commences an intricate narrative pattern that points to a series of tensions in ancient Israelite worldview involving gender, polity, and the causes and conduct of war. Women are treated as items of exchange or chattel and yet are most valuable and desirable commodities; Israel is one people, "the descendants of Israel," and yet more local, tribal kinship bonds sometimes override loyalty to the larger group or "family"; war is in the hands of Yhwh and yet is a quintessentially human event, disorganized and uncontrolled; war appears to be fought for a just cause, to avenge the rape and murder of a woman and to assert the legal prerogatives of a fledgling Israelite political entity, and yet the conduct of the war is patently unjust.

The nuclear family of ch. 19 serves as a symbol of the family of Israel. A relationship between a dysfunctional couple is followed by heinous aggression by individual Israelites against a few of their kin. This act of violence in turn leads to a destructive civil war and massive slayings in battle. The composer of this and subsequent chapters may well be using ancient narrative material that suits the epic themes and outlooks of Judges. The point of view expressed, however, also tallies well with that of the thoughtful humanist voice, which is astutely aware of the tensions and self-contradictions that are implicit in Israelites' views of their people's identity and history. Moore suggests, in a somewhat similar vein, that a contemporary of the Chronicler has shaped this material (405, 407).

Judges 19, like the two previous and two subsequent chapters, departs from the judge-centered format of the tales in chs. 3–16 and lacks the frame of the theologian that now introduces tales of the judges. Most of the verses in this disturbing tale of murder break easily into discrete cola that convey complete thoughts. The use of subordination in 19:30 underscores the present shocking episode by contrasting it with the shared, recollected past (cf. 9:17–18).

[1–10] The recurring line concerning an earlier time in the history of Israel (cf. 17:6; 18:1; and 21:25) links the tale of war in chs. 19–21 with the Danite founding myth and sets the tone for a particular attitude to the past. While some regard the variations upon this line as a critique of chaotic times before the establishment of the monarchy, they are better understood as more neutral allusions to early days in Israel's foundation history. Such are the ways of olden times, long past but intriguing. The line at v. 1 introduces a late author's version of compelling stories that underscore issues relevant to a uniquely Israelite process of self-definition and that draw upon more universal features of human experience.

As in the Danite foundation tale (17:8), a Levite from Judah who sojourns in the hill country of Ephraim figures prominently. The term *pîleges̆*, translated "concubine," is of uncertain etymological origins (see Rabin 1974). In the Hebrew Bible, she is often a second wife and appears to have a status lower than that of a "wife" but higher than that of a "harlot." Secondary wives frequently serve as sources of additional fertility for their husbands (Gen 22:24; 25:6; 36:12). Their status in the family is suggested by their mention in genealogical notices (Judg 8:31). Reuben seeks to enhance his status by having sex with his father's "concubine" (Gen 35:22), and Abimelech's status with powerful relatives is rooted in that of his mother, "concubine" of Gideon (8:31; 9:1ff.). She appears to have been "a free woman with an influential family" (Rabin 1974: 363; Moore 234). Social obligation and a contract of some kind are implicit in the marriage bond, as the relationship with the father-in-law suggests.

A literal reading of the woman's "playing the harlot" (19:2) would suggest marital infidelity or acting as a "loose woman," as in Gen 38:24 and Deut 22:21. The term, however, can also be used metaphorically to describe other acts of unfaithfulness (e.g., Hos 2). In a world in which men arrange the exchange of women, the woman's departure, in accordance with her own decision, could be regarded as an act of defiance (see also Yee 1995: 162). The departure could be regarded either as a kind of "harlotry," viewed as disloyalty, or as a protest against a situation of abuse. Alternate manuscript traditions imply an argument between the partners and perhaps a somewhat more equal footing in the marriage (see note b). Familial fissures or acts of abuse are frequently followed by attempts at reconciliation in the Hebrew Bible, as in 19:3 (cf. Gen 34:3; Hos 2:14 [MT 16]).

Five days of eating, drinking, and rejoicing at the home of the father-in-law mark the scene as one of convivial hospitality, as befits affinal kin. The dense repetition serves to emphasize the interaction, broken by the visitor's insistence on departure even as the day declines. The contrast between the day and the night adumbrates the frightening events that await the travelers. The woman has no voice throughout the men's conversation, a reminder that the tale has to do with relations between the men.

[11–25] The interaction between the Levite and his aide point to the contrast between "inside" and "outside" the group. Certain expectations for treatment influence the Levite's decision in a world of "us versus them." The Levite's refusal to accept the lad's suggestion to stop among non-Israelites and his insistence upon reaching an Israelite town set up tremendous irony in light of the vicious treatment he and his wife receive among those who are supposedly members of his own group. It has been suggested that the locations of Gibeah and Benjamin have implications for an anti-Saulide polemic (see discussion in Moore 407), given the first king's origins in the tribe of Benjamin and frequent mention of his connection with sacred spaces and trees in Gibeah (1 Sam 10:26; 11:4; 14:2; 22:6; 26:1). Such a nuance is certainly possible in this particular telling of the narrative, but the tale of broken hospitality in Judges 19 shares a tale type with the story of the Sodomites in Genesis 19, the better-known Israelite version of this traditional narrative.

Arguments have been made for relative chronology or borrowing between Judges 19 and Genesis 19 (see Niditch 1982; Lasine 1984). Each version, however, is best regarded as a variation on a theme, used for specific purposes in each context. The international folktale pattern involves weary travelers who seek succor but instead are treated with virulent hostility, thereby casting their "hosts" as the quintessentially antisocial "other." The Greek tales of the Cyclops and the Lestragonians provide comparable examples.

The Israelite versions include the motif of the one helpful man, further heightening the evil of the other townsfolk. Both the helpers, Lot in Genesis 19 and an unnamed man here, are resident aliens, somewhat marginal folk who are imagined as sympathetic to others like themselves. Notice language shared by the accounts (Gen 19:2 and Judg 19:20; Gen 19:3 and Judg 19:21; Gen 19:2 and Judg 19:15; see Burney 444–45). The versions thus share texture and text in traditional style. In Genesis the tale serves to condemn the Sodomites and extols the power of God, who stops the evildoers with blindness. In Judges 19, however, the narrative points to fissures within the would-be community of Israelites. Benjaminites are inhospitable to people headed further northward. Only the local northerner helps them. Benjaminites then support the evildoers over against the victims' rights to just vengeance and refuse the demands of the larger community of tribes to unite and extirpate the evil within their midst.

As in Genesis 19, the aggressive and violent demands of the mob involve homosexual rape (Judg 19:22). As discussed in connection with Ehud, Samson, and the the death of Sisera in 5:27, the man who defeats his enemy has metaphorically raped his enemy; he is empowered, his enemy a "mere" woman (see Vermeule 1979: 101–2; Niditch 1989; and Yee 1995: 164). By the same token, the man who is actually raped is made into the woman, the quintessential defeated enemy. Issues of shame and honor are at play. The worthless men seek to assert their power over against the outsider, whom they seek to humiliate. Also at play is an abusive sexual ethic in which the rape of women in battle and other contexts (e.g., Gen 34) is applied to the subduing of men. This passage is perhaps less about views of homosexuality, which priestly writers do condemn (Lev 18:22), than about a larger theme in sexual ethics in which one partner subdues, owns, and holds unequal power over the other (see Trible 1978: 105–39). A most troubling feature of the Israelite version of the tale type is the apparent willingness of the men to hand over their women to violent miscreants. Implicit is a worldview in which women are regarded as disposable and replaceable. On the other hand, the narration that follows implies that the author does not condone the men's behavior. They emerge as cowardly, and their complicity in the rape and murder of the woman is a clear and reprehensible violation of covenant. The tale as told also emphasizes the ways in which women, the mediating gender, provide doorways in and out of war.

[26–30] The scene of death and the discovery of the murder are filled with pathos. The woman collapses at the threshold. The author implicitly contrasts her condition, dying, abandoned, outside, with the husband's security in "the house of the man" until morning. His staying within until the morning is mentioned twice (19:26, 27). He is pictured to start his day without a care, ready to go on his way. She, again in contrast, is described as frozen in a state of desperation, "fallen," her hands clinging to the entrance of the safe zone. He does not even notice that she is dead. In two short words in the Hebrew, he orders her up. Her death is marked by the absence of her voice—indeed, we have not heard a word from her at all in the narrative.

The image of dividing the woman's corpse into twelve pieces, which are then sent to the twelve tribes, is a macabre parallel to Saul's divvying up his father's oxen and sending the pieces abroad to the territories of Israel with a stated threat that they must join him in battle lest he slaughter their cattle (1 Sam 11:7). Of course, here the enemy is internal and the sacrificial victim is now doubly sacrificed, victimized twice. The Israelites themselves are pictured as aghast at the

man's grotesque gesture, as indicated by their words in v. 30. The slow pace of
the Hebrew in v. 30 with its enjambed grammatical structures makes one pause.
Both 19:29 and Saul's action reflect ritualized methods of calling up allies to
arms, the constituent members of the people Israel that Martin Noth described
as a confederation, league, or amphictyony (1966: 53–75, 93).

Many consider the scene an indicator of the chaos that requires the establishment of a monarchy with a centralized government and an assumed capacity better to enforce the rule of law (Yee 1995: 158; Lasine 1984; Trible 1984:
84). Phyllis Trible sensitively points to the similarity between the language at
17:16 and 21:25 and the host's words to the murderous throng at 19:24 (1984:
84). The monarchy might be seen to limit people's capacity to do what is "good"
or "right" in their own eyes. If the sacrificial scene and the larger story of the
traveling Levite and his wife are understood as foundation myth, an alternate
interpretation emerges that is less bound to suggestions concerning a promonarchic stance. The woman is a visceral symbol of Israel's body politic, anticipating the way in which Israel is to be torn asunder by the civil war that follows
her murder. This sort of chaos, often including murder within the family followed by battle, is necessary to contrast with and motivate the foundation of a
new order. The woman's dismemberment, like a world-altering event, leads to
actual war out of which emerge a new order, peace, and reconciliation between
men. The reconciliation is achieved through the distribution of women. The
women are viewed as captured commodities; they are exchange items that
achieve unity between those who participate in the exchange, as are the pieces
of an animal carcass that create community at a sacrificial feast. Thus this story
begins with the sacrifice of a woman, continues with demands for shared responsibility, and ends with the sacrifice of women, the exchanges by which men
form or symbolize relationships. In Judges 19–21 the women themselves have
no say in the matter.

The tearing apart of the wife, however, also condemns her husband, for he
desecrates his wife's body and shows himself capable of mad violence. He perhaps reveals his own guilty anger in the enraged attack upon the body of the
one whom he himself had thrown to the angry, murderous mob.

Judges 20:1–48
Civil War

20:1   And all the descendants of Israel went forth,
      and the congregation assembled as one man,[a]
         from Dan[b] until Beer-sheba and the land of Gilead
            unto Yhwh at Mizpah.

2   And the chiefs[c] of all the people stationed themselves,
          all the tribes of Israel,
                in the assembly of the people of God,
          four hundred thousand men on foot,
                each drawing a sword.
3   And the descendants of Benjamin heard
          that the descendants of Israel were going up to Mizpah,
      and the descendants of Israel said,
      "Speak!
      How[d] came about this evil?"
4   And the Levite man answered,
          the husband of the woman who was murdered,
      and he said,
      "To Gibeah that belongs to Benjamin I came,
          myself and my concubine to spend the night.
5   And the lords[e] of Gibeah rose up against me,
      and they surrounded me at the house by night.
      They thought to kill me,
      and my concubine they raped,[f]
      and she died.
6   And I laid hold of my concubine,
      and I cut her into pieces,
      and I sent her to all the open territory of the inheritance of Israel
          because they committed[g] wickedness[h] and wanton folly in Israel.
7   Behold, you are all descendants of Israel.
      Provide yourselves discussion and counsel here."
8   And all the people rose up as one man saying,
      "We will not go, not one man, to his home,[i]
      and no man will turn toward his house.
9   And now, this is the thing that we will do to Gibeah.
      Against it by lot![j]
10   And we will take ten men of a hundred
          in all the tribes of Israel,
                and a hundred of a thousand,
                and a thousand of ten thousand,
                      to take provisions to the people
                      to make ready for their coming to Gibeah in Benjamin
                            for all the wanton folly that they did in Israel."
11   And every man of Israel was gathered to the town
          as one man, united.
12   And the tribes of Israel sent men
          throughout all the tribes of Benjamin, saying,

"What is this evil that has been done among you?

13   And now, give over the men,
     worthless men who are in Gibeah,[k]
   and we will put them to death,
   and we will burn out the evil from Israel."
   But the descendants of Benjamin were not willing
     to listen to the voice of their kin, the descendants of Israel.

14   And gathered were the descendants of Benjamin, from the towns
      toward Gibeah,
     to go forth to war against the descendants of Israel.

15   And the descendants of Benjamin mustered[l] on that day from the towns,
     twenty-six thousand sword-drawing men.
   Apart from the dwellers of Gibeah were mustered
     seven hundred chosen men.[m]

16   From all this people,
     seven hundred chosen men were left-handed;[n]
   every one was someone who could sling with a stone
     at a hair and not miss.[o]

17   And the men of Israel mustered, apart from Benjamin,
     four hundred thousand sword-drawing men,
      every one of these a battle-hardened man.[p]

18   And they rose and went up to Bethel,
   and they inquired of God,[q]
   and the descendants of Israel said,
   "Who will go up for us at the beginning[r]
     to war against the descendants of Benjamin?"
   And Yhwh said,
   "Judah will be at the beginning."[s]

19   And arise did the descendants of Israel in the morning,
   and they encamped against Gibeah.

20   And go forth did the men of Israel
     to war against Benjamin,
   and the men of Israel arrayed[t] against them,
     war at Gibeah.

21   [u] And the descendants of Benjamin went forth from Gibeah,
   and they brought to ruin in Israel on that day,
     twenty-two thousand men to the ground.

22   And the people strengthened the men of Israel,
   and they again arrayed for war
     in the place where they had arrayed on the first day.

23   And the descendants of Israel went up,
   and they cried before Yhwh until the evening,

and they inquired of Yhwh, saying,[v]
"Shall we again draw forth to war
   with the descendants of Benjamin, our kin?"
And said Yhwh,
"Go up against him."

24   And the descendants of Israel drew near
   to the descendants of Benjamin
      on the second day.

25   And Benjamin went forth to meet them
   from Gibeah
      on the second day.
And they brought to ruin among the descendants of Israel,
   an additional eighteen thousand men to the ground,
      all of these sword-drawers.

26   And all the descendants of Israel went up,
   and all the people,
and they went to Bethel,
and they cried and sat there before Yhwh,
and they fasted on that day until evening;
they raised up whole burnt offerings and well-being offerings
   before Yhwh.[w]

27   And the descendants of Israel inquired of Yhwh,
and there was located the ark of the covenant of God in those days.

28   And Phinehas, son of Eleazar, son of Aaron,
   was in attendance before it in those days saying,
"Shall we[x] again go forth to war
   against the descendants of Benjamin our kin,
or shall we stop?"
And Yhwh said,
"Go up, because tomorrow I will give them into your hand."

29   And Israel set ambushes at Gibeah round about.

30   And the descendants of Israel went up
   against the descendants of Benjamin
      on the third day,
and they arrayed against Gibeah as formerly.

31   And the descendants of Benjamin went forth to meet the people.
They were drawn away from[y] the town,
and they began to strike down some of the people, slain,[z]
   as before on the highways
      (the one that goes up to Bethel
      and the one to Gibeah in the open country),
         about thirty men in Israel.

32   And the descendants of Benjamin said,
    "They are smitten before us, as at first."
    And the descendants of Israel said,
    "Let us flee and draw them away[aa]
        from the town to the highway."

33   And all the men of Israel rose from their place
    and arrayed themselves at Baal-tamar,
    and the ambush of Israel came bursting forth from its place,
        from Maareh-geba.

34   And go against Gibeah
        did ten thousand chosen men from all of Israel.
    And the battle was difficult,
    and they did not know
        that calamity was about to reach them.

35   And Yhwh smote Benjamin before Israel,
    and the descendants of Israel brought Benjamin to ruin on that day,
        twenty-five thousand, one hundred men,
            all of these sword-drawers.

36   And the descendants of Benjamin saw that they were smitten,
    and the men of Israel gave room to Benjamin
        because they trusted in the ambush
            that they had set at Gibeah.

37   And the ambush group came quickly,
    and they made a dash[bb] to Gibeah,
    and move in[cc] did the ambush,
    and they struck all the town with the mouth of the sword.

38   And the appointed signal was between the men of Israel
          and the ambushers:[dd]
        their sending up a beacon[ee] of smoke from the town.

39   [ff] And the men of Israel turned in battle,
    and Benjamin began to strike down slain
        among the men of Israel about thirty men,
    for they said,
    "Smitten he is smitten before us
        as in the first battle."

40   And the beacon began to go up[gg] from the town,
        a column of smoke.
    And Benjamin looked behind them,
    and behold, the whole[hh] town was going up, a holocaust toward heaven.

41   And the men of Israel turned,
    and dismayed[ii] were the men of Benjamin,
    for they saw that calamity was about to reach them.

42   And they turned away from the men of Israel,
         to the way of the wilderness,[ii]
      but the battle clung[kk] to them,
      and those who were from the town were bringing ruin to them
         in their midst.
43   They encircled Benjamin.
      They pursued him.
      They trampled peace,[ll]
         until Nohah toward Gibeah
            from the east of the sun.
44   And eighteen thousand men fell from Benjamin,
         all of these, men of valor.
45   And they turned and fled toward the wilderness,
         to the Rock of Rimmon,
      and gleaned[mm] on the highways were five thousand men,
      and they stuck close[nn] to them until Gidom,
      and they struck down from them two thousand men.
46   And it was that all who fell from Benjamin
         were twenty-five thousand sword-drawing men,
            on that day,
         all of these men of valor.
47   And they turned and fled toward the wilderness,
         to the Rock of Rimmon,
            six hundred men,
      and they stayed at the Rock of Rimmon four months.
48   And the men of Israel returned against the descendants of Benjamin,
      and they struck them by the mouth of the sword, the town in its entirety,[oo]
            including animals and all that was found.
      Also all the towns that were found, they sent up in fire.

a. The opening lines in OL expand on the consultative nature of the gathering and read, "And all the house of Israel gave instruction, and all the congregation made an assembly like one man."

b. MT may be read "to Medan" or "from Dan," as in Vat and OL.

c. Literally, "corner, support, or defense" (BDB 819). Vat and OL omit "all the chiefs," reading the subject as "all the tribes of Israel." Vat continues, "stationed themselves before the face of the Lord in a congregation," thus emphasizing the oracular motivation for the gathering.

d. Vat has a word that can mean "how" or "where." OL reads, "where." Note that the following verse responds to the question "where."

e. The term used is *ba'al*, literally, "master." OL translates or reads, "chiefs," and Vat, "men."

f. OL expands, "and mocked her," i.e., made sport of her sexually.

g. Literally, "did."

h. Vat translates the Hebrew term for "wickedness" as literally, "boiling" or "fermentation," because the Greek word sounds like Hebrew *zimmâ* and is a good metaphor for unbridled wickedness.

i. Literally, "tent."

j. Vat and OL read more fully, "We will go up against her by lot." This reading may be a gloss on the same Hebrew or a longer version.

k. OL reads, "give the guilty men from the sons of Benjamin," making clear that only those who committed the crime will be punished. MT is more ambiguous.

l. Vat translates the root *pqd* as "reviewed." OL translates, "numbered."

m. OL and Vat combine the end of v. 15 and the beginning of v. 16, leaving out one of the references to "seven hundred chosen men."

n. Literally, "bound with regards to the right hand." On left-handedness see the discussion of Ehud (ch. 3). Vat and OL translate, "ambidextrous."

o. Literally, "sin," i.e., "make a mistake."

p. Literally, "a man of war."

q. Notice the echo of 1:1 and the formulaic language for requesting an oracle.

r. OL translates, "play a leadership role," emphasizing status rather than chronology. The parallel with the opening of Judges continues.

s. OL translates, "Judah will go up as leader."

t. Literally, "set in rows."

u. OL reads, "And the sons of Israel gave to them one thousand men to besiege the cities. And they placed themselves on the way to Gibeah, and all the congregation commanded them saying, 'Go to that place which is above the ambushes, and it will be when the sons of Benjamin begin to come out from the city, you will mingle secretly, and you will enter it, and you will take away peace, and we will turn back hard upon their heels, and we will strike them.' And Benjamin went out from Gibeah, and all the men of Israel went out to Benjamin, all of Israel meeting with them in war against Gibeah, and Benjamin went out and exterminated from Israel in that day twenty-two thousand men, and Israel was overcome, and again they arrayed to fight there in the valley as on the first day." The content is similar to that of MT 20:21–22, but includes a description of a planned ambush and deception by which the battle is to succeed. The text is more pictorial as a narrative.

v. Notice the continuation of formulaic language indicating a request for an oracle.

w. The end of MT v. 26 begins v. 27 OL ("before the Lord"). OL picks up the thread found halfway though MT v. 28. Omitting "And Phinehas . . . saying," OL provides the content of MT 20:27–28 thus: "And they inquired of the Lord and they said 'Why, O Lord, has indignation and wrath been committed against Israel, and we your children have gathered together to take away the sons of iniquity who did impiety in Israel, and behold, we have fled from their face twice and now shall we set up again to go . . . ?'" OL thus provides a theological justification from the mouths of the Israelites. In content and structure, this little monologue is reminiscent of the lament; good deeds appear to have been rewarded with undeserved suffering. MT and Vat describe a simpler request for military advice by means of an oracle. Vat leaves out MT v. 27: "And the descendants . . . of Yhwh," and places a similar phrase in v. 28. Instead of Phinehas "saying," Vat has, "They inquired." Perhaps this simpler variant is less priestly in orientation and allows the people to approach the oracle themselves with their question.

x. MT employs the singular literally, "shall I," as if Phinehas speaks for himself as leader.

y. Vat translates, "were emptied out from."

z. OL reads, "And the sons of Benjamin went out to the people, and they were drawn out from the city and they began to fall wounded." Here the Lyons Manuscript ends.

aa. Vat reads, "empty them out," as in v. 31.

bb. Translated elsewhere, "raid." See 9:44, "strip off."

cc. Translated elsewhere as "march" (e.g., 5:14), literally, "draw out."

dd. Vat reads, "the ambush of/concerning the battle." MT has an untranslatable word, *hrb*, after "ambush," omitted in Vat. A reads a *ḥ* and translates "ambush of the sword," thus presenting an excellent war image. A may reflect an alternate Hebrew *Vorlage* that made more sense or a text that had been corrected to make more sense. It is also possible that the translator in A engaged in a form of creative exegesis in order to make sense of the same difficult Hebrew text found in MT.

ee. Literally, "a raising up of." Vat translates or reads, "signal."

ff. Vat begins, "And the sons of Israel saw that the ambush had captured Gibeah, and they stood in battle array, and Benjamin . . . ," painting the scene with a longer variant.

gg. Vat reads, "go up even more," conveying a sense of progress in this difficult-to-follow pattern of battle.

hh. The Hebrew term for completeness is used in sacrificial contexts to connote a whole burnt offering, hence our translation "holocaust." Vat translates, "the completeness/consummation of the city went up."

ii. Vat translates "rush" for the root that can also be translated "dismayed." Vat thus conveys a sense of mayhem.

jj. Vat translates literally and expands slightly, "They faced the men of Israel toward the way of the desert, and they fled."

kk. Literally, "embraced."

ll. The syntax and meaning of MT is difficult at this point. Vat reads, "They cut Benjamin into pieces, and they pursued him, from Nohah at his heel until opposite Gibeah."

mm. Vat reads, "gathered up the stragglers."

nn. Cf. 18:22, where I translated the term "overtook."

oo. Vat translates, "from the city of Methla."

Chapter 20 describes Israel's descent into civil war as the bonds of kinship trump the community of statehood. Benjamin refuses to join the rest of Israel in rooting out the evil in their midst, siding instead with its closer kin in Gibeah. The narrative thus offers a test of Israel's unity, as the events described challenge the very notion of peoplehood under the covenant. This interest in the forms of polity and the tensions between them is typical of the humanist voice of Judges.

The huge numbers of participants, dead, and wounded and the often difficult-to-follow stalemate that characterizes the war are reflected in the highly repetitive and jagged style of the account. Various sentences reveal dense subordination and lengthy noun strings, typical of a late Hebrew register (e.g., 20:2, 3, 10, 31, 36), and the rough edges of the Hebrew have led to interesting variations in the manuscript traditions, some of which provide alternate versions of portions of the epic battle account. The style of vv. 2 and 10 captures the arduous process of preparations for war. Verse 31 provides another example of unfolding geographic content, a verbal map of sorts (cf. 3:3; 4:5, 6, 11). The register thus suits the content.

[1–7] A formal gathering of military forces at Mizpah is imagined, having ritual and legal dimensions. Mizpah, meaning "outlook point" or "height," is a hilltop location in the territory of Benjamin. A consensus of modern scholars suggests a possible identification with Tell en-Naṣbeh, located about 7.5 miles north of Jerusalem. Like Gibeah, another hilltop location north of Jersusalem, Mizpah has significance as a sacred site associated with the transition to the monarchy, in particular with the judgeship of Samuel. Samuel prays for the people at Mizpah after they demand a king (1 Sam 7:5), and he is said "to judge" there. From this border fortress and holy place Israel goes forth to battle against the Philistines (1 Sam 7:11). Similarly, in Judg 20:1 Mizpah is the locus of ritual, legal, and political activity, for here miscreants from Gibeah are accused and judged guilty and here the Israelites consider undertaking a war of vengeance that would affect the group as a whole. The scene in Judg 20:1–7 suggests the instructions of Deut 13:12–18 concerning the responsibility of Israelites to root out from among the people those who break covenant. An inquiry is to be made and guilt ascertained. This is precisely what happens in Judges 20 as the Levite offers testimony.

The Levite dissimulates. He does not mention the threat of rape directed at his own person, nor does he admit that he himself threw his wife to the mob to save his own skin. He implies that the miscreants sought to kill him and somehow took his wife, who was then raped and killed. His misrepresentation of the events contributes further to a negative portrayal of the Levite; readers and hearers of this tale already know about his despicable treatment of his wife and her body. The Levite urges the people as a whole to seek vengeance and implies that the sending out of her body in parts was a visceral cry to action. Israel will be unified, each tribe implicitly responsible for her body. Somewhat comparable are the instructions in Deut 21:1–9 concerning bloodguilt for a person murdered without witnesses. The people, represented by the elders, symbolically take responsibility for an unsolved murder and thereby cleanse the group of corporate guilt and sin. In Deuteronomy 21, however, an animal plays the sacrificial role as substitution for the victim. In a pattern evocative of creation myths in which the cosmos is imagined as a body divided, the murdered woman has literally been split and distributed (see on 19:30).

The gathering at Mizpah where the tribes consider a joint exercise of martial power to enforce the will of the group is precisely the sort of scene imagined by Martin Noth and others who have suggested the existence of a twelve-tribe, pan-Israelite league or confederation. While aspects of the theory have rightly come under criticism, the notion that some means existed for allied military action on the part of various segments of Israel seems likely. The scene at Mizpah, however, explores how difficult such alliances are to maintain.

[8–13] The group appears to unify for battle and vengeance. The apportioning by lot is frequent in biblical accounts (e.g., Josh 18:10; 1 Chron 24:5, 7; Neh 11:1) and here is seen in a military context. Casting lots allows for divinely ordained decisions. The elongated style of v. 10 contributes to the sense of preparation in the amassing of troops. Implicit is the message that all of this work is worth the goal to punish "the wanton folly." The Hebrew at v. 13 is ambivalent. Do the Israelites seek only those who committed the outrage, or does the phrase "worthless men who are in Gibeah" imply that all in Gibeah are now contaminated by sin? In a similar fashion, the family of Achan (Josh 7:24–26) is placed under the ban in a process of guilt by association in which uncleanness is contagious. Achan himself had stolen objects devoted to the deity, but those related to him must also suffer his punishment, even his children. The refusal of the Benjaminites to cooperate is somewhat more understandable if the model of the ban is at play. In any event, they place loyalty to their tribal kin over justice for all; loyalty to a pan-Israelite entity, also acknowledged and described literally as "their brothers" or kin, is less important to them than loyalty to their more immediate kin. The kinship of all Israelites is an important theme of the tale, emphasized in the conclusion in ch. 21.

[14–48] The civil war is characterized by the recurring pattern of war: muster of each side (vv. 14, 15, 17, 19, 22, 29, 32), request for an oracle by the Israelites (vv. 18, 23, 26–28), response of the deity (vv. 18, 23, 28), going forth to battle (vv. 20, 21, 24, 25, 30, 31), the battle (vv. 25, 31, 33, 34, 35, 36–37, 39), and the outcome (vv. 39–48). The majority eventually take control of the crack troops of the enemy, the left-handed men of Benjamin.

As in great ancient epics or modern films that invoke them, victory in battle favors one side and then the other in the oscillation of military stalemate. Some, such as Gray (280–282), Soggin (294), and Burney (447–58), see recurring references to muster, oracle, and engagement as an indication of separate sources. Repetition, in their view, has resulted from the combining of versions of the same account; and Burney, in particular, provides intricate suggestions for the earlier sources and the process that led to the current account. The repetitions in the present version, however, are thematically important, pointing to the very nature of war as an often pointless round of battles; power rises and falls, and justice is difficult to determine. The repetition of language exemplifies a variety of traditional registers but also helps to emphasize the push-and-pull dynamic of war.

The author appears to take pleasure in describing the battle as a competition with recurring patterns of military contest that serve to heighten drama and tension, but the passage does suggest that the resulting stalemate produces ethical dilemmas. The repeated requests for divine advice suggest confusion and severe uncertainty about the war undertaken. This self-doubting attitude to war is not only found in an international corpus of epic literature, but is of special interest to the humanist voice of Judges.

[14–25] The skill of the left-handed Benjaminites is beautifully articulated in v. 16 (see 3:15 concerning Ehud above). Literally "sons of the right," the Benjaminites are often left-handed, due to training (see Halpern 1988b: 34–35) or genetics. Obvious respect is shown the enemy, as is typical in epic literatures (see 8:18–21). Verse 18 reprises the opening line of Judges 1, as the Israelites request via an oracle to know who should be at the forefront of the force, and Judah is portrayed as the chosen leader. This reprise perhaps suggests not only a southern writer but also a voice different from those that frame and express the corpus of tales of northern judges from chs. 3–16. Thus language, in addition to matters of content and theme, discussed above, support the suggestion that the voice responsible for chs. 17–21 is also responsible for the introduction in ch. 1. This section ends at 20:21 with Israel suffering huge losses.

Rallying and again requesting an oracle of God, the Israelites ask if they should persevere. The deity answers in the affirmative, but following his advice ironically leads only to further devastation (20:25). While the author in typical biblical narrative fashion provides no overt value judgment concerning the advice or its unfortunate outcome, the reader is left to ponder the divine wisdom. The next section, describing the third leg of the war, does suggest the Israelites' frustration.

[26–48] This version of the request for an oracle is the lengthiest and, in tone, the most desperate. The Israelites "cry," fast," and "raise up offerings." The emotion has intensified at each request (vv. 18, 23, and 26). No less than the prestigious heir of Aaron's mantle makes inquiry, Phinehas, son of Eleazar, son of Aaron, the zealous Yahwist who slew the Israelite man and his Midianite woman accused of non-Yahwistic practices in Numbers 25. Again Yhwh urges them to battle.

The tactics in the third attempt involve ambush and deception rather than direct confrontation (vv. 29, 32, 37). Places where the Israelite army arrays, bursts upon, or routs the enemy (Baal-tamar, v. 33; Maareh-geba, v. 33; Nohah, v. 43) are set in the environs of Gibeah. All the action takes place in Benjamin. Rimmon has been identified with modern Rammun, four miles east of Bethel (Boling 288). The fate of the Benjaminites is described in dramatic and ironic terms. They do not realize that "calamity" is upon them (vv. 32, 34, 41). The language exquisitely describes the difficulty of battle (v. 34), the speed with which the battle changes course (v. 37), the dismay (v. 41), and the way that battle "clings" to combatants (v. 42). The third encounter is evocative of the ban, the totalistic devotion to destruction so often invoked in the book of Joshua. The term "holocaust," the totality of the destruction, and the ascent of the smoke toward heaven (v. 40) all suggest total devotion to destruction, as do references in v. 48 to "striking by the mouth of the sword, the town in its entirety" (see also v. 37), including animals, and the sending up in fire of all the remaining towns. There are, however, survivors. Chapter 21 deals with their disposition.

Judges 21:1–25
The Reconciliation of Men
through "the Traffic in Women"

21:1 And the men of Israel had taken an oath in Mizpah, saying,
 "A man from among us will not give his daughter
  to Benjamin as wife."

2 And the people came to Bethel,
 and they sat there until the evening before God,
 and they lifted up their voice,
 and they wept a great weeping.

3 And they said,
 "Why, Yhwh, God of Israel,
  has this happened in Israel,
   for one tribe to be picked out[a] today from Israel?"

4 And it was the next day,
 and the people rose early,
 and they built there an altar,
 and they raised up whole burnt offerings and well-being offerings.

5 And said the descendants of Israel,
 "Who is it that did not go up in the assembly of Israel
  from all the tribes of Israel to Yhwh?"
 For a great oath was taken
  against whomever did not go up to Yhwh at Mizpah,
   saying, "Die he will die."

6 And the descendants of Israel had compassion upon Benjamin, their kin,
 and they said,
 "Hewn off today is one tribe in Israel.

7 What can be done for them, for those who remain, for wives?
 And we took an oath by Yhwh,
  not to give them from our daughters as wives."

8 And they said,

"Which is one from the tribes of Israel
   that did not go up to Yhwh at Mizpah?"
And behold, no man had come to the encampment
   from the dwellers of Jabesh-gilead to the congregation.

9   And the people were mustered,
      and behold, no man was there
         from the dwellers of Jabesh-gilead.

10   And the congregation sent there
         twelve thousand men from the sons of valor,
      and they commanded them saying,
      "Go and strike the dwellers of Jabesh-gilead
         by the mouth of the sword,
            and the women and the children.[b]

11   And this is the thing you will do.
         Every male and every woman
            who has known the bed of a male,
               you shall devote to destruction."[c]

12   And they found from among the dwellers of Jabesh-gilead,
         four hundred virgin lasses
            who had not known a man, for bedding with a male,
      and they brought them to the encampment of Shiloh,
         which was in the land of Canaan.

13   And all the congregation sent,
      and they spoke to the descendants of Benjamin,
         who were at the Rock of Rimmon,
      and they called out to them peace.

14   And Benjamin returned at that time,
      and they gave to them the women whom they had let live,
         from the women of Jabesh-gilead,
      but they did not find enough for them.[d]

15   And the people had compassion upon Benjamin
         because Yhwh made a breach in the tribes of Yhwh.

16   And the elders of the congregation said,
      "What shall we do for wives for the remainder,
      for women are eliminated[e] from Benjamin."

17   And they said,
      "The inheritance of the escaped remnant of Benjamin!
      And a tribe will not be blotted out from Israel,

18   but we cannot give them wives from our daughters.
      For the descendants of Israel have taken an oath, saying,
      'Cursed be anyone who gives a woman to Benjamin.'"

19   And they said,

"Behold, there is a yearly[f] festival of Yhwh in Shiloh,
   which is north of Bethel,
      from east of the sun to the highway
         that goes up from Bethel toward Shechem,
            and from the south of Lebonah."
20   And they commanded the descendants of Benjamin, saying,
   "Go and prepare an ambush in the vineyards.
21   And you will see and behold,
   if the daughters of Shiloh come forth to whirl in whirling dances,
      then come forth from the vineyards,
   and seize for yourselves, each man his woman,
      from the daughters of Shiloh,
   and go to the land of Benjamin.
22   And let it be if their fathers or brothers come
      to quarrel with us,[g]
   we will say to them,
   'Be gracious to them,
   for we did not take a woman for each man in warring,
   neither did you give to them,
      in such a way[h] that you incurred guilt.'"[i]
23   And the descendants of Benjamin did thus,
   and they carried off women in accordance with their numbers,
      from the whirling dancers whom they stole.
   And they went and returned to their inheritance,
   and they built cities,
   and they dwelled in them.
24   And the descendants of Israel sallied forth from there at that time,
      each man to his tribe and clan,
   and they went forth from there,
      each man to his inheritance.
25   In those days, there was no king in Israel.
   A man would do what was right in his eyes.[j]

a. Vat translates, "to be visited with." The root *pqd* has been translated in military contexts above as "muster" and literally means "to appoint."

b. Vat omits "and the women and the children," a phrase that does seem misplaced or fragmentary in MT.

c. Vat continues, "'but you will preserve for yourselves the virgins,' and they did so."

d. Vat reads the assessment more positively: "and it pleased [or conciliated] them."

e. Literally, "destroyed from."

f. Literally, "from days to days/time to time." Cf. Exod 13:10; Judg 11:40; 1 Sam 1:3.

g. The root of "quarrel" (*ryb*) is used in various juridical settings (e.g., Deut 19:17; 1 Sam 24:16; Hos 2:2 [MT 4]). Vat reads "you," not "us."

h. Literally, "now."

i. Vat reads, "Have some compassion on us as regards to them because we did not take a man his wife in battle. You did not give them. You incurred guilt as by lot." In other words, it was not their fault. No warriors were killed. They should accept the event as if it were an act of nature.

j. Variations on this refrain are found also in Judg 17:6; 18:1; and 19:1.

In an influential essay, feminist scholar Gayle Rubin (1975) suggests that the relationships between men in a wide variety of societies are created, maintained, and transformed by the exchange of females, a process that Rubin trenchantly and subversively calls "the traffic in women." Judges 21 describes such a process for the purposes of reconciliation between warring groups of men. A violent but socially sanctioned "traffic in women" takes nubile females out of the hands of one set of men and into the control of another. The women themselves, as in the tale of the murdered concubine, are voiceless. Their transfer, however, completes the mythic cycle of tales about the formation of the people, much as the concubine's murder began it. To read Judges 19–21 as a narrative about chaos is correct, but chaos does not end the story, making necessary a new order under kings. Rather, the cycle ends with a victory, the cessation of hostilities, the reintegration of the internecine enemy, and the transfer of women. At the end, harmony prevails, at least in the view of the androcentric author: the warriors are domesticated, building houses, dwelling in them, and returning home. A renewal of order has taken place.

[1–14] For the first time in the story cycle, the reader learns about an oath barring the exchange of women with Benjamin. In a traditional culture, the transfer of women creates peace through political and economic interdependence. To deny such prized commodities is to break ties and prevent positive interaction. The Israelites are pictured as regretting having taken this step against Benjamin, "their kin," and seek a means of restoring the wholeness of the group, the descendants of Israel. This theme of reconciliation is found also in 1 and 2 Chronicles, in which writers long for the reunification of the northern and southern kingdoms, so long divided (see Japhet 1989: 270–324). Reconciliation between kin is thus an important late biblical theme, but it appears also in earlier or less datable biblical material. The inevitable rivalry between brothers in Israel regularly ends in reconciliation, as in the tales of Esau and Jacob (Gen 33:1–4) and of Joseph and his brothers (Gen 45:1–9). In Judges 21 the process of reconciliation begins. Perhaps the divisive vow is not mentioned until ch. 21 for dramatic effect, in order to underscore the passage from war to peace, from enmity to reconciliation. Alternatively, the vow alludes to a piece of the story assumed by traditional receivers of the narrative familiar with the full range of motifs that constitute the tradition.

The people's weeping, the question to God, the building of an altar and offering sacrifices suggest a request for an oracle (21:3–4), as throughout ch. 20, but no direct response comes from the deity. In this case, ritual action seems to inspire a witch hunt for those who did not heed the call to participate in the fighting against Benjamin (21:5). The act of reconciliation requires scapegoating. The scapegoating of one group allows for rehabilitation of the real source of tension, the Benjaminites who refused to give up miscreants in their midst. Within the large Transjordanian holding of Manasseh is a group, the inhabitants of Jabesh-gilead, who are sacrificed to achieve reunification of the larger people, Israel.

Like Gibeah, Jabesh-gilead is another place associated with Israel's first king, Saul of Benjamin. He is the rescuer of the townspeople when they are threatened by the Ammonites (1 Sam 11:1–11), and they, in turn, retrieve the exposed corpses of Saul and his sons after they are killed in battle with the Philistines. In Judges 21, however, they are portrayed as disloyal members of the Israelite military alliance, having failed to heed the call to arms in response to the murder in Gibeah. Perhaps, as in the portrayal of Gibeah and Benjamin, an anti-Saulide polemic is implicit. Another interpretation might treat the people of Jabesh-gilead as unlucky victims.

As in the case of ch. 20, scholars have treated repetition as evidence of sources (Soggin 300), but the repetitions serve vital narrative functions. Variations upon a repeated phrase at vv. 5 and 8 concerning "who did not go up" create the impression of the heightening drumbeat of a witch hunt, while vv. 3, 6, and 7 emphasize the supposedly righteous cause behind the elimination of males and adult women in Jabesh-gilead. This search for women to allow for Benjamin's reincorporation into the twelve tribes of Israel involves a partial invocation of the ban, "the devoting to destruction" (21:11) of people. Language of "striking by the mouth of the sword" men, women, and children (presumably male children) (21:10) is typical of banning texts (e.g., Deut 2:34; Josh 6:21). Those who disloyally shirk military obligations under the bonds of the covenant must die, but no one seems to think of hunting down disloyal members of the league until the need for women becomes clear. The banlike action is really invoked in order to free up virgin girls for Benjamin. As in Numbers 31, a special category of banning obtains involving virgin girls. The central characteristic of the war ideology of the ban is the destruction of all human beings, regardless of gender, age, or military status. The killing is a totalistic devotion to sacrifice equated with "a whole burnt offering" to God in Deut 13:16. In Judg 20:10–12, as in Num 31:17–18, banning allows for the sparing of pure women as booty, unsullied and unmarked by men's sexual branding (see Niditch 1993b: 78–89). They are blank slates available to be possessed and defined by marriage with the men of Benjamin. Ironically, the women stolen under the cover of these convenient charges, themselves sacrificial offerings of another kind, are insufficient to provide women for Benjamin and seal reconciliation. Further sacrifice is needed.

[15–25] The author restates the problem surrounding Benjamin's restoration to the group via wives (vv. 15–17) and reiterates the curse preventing a voluntary reintroduction of normal customs of exchange (v. 18). In this section, "elders" of the congregation play a leadership role as the storyteller projects an image of polity in the days before there were kings in Israel. In a traditional pattern reminiscent of the Latin rape of the Sabine women (see Gaster 1981: 2:444–46), Israel comes up with the idea of allowing and encouraging the Benjaminites to help themselves to the damsels of Shiloh who engage in whirling dances at a yearly festival related to wine growing and vineyards.

The verbal map drawn for the location of Shiloh (21:19) is significant. The ancient cult center is situated with reference to other central northern sites, Bethel to its south (see 1:22; 4:5; 20:18, 26, 31), and Shechem to the north (see 9:2). Lebonah is not mentioned elsewhere in the Hebrew Bible. Located about three miles north-northwest of Shiloh and identified with modern Lubban, it too belongs to a route used for travel, trade, and perhaps for pilgrimage (cf. Exod 34:23). In a foundation tale, such an important sacred trail emphasizes national identity and maps an important means of religious self-definition. The author thereby emphasizes that the roots of Israelite identity are ancient and deep. The literary form of the map is similar to Num 21:11–20, especially material said to be quoted from "the Book of the Wars of the Lord" at Num 21:14–15. In Numbers the sites mark ancient borders, an equally important aspect of situating national geography and mapping group identity. The oral maps are parallelistic in the style of ancient Hebrew poetry and employ colorful descriptions of direction, for example, "east of the sun" (Judg 21:19).

The men of Benjamin are told that if the girls' fathers object, the Israelites will try to convince them of the wisdom of not opposing the seizure of their daughters. No one will have broken the oath (21:1); no blood will have been shed in Shiloh. Why not aid in the process of reconciliation? Like the tale of Jephthah's daughter, the tale of the women of Shiloh may well be an etiology for customs involving marriage, key passages in the lives of young women. In this case, the story describes a yearly "wife-stealing" ritual in which matches are made between men of Benjamin and daughters of Shiloh. Such rituals are common in other cultures (see Gaster 1981: 2:444–46).

With wives obtained, the Benjaminites go off to build cities and dwell in them. Reunited with their kin and their problems resolved, the Israelites return as well to their various tribes and clans. The final imagery is not of chaos but of cosmogony. The world is set and ordered, cities inhabited, and people properly and peacefully divided into social kinship groups, even while recognizing the ties that unify all Israelites. For the time being, the group as a whole has asserted itself over against more circumscribed kin-based loyalties within one tribe.

Women are manipulated, seized, and raped at the end of the cycle in Judges 19–21, as at the beginning of the cycle. They are the doorways through which chaos descends and order is reestablished, critical to tales of creation and foundation. The narrative is told from a male-dominated perspective, and little comfort is provided for feminist appropriation (in contrast to responses invited by the portrayal of other women in Judges, such as Achsah, Deborah, and Jael), but women are vitally important to the men's tales. There will be no Israel without them. Marginal, they are nevertheless critical portals in tales of nationhood. The author himself may reveal some embarrassment about the old stories, much as he relishes telling them. It was all so long ago when each man did what was right in his own eyes (21:25). Yet Judges does not end with chaos; it ends with wholeness, reconciliation, rehabilitation, and peace, made possible in men's eyes through the taking of women.

APPENDIX
A LITERAL TRANSLATION OF JUDGES

Judges 1:1–36
Introduction by Means
of Explicit Ambivalence

1:1　And it was after the death of Joshua,
　　　and ask did the descendants of Israel of Yhwh, saying,
　　　"Who will go up for us against the Canaanites, at the beginning,
　　　　　to wage war against them?"

2　　And said Yhwh,
　　　"Judah will go up.
　　　Behold, I have given the land into his hand."

3　　And said Judah to his brother Simeon,
　　　"Go up with me into my allotment,
　　　and let us wage war against the Canaanites,
　　　and I will come, also I, with you into your allotment."
　　　And go with him did Simeon.

4　　And up went Judah,
　　　and Yhwh gave the Canaanites and the Perizzites into their hand.
　　　They struck down in Bezek ten thousand men.

5　　And they encountered Adoni-bezek in Bezek,
　　　and they waged war against him,
　　　and they struck down the Canaanites and the Perizzites.

6　　And flee did Adoni-bezek;
　　　they followed after him;
　　　they seized him;
　　　they cut off the large digits of his hands and feet.

7　　And said Adoni-bezek,
　　　　"Seventy kings,
　　　　　　the large digits of their hands and feet cut off,

used to glean under my table.
As I did,
so God has repaid me."
And they brought him to Jerusalem,
and he died there.

8   And wage war did the descendants of Judah against Jerusalem,
they captured it;
they struck it down by the mouth of the sword;
and the city, they sent up in fire.

9   And thereafter, go down did the descendants of Judah
to wage war against the Canaanites
dwelling in the hill country, the south, and the lowlands.

10 And go did Judah against the Canaanites
who dwelled in Hebron
(and the name of Hebron formerly was Town-of-Four [Kiriath-arba])
and they struck down Sheshai, Ahiman, and Talmai.

11 And go did they from there against the dwellers of Debir
(and the name of Debir formerly was Town-of-Document
[Kiriath-sepher]).

12 And said Caleb,
"He who strikes down Town-of-Document and captures it,
I will give to him Achsah, my daughter, as wife."

13 And capture it did Othniel, son of Kenaz,
the brother of Caleb (the one younger than he),
and he gave to him Achsah, his daughter, as a wife.

14 And it was when she came that she urged him
to ask from her father for a piece of open country.
And she pounded down from upon the donkey,
and say to her did Caleb,
"What is with you!?"

15 She said to him,
"Give to me a blessing;
for the Southland you have given me,
but give to me ponds of water."
And give to her did Caleb
the upper ponds and the lower ponds.

16 And the descendants of Keni, father-in-law of Moses,
went up from the City of the Palms
with the descendants of Judah
into the wilderness of Judah
that is in the south toward Arad;
they went and dwelled with the people.

17 And go did Judah with Simeon his brother,
    and they struck down the Canaanites who dwelled in Zephath,
    and they devoted it to destruction
    and called the name of the city "Devoted to Destruction" (Hormah).

18 And capture did Judah, Gaza and its border region
        and Ashkelon and its border region
        and Ekron and its border region.

19 And Yhwh was with Judah,
    and he took possession of the hill country,
    for he could not dispossess the dwellers of the valley
        because chariotry of iron was theirs.

20 And they gave to Caleb Hebron
        as had spoken Moses,
    and he dispossessed from there the three sons of the Anak,

21 and the Jebusites dwelling in Jerusalem,
        the descendants of Benjamin did not dispossess.
    And dwell do the Jebusites
        with the descendants of Benjamin
        in Jerusalem until this day.

22 And go up did the house of Joseph,
        they too, against Bethel,
    and Yhwh was with them.

23 And go espying did the house of Joseph, in Bethel,
    and the name of the town formerly was Luz.

24 And see did the guards a man going forth from the town,
    and they said to him,
    "Let us see, I pray you, the entryway of the town,
    and we will make with you a mercy pact."

25 And he let them see the entryway of the town,
    and they struck down the town by the mouth of the sword,
    but the man and all his family they sent free.

26 And went the man to the land of the Hittites,
    and he built a town and called its name Luz.
    That is its name until this day.

27 And Manasseh did not dispossess Beth-shean and its suburbs,
        nor Taanach and its suburbs,
        nor the dwellers of Dor and its suburbs,
        nor the dwellers of Ibleam and its suburbs,
        nor the dwellers of Megiddo and its suburbs,
    and persist did the Canaanites to dwell in this land.

28 And when it was that grew strong did Israel,
        they set the Canaanites at forced labor,

but dispossess they did not dispossess them.

29   And Ephraim did not dispossess
         the Canaanites who dwell in Gezer,
     and dwelled the Canaanites in his midst in Gezer.

30   Zebulun did not dispossess the dwellers of Kitron
         nor the dwellers of Nahalol,
     and the Canaanites dwelled in his midst,
     and they became forced labor.

31   Asher did not dispossess the dwellers of Acco,
         nor the dwellers of Sidon,
         nor Ahlab, nor Achzib
         nor Helbah, nor Aphik, nor Rehob.

32   And dwell did the Asherites in the midst of the Canaanites,
         dwellers of the land,
     for they did not dispossess them.

33   Naphtali did not dispossess the dwellers of Beth-shemesh,
         nor the dwellers of Beth-anath,
     and they dwelled in the midst of the Canaanites,
         dwellers of the land,
     and the dwellers of Beth-shemesh and Beth-anath
         became to them forced labor.

34   And press did the Amorites,
         the descendants of Dan to the hill country,
     for they did not allow them to go down into the valley.

35   And persist did the Amorites to live in Mount Heres (Har-heres),
         in Aijalon, and in Shaalbim,
     and grew heavy did the hand of the house of Joseph,
     and they became forced labor.

36   And the border of the Amorites was from Scorpion-rise (Akrabbim),
         from the Rock (Sela) and upward.

Judges 2:1–23
From "Weeping" to the Death of Joshua

2:1   And go up did a messenger of Yhwh
          from Gilgal to Bochim,
      and he said,
      "I caused you to go up from Egypt
      and I brought you to the land

that I swore to your ancestors,
and I said,
'I will not break my covenant with you, forever,

2 and you will not cut a covenant
with the dwellers of this land.
Their altars you will pull down.'
But you did not listen to my voice.
What is this you have done?

3 And also I said,
'I will not drive them out from before you,
and they will be to you a trap,
and their gods will be to you a lure.'"

4 And it was, when spoke the messenger of Yhwh these words,
to all of the descendants of Israel,
lift up did the people their voice and weep.

5 And they called the name of that place "Weeping" (Bochim),
and they sacrificed there to Yhwh.

6 And send did Joshua the people,
and go did the descendants of Israel,
each to his inheritance,
to take possession of the land.

7 And serve did the people Yhwh
all the days of Joshua
and all the days of the old men
who prolonged their days beyond Joshua,
who saw all the great deeds of Yhwh
that he did for Israel.

8 And die did Joshua, son of Nun, servant of Yhwh,
a son of one hundred and ten years.

9 And they buried him within the borders of his inheritance
in "Portion of the Sun" (Timnath-heres),
in the hill country of Ephraim,
north of Mount Gaash.

10 And also all of that generation was gathered to its ancestors,
and there arose another generation after them
who did not know Yhwh,
and also the deeds that he did for Israel.

11 And do evil did the descendants of Israel in the eyes of Yhwh,
and they served the baals,

12 and they forsook Yhwh, the god of their ancestors,
who brought them out of the land of Egypt.
And they went after other gods

from the gods of the peoples who were round about them,
and they bowed down to them,
and they angered Yhwh.

13   And they forsook Yhwh,
and they served the baal and the ashtarot.

14   And kindled was the anger of Yhwh against Israel,
and he gave them into the hand of plunderers,
and they plundered them,
and he sold them into the hand of their enemies round about,
and they could no longer stand before their enemies.

15   Every time that they went forth,
      the hand of Yhwh was against them for evil,
         as Yhwh had spoken to them
         and as had sworn Yhwh to them,
and they were in very sore straits.

16   And raise up did Yhwh judges,
and they delivered them from the hand of their plunderers.

17   But even to their judges they did not listen,
for they whored after other gods,
and they bowed down to them.
They turned quickly from the way
      that their ancestors had walked
         to listen to the commandments of Yhwh.
They did not do likewise.

18   And when Yhwh raised up for them judges,
      Yhwh would be with the judge,
and he would deliver them from their enemies
      all the days of the judge;
for Yhwh would have compassion over their groaning
      because of their torturers and oppressors.

19   And it was at the death of the judge
      that they would return to go to ruin, worse than their ancestors,
         to walk after other gods,
         to serve them,
         and to bow down to them.
They did not let go of any of their practices or their rough ways.

20   And kindled was the anger of Yhwh against Israel,
and he said,
"Because this nation has crossed my covenant
      that I commanded their ancestors,
      and did not listen to my voice,

21   for my part, I will not continue

to dispossess one person from before them
from among the nations that Joshua did leave
when he died
22   in order to test Israel by means of them.
Do they keep to the way of Yhwh, to walk upon it
as their ancestors had kept,
or do they not?"
23   And leave in place did Yhwh these nations,
not dispossessing them quickly,
for he did not give them into the hand of Joshua.

Judges 3:1–31
A Covenantal Introduction and the Judges Othniel, Ehud, and Shamgar

3:1   And these are the nations that leave in place did Yhwh
in order to test by means of them Israel,
all those who had no knowledge
of all the wars of Canaan.
2   It was only for the sake of the knowledge
of generations of the descendants of Israel,
in order to teach them war,
only because previously they did not have knowledge.
3   The five tyrants of the Philistines and all the Canaanites
and the Sidonians and the Hivites,
who dwell in the mountain of Lebanon,
from the mountain of Baal-hermon
to the entrance of Hamath.
4   They existed to test Israel by means of them
in order to know whether they would listen
to the commandments of Yhwh,
which he commanded to their ancestors
by the hand of Moses.
5   And the descendants of Israel dwelled in the midst of the Canaanite,
the Hittite, the Amorite, the Perizzite,
the Hivite, and the Jebusite.
6   And they took their daughters to them for wives,
and their daughters they gave to their sons,
and they served their gods.

7   And do evil did the descendants of Israel in the eyes of Yhwh,
     and they forgot Yhwh their god,
     and they served the baals and the asherot.
8   And kindled was the anger of Yhwh against Israel,
     and he sold them into the hand of Cushan-rishathaim,
          king of Aram-naharaim,
     and serve did the descendants of Israel, Cushan-rishathaim
          for eight years.
9   And call out did the descendants of Israel to Yhwh,
     and raise up did Yhwh a deliverer for the descendants of Israel.
     And he delivered them: Othniel, son of Kenaz,
     the brother of Caleb (the one younger than he).
10   And there was upon him the spirit of Yhwh,
     and he judged Israel,
     and he went forth to war,
     and did give Yhwh into his hand Cushan-rishathaim,
          king of Aram,
     and his hand was strong against Cushan-rishathaim.
11   And quiet was the land for forty years,
     and die did Othniel, son of Kenaz.
12   And act again did the descendants of Israel
          to do evil in the eyes of Yhwh,
     and Yhwh strengthened Eglon, king of Moab, over Israel
          because they had done evil in the eyes of Yhwh.
13   And he gathered to him the descendants of Ammon and Amalek,
     and he went and struck Israel,
     and they took possession of the City of Palms.
14   And serve did the descendants of Israel Eglon, king of Moab,
          for eighteen years.
15   And call out did the descendants of Israel to Yhwh,
     and raise up for them did Yhwh a deliverer,
          Ehud, son of Gera, a Benjaminite,
               a left-handed man.
     And send did the descendants of Israel in his hand
          a tribute offering to Eglon, king of Moab.
16   And make for himself did Ehud a sword,
     and it had two edges,
          a short cubit its length.
     And he girded it on under his garment,
          upon his right thigh.
17   And he presented the tribute offering to Eglon, king of Moab.
     Eglon was a very fat man.

18   And it was when he finished presenting the tribute offering
       that he sent away the people bearing the tribute offering.
19   And he returned by way of the hewn images
      that were at the circle,
   and he said,
   "Something secret I have for you, O king,"
   and he said,
   "Silence."
   And go away from him did all those who attended him.
20   And Ehud came to him,
   and he was sitting in the cool upper chamber
      that he had,
         alone.
   And said Ehud,
   "Something from God I have for you."
   And he rose up from upon the throne.
21   And send forth did Ehud his left hand,
   and he took the sword from upon his right thigh,
   and he drove it into his belly.
22   And go in did the hilt after the blade,
   and close did the fat behind the blade,
   for he did not draw out the sword from his belly,
   and out he went by the exit way.
23   And go out did Ehud to the colonnaded portico,
   and he shut the doors of the upper chamber behind him,
   and he bolted them.
24   And he went off.
   But his servants came.
   They saw and behold, the doors of the upper chamber were bolted.
   And they said,
   "He must be 'indisposed' in the cool room."
25   And they waited until the point of embarrassment,
   and behold, he did not open the doors of the upper chamber,
   and they took the key and opened up,
   and behold, their lord was fallen on the ground dead.
26   And Ehud escaped during their tarrying,
   and he crossed by the hewn images
   and escaped to Seirah.
27   And it was at his coming,
   he blasted the shofar in the hill country of Ephraim.
   And go down with him did the descendants of Israel,
   from the hill country,

and he was in front of them.
28   And he said to them,
"Follow after me
because Yhwh has given your enemies, Moab, into your hands."
And they followed after him,
and they captured the fords of the Jordan
    over against Moab,
and they let no one cross.
29   And they struck Moab at this time,
        about ten thousand men,
        all robust, all men of valor,
and not a man escaped.
30   And humbled was Moab on that day beneath the hand of Israel,
and quiet was the land for eighty years.
31   And after him, there was Shamgar, son of Anat,
and he struck the Philistines,
        six hundred men, with an oxgoad,
and delivered also he Israel.

Judges 4:1–24
Tales of Deborah and Jael, Warrior Women

4:1   And act again did the descendants of Israel
        to do evil in the eyes of Yhwh,
for Ehud was dead.
2   And sell them did Yhwh into the hand of Jabin,
        king of Canaan, who ruled in Hazor,
and the captain of his army was Sisera,
and he was dwelling in Harosheth-ha-goiim.
3   And call out did the descendants of Israel to Yhwh,
because nine hundred chariots of iron did he have,
and he oppressed the descendants of Israel with force,
        for twenty years.
4   And Deborah, a woman who was a prophet—
        a woman of fire was she—
she was judging Israel at that time.
5   And she would sit under the palm of Deborah,
        between Ramah and between Bethel,
        in the hill country of Ephraim,
and go up to her would the descendants of Israel for judgment.

6   And she sent and called to Barak, son of Abinoam,
        from Kedesh-Naphtali,
     and she said to him,
        "Has not commanded Yhwh, god of Israel,
            'Go and march to Mount Tabor
            and take with you ten thousand men,
                from the descendants of Naphtali
                and from the descendants of Zebulun.
7   And I will march to you, at the Torrent of (Wadi) Kishon,
                Sisera, captain of the army of Jabin,
                and his chariots and his horde,
            and I will give him into your hand.'"
8   And say to her did Barak,
        "If you will go with me, I will go,
        and if you will not go with me, I will not go."
9   And she said,
        "Go, I will go with you;
        however, glory for you will not be on the way that you are walking,
        for into the hand of a woman will Yhwh sell Sisera."
     And rise up did Deborah,
     and she went with Barak to Kedesh.
10   And call up did Barak, Zebulun and Naphtali to Kedesh.
     And go up on foot did ten thousand men,
     and go up with him did Deborah.
11   And Heber the Kenite had separated from Kayin
         who was from the descendants of Hobab, father-in-law of Moses.
     And he stretched out his tent as far as the Oak in Zaanannim
             (Elan-bezaanannim)
         which is near Kedesh.
12   And they told Sisera
         that up had gone Barak, son of Abinoam,
             to Mount Tabor.
13   And call out did Sisera all his chariotry,
         nine hundred chariots of iron,
         and all the people that were with him,
             from Harosheth-ha-goiim to the Torrent of Kishon.
14   And said Deborah to Barak,
        "Rise up, because this is the day
            that Yhwh has given Sisera into your hands.
        Is Yhwh not going before you?"
     And go down did Barak from Mount Tabor,
         and twenty thousand men after him.

15   And cause to panic did Yhwh
         Sisera and all his chariotry,
         and the whole company,
             by the sword's mouth, before Barak.
     And go down did Sisera from upon the chariot,
     and flee did he on foot.

16   And Barak followed after the chariotry
         and after the company,
             until Harosheth-ha-goiim.
     And fall did the whole company of Sisera by the sword's mouth,
     and there did not remain as much as one.

17   And Sisera fled on foot
         to the tent of Jael,
             the wife of Heber the Kenite,
     because peace there was between Jabin, king of Hazor,
         and between the house of Heber the Kenite.

18   And out came Jael to meet Sisera,
     and she said to him,
     "Turn aside, my lord,
     turn aside to me.
     Be not afraid."
     So he turned aside to her, to the tent,
     and she hid him with a covering.

19   And he said to her,
     "Give me to drink, I pray you, a bit of water
     for I am thirsty."
     And she opened a skin bottle of milk,
     and gave him to drink,
     and she hid him.

20   And he said to her,
     "Stand at the opening of the tent,
     and let it be if a person comes,
         and asks you and says,
             'Is there here a man?'
         you say,
             'There is not.'"

21   And take, did Jael, the wife of Heber, a tent stake,
     and she put the hammer into her hand,
     and she came to him softly,
     and drove the stake into his temple,
     and pounded it into the ground.
     He had been sleeping,
     he was tired,

and he died.

22   And behold, Barak was following after Sisera,
and out went Jael to meet him,
and she said to him,
"Come and I will show you the man whom you seek,"
and he came with her,
and behold, Sisera was fallen, dead,
and the stake was in his temple.

23   And humble did God on that day, Jabin, king of Canaan,
     before the descendants of Israel.

24   And go did the hand of the descendants of Israel,
     going harder and harder upon Jabin, king of Canaan,
     until they cut off Jabin, king of Canaan.

Judges 5:1–31
The Song of Deborah

5:1   And sing did Deborah
      and Barak, son of Abinoam,
         on that day, saying,

2   "When flow, did the flowing locks in Israel,
        when freely offered themselves did the people,
     bless Yhwh.

3   Listen, kings!
     Lend an ear, potentates!
     I to Yhwh, I will sing.
     I will make music for Yhwh, god of Israel.

4   Yhwh, at your going forth from Seir,
        at your marching from the open country of Edom,
        earth shook,
        even the skies spouted,
        even the dark clouds spouted water.

5   The mountains streamed from before Yhwh—
            this is Sinai—
        from before Yhwh, god of Israel.

6   In the days of Shamgar, son of Anat,
        in the days of Jael,
     come to a halt did high roads,
        and walkers on pathways
        walked on back roads.

7   Come to a halt did ways of life in the unwalled towns.

In Israel, they came to a halt
    until I arose, Deborah,
    until I arose, a mother in Israel.

8   When they choose new gods,
        then war is in the gates.
    Shield was not seen, upon my oath, nor spear
        in the forty thousand in Israel.

9   My heart is with the commanders of Israel
        who freely offer themselves among the people.
    Bless Yhwh!

10   Riders on tawny donkey mares,
        those who dwell near Midian,
        those who walk on the way,
    tell one another!

11   From the sound of tambourines between watering holes,
        there they recount the justice-bringing acts of Yhwh,
            just acts for those in his unwalled towns in Israel.
    Then subdue the gated cities do the people of Yhwh.

12   Awake, awake, Deborah!
    Awake, awake, tell a lyric tale.
    Rise up, Barak.
    Capture your captives, son of Abinoam!

13   Then a survivor subdues the chieftains.
    The people of Yhwh subdue for me the mighty.

14   From Ephraim—their root is in Amalek.
    Behind you, Benjamin, with your people.
    From Machir go down the commanders
    and from Zebulun they march to the baton of the muster officer.

15   And the princes of Issachar are with Deborah.
    And Issachar, support of Barak
        in the valley was sent on foot.
    In the divisions of Reuben,
        great are the stout of heart.

16   Verily you dwell between the settlements
        to hear the whistling for the flocks.
    Concerning the divisions in Reuben,
        great are the stout of heart.

17   Gilead in Transjordan plies his tent,
    and Dan, verily, he resides in ships.
    Asher dwells on the shore of the sea,
    and on its promontories, he plies his tent.

18   Zebulun is a people whose soul taunts Death

and Naphtali on the heights of the open country.

19 Came kings; they waged war.
Then wage war did the kings of Canaan,
    in Taanach at the waters of Megiddo.
Plunder of silver they did not take.

20 From the heavens wage war did the stars.
From their orbits, they fought with Sisera.

21 The Torrent of Kishon swept them away,
    the torrent of primordial times,
    the Torrent of Kishon.
You will tread down the life force of the strong.

22 Then hammer did the horse hooves,
    the stampeding, stampeding of their stallions.

23 Curse Meroz, says the messenger of Yhwh.
Curse a cursing upon her indwellers
because they did not come to the aid of Yhwh,
    to the aid of Yhwh among the mighty.

24 More blessed than women is Jael,
    the wife of Heber, the Kenite,
more than tent-dwelling women is she blessed.

25 Water he asked for,
milk she gave,
    in a basin fit for chieftains,
she brought near curds of cream.

26 Her hand she sent for the tent stake,
    her right hand for the workman's hammer,
and she hammered Sisera.
She destroyed his head.
She shattered, she pierced his temple.

27 Between her legs, he knelt, he fell, he lay.
Between her legs, he knelt, he fell.
Where he knelt, there he fell, despoiled.

28 Through the window she looked down.
Wail did the mother of Sisera from behind the latticework.
'Why delay his chariotry to come?
Why tarry the clatterings of his chariots?'

29 The wise women among her ladies answer.
Yea, she returns her words to herself.

30 'Are they not finding, dividing spoil?
A wench, two wenches for each man.
Spoil of dyed stuff for Sisera,
    spoil of dyed stuff,

      embroidered dyestuff,
      doubly embroidered stuff
        for my neck, spoil.'

31   Thus may perish all your enemies, Yhwh,
      and those who love him, like the going forth of the sun in his strength."
      And quiet was the land for forty years.

Judges 6:1–40
The Call of Gideon

6:1   And evil did the descendants of Israel in the eyes of Yhwh,
      and give them did Yhwh into the hands of Midian
        for seven years.

2   And strong was the hand of Midian upon Israel.
      Because of Midian, did the descendants of Israel make use
        for themselves
        of river gorges that were in the mountains,
          caves, and hidden strongholds.

3   And it was if sow seed did Israel,
        go up would Midian and Amalek and the Easterners,
        and go up against it.

4   And they would encamp against them,
      and they would ruin the produce of the land
        until the vicinity of Gaza,
      and there did not remain a source of livelihood in Israel,
        even a sheep, even a bull, or even a donkey.

5   For they and their cattle would go up,
      and their tents would come as many as locusts,
      and to them and their camels there was no number,
      and they came against the land to ruin it.

6   And Israel was laid very low because of Midian,
      and call out did the descendants of Israel to Yhwh.

7   And it was when call out did the descendants of Israel to Yhwh,
        because of Midian,

8   that send did Yhwh a man who was a prophet
          to the descendants of Israel,
      and he said to them,
      "Thus says Yhwh, god of Israel,
      'I brought you up from Egypt

and brought you out from the domain of slaves,

9   and I saved you from the hand of Egypt,
    and from the hand of all your oppressors,
  and I drove them out from before you,
  and I gave to you their land.'

10   And I said to them,
  'I am Yhwh, your god.
  Do not reverence the gods of the Amorites
    in whose land you live,'
  and you did not listen to my voice."

11   And go did the messenger of Yhwh
  and he sat under the oak
    that was in Ophrah
    that belonged to Joash the Abiezerite,
  and Gideon, his son, was beating out wheat in the winepress,
    to hide it from Midian.

12   And appear to him did the messenger of Yhwh,
  and he said to him,
  "Yhwh is with you, mighty man of valor."

13   And say to him did Gideon,
  "With all due respect, my lord,
  if Yhwh is with us,
    why have we encountered all this?
  And where are all the wonderful acts
    that tell us about did our ancestors, saying,
      'Has not Yhwh brought us up from Egypt?'
  And now forsaken us has Yhwh,
  and he has given us into the hand of Midian."

14   And turn to him did Yhwh,
  and he said,
  "Go in this your strength,
  and you will deliver Israel from the hand of Midian.
  Have I not sent you?"

15   And he said to him,
  "With due respect, my lord,
  by what means will I deliver Israel?
  Behold, my clan is the lowliest in Manasseh,
  and I am the youngest in my extended household."

16   And say to him did Yhwh,
  "Because I will be with you,
  and you will strike down Midian
    as if they were one man."

17   And he said to him,
      "If, I pray you, I have found favor in your eyes,
         make for me a sign
            that you are the one speaking with me.
18   Don't, I pray you, depart from here
         until I come to you.
      And I will bring my offering,
      and I will set it before you."
      And he said,
      "I will sit still
         until you return."
19   And Gideon came,
      and he did up a she-goat kid,
         and matzo cakes of an ephah's measure of flour.
      The meat he put in a basket,
      and the broth he put in a pot,
      and he brought them out to him,
         to under the oak,
      and he approached.
20   And say to him did the messenger of God,
      "Take the meat and the matzos,
      and set them on this rock,
      and the broth, pour out";
      and he did so.
21   And send forth did the messenger of Yhwh,
         the end of the staff that was in his hand,
      and he touched the meat and the matzos.
      And up went the fire from the stone,
      and it consumed the meat and the matzos,
      and the messenger of Yhwh went out of his sight.
22   And see did Gideon that a messenger of Yhwh was he,
      and said Gideon,
      "Alas, my Lord Yhwh,
      for I have seen the messenger of Yhwh, face-to-face."
23   And say to him did Yhwh,
      "Peace to you.
      Do not be afraid.
      You will not die."
24   And build there did Gideon an altar to Yhwh,
      and he called it "Yhwh is peace."
      Until this day, it is still at Ophrah of the Abiezerites.
25   And it was on that night,

and say to him did Yhwh,
"Take the steer of the head of cattle that belongs to your father,
    the second steer, seven years old,
and tear down the altar of the baal that belongs to your father,
and the asherah that is next to it, cut down.

26   And build an altar to Yhwh your God,
        on top of this stronghold in the row,
    and take the second steer,
    and raise up a burnt offering
        with the wood of the asherah that you cut down."

27   And take did Gideon ten men from his servants,
    and he did as speak to him did Yhwh.
    And it was because he feared the household of his father
        and the men of the town
            too much to do it by day,
        that he did it by night.

28   And rise early did the men of the town in the morning,
    and behold, broken down was the altar of the baal,
    and the asherah that was next to it was cut down,
    and the second steer was being raised up in sacrifice
        upon the altar that had been built.

29   And each person said to his neighbor,
    "Who did this thing?"
    And they searched and sought out,
    and they said, "Gideon, son of Joash, did this thing."

30   And said the men of the town to Joash,
    "Bring out your son and he will die
    because he broke down the altar of the baal
    and because he cut down the asherah that was next to it."

31   And said Joash to all who stood against him,
    "Will you contend for the baal?
    Will you deliver him?
    Whoever contends with him,
        let him die by morning.
    If he is a god,
        he will contend for himself
        because someone broke down his altar."

32   And they called him on that day Jerubbaal, saying,
    "Let the baal contend with him
    because he broke down his altar."

33   And all of Midian and Amalek and the Easterners gathered together,
    and they crossed over and made camp in the Valley of Jezreel.

34   And the spirit of Yhwh clothed Gideon,
and he blasted the shofar,
and called out was Abiezer after him.

35   And messengers he sent into all Manasseh,
and they too were called out after him,
and messengers he sent into Asher, and Zebulun, and Naphtali,
and they went up to meet them.

36   And said Gideon to God,
"If you have a deliverer for Israel by my hand
      as you spoke,

37   behold, I am placing the woolen fleece on the threshing floor.
If there is dew on the fleece alone,
    and on the whole ground, dryness,
        I will know that you are delivering by my hand, Israel,
            as you spoke."

38   And it was thus,
and he rose early the next morning,
and he pressed down the fleece,
and he squeezed dew from the fleece,
    a bowlful of water.

39   And said Gideon to God,
"Let not burn your anger against me,
but let me speak, just one more time.
May I test, I pray you, just once more with the fleece.
Let it be dry on the fleece alone,
and on the ground let there be dew."

40   And God did thus on that night,
and it was dry on the fleece alone,
and on all the ground there was dew.

Judges 7:1–25
The Battle with Midian

7:1   And rise up early did Jerubbaal, that is, Gideon,
      and all the people who were with him,
and they encamped by the spring of Harod,
and the camp of Midian was to the north of him,
      down from the hill of Hammoreh in the valley.

2   And said Yhwh to Gideon,

"Too many are the people who are with you
to allow me to give Midian into their hands,
lest Israel glorify itself at my expense saying,
'My hand has delivered me.'

3 And now, call, I pray you, in the ears of the people saying,
Whoever is afraid and trembling, let him return
and let him fly away from the mountain of Gilead.'"
And there returned from the people twenty-two thousand,
and ten thousand remained.

4 And said Yhwh to Gideon
"Still the people are too many.
Bring them down to the water,
and I will smelt away some from you there,
and it will be, those about whom I say to you,
'This one will go with you,'
he will go,
and about whom I say to you,
'This one will not go with you,'
he will not go."

5 And he brought the people down to the water.
And said Yhwh to Gideon,
"Everyone who laps with his tongue from the water,
as a dog would lap,
place him to one side,
and everyone who kneels on his knees to drink. . . ."

6 And the number of lappers
(their hands to their mouths)
was three hundred men,
and all the rest of the people
kneeled on their knees to drink water.

7 And said Yhwh to Gideon,
"With the three hundred men who lapped, I will deliver you,
and I will give Midian into your hand.
And as for all the people, let each man go back to his place."

8 And take provision did the people in hand,
and their trumpets,
and every Israelite man he sent off,
each man to his tent.
And the three hundred men he retained,
and the camp of Midian was below him in the valley.

9 And it was on that night,
and said to him Yhwh,

"Arise, go down to the encampment,
because I have given it into your hand.
10   And if you are afraid to go down,
          go down, you and Puah, your lad, to the encampment.
11   And listen to what they say,
      and afterward, strengthened will be your hands,
      and you will go down against the encampment."
      And down went he and Puah, his lad,
          to the edge of the battle arrays that were in the camp.
12   And Midian and Amalek and all the Easterners
          lay in the valley as many as locusts,
      and to their camels there was no numbering,
          as many as the sands that are on the shore of the sea.
13   And go did Gideon,
      and behold, a man was telling his companion a dream,
      and he said,
      "Behold, a dream I dreamed,
      and behold, a round barley bread
          was turning over and over in the encampment of Midian,
      and it came to the tent and struck it and it fell.
      It upturned it, and the tent fell down."
14   And answer did his companion and he said,
      "This is none other than the sword of Gideon,
          son of Joash, man of Israel.
      Given has God into his hand,
          Midian and all the encampment."
15   And it was when hear did Gideon
          the telling of the dream and its breakdown,
              he bowed down.
      And he returned to the camp of Israel,
      and he said,
      "Arise, because given has Yhwh into your hand,
          the camp of Midian."
16   And he divided the three hundred men into three units,
      and he gave trumpets into the hand of all,
          and empty jars, and torches in the jars.
17   And he said to them,
      "Me you will see, and likewise you shall do,
      and behold, I am going to the edge of the encampment,
      and let it be, as I do, likewise you shall do.
18   And when blow on the trumpet do I and all who are with me,

then you blow on the trumpets, also you,
  around the whole encampment,
and say, 'For Yhwh and for Gideon.'"

19 And go did Gideon, and the hundred men who were with him,
  to the edge of the encampment, at the beginning of the
    middle watch.
Indeed, they had just posted the guards.
And they blasted the trumpets
and shattered the jars that were in their hands.

20 And blast did the three units on the trumpets,
and they broke the jars,
and they held in their left hand the torches,
and in their right hand the trumpets to blast,
and they called out,
"A sword for Yhwh and for Gideon."

21 And stand did each man in his place, around the encampment,
and run did the whole camp,
and they raised the alarm and fled.

22 And blast did they the three hundred trumpets,
and set did Yhwh the sword of each man against his neighbor,
  and against the whole company,
and flee did the company, until Beth-shittah, toward Zererah
  until the edge of Abel-meholah until Tabbath.

23 And called out were the men of Israel, from Naphtali,
  and from Asher, and from all Manasseh,
and they followed after Midian.

24 And messengers send did Gideon
  in all the hill country of Ephraim saying,
  "Go down to meet Midian,
  and capture them against the waters,
    until Beth-barah and the Jordan."
And called out was every man of Ephraim,
and they captured the waters
  until Beth-barah and the Jordan

25 And they captured the two chieftains of Midian,
  Oreb and Zeeb,
and they killed Oreb at the Rock of Oreb,
and Zeeb they killed at the Winevat of Zeeb,
and they followed after Midian,
and the heads of Oreb and Zeeb they brought to Gideon,
  across the Jordan.

Judges 8:1–35
Inner-Group Tensions, the Rejection
of Kingship, and a Hero's Burial

8:1 And say to him did the men of Ephraim,
 "What is this thing you have done to us
  not to call us
   when you went to wage war against Midian?"
 And they contended with him forcefully.
2 And he said to them,
 "What have I done now compared to you?
 Are not the gleanings of Ephraim better
  than the vintage of Abiezer?
3 Into your hands did Yhwh give the chieftains of Midian,
  Oreb and Zeeb,
 and what have I been able to do compared to you?"
 Then abated their temper from against him
  when he spoke this thing.
4 And went Gideon toward the Jordan,
  crossing was he,
 and the three hundred men who were with him
  were exhausted and in pursuit.
5 And he said to the men of Succoth,
 "Give, I pray you, round loaves of bread
  to the people who follow in my footsteps,
   because they are exhausted,
 and I am following after Zebah and Zalmunna,
  kings of Midian."
6 And said the chieftains of Succoth,
 "Is the palm of Zebah and Zalmunna now in your hands
  that we should give to your army bread?"
7 And said Gideon,
 "Therefore, when Yhwh gives Zebah and Zalmunna into my hand,
  I will thresh your flesh
   with the thorns of the wilderness and with briars."
8 And he went up from there to Penuel,
 and spoke to them like this,
 and answer him did the men of Penuel
  as had answered the men of Succoth.
9 And he said also to the men of Penuel, saying,

"When I return in peace,
    I will break down this tower."
10 And Zebah and Zalmunna were in Karkor,
    and their company was with them,
        around fifteen thousand men,
        all who remained
            from all the company of the Easterners,
    for those who had fallen
        were one hundred and twenty thousand sword-drawing men.
11 And go up did Gideon on the way of the tent dwellers,
        east of Nobah and Jogbehah,
    and he struck the encampment,
    for the camp was unsuspecting.
12 And flee did Zebah and Zalmunna,
    and he followed after them,
    and he captured the two kings of Midian,
        Zebah and Zalmunna,
    and all the camp he made tremble.
13 And return did Gideon son of Joash from the war scene,
        at the ascent of Heres.
14 And he captured a lad from the men of Succoth
    and he questioned him,
    and he wrote down for him the chieftains of Succoth and her elders,
        seventy-seven men.
15 And he went to the men of Succoth and said,
    "Here are Zebah and Zalmunna,
        about whom you reproached me saying,
            'Is the palm of Zebah and Zalmunna now in your hands
                that we should give to your exhausted men, bread?'"
16 And he took the elders of the town,
        and wilderness thorns and briars,
    and he "educated" with them the men of Succoth.
17 And the tower of Penuel he broke down
    and he killed the men of the city.
18 And he said to Zebah and Zalmunna,
    "Where are the men whom you killed in Tabor?"
    And they said, "As you are, so were they.
    Each one had the form of the sons of a king."
19 And he said,
    "My brothers, the sons of my mother, they were.
    As Yhwh lives, had you left them alive,
        I would not kill you."

20   And he said to Jether his eldest,
     "Rise and kill them."
     But the lad could not draw his sword,
     because he was afraid
     because he was still a lad.
21   And said Zebah and Zalmunna,
     "You rise yourself,
     and strike us down,
     for as is the man, so his strength."
     And rise did Gideon,
     and he killed Zebah and Zalmunna,
     and he took the crescents
          that were on the neck of their camels.
22   And said the men of Israel to Gideon,
     "Rule over us, also you and also your son,
          and also the son of your son
     because you delivered us from the hand of Midian."
23   And said to them did Gideon,
     "I will not rule over you
     and my son will not rule over you.
     Yhwh will rule over you."
24   And said to them Gideon,
     "Let me ask you an asking,
     and give to me, each man, an earring of his booty."
     (For earrings of gold they had
     because they were Ishmaelites.)
25   And they said,
     "Give we will surely give."
     And they spread out the mantle,
     and they threw there, each man, an earring of his booty.
26   And the weight of the earrings of gold for which he asked was
          one thousand seven hundred gold-weight,
               apart from the crescents and the pendants
               and the clothing of purple
                    that was upon the kings of Midian,
               and apart from the neck pendants
                    that were on the necks of their camels.
27   And make it did Gideon into an ephod,
     and he stationed it in his town, in Ophrah,
     and whore did all Israel after it,
     and it was to Gideon and his family a lure.
28   And humbled was Midian before the descendants of Israel,

and they did not continue to lift their heads,
and quiet was the land for forty years in the days of Gideon.

29 And go did Jerubbaal, son of Joash,
and he dwelled in his homestead.

30 And Gideon had seventy sons,
  the issue of his loins,
for many wives had he.

31 And his concubine who was in Shechem bore him, also she, a son,
and he set his name as Abimelech.

32 And die did Gideon, son of Joash, at a good old age,
and he was buried in the burial place of Joash, his father,
  in Ophrah of the Abiezerites.

33 And it was when die did Gideon
  that the descendants of Israel returned
    to whoring after the baals,
and they set up for themselves Baal of the Covenant as a god.

34 And the descendants of Israel did not remember Yhwh their god,
  who saved them from the hand of all their enemies round about.

35 And they did not do acts of fealty
  toward the house of Jerubbaal Gideon
    in accord with all the good that he had done for Israel.

Judges 9:1–57
The Rise and Fall of Abimelech,
the Would-be King

9:1 And go did Abimelech, son of Jerubbaal, to Shechem
  to the kin of his mother,
and he spoke to them and to all the clan members
  of the extended household of his mother, saying,

2 "Speak, I pray you, in the ears of all the lords of Shechem.
What is better for you,
  if rule over you do seventy men,
    all the sons of Jerubbaal,
  or if rule over you does one man?
And remember that your bone and flesh am I."

3 And speak did the kin of his mother concerning him
  in the ears of all the lords of Shechem,
    all these words.

And stretch did their hearts after Abimelech,
for they said, "Our kin he is."
4 And they gave him seventy pieces of silver
    from the house of Baal of the Covenant;
and hire with them did Abimelech,
    worthless and reckless men,
and they went after him.
5 And he came to his father's extended household at Ophrah,
and he killed his brothers, the sons of Jerubbaal,
    seventy men on one stone,
but there remained Jotham, son of Jerubbaal, the youngest,
for he hid himself.
6 And gathered were all the lords of Shechem
    and all of Beth-millo,
and they went and kinged Abimelech as king
    at the oak of the standing stone that was in Shechem.
7 And they told Jotham,
and he went and stood on the top of Mount Gerizim,
and he lifted his voice,
and he called and said to them,
"Listen to me, lords of Shechem,
and listen to you will God.
8 Go did go the trees
    to anoint over them a king,
and they said to the olive tree,
    'Be king over us.'
9 And said to them the olive tree,
'Would I halt producing my luxuriant oil,
    which, by me, they honor gods and men,
and go to sway over the trees?'
10 And said the trees to the fig tree,
    'Come you, be queen over us."
11 And said to them did the fig tree,
'Would I halt producing my sweetness
    and my good fruit
and go sway over the trees?'
12 And said the trees to the vine,
    'Come you, be queen over us.'
13 And said to them the vine,
'Would I halt producing my new wine
    that makes rejoice gods and men
and go to sway over the trees?'

14 And said all the trees to the bramble,
   'Come you, be king over us.'
15 And said the bramble to the trees,
   'If in truth you are anointing me
       to be king over you,
   come, seek refuge in my shade,
   but if not, may a fire go forth from the bramble
   and consume all the cedars of Lebanon.'
16 And now, if in truth and integrity you have done
       when you kinged Abimelech,
   and if good things you did for Jerubbaal and his extended household
   and if in accordance to his dealings with his hands,
       you have done for him
17   (in that my father waged war for you
       and risked his life to the limit,
       and saved you from the hand of the Midianites.
18 And you have risen up against the household of my father today,
       and you have killed his sons,
           seventy men on one stone,
       and you have kinged Abimelech, son of his concubine,
           over the lords of Shechem,
       for your kin is he).
19 But if in truth and integrity you have done with Jerubbaal
       and with his extended household this day,
   rejoice in Abimelech,
   and let him rejoice, also he, in you.
20 And if not, may fire go forth from Abimelech,
   and let it consume the lords of Shechem and Beth-millo,
   and may fire go forth from the lords of Shechem and from Beth-millo,
   and let it consume Abimelech."
21 And escape did Jotham,
   and he fled and went to Beer,
   and he dwelled there
       because of Abimelech his brother.
22 And become chief did Abimelech over Israel three years.
23 And send did God an evil spirit
       between Abimelech and the lords of Shechem
   and deal treacherously did the lords of Shechem with Abimelech,
24   in order that the violence toward
           the seventy sons of Jerubbaal, and their blood,
               be put upon Abimelech, their brother,
                   who killed them

and upon the lords of Shechem,
who made his hands strong
to kill his brothers.

25 And set for him did the lords of Shechem ambushes
on the tops of the mountains,
and they robbed all who would cross them on the way,
and it was told to Abimelech.

26 And come did Gaal, son of Ebed, and his kin,
and they crossed over to Shechem,
and trust in him did the lords of Shechem.

27 And they went out into the open country,
and they gathered grapes from their vineyards,
and they trod down
and made thanksgiving praises,
and they came to the house of their god,
and they ate, and drank, and cursed Abimelech.

28 And said Gaal, son of Ebed,
"Who is Abimelech
and who is Shechem that we should serve him?
Did not the son of Jerubbaal and Zebul his deputy
serve the men of Hamor, father of Shechem,
and why serve him should we?

29 Would that someone give this people into my hand,
and I would remove Abimelech."
And he said to Abimelech,
"Make many your army and go forth!"

30 And listen did Zubal, chieftain of the city,
to the words of Gaal, son of Ebed,
and he became angry.

31 And he sent messengers to Abimelech in Torma saying,
"Behold, Gaal, son of Ebed, and his kin have been coming to Shechem,
and behold, they are making the city an enemy against you.

32 And now, arise tonight,
you and the people who are with you,
and set an ambush in the open country.

33 And when it is in the morning,
when the sun rises,
you rise early and make a raid on the city;
and behold, he and the people who are with him will go forth against you,
and do to him as your hand finds."

34 And rise up did Abimelech
and all the people who were with him in the night,

and they set an ambush for Shechem, four units.

35 And go did Gaal, son of Ebed,
and he stood at the entrance of the gate of the city.
And rise up did Abimelech, and the people who were with him,
from the ambush site.

36 And see did Gaal the people,
and he said to Zebul,
"Behold, the people are coming down from the tops of the mountains."
And say to him did Zebul,
"The shadow of the mountains you see as men."

37 And Gaal spoke again some more,
and he said,
"Behold, the people are coming down from Tabbur-erez,
and one unit is coming from the way of Elon-meonenim."

38 And said to him did Zebul,
"Where oh where is your mouthiness as you said,
'Who is Abimelech that we should serve him?'
Is this not the people that you despised?
Go out, I pray you, now,
and wage war against him."

39 And go forth did Gaal before the lords of Shechem,
and he waged war against Abimelech.

40 And follow after him did Abimelech,
and he fled from before him,
and fall, pierced through, did many
against the entranceway of the gate.

41 And dwell did Abimelech in Arumah,
and Zebul drove out Gaal and his kin
from dwelling in Shechem.

42 And it was the next day,
and go forth did the people to the open country,
and they told Abimelech.

43 And he took the people
and divided them into three units,
and they set an ambush in the open country.
And he saw,
and behold, the people going forth from the city,
and he rose up against them,
and he struck them down.

44 And Abimelech and the units that were with him made a raid,
and they took a stand at the entranceway of the gate of the city,
and two units made a raid on all who were in the open country,

and they struck them down.

45 And Abimelech waged war against the city, all that day,
and he captured the city,
and the people who were in it he killed,
and he broke down the city,
and he sowed it with salt.

46 And hear did all the lords of the Tower of Shechem,
and they went to the hideout of house of El of the Covenant.

47 And it was told to Abimelech,
that gathered together
were all the lords of the Tower of Shechem.

48 And go up did Abimelech to Mount Zalmon,
he and all the people who were with him,
and take did Abimelech the axes in his hand,
and he cut tree brush and lifted it,
and placed it on his shoulder,
and he said to the people who were with him,
"What you see me do,
quickly, do as I do."

49 And cut also all the people, each man, brushwood,
and they went after Abimelech,
and they put them against the hideout,
and they kindled with them the hideout in fire,
and die did also all the people of the Tower of Shechem,
about a thousand men and women.

50 And go did Abimelech to Thebez,
and he encamped in Thebez, and captured it.

51 And a strong tower was in the midst of the city,
and flee there did all the men and women
and all the lords of the city,
and they closed it up behind them,
and they went up to the roof of the tower.

52 And come did Abimelech up to the tower,
and waged war against it,
and he approached unto the entranceway of the tower,
to burn it with fire.

53 And throw down did one woman an upper millstone
on the head of Abimelech,
and she crushed his skull.

54 And he called quickly to the lad who carried his gear,
and he said to him,
"Draw your sword and kill me,

lest they say of me,
   'A woman killed him.'"
And pierce him through did his lad,
and he died.

55   And see did the men of Israel
     that dead was Abimelech,
and went each man back to his place.

56   And return did God the evil of Abimelech
     that he did to his father,
      to kill seventy of his kin.

57   And all the evil of the men of Shechem,
     return did God upon their heads,
and there came upon them,
     the curse of Jotham, son of Jerubbaal.

Judges 10:1–18
The Judges Tola and Jair,
and Israel's Subsequent Decline

10:1   And there arose after Abimelech,
     to deliver Israel,
      Tola son of Puah, son of Dodo,
       a man of Issachar,
and he dwelled in Shamir
     in the hill country of Ephraim.

2   And he judged Israel twenty-three years,
and he died and was buried in Shamir.

3   And there arose after him Jair the Gileadite,
and he judged Israel twenty-two years.

4   And there were to him thirty sons
     who rode on thirty donkeys,
and thirty villages there were to them,
them they call the villages of Jair,
     —until this day—
      which are in the land of Gilead.

5   And die did Jair,
and he was buried in Kamon.

6   And act again did the descendants of Israel
     to do evil in the eyes of Yhwh,

and they served the baals and the ashtarot,
    and the gods of Aram, and the gods of Sidon,
    and the gods of Moab, and the gods of the descendants of Ammon,
    and the gods of the Philistines,
and they forsook Yhwh
and did not serve him.

7   And kindled was the anger of Yhwh against Israel,
and he sold them into the hand of the Philistines
    and into the hand of the descendants of Ammon.

8   And they shattered and crushed the descendants of Israel,
        in that year —for eighteen years—
            all the descendants of Israel
                who were in Transjordan
                    in the land of the Amorites,
                        which is in Gilead.

9   And cross did the descendants of Ammon the Jordan
        to wage war also with Judah and Benjamin
            and with the house of Ephraim,
and it was very dire straits for Israel.

10   And call out did the descendants of Israel to Yhwh saying,
"We have sinned against you,
for we have forsaken our god
and have served the baals."

11   And said Yhwh to the descendants of Israel,
        "Did not (I deliver you) from Egypt and from the Amorites
and from the descendants of Ammon and from the Philistines?

12   And the Sidonians, and Amalek, and Maon oppressed you,
and you called out to me,
and I delivered you from their hands.

13   But you have forsaken me,
and have served other gods.
Therefore I will not act again to deliver you.

14   Go and call to the gods whom you have chosen.
Let them deliver you in the time of your dire straits."

15   And said the descendants of Israel to Yhwh,
"We have sinned.
Do with us whatever seems good in your eyes,
but save us, I pray you, this day."

16   And they removed the foreign gods from their midst,
and they served Yhwh,
and his soul was cut to the quick over the trouble of Israel.

17   And called to arms were the descendants of Ammon

and they encamped in Gilead,
and gathered were the descendants of Israel,
and they encamped at Mizpah.
18 And said the people, the chiefs of Gilead,
 each man to his companion,
"Whoever is the man who begins to wage war
 against the descendants of Ammon,
 he will be head of all those who dwell in Gilead."

Judges 11:1–40
Jephthah, Epic Hero

11:1 And Jephthah the Gileadite was a mighty man of valor,
and he was the son of a whore woman,
and beget did Gilead, Jephthah.
2 And bear did the wife of Gilead to him sons,
and grow up did the sons of the wife,
and they drove away Jephthah,
and said they to him,
"You will not share inheritance with our paternal household,
for the son of another woman you are."
3 And flee did Jephthah from before his brothers,
and he dwelled in Goodland (the land of Tob),
and gather around Jephthah did worthless men,
and they went forth with him.
4 And it was after a time,
wage war did the descendants of Ammon with Israel.
5 And when wage war did the descendants of Ammon with Israel,
 go did the elders of Gilead to take Jephthah back from Goodland.
6 And they said to Jephthah,
"Come and be to us chief,
and let us wage war against the descendants of Ammon."
7 And said Jephthah to the elders of Gilead,
"Did you not treat me as an enemy,
and drive me out from my paternal household,
and why do you come to me now
 when you are in dire straits?"
8 And said the elders of Gilead to Jephthah,
"Even so, now we have returned to you.

Go with us
and wage war against the descendants of Ammon,
and you will be to us the head of all who dwell in Gilead."

9   And say did Jephthah to the elders of Gilead,
"If you are bringing me back
    to wage war against the descendants of Ammon,
and if Yhwh gives them over to me,
    I will be to you a headman."

10 And said the elders of Gilead to Jephthah,
"May Yhwh be the listener between us
    if we do not do according to your word."

11 And go did Jephthah with the elders of Gilead,
and the people set him over them as headman and chief,
and speak did Jephthah all his terms
    before Yhwh in Mizpah.

12 And send did Jephthah messengers
    to the king of the descendants of Ammon saying,
"What is between me and you
    that you have come to me to wage war against my land?"

13 And said the king of the descendants of Ammon
    to the messengers of Jephthah,
"Indeed, take did Israel my land
    when he came up from Egypt,
        from the Arnon until the Jabbok and until the Jordan.
And now, return it in peace."

14 And again Jephthah sent messengers
    to the king of the descendants of Ammon,

15 and he said to him,
"Thus says Jephthah:
Israel did not take the land of Moab
    and the land of the descendants of Ammon.

16 Rather, in their going up from Egypt,
    Israel went in the wilderness until the Red Sea,
and they came toward Kadesh.

17 And send did Israel messengers
    to the king of Edom saying,
'Let me cross, pray, over your land,'
but the king of Edom would not listen;
and also to the king of Moab they sent,
but he was not willing,
and stay did Israel in Kadesh.

18 And they made their way in the wilderness,

and they went around the land of Edom,
    and the land of Moab,
and they came to the sunrise side of the land of Moab,
and they encamped across the Arnon,
and they did not go within the boundary of Moab,
for Arnon is the boundary of Moab.

19   And send did Israel messengers to Sihon,
        king of the Amorites, king of Heshbon,
    and said to him Israel,
    'Let us cross, pray, over your land, to our destination.'

20   And trust not did Sihon Israel
        to cross over his boundary,
    and gather did Sihon all his people,
    and they encamped in Jahaz
    and waged war against Israel.

21   And give over did Yhwh, god of Israel,
        Sihon and all his people,
            into the hand of Israel.
    And he struck him
    and take possession did Israel
        of all the land of the Amorites
            who were dwelling in that land.

22   And they took possession of all the boundary of the Amorites,
        from the Arnon to the Jabbok
        and from the wilderness to the Jordan.

23   And now Yhwh, god of Israel,
        has dispossessed the Amorites
            for the sake of his people Israel,
    and you would take possession of us!

24   Is it not the case that whatever Chemosh your god dispossesses for you,
        it, you should possess,
    and all that Yhwh our god dispossesses for our sake,
        it, we should possess?

25   And now, are you good and better than Balak, son of Zippor,
        king of Moab?
    Did he quarrel a quarrel with Israel?
    Did he wage a war against them?

26   While Israel dwelled in Heshbon and its suburbs,
        and in Aroer and its suburbs,
            and in all the towns that are next to the Arnon,
                for three hundred years,
    why did you not engage in recovery in that time?

27   And I, I have not sinned against you,
      but you are doing me wrong
            to wage war against me.
      Let Yhwh the judge judge today
            between the descendants of Israel
                  and between the descendants of Ammon."

28   And listen not would the king of the descendants of Ammon,
            to the words of Jephthah
                  that he had sent to him.

29   And there was upon Jephthah the spirit of Yhwh,
      and he crossed over to Gilead and to Manasseh,
      and he crossed to Mizpah of Gilead,
      and from Mizpah of Gilead,
            he crossed over to the descendants of Ammon.

30   And vow did Jephthah a vow to Yhwh and he said,
      "If give you give the descendants of Ammon into my hand,

31   and it will be: the emerging thing that emerges
                  from the doors of my house to meet me
                        upon my returning in peace
                              from the descendants of Ammon,
                  shall be for Yhwh,
            and I shall offer it up as a whole burnt offering."

32   And cross over did Jephthah to the descendants of Ammon,
            to wage war against them,
      and give them did Yhwh into his hand.

33   And he struck them from Aroer until the vicinity of Minnith,
            twenty towns,
            and until Greenland of the Vineyards (Abel-Keramim),
                  a very great striking,
      and humbled were the descendants of Ammon
            before the descendants of Israel.

34   And go did Jephthah to Mizpah, to his home base.
      And behold, his daughter was coming forth
            to greet him with timbrels and whirling dances.
      And only she was the one.
      No others did he have but for her,
            son or daughter.

35   And it was when he saw her,
            he tore his garment,
      and he said,
      "Alas, my daughter.
      Causing me to kneel, you have knelt me down.

You have become (enmeshed) in my troubles.
And I have opened my mouth to Yhwh,
and I cannot turn back."
36 And she said to him,
"My father, you have opened your mouth to Yhwh.
Do according to what came forth from your mouth,
now that done for you has Yhwh
   acts of vengeance upon your enemies,
     upon the descendants of Ammon."
37 And she said to her father,
"Let this thing be done for me.
Allow me two months,
and I will go,
and I will go down into the mountains,
and I will cry over my maidenhood,
   myself and my companions."
38 And he said, "Go."
And he sent her for two months.
And she went, she and her companions,
and she cried over her maidenhood upon the mountains.
39 And it was at the end of two months,
and she returned to her father,
and he did to her the vow that he had vowed.
And she had never known a man.
And it became a rule in Israel:
40 From year to year,
   go would the daughters of Israel
     to tell of the daughter of Jephthah the Gileadite,
     four days each year.

Judges 12:1–15
Internecine Strife and Brief Annals of Ibzan, Elon, and Abdon

12:1 And the men of Ephraim were called out,
and they crossed northward,
and they said to Jephthah,
"Why did you cross to wage war with the descendants of Ammon,

and us you did not call to go with you?
Your home base we will burn upon you with fire."
2   And did say Jephthah to them,
"I was a man involved in an egregious dispute,
    myself, my people, and the descendants of Ammon,
and I called out to you,
and you did not deliver me from their hand.
3   And I saw that you were not acting as deliverer,
and I put my life in my palm,
and I crossed over to the descendants of Ammon,
and give them did Yhwh into my hand.
And why have you come up to me
    this day to wage war against me?"
4   And gather did Jephthah all the men of Gilead,
and wage war did Jephthah against Ephraim,
and strike down Ephraim did the men of Gilead,
for they said, "Fugitives of Ephraim are you, Gilead,
    in the midst of Ephraim, in the midst of Manasseh."
5   And capture did Gilead the fords of the Jordan against Ephraim.
And it was when the fugitives of Ephraim would say,
"Let me cross,"
say to him would the men of Gilead,
"An Ephraimite are you?"
And he would say, "No."
6   And they would say to him,
"Say, pray, 'shibboleth,'"
and he would say "sibboleth."
And he could not accomplish to say it thus,
and they would seize him and slaughter him
    at the fords of the Jordan.
And fall at that time from Ephraim
    did forty-two thousand.
7   And judge Israel did Jephthah for six years,
and die did Jephthah the Gileadite,
and he was buried in the towns of Gilead.
8   And judge Israel after him did Ibzan from Bethlehem.
9   And there were to him thirty sons.
And thirty daughters he sent outside,
and thirty daughters he brought in for his sons from outside.
And he judged Israel for seven years.
10 And die did Ibzan,
and he was buried in Bethlehem.

11   And judge Israel after him did Elon the Zebulunite,
      and he judged Israel for ten years.
12   And die did Elon the Zebulunite,
      and he was buried in Aijalon in the land of Zebulun.
13   And judge Israel after him did Abdon,
         son of Hillel the Pirathonite.
14   And there were to him forty sons and thirty grandsons
         who rode on seventy donkeys.
      And he judged Israel for eight years.
15   And die did Abdon,
         son of Hillel the Pirathonite,
      and he was buried in Pirathon in the land of Ephraim,
         in the hill country of the Amalekites.

Judges 13:1–25
The Birth Story of Samson, Superhero

13:1   And act again did the descendants of Israel
          to do evil in the eyes of Yhwh.
       And give them did Yhwh into the hands of the Philistines
          for forty years.
2   And there was a certain man from Zorah
          from the clan of the Danites,
       and his name was Manoah.
       And his woman was barren,
       and she had not given birth.
3   And appear did the messenger of Yhwh to the woman,
       and he said to her,
       "Behold, you are barren
       and have not given birth,
       but you are pregnant,
       and will give birth to a son.
4   And now, keep on your guard, pray,
       and do not drink wine or strong drink,
       and do not eat anything unclean,
5   for behold, you are pregnant,
       and will give birth to a son,
       and a razor will not go up upon his head,
       for a *Nazir* to God will be the lad from the womb,

and he will begin to deliver Israel
   from the hand of the Philistines.""

6   And go did the woman,
and she said to her man, saying,
"A man of God came to me,
and his appearance was like the appearance of the messenger of God,
   exceedingly awe-inspiring.
I did not ask where from he was,
and his name he did not tell me.

7   And he said to me,
'Behold, you are pregnant
and will give birth to a son,
and now do not drink wine or strong drink,
and do not eat anything unclean,
for a *Nazir* of God will be the lad,
   from the womb until the day of his death.'"

8   And make supplication did Manoah to Yhwh,
and said, "Please, Lord,
the man of God whom you sent,
   may he come, pray, again to us, and teach us
      what we should do for the lad to be born."

9   And listen did God to the voice of Manoah,
and go did the messenger of God again to the woman.
And she was sitting in the open country,
and Manoah her man was not with her.

10   And hurry did the woman,
and she ran and told her man,
and she said to him,
"Behold, appeared to me the man
   who came today to me."

11   And rise and go did Manoah after his woman,
and he went to the man,
and he said to him,
"Are you the man who spoke to the woman?"
And he said, "I am."

12   And said Manoah,
"Now, should come your words to be,
   what will be the rule of the lad and his deeds?"

13   And said the messenger of Yhwh to Manoah,
"Of everything that I said to the woman, she shall keep guard.

14   Of everything that comes from the vine of wine, she shall not eat,
and wine and strong drink she shall not drink,
and all unclean things she shall not eat.

      All that I command her she shall keep."

15   And said Manoah to the messenger of Yhwh,
      "Let us, pray, detain you,
      and make before you a she-goat kid."

16   And said the messenger of Yhwh to Manoah,
      "If you would detain me, I will not eat your bread,
      And if you would make a burnt offering, to Yhwh send it up,"
      for know not did Manoah
         that a messenger of Yhwh was he.

17   And said Manoah to the messenger of Yhwh,
      "What is your name,
         so that, if come to be your words, we may honor you?"

18   And said to him the messenger of Yhwh,
      "Why do you ask concerning my name,
      for it is wonderful."

19   And take did Manoah the she-goat kid and the grain offering,
      and he raised (them) upon the rock to Yhwh—
         he who makes things wondrous to do—
      and Manoah and his wife were watching.

20   And it was as the flame arose from upon the altar skyward,
         that upward went the messenger of Yhwh in the flame of the altar,
      and Manoah and his woman were watching,
      and they fell on their faces to the ground.

21   And not act again did the messenger of Yhwh
         to appear to Manoah and his woman.
    Then know did Manoah
         that a messenger of Yhwh was he.

22   And said Manoah to his woman,
      "To die we will die,
      for God we have seen."

23   And said to him did his woman,
      "If desire did Yhwh to kill us,
         he would not have taken from our hands
            a burnt offering and a grain offering,
      and would not have shown us all this,
      and now he would not have had us hear things such as this."

24   And give birth did the woman to a son,
      and she called his name Samson,
      and grow up did the lad,
      and bless him did Yhwh.

25   And began the spirit of Yhwh to impel him,
         in the encampment of Dan
            between Zorah and Eshtaol.

Judges 14:1–15:20
Samson and Marriage with the Philistines

14:1 And down went Samson to Timnah,
    and he saw a woman in Timnah
        from the daughters of the Philistines.

2 And he went up and told his father and his mother,
    and he said,
    "A woman I saw in Timnah
        from the daughters of the Philistines,
    and now take her for me as a wife."

3 And say to him did his father and his mother,
    "Is there not among the daughters of your kin
        and in all our people a woman
            that you must go to take a woman
                from the Philistines, the uncircumcised?"
    And said Samson to his father,
    "Her, take for me,
        because she is right in my eyes."

4 And his father and his mother did not know
        that from Yhwh it was,
    for an opportunity he was seeking against the Philistines,
    and at this time the Philistines were ruling Israel.

5 And down went Samson, and his father and his mother, to Timnah,
    and they went to the vineyards of Timnah,
    and behold, a whelp of the lions roaring to meet him.

6 And rush upon him did the spirit of Yhwh,
    and he tore him in two like the tearing of a kid,
    and nothing was there in his hand,
    and he did not tell his father and his mother
        that which he had done.

7 And he went down and spoke to the woman,
    and she was right in the eyes of Samson.

8 And he returned after some days to take her,
    and he turned to see the fallen body of the lion,
    and behold, a swarm of bees
        in the carcass of the lion, and honey.

9 And he scraped it out into his palms,
    and he walked along, walking and eating,
    and he went to his father and to his mother,
    and he gave to them and they ate,

and he did not tell them
   that from the carcass of the lion
      he had scraped the honey.

10   And go down did his father to the woman,
and make there did Samson a feast,
for thus would do the young men.

11   And it was when they saw him,
they took thirty companions,
and they were with him.

12   And say to them did Samson,
"Let me, pray, riddle you a riddle.
If to tell you tell it to me
   within the seven days of the feast,
and you find out,
     I will give to you thirty linen garments
      and thirty changes of clothing.

13   And if you are not able to tell me,
   give will you to me thirty linen garments
     and thirty changes of clothing."
And they said to him,
"Riddle your riddle and let us listen."

14   And he said to them,
"From the eater came forth eats,
and from the strong came forth sweets."
And they could not tell the riddle for three days.

15   And it was on the seventh day,
and they said to the woman of Samson,
"Seduce your man, and let him tell us the riddle,
lest we burn you and the household of your father in fire.
Was it to dispossess us you called us together or not?"

16   And weep did the woman of Samson over him,
and she said,
"You only hate me and do not love me.
The riddle you have riddled to my kinfolk,
but me you have not told."
And he said to her,
"Behold, my father and my mother I have not told,
and you shall I tell?"

17   And she wept over him for the seven days
   that they had for the party,
and it was on the seventh day that he told her
because she pressed him.

And she told the riddle to her own folk.

18   And say to him did the men of the town on the seventh day,
         before the setting of the sun,
      "What is sweeter than honey,
      and what is stronger than the lion?"
      And he said to them,
      "If you had not plowed with my heifer,
         you would not have found out my riddle."

19   And rush upon him did the spirit of Yhwh,
      and he went down to Ashkelon,
      and he struck from among them thirty men.
      And he took their gear,
      and he gave the clothing to the tellers of the riddle.
      And kindled was his anger,
      and he went up to his father's household.

20   And the woman of Samson was for his companion,
         who had served as companion to him.

15:1 And it was after some days, in the harvest of the wheat,
      and visit did Samson his woman with a she-goat kid.
      And he said,
      "I would go to my woman in the chamber,"
      but not give to him permission would her father to go.

2   And said her father,
      "To say I said, for a hating you hate her,
      and I gave her to your companion.
      Is not her younger sister better than she?
      Let her, pray, be for you in place of her."

3   And say to them did Samson,
      "I am clean from guilt this time as regards the Philistines,
      for I am going to do with them mischief."

4   And went Samson,
      and he captured three hundred foxes,
      and he took torches,
      and he turned tail to tail,
      and he put one torch
         between two tails, in the middle.

5   And he caused fire to burn in the torches,
      and he sent (them) among the standing grain of the Philistines,
      and he caused to burn from stacks to standing grain
         and to vineyards, olive groves.

6   And said the Philistines,
      "Who did this?"

And they said, "Samson, son-in-law of the Timnite,
because he took his woman,
and he gave her to his companion."
And up went the Philistines
and they burnt her and her father in fire.

7   And say to them did Samson,
"If you do something like this,
    surely I will take vengeance upon you,
and afterward I will stop."

8   And he struck them leg upon thigh,
    a great striking.
And he went down and dwelled in the cleft of the Rock of Etam.

9   And up went the Philistines,
and they encamped in Judah,
and they spread abroad in Lehi.

10   And said the men of Judah,
"Why have you come up upon us?"
And they said, "To bind Samson we have come up,
    to do to him as he did to us."

11   And down went three thousand men from Judah,
    to the cleft of the Rock of Etam,
and they said to Samson,
"Do you not know that ruling over us are the Philistines,
and what is this you have done to us?"
And he said to them,
"As they did to me so I did to them."

12   And they said to him,
"To bind you we have come down,
    to give you into the hand of the Philistines."
And say to them did Samson,
"Swear to me, lest assail me do you."

13   And they said to him saying,
"No, for to bind we will bind you,
and we will give you into their hands,
but kill we will not kill you."
And they bound him with two new ropes,
and they brought him up from the rock.

14   He came to Lehi,
and the Philistines raised a war cry to meet him.
And rush upon him did the spirit of Yhwh
and were the ropes that were on his arms
    like flax that was burning in fire,

and melt did the bindings from upon his hands.
15 And he found the fresh jawbone of a donkey,
    and he sent his hand,
    and he took it and struck with it a thousand men.
16 And said Samson,
    "With the jawbone of a donkey
        a heap, two heaps,
    with the jawbone of a donkey,
        I struck one thousand men."
17 And when he finished speaking,
    he threw the jawbone from his hand,
    and he called the place "The Height of the Jawbone" (Ramoth-Lehi).
18 And he was very thirsty,
    and he called to Yhwh, and he said,
    "You gave into the hand of your servant
    this great deliverance,
    and now I will die of thirst,
    and I will fall into the hand of the uncircumcised."
19 And split did God the hollow that is in Lehi,
    and came forth from it water,
    and he drank, and return did his spirit,
    and he lived.
    For this reason, he called its name "Well of One Who Calls" (En-hakkore),
        which is in Lehi to this day.
20 And he judged Israel
        in the days of the Philistines
            for twenty years.

Judges 16:1–31
The Female "Other," Delilah, and Death

16:1 And walk did Samson to Gaza,
      and there he saw a whore woman,
      and he went to her.
2   To the Gazites it was told, saying,
      "Come has Samson here."
      And they formed a circle and lay in wait for him all the night
          at the gate of the city.
      And they kept themselves quiet all the night, saying,

"Until the light of morning, and we will kill him."

3 And sleep did Samson until the middle of the night,
and he arose in the middle of the night,
and he seized the doors of the gate of the city
    and the two doorposts,
and he pulled them up with the bar,
and he put (them) on his shoulders,
and he took them up to the head of the hill
    that was in front of Hebron.

4 And it was after this
that he loved a woman in the Valley of Sorek,
and her name was Delilah.

5 And went up to her did the lords of the Philistines,
and they said to her,
"Seduce him
and see by what means is his great strength,
and by what means we may have power over him,
and we will bind him to humble him,
and we will give to you, each man,
    one thousand one hundred in silver."

6 And said Delilah to Samson,
"Tell me, pray, by what means is your great strength,
and by what means may you be bound in order to humble you."

7 And said to her Samson,
"If they bind me with seven fresh gut cords
    that have not been dried out,
I will become weak,
and I will be like any human being."

8 And bring up to her did the lords of the Philistines
        seven fresh gut cords
            that had not been dried out,
and she bound him with them.

9 The ambushers waited for her in the inner chamber,
and she said to him,
"Philistines are upon you, Samson."
And he tore the gut cords
    as is torn a twisted thread of tow at the very scent of fire,
and not known was his strength source.

10 And said Delilah to Samson,
"Behold, you have mocked me,
and you have spoken to me lies.
Now tell me by what means you may be bound."

11   And he said to her,
    "If to bind they would bind me with new ropes,
       with which work has not been done,
    I will become weak,
    and I will be like any human being."

12   And take did Delilah new ropes,
    and she bound him with them,
    and she said to him,
    "Philistines are upon you, Samson."
    And the ambushers were waiting in the inner chamber;
    and he tore them from upon his arms like a thread.

13   And said Delilah to Samson,
    "Until now you have mocked me,
    and you have spoken to me lies.
    Tell me by what means may you be bound!"
    And he said to her,
    "If you weave the seven plaits of my head
       with the loom stuff."

14   And she thrust with the pin,
    and she said to him,
    "Philistines are upon you, Samson."
    And he awoke from his sleep,
    and he pulled out the pin of the loom and the loom stuff.

15   And she said to him,
    "How can you say, 'I love you'?
    And your heart is not with me.
    This is three times you have mocked me,
    and you have not told me
       by what means is your strength great."

16   And it was because she pressed him
       with her words all the days,
    and she urged him,
    and cut short was his soul to death.

17   And he told her all his heart,
    and he said to her,
    "A razor has not come upon my head,
    because a *Nazir* of God I have been
       from the womb of my mother.
    If I am shaven,
       then turn away from me will my strength,
    and I will become weak,
    and I will be like every human being."

18 And see did Delilah
        that he told her his whole heart,
    and she sent and she called to the lords of the Philistines saying,
    "Go up this time,
    for he has told me all his heart."
    And up to her went the lords of the Philistines,
    and they brought up the silver in their hands.

19 And she made him sleep on her knees.
    And she called the man,
    and she shaved off the seven plaits of his head,
    and she began to humble him,
    and turn away did his strength from him.

20 And she said,
    "Philistines are upon you, Samson."
    And he awoke from his sleep,
    and he said,
    "I will go forth like the other times and be shaken free,"
    but he did not know that Yhwh had turned away from him.

21 And seize him did the Philistines,
    and they gouged out his eyes,
    and they brought him down to Gaza,
    and they bound him with bronze shackles,
    and he became one who grinds in the prison house.

22 And began did the hairs of his head to grow
        after he was shaven.

23 And the lords of the Philistines gathered
        to sacrifice a great sacrifice
            to Dagon their god and to joy,
    and they said,
    "Given has our god into our hands,
    Samson our enemy."

24 And see him did the people,
    and they praised their god,
    for they said,
    "Given has our god into our hands
        our enemy and the devastator of our land
            who made many our fatally wounded."

25 And it was when merry was their heart,
    they said, "Call Samson,
    and let him sport before us."
    And they called Samson from the prison house,
    and he sported before them,

and they stood him between the pillars.

26   And said Samson to the lad who held his hand,
     "Allow me to touch the pillars
          upon which the house is set,
     and I will lean upon them."

27   And the house was full of men and women,
     and there were all the lords of the Philistines,
     and on the roof were about three thousand men and women,
          those watching the sporting of Samson.

28   And call did Samson to Yhwh,
     and he said, "My Lord, Yhwh,
     remember me, pray, and strengthen me, pray,
          just this one time, O God,
     and I will take vengeance in a single vengeance
          for my two eyes, on the Philistines."

29   And grasp did Samson the two pillars of the central portion
          upon which the house was set,
     and he leaned upon them,
          one in his right hand and one in his left.

30   And said Samson,
     "May my soul die with the Philistines,"
     and he stretched out with his strength,
     and fall did the house upon the lords,
          and upon all the people who were within,
     and the dead whom he made die in his death
          were more than he made to die in his life.

31   And down went his brothers and all his father's extended household,
     and they lifted him and went up,
     and they buried him between Zorah and Eshtaol
          in the sepulchre of Manoah, his father.
     And he had judged Israel for twenty years.

Judges 17:1–18:31
Micah's House Shrine
and the Founding of Dan

17:1   And there was a man
          from the hill country of Ephraim,
       and his name was Micaiah.

2 And he said to his mother,
  "The one thousand and one hundred in silver
    that were taken from you
      and you uttered a curse,
      and also you mentioned it in my ears,
    behold, the silver is with me.
    I took it."
  And said his mother,
  "Blessed be my son to Yhwh."

3 And he returned one thousand and one hundred in silver to his mother.
  And said his mother,
  "To be holy, I have made holy the silver to Yhwh,
    from my hand to my son
      to make a hewn icon and a cast icon,
  and now I return it to you."

4 And he returned the silver to his mother,
  and take did his mother two hundred in silver,
  and she gave it to the smelter,
  and he made them into a hewn icon and a cast icon,
  and it was in the house of Micaiah.

5 And the man Micah had a house of God,
  and he made an ephod and teraphim,
  and he consecrated one of his sons,
  and he became for him a priest.

6 In those days there was no king in Israel.
  A man, what was right in his eyes, he would do.

7 And there was a lad from Bethlehem of Judah,
    from the clan of Judah,
  and he was a Levite,
  and he sojourned there.

8 And go did the man from the town,
    from Bethlehem of Judah,
      to sojourn wherever he would find,
  and he came to the hills of Ephraim
    until the household of Micah
      to make his way.

9 And say to him did Micah,
  "From where do you come?"
  And he said to him,
  "A Levite I am
    from Bethlehem in Judah,
  and I am going to sojourn wherever I might find."

10   And say to him did Micah,
      "Dwell with me,
      and be to me a father and a priest,
      and I will give to you ten pieces of silver for the days
          and an estimate for clothing and your sustenance."
      And go did the Levite.

11   And willing was the Levite to dwell with the man,
      and become did the lad to him like one of his sons.

12   And consecrate did Micah the Levite,
      and become to him, did the lad, a priest,
      and he was in the household of Micah.

13   And said Micah,
      "Now I know that make it go well with me will Yhwh,
      because I have the Levite as a priest."

18:1 In those days, there was no king in Israel,
      and in those days, the tribe of Dan was seeking for itself
          an inheritance to dwell in,
      for there had not fallen to him
          until that day
              an inheritance in the midst of the tribes of Israel.

2   And send did the descendants of Dan
          from their clan five men,
              from the whole of them, valiant men,
                  from Zorah and from Eshtaol,
                      to spy out the land and to search it,
      and they said to them,
      "Go, search out the land."
      And they went to the hill country of Ephraim,
          until the house of Micah,
      and they spent the night.

3   They were with the household of Micah,
      and they recognized the voice of the Levite lad,
      and they turned there,
      and they said to him,
      "Who brought you here,
      and what are you doing in this (place),
      and what is for you here?"

4   And he said to them,
      "Thus and such did for me Micah,
      and he hired me,
      and I became for him a priest."

5   And they said to him,

"Inquire, pray, of God,
and we would know,
will our way lead to success,
    the one upon which we are walking?"

6   And say to them did the priest,
"Go in peace.
Before Yhwh is your way
    upon which you walk."

7   And walk did the five men,
and they went to Laish,
and they saw the people who were in her midst
    living in trust after the custom of the Sidonians,
    quiet and trusting,
    and not plotting a thing in the land,
    possessing restraint,
and far were they from the Sidonians,
and dealings they did not have with any human.

8   And they went to their kin at Zorah and Eshtaol,
and say to them did their kin,
"What (do) you (think)?"

9   And they said,
"Rise up and let us go up against them,
for we have seen the land,
and behold, it is very good,
and you are being silent!
Do not be sluggish to set out to go
    to possess the land.

10   And when you go,
    you will come to a trusting people,
and the land is wide-handed,
for given has God into your hands
    a place where there is no lack
        of anything on earth."

11   And travel from there did the clan of the Danites,
    from Zorah and from Eshtaol,
        six hundred men,
            girded with the instruments of war.

12   And they went up and they encamped
    in the Town of Forests (Kiriath-jearim) in Judah.
For this reason,
    they have called that place "Encampment of Dan" (Mahaneh-dan)
        until this day.

Behold it is at the back of Town of Forests.

13 And they crossed over from there to the hill country of Ephraim,
and they came to the house of Micah.

14 And answer did the five men
who had been going to spy out the land Laish.
And they said to their kinfolk,
"Did you know that there is in these houses,
an ephod and teraphim, and a hewn icon and a cast icon?
And now, know what you will do."

15 And they turned here,
and came to the house of the Levite lad,
at the household of Micah,
and they inquired of him as to his well-being.

16 And six hundred men
girded with instruments of war
were standing at the entrance of the gate
who were from the descendants of Dan.

17 And up went the five men
who had been going to spy out the land;
they came there;
they took the hewn icon and the ephod
and the teraphim and the cast icon,
and the priest was standing at the entrance of the gate,
and the six hundred men,
girded with the instruments of war.

18 And these came to the house of Micah,
and they took the hewn icon and the ephod,
and the teraphim and the cast icon,
and say to them did the priest,
"What are you doing?"

19 And they said to him, "Be silent.
Put your hand on your mouth,
and go with us,
and be to us a father and a priest.
Is it better your being priest to the household of one man
or your being priest to a tribe and clan in Israel?"

20 And the priest felt good at heart,
and he took the ephod and the teraphim and the hewn icon,
and he went in the midst of the people.

21 And they turned and went,
and they put the children
and the cattle and the riches
in front of them.

22 They went a distance from the household of Micah,
and the men who were among the households
that were with the household of Micah
were called out,
and they overtook the descendants of Dan.

23 And they called to the descendants of Dan,
and they turned their faces,
and they said to Micah,
"What's with you that you called to arms?"

24 And he said,
"My gods that I made you have taken
and the priest,
and you have gone off,
and what do I have left,
and what is this that you say to me,
'What's with you?'"

25 And say to him did the descendants of Dan,
"You better not make your voice heard among us,
lest strike you down do bitter-souled men,
and you will gather up your soul and the souls of your household."

26 And go did the descendants of Dan on their way,
and see did Micah that they were stronger than he,
and he turned and returned to his household.

27 And they took what Micah had made,
and the priest that he had had,
and they went to Laish,
against a people quiet and trusting,
and they struck them by the mouth of the sword,
and the town they burned with fire.

28 And there was no savior,
for far away it was from Sidon,
and dealings they had not with any human,
and it was in the valley that belongs to Beth-rehob,
and they built up the town,
and they dwelled in it.

29 And they called the name of the town Dan
in the name of Dan their ancestor
who was born to Israel,
but Laish was the name of the town at first.

30 And raise up for themselves did the descendants of Dan the hewn icon,
and Jonathan, son of Gershom, son of Moses,
he and his sons, became priests to the tribe of the Danites,
until the day of the exile of the land.

31   And they set up for themselves the hewn icon of Micah
         that he made,
              all the days that the house of God was in Shiloh.

Judges 19:1–30
The Rape and Murder
of the Levite's Concubine

19:1   And it was in those days,
         and king there was not in Israel.
         And there was a Levite man
              living in the recesses of the hill country of Ephraim,
         and he took for himself a concubine woman
              from Bethlehem of Judah.
2   And play the whore against him did his concubine,
         and she went from him to the house of her father,
              to Bethlehem of Judah,
         and she was there four months of days.
3   And rise up did her husband,
         and he went after her
              to speak upon her heart,
              to bring her back.
         And his lad was with him and a pair of donkeys.
         And she brought him to the house of her father,
         and see him did the father of the lass,
         and he rejoiced to meet him.
4   And lay hold of him did his father-in-law,
              father of the lass,
         and he dwelled with him three days,
         and they ate, and drank, and spent the night there.
5   And it was on the fourth day,
         and they rose up early in the morning,
         and he arose to go.
         And said the father of the lass to his son-in-law,
         "Sustain your heart with a morsel of bread,
         and afterward you may go."
6   And they sat and they ate,
              the two of them together,

and they drank.
And said the father of the lass to the man,
"Be willing, pray, and spend the night,
and may your heart be glad."

7   And rise up did the man to go,
and urge him did his father-in-law,
and he stayed and spent the night there.

8   And he rose up early in the morning,
      on the fifth day to go,
and said the father of the lass,
"Sustain, pray, your heart."
And they tarried until the stretching forth of the day,
and eat did the two of them.

9   And arise did the man to go,
      he, and his concubine, and his lad.
And say to him did his father-in-law,
      the father of the lass,
"Behold, pray, withdrawn has the day to become evening.
Stay, pray, the night.
Behold, the declining of the day.
Stay the night here,
and let your heart be glad,
and you will rise up early tomorrow to be on your way,
and go to your home."

10   And not willing was the man to stay the night,
and he arose and went,
and he came up to Jebus,
      that is, Jerusalem,
and with him was the pair of saddled donkeys,
and his concubine was with him.

11   They were at Jebus,
and the day was mostly gone,
and said the lad to his lord,
"Let us turn
      into this city of the Jebusites,
and spend the night there."

12   And say to him did his lord,
"We will not turn into a foreign town
      that does not belong to the descendants of Israel,
but we will go to Gibeah."

13   And he said to his lad,
"Come and let us draw near to one of the places,

and let us spend the night in Gibeah or Ramah."
14   And they crossed over and went,
and go down upon them did the sun nearby Gibeah
     that belonged to Benjamin.
15   And they turned there to go to spend the night in Gibeah,
and he went and sat in the plaza of the town,
and there was no man gathering them
     into the house to spend the night.
16   And behold, an old man came from his work,
     from the field in the evening.
And the man was from the hill country of Ephraim,
and he resided in Gibeah,
but the men of the place were descendants of Benjamin.
17   And he raised his eyes,
and he saw the wayfaring man in the plaza of the town,
and said the old man,
"Where are you going,
and from where do you come?"
18   And he said to him,
"Crossing over are we, from Bethlehem of Judah
     to the recesses of the hill country of Ephraim.
I am from there,
and I had gone to Bethlehem of Judah,
and with the house of Yhwh I walk,
and there is no man gathering us into his house.
19   And even straw, even fodder there is for our donkeys,
and even bread and wine there are for me,
     for your maidservant, and for the lad.
With your servants there is lacking not a thing."
20   And the old man said,
"Peace to you.
Only let all you lack be upon me,
only in the plaza do not spend the night."
21   And he brought him to his house,
and he gave provender to the donkeys,
and they washed their feet,
and they ate and drank.
22   And they were making glad their heart,
and behold, the men of the town,
     worthless men,
          surrounded the house.
They were beating violently on the door,

and they said to the man,
> the old master of the household, saying,

"Bring out the man who came to your house,
and we would know him."

23 And out to them went the man, master of the household,
and he said to them,
"Don't, my brothers,
don't do evil, I pray you,
> after this man has come to my house.

Do not do this wanton folly.

24 Behold, my maiden daughter and his concubine.
I will bring them out, I pray you,
and you humiliate them,
and do to them what is good in your eyes,
but to this man
> do not do this deed of wanton folly."

25 And not willing were the men to listen to him,
and take hold did the man of his concubine,
and he forced (her) to go out to them outside,
and they knew her,
and they abused her all the night until morning,
and they sent her away at the rise of dawn.

26 And go did the woman at the turning of the morning,
and she fell at the entrance of the house of the man,
> where her lord was until the light (of day).

27 And arise did her lord in the morning,
and he opened the doors of the house,
and he went forth to go on his way,
and behold, the woman his concubine was fallen
> at the entrance of the house,

and her hands were on the threshold.

28 And he said to her
"Get up, let's go."
But there was no answerer.
And he took her on the donkey,
and arise did the man,
and he went home.

29 And he went to his house,
and he took the knife,
and he lay hold of his concubine,
and he cut her in pieces, limb by limb,
> into twelve cut pieces,

and he sent her into all the territory of Israel.
30 And it was that all who saw it said,
"There has not been done nor been seen anything like this,
    from the day of the going up of the descendants of Israel
        from the land of Egypt
            until this day.
Set yourselves upon it,
take counsel and speak."

Judges 20:1–48
Civil War

20:1 And go forth did all the descendants of Israel,
and assemble did the congregation as one man,
    from Dan until Beer-sheba and the land of Gilead
        unto Yhwh at Mizpah.
2 And station themselves did the chiefs of all the people,
    all the tribes of Israel,
        in the assembly of the people of God,
    four hundred thousand men on foot,
        drawing a sword.
3 And hear did the descendants of Benjamin
    that going up were the descendants of Israel to Mizpah,
and say did the descendants of Israel,
"Speak!
How came about this evil?"
4 And answer did the Levite man,
    the husband of the woman who was murdered,
and he said,
"To Gibeah that belongs to Benjamin I came,
    myself and my concubine to spend the night.
5 And rise up against me did the lords of Gibeah,
and they surrounded me at the house by night.
Me, they thought to kill,
and my concubine they raped,
and she died.
6 And I laid hold of my concubine,
and I cut her into pieces,
and I sent her to all the open territory of the inheritance of Israel
    because they committed wickedness and wanton folly in Israel.

7 Behold, you are all descendants of Israel.
Provide yourselves discussion and counsel here."

8 And rise up did all the people as one man saying,
"We will not go, not one man, to his home,
and no man will turn toward his house.

9 And now, this is the thing that we will do to Gibeah.
Against her by lot!

10 And we will take ten men of a hundred
in all the tribes of Israel,
and a hundred of a thousand,
and a thousand of ten thousand
to take provisions to the people
to do for their coming to Gibeah in Benjamin
for all the wanton folly that they did in Israel."

11 And gathered was every man of Israel to the town
as one man, united.

12 And send did the tribes of Israel men
throughout all the tribes of Benjamin, saying,
"What is this evil that has been done among you?

13 And now, give over the men,
worthless men who are in Gibeah,
and we will put them to death,
and we will burn out the evil from Israel."
But not willing were the descendants of Benjamin
to listen to the voice of their kin, the descendants of Israel.

14 And gathered were the descendants of Benjamin, from the towns
toward Gibeah,
to go forth to war against the descendants of Israel.

15 And muster did the descendants of Benjamin on that day from the towns,
twenty-six thousand sword-drawing men.
Apart from the dwellers of Gibeah were mustered
seven hundred chosen men.

16 From all this people,
seven hundred chosen men were left-handed;
every one was someone who could sling with a stone
at a hair and not miss.

17 And the men of Israel mustered, apart from Benjamin,
four hundred thousand sword-drawing men,
every one of these a battle-hardened man.

18 And they rose and went up to Bethel,
and they inquired of God,
and said the descendants of Israel,

"Who will go up for us at the beginning,
    to war against the descendants of Benjamin?"
And said Yhwh,
"Judah will be at the beginning."

19   And arise did the descendants of Israel in the morning,
    and they encamped against Gibeah.

20   And go forth did the men of Israel
        to war against Benjamin,
    and array against them did the men of Israel,
        war at Gibeah.

21   And go forth did the descendants of Benjamin from Gibeah,
    and they brought to ruin in Israel on that day,
        twenty-two thousand men to the ground.

22   And the people strengthened the men of Israel,
    and they again arrayed for war
        in the place where they had arrayed on the first day.

23   And up went the descendants of Israel,
    and they cried before Yhwh until the evening,
    and they inquired of Yhwh, saying,
    "Shall we again draw forth to war
        with the descendants of Benjamin, our kin?"
    And said Yhwh,
    "Go up against him."

24   And draw near did the descendants of Israel
        to the descendants of Benjamin
            on the second day.

25   And go forth did Benjamin to meet them
        from Gibeah
            on the second day.
    And they brought to ruin among the descendants of Israel,
        an additional eighteen thousand men to the ground,
            all of these sword-drawing.

26   And up went all the descendants of Israel,
        and all the people,
    and they went to Bethel,
    and they cried and sat there before Yhwh,
    and they fasted on that day until evening;
    they raised up whole burnt offerings and well-being offerings before Yhwh.

27   And inquire did the descendants of Israel of Yhwh,
    and there was located the ark of the covenant of God in those days.

28   And Phinehas, son of Eleazar, son of Aaron,
        was in attendance before it in those days saying,

"Shall we again go forth to war
  against the descendants of Benjamin our kin,
or shall we stop?"
And said Yhwh,
"Go up because tomorrow I will give them into your hand."

29 And set did Israel ambushes at Gibeah round about.

30 And up went the descendants of Israel
  against the descendants of Benjamin
    on the third day,
and they arrayed against Gibeah as formerly.

31 And go forth did the descendants of Benjamin to meet the people.
They were drawn away from the town,
and they began to strike down some of the people, slain,
  as before on the highways
    (one that goes up to Bethel
    and one to Gibeah in the open country),
      about thirty men in Israel.

32 And said the descendants of Benjamin,
"Smitten are they before us as at first."
And the descendants of Israel said,
"Let us flee and draw them away
  from the town to the highway."

33 And all the men of Israel rose from their place
and arrayed themselves at Baal-tamar,
and the ambush of Israel came bursting forth from its place,
  from Maareh-geba.

34 And go against Gibeah
  did ten thousand chosen men from all of Israel.
And the battle was difficult,
and they did not know
  that about to reach them was calamity.

35 And smite did Yhwh Benjamin before Israel,
and bring Benjamin to ruin did the descendants of Israel on that day,
  twenty-five thousand, one hundred men,
    all of these sword-drawers.

36 And see did the descendants of Benjamin that they were smitten,
and give did the men of Israel room to Benjamin
  because they trusted to the ambush
    that they had set at Gibeah.

37 And the ambush group came quickly,
and they made a dash to Gibeah,
and move in did the ambush,

and they struck all the town with the mouth of the sword.

38   And the appointed signal was between the men of Israel and the
          ambushers:
       their sending up a beacon of smoke from the town.

39   And turn did the men of Israel in battle,
     and Benjamin began to strike down slain
          among the men of Israel about thirty men,
     for they said,
     "To be smitten he is smitten before us
          as in the first battle."

40   And the beacon began to go up from the town,
          a column of smoke.
     And look did Benjamin behind them,
     and behold, going up was the whole town, a holocaust toward heaven.

41   And the men of Israel turned,
     and dismayed were the men of Benjamin,
     for they saw that about to reach them was calamity.

42   And they turned away from the men of Israel,
          to the way of the wilderness,
     but the battle clung to them,
     and those who were from the town were bringing ruin to them
               in their midst.

43   They encircled Benjamin.
     They pursued him.
     Rest they trampled,
          until Nohah toward Gibeah
               from the east of the sun.

44   And fall from Benjamin did eighteen thousand men,
          all of these, men of valor.

45   And they turned and fled toward the wilderness,
          to the Rock of Rimmon,
     and gleaned on the highways were five thousand men,
     and they stuck close to them until Gidom,
     and they struck down from them two thousand men.

46   And it was that all who fell from Benjamin
          were twenty-five thousand sword-drawing men,
               on that day,
          all of these men of valor.

47   And they turned and fled toward the wilderness,
          to the Rock of Rimmon,
               six hundred men,
     and they stayed at the Rock of Rimmon four months.

48   And the men of Israel returned against the descendants of Benjamin,
       and they struck them by the mouth of the sword, the town in its entirety,
          including animals and all that was found.
       Also all the towns that were found, they sent up in fire.

Judges 21:1–25
The Reconciliation of Men
through "the Traffic in Women"

21:1   And the men of Israel had taken an oath in Mizpah, saying,
       "A man from among us will not give his daughter
          to Benjamin as wife."
2   And come did the people to Bethel,
       and they sat there until the evening before God,
       and they lifted up their voice,
       and they wept a great weeping.
3   And they said,
       "Why, Yhwh, God of Israel,
          has this happened in Israel,
             for one tribe to be picked out today from Israel?"
4   And it was the next day,
       and rise early did the people,
       and they built there an altar,
       and they raised up whole burnt offerings and well-being offerings.
5   And said the descendants of Israel,
       "Who is it that did not go up in the assembly of Israel
          from all the tribes of Israel to Yhwh?"
       For a great oath there was
          against whomever did not go up to Yhwh at Mizpah,
             saying, "To die he will die."
6   And have compassion did the descendants of Israel upon Benjamin, their kin,
       and they said,
       "Hewn off today is one tribe in Israel.
7   What can be done for them, for those who remain, for wives?
       And we took an oath by Yhwh,
          not to give them from our daughters as wives."
8   And they said,
       "Which is one from the tribes of Israel

that did not go up to Yhwh at Mizpah?"
And behold, no man had come to the encampment
　　from the dwellers of Jabesh-gilead to the congregation.
9　　And the people were mustered,
and behold, no man was there
　　from the dwellers of Jabesh-gilead.
10　　And send there did the congregation
　　twelve thousand men from the sons of valor,
and they commanded them saying,
"Go and strike the dwellers of Jabesh-gilead
　　by the mouth of the sword,
　　　　and the women and the children.
11　　And this is the thing you will do.
　　Every male and every woman
　　　　who has known the bed of a male,
　　　　　　you shall devote to destruction."
12　　And they found from among the dwellers of Jabesh-gilead,
　　　　four hundred virgin lasses
　　　　　　who had not known a man, for bedding with a male,
and they brought them to the encampment of Shiloh,
　　which was in the land of Canaan.
13　　And send did all the congregation,
and they spoke to the descendants of Benjamin,
　　who were at the Rock of Rimmon,
and they called out to them peace.
14　　And return did Benjamin at that time,
and they gave to them the women whom they had let live,
　　from the women of Jabesh-gilead,
and they did not find enough for them.
15　　And the people had compassion upon Benjamin
　　because make did Yhwh a breach in the tribes of Yhwh.
16　　And said the elders of the congregation,
"What shall we do for wives for the remainder,
for eliminated from Benjamin are women?"
17　　And they said,
"The inheritance of the escaped remnant of Benjamin!
And not blotted out will be a tribe from Israel,
18　　but we cannot give them wives from our daughters.
For taken an oath have the descendants of Israel, saying,
'Cursed be anyone who gives a woman to Benjamin.'"
19　　And they said,
"Behold, there is a yearly festival of Yhwh in Shiloh,

which is north of Bethel,
> from east of the sun to the highway
> > that goes up from Bethel toward Shechem,
> > > and from the south of Lebonah."

20 And they commanded the descendants of Benjamin saying,
"Go and prepare an ambush in the vineyards.

21 And you will see and behold,
if come forth do the daughters of Shiloh to whirl in whirling dances,
then come forth from the vineyards,
and seize for yourselves, each man his woman,
from the daughters of Shiloh,
and go to the land of Benjamin.

22 And let it be if come their fathers or brothers
to quarrel with us,
we will say to them,
'Be gracious to them,
for we did not take a woman for each man in warring,
neither did you give to them
in such a way that you incurred guilt.'"

23 And do thus did the descendants of Benjamin,
and they carried off women in accordance with their numbers,
from the whirling dancers whom they stole.
And they went and returned to their inheritance,
and they built cities,
and they dwelled in them.

24 And sally forth from there did the descendants of Israel at that time,
each man to his tribe and clan,
and they went forth from there,
each man to his inheritance.

25 In those days there was no king in Israel.
A man, what was right in his eyes, he would do.

INDEX